An Association of the U.S. Army Book

Where Are the
WMDs?

THE REALITY OF CHEM-BIO THREATS
ON THE HOME FRONT AND THE BATTLEFRONT

Al Mauroni

NAVAL INSTITUTE PRESS
ANNAPOLIS, MARYLAND

Naval Institute Press
291 Wood Road
Annapolis, MD 21402-5034

Library of Congress Cataloging-in-Publication Data
Mauroni, Albert J., 1962–
Where are the WMDs?: the reality of chem-bio threats on the home front and the battlefront/Al Mauroni.
   p. cm.
  Includes bibliographical references and index.
  ISBN 1-59114-486-8 (alk. paper)
  1. Weapons of mass destruction. 2. Iraq War, 2003—Causes. 3. United States—Defenses. 4. United States—Military policy. 5. World politics—21st century I. Title.
  U793.M38 2006
  358.30973—dc22

                                       2005037935

Printed in the United States of America on acid-free paper ∞

12 11 10 09 08 07 06   9 8 7 6 5 4 3 2
First printing

This book is dedicated to a former colleague, Gerald "Geep" Fisher, a Booz-Allen consultant who was with Lt. Gen. Timothy Maude in his office on September 11, 2001, and to the other military and civilian victims of American Airlines Flight 77's crash into the Pentagon.

CONTENTS

Tables and Figures

PREFACE

*All history becomes subjective; in other words
there is properly no history, only biography.*

—RALPH WALDO EMERSON, U.S. PHILOSOPHER

I have a reputation, not completely undeserved, for sounding off with brash observations and untested concepts. In a small, insular group such as the DoD chemical and biological (CB) defense community, that can be a liability as much as an asset. I do not intend to offend, but rather to illuminate a rarely discussed and highly specialized field. I do not apologize for my rather blunt view of the activities taking place within this military profession. This book is first and foremost a history of some fairly significant events in the DoD CB defense community, and includes opinions of what must be done to develop a much-needed capability for the armed forces. The history is presented as I saw it; the opinions are mine alone.

Throughout its history, the DoD CB defense community has been impacted by particular nexuses of national and international events, the military's desire to radically change its operations, and influential leadership motivated to make changes that have radically changed its way of doing business. The first modification occurred when the Army realized it needed a dedicated force of specialists to fight on the chemical battlefields of Europe, and created a Chemical Warfare Service. The second critical nexus was at the start of World War II, when the Chemical Warfare Service had to develop CB warfare capability for a two-front global war practically from scratch. Prior to 1941, these defense experts had been ignored; afterward, they played a major role in Cold War research and development of unconventional weapons and related defense equipment. A series of events between 1968 and 1972 changed their status, including the Dugway sheep incident of 1968, the media coverage of Agent Orange and napalm use in Vietnam, the public discovery that the U.S. government had chemical weapons in Germany and Okinawa, and the outcry over burying chemical munitions in the ocean, to name a few. The Army disestablished the Chemical Corps in 1973 and nearly eliminated its defensive capability from the armed forces. Then a series of persuasive defense studies in 1976 following the Arab-Israeli war gave the Chemical Corps a second chance. This nexus caused a fundamental shift within the Chemical Corps from their role as lab technicians to field combat supporters. Between 1981 and 1990, the Chemical Corps regained and then lost its offensive chemical weapons program, but rebuilt a strong chemical defense capability. Following the first Gulf War, the other services joined the Army in a joint service CB Defense Program, probably the first truly joint acquisition program in DoD history.

Although the 1980s and 1990s were good years for the DoD CB defense community, they were far from ideal. The budget between 1981 and 1995 remained at less than one half of one percent of the total DoD budget. In part, this was because combat arms leaders were focused on more immediate priorities; but another reason was that the Chemical Corps specialties failed to become a critical part of combat operations. CB defense has always been hard to integrate into normal military training and exercises because simulating realistic nuclear, biological, and chemical (NBC) warfare conditions is difficult and relies on specialized equipment. The Chemical Corps' technical focus also alienated them from combat forces. Although military leaders understand the general NBC warfare threat, they have never accepted it as a routine part of military operations, especially since the end of the Cold War.

The fourth critical nexus for the CB defense community was a one-two punch: first the March 1995 Tokyo subway sarin attack and then September 11, 2001. Today, second- and third-tier adversarial nations may develop and use CB weapons, and threats of nuclear retaliation against nonnuclear countries aren't credible. The military has to support homeland security efforts that address the possibility of terrorist use of chemical, biological, radiological, or nuclear (CBRN) hazards against civilian populations, and the four services are worried that terrorists might use these hazards against their military installations and facilities. This is an opportunity for the DoD CB defense community to offer a new concept to address these needs. The approach cannot, however, be that WMDs are a catastrophic threat that will be addressed separately from everyday operational missions.

CB warfare in and of itself does not change the outcome of battles in which U.S. military forces may participate. A sound CBRN defense reduces the number of potential casualties and the time required to win a conflict. But unless we have to face Russia or China on the battlefield, CB warfare will not cause U.S. forces to lose a conflict, and the field commanders know it. As a military acquisition effort, the DoD CB Defense Program is small potatoes; as a military training topic, no commanders lost their command because they failed the CB defense evaluation at their combat training centers. For all the "what if" discussions and declarations that "it's not a question of if but when," U.S. military forces have not been attacked with NBC weapons since World War I. So their leaders reason that this luck will continue. The question becomes, how do we develop CBRN defense if the military leadership does not believe that NBC weapons are a real and present danger?

To take advantage of this situation, we must recognize that the term WMD is a relic of the Cold War and needs to go. The future CBRN defense specialist must first address the general and specific needs of nonproliferation and counterproliferation threats of NBC weapon use on the battlefield. Second, these specialists need to understand antiterrorism programs as distinctly different from traditional warfighting concepts—the threat and risk assessments conducted at military installations, and the cost/benefit analyses of applying scarce operations funds to a general, year-long threat of terrorism. Homeland security is another emerging area involving federal agencies with different agendas, resulting in yet another set of acronyms and a complex relationship between the federal, state, and local governments. These three groups are the new customers for CBRN defense expertise.

I do not adequately address all the changes and issues in the area of CBRN defense within homeland security, especially following the 9/11 attacks. There is just too much material, too many issues, and a lot of history surrounding these topics to adequately address the military's role in both antiterrorism and civil support actions, the creation of the Department of Homeland Security, and the supporting roles of other government agencies regarding their attempts to address the issue of terrorist CBRN attacks. The best I can do in this book is outline the early geneses of those efforts and, perhaps, revisit that issue later.

I have stressed the need for leadership, and I wish to clarify that there is a difference between the senior DoD leadership and the Chemical Corps leadership. By senior DoD leadership, I mean the influential three- and four-star generals, flag officers, and civilian political appointees who make policies and major decisions. These people decide whether or not CBRN defense is being underfunded. The Chemical Corps leadership and others who strive to develop CBRN defense products can only work with the resources and direction given to them. To be successful, the DoD CB defense leadership must recognize the necessity for change, develop an agenda to improve understanding of the nature of CBRN defense, and articulate clearly the need for additional resources and support from higher authorities.

As with any effort of this magnitude, I have to thank the many people who have supported the writing of this book. Any errors of omission or commission are mine alone. These supporters include Col. Ted Newing (Ret.), Col. Ray Van Pelt, Col. Tom Woloszyn, Col. Gene Fuzy (Ret.), Col. Brian Lindamood, Lt. Col. Ed Cotton, Lt. Col. Shirley DeGroot, Lt. Col. William King, Lt. Col. John Kulifay, Lt. Col. Brian Lynch, Lt. Col. Jim Placke, Lt. Col. David Velacruz, Maj. Scott Estes, Maj. Mark Lee, Maj. Peter Lofy, Cap. Scott Gould, Cap. David Osborne, Command Sgt. Maj. Maryeva Beesley, Staff Sgt. Joe Parrish, David Evans, Bill Heisel, Rich Saunders, Rick Turville, and many others who have supported my research. Thanks to Roger Cirillo at AUSA and Eric Mills and Linda O'Doughda of the Naval Institute Press for their support and endorsement. Thanks to Alicia Williams, Kevin Sullivan, and the Argosy staff for their great editing support, which has vastly improved my manuscript. Special thanks to my wife Roseann, who has done so much to assist and encourage me. Without her constant support, I would be nowhere close to achieving my goal of becoming a successful writer.

Al Mauroni
Alexandria, Virginia

Where Are the
WMDs?

CHAPTER 1

HERE BE DRAGONS!

*Children today laugh at fathers who tell them about dragons. It is necessary
to make fear a required subject; otherwise children will never learn it.*

—KARL KRAUS, AUSTRIAN WRITER

There is a popular belief that ancient cartographers would label the unexplored areas at the edges of their maps with the phrase "here be dragons" to warn seafarers of potential, but unseen dangers. Actually, there is perhaps only one known case where the term *hic sunt dracones* was used on an ancient map; more commonly cartographers used illustrations of monsters or fierce beasts to note turbulent or unexplored waters.[1] In any event, the use of the term "here be dragons" or similar phrases and illustrations have been associated with our deep emotional fears of the unknown, referring to a time when ignorance or superstition ruled our actions more often than logic and boldness did.

Legends and myths about dragons can be traced back thousands of years. Perhaps the earliest were the mythical and divine dragons of Chinese culture that brought abundance, good fortune, and prosperity. These Eastern dragons were worshiped as life-giving protectors, symbols of great fortune, and very powerful deities. In Greek mythology, a dragon (or, in some accounts, a hydra) guarded the golden apples in the garden of the Hesperides, the daughters of Atlas and Hesperis. The Greek word *drakon* comes from a verb meaning "to see" or "to look at," referring to a creature with a deadly gaze rather than a fire-breathing serpent with clawed feet and wings.

Western dragons described in thirteenth-century literature had a more sinister aspect, often associated with reptilian creatures that breathed fire and poisonous fumes, guarding mounds of treasure and expecting annual sacrifices of virginal maidens. Beowulf was slain in the twilight of his rule by a fire-breathing dragon, according to the tales. Interpretations of the Bible often interchange the terms "dragon" and "serpent," with Middle Age usage referring to the dragon as a symbol of sin and paganism.[2] Smaug in *The Hobbit* is another famous example of a sinister dragon. Yet while medieval tales refer to heroic knights rescuing fair dames from fierce dragons, in Western Europe the dragon was often chosen as a symbol of strength and might. Perhaps the most famous of these is the red dragon on King Arthur's standard. The current standard of the Principality of Wales is also a red dragon. Many heraldic coats of arms display a dragon as a creature with a horny head, barbed tongue, scaly back, armored rolls on the chest and belly, two bat-like wings, four legs with talons like an eagle's, and a pointed tail, often with an arrowhead tip (not to be confused with the two-legged wyvern or the eagle-headed griffin).

In a fashion, the current obsession with weapons of mass destruction (WMD) has become the modern equivalent of "here be dragons" for three reasons. The most obvious reason is the symbolism of WMD employment: immoral opponents using sinister devices to discharge deadly poisons against the unprotected public and those knights of modern day, soldiers, sailors, airmen, and Marines, or local emergency responders reacting to a terrorist event. These knights must don cumbersome armor and employ expensive, arcane tools to operate in the dragon's lair and to defeat the dragon. Most military professionals are unnerved by the thought of an enemy's ability to send invisible, odorless clouds of death rolling toward an unprepared force. Few military professionals know the long history and deliberate development of these weapons within the United States and the Soviet Union, an education that would outline the actual potential and limitations of their use on the battlefield and diminish much of the mystery.

During the Cold War, the words "weapons of mass destruction" meant something; they were backed up by the massive destructive capability of a superpower's well-funded and extensive unconventional weapons program. Megaton nuclear weapons could have destroyed entire metropolitan areas, and clouds of strategic bombers carrying tons of biological agents could have laid waste to a country's agricultural industry. Hundreds of Soviet tactical ballistic missiles with warheads amounting to tons of chemical agents could have tilted the entire operational battle in Europe. Invisible, deadly, and far-reaching, these nuclear, biological, and chemical (NBC) weapons were tested and were lethal tools of war for both the United States and the Soviet Union up to the mid-1990s. The fact that no other nation-state in the world has been able to develop, store, or use WMDs on the scale envisioned by the major superpowers is often ignored in favor of discussing the exaggerated potential effects of these weapons.

The second reason WMDs are the modern dragons is the deliberate generation of fear and perpetuation of ignorance by the media and talking heads discussing the technical nature of NBC weapons. The media uses terms such as "deadly nerve agents" and "germ warfare" not just in articles about the potential threat of chemical and biological (CB) warfare agents employed on the battlefield, but also in articles discussing the U.S. government's efforts to destroy its aging chemical munitions stockpile or to develop vaccines for biological warfare agents. Even a few grams or an ounce of a chemical or biological warfare agent can be labeled as a WMD, because that news line will dominate the front page. Hollywood and television movies enhance the myth with ludicrous plots detailing how a plane carrying a briefcase of nerve agent could wipe out the East Coast, or how a secret government laboratory created a biological agent that nearly destroys civilization. The anthrax-filled letter sent to Senator Patrick Leahy in the fall of 2001 was assessed as holding enough spores to kill 100,000 people, but even if someone had opened the letter in an unenclosed space, would it have indeed killed that many? Of course not, unless those 100,000 people lined up like sheep to receive their minimum lethal dose of 8,000 to 10,000 spores. Similarly, in 1995 the Aum Shinrikyo used enough sarin in the Tokyo subway to kill more than 1,500 people, yet only 12 died. These cases were not mass casualty events. But newspapers have to be sold and television news anchors need sensational stories to draw in viewers.

As the relatively new threat of chemical, biological, radiological, and nuclear (CBRN) terrorism has emerged, numerous talking heads, including so-called subject-matter experts as well as politicians recruited by the media, ominously drone "it's not a question of if, but when. . . ." Of course, they have been using that same phrase for more than a decade. Strangely enough, there have been only two instances of successful biological terrorism in more than twenty years, neither of which caused mass casualties, and there have been no cases of successful chemical terrorism on U.S. territories. Lots of hoaxes, yes; actual terrorist chemical incidents, no. So when is "when," exactly? Does "when" mean one year from now, five, ten, twenty years? After a while, "it's not a question of if, but when . . ." loses its credibility.

Last, WMDs are the new "dragon" in terms of their symbolism in the U.S. military. The U.S. Army's Chemical Warfare Service (predecessor to the current Chemical Corps) employed chemical munitions, thermite, and high explosives in support of combat operations beginning in World War I and through World War II. Army chemical units and defense agencies adopted the symbol of the Western dragon in the 1940s, as embodying the fire and destructive power of chemical and incendiary munitions and flamethrowers. When the Army went to a regimental system in the mid-1980s, the Chemical Corps submitted a design for a coat of arms consisting of a shield "blazoned as follows: Per bend Or and Azure [half gold and half cobalt blue] a dragon rampant Vert [standing on one leg and gesturing with the other three] and in base a tree trunk scarred by war eradicated of the first [symbolizing the birth of the Chemical Corps during World War I]." [3] While the Army no longer employs chemical weapons and flamethrowers, the Dragon Soldiers continue the legacy.

The Chemical Corps is the Department of Defense's (DoD) expert agency on CBRN defense issues. Its soldiers specialize in what has traditionally been termed "NBC defense" during military combat operations, one aspect of what DoD today calls counterproliferation. According to the 2002 National Strategy to Combat WMD, counterproliferation is one of the three pillars of combating WMD, and includes counterforce, active defense, and passive (NBC) defense. We'll talk more about this operational architecture later in the book. Today's Chemical Corps specialists are not experts in WMD issues as much as they are general CBRN defense experts addressing aspects within counterproliferation, antiterrorism, and homeland defense. There are other military experts outside the Army who address CBRN defense aspects and still others who deal with specific WMD issues other than CBRN defense; later we will identify these experts as well.

We need to dispel the myths surrounding WMDs to realistically address the challenge of these weapons, but that is not an easy or simple task. The need to address the strategic threat of CB weapons has been eclipsed by the larger threat of nuclear weapons. At the tactical level, CBRN defense is an unglamorous aspect of combat drills, usually involving long periods of sitting around in heavy protective suits and masks and pretending that an invisible cloud of agent is passing by. The topic does not command a great deal of attention, unless there is some sort of public controversy, and it has never occupied that much of the military budget. CB warfare has always been a distinct possibility and most people understood that. No one liked the idea of having to fight the Soviets in the presence of CB warfare agents during the long Cold War, but it was a known and accepted facet of military operations. Nations designed these weapons to be used on a tactical battleground (as opposed to most nuclear weapons), and over time, the United States developed a credible offensive capability that was both effective and lethal. Military and civilian planners developed logical, executable policies to guide deterrence and defense against adversarial use of CB weapons because the Soviet threat was seen as real and credible. Between 1941 and 1990, there were many experts in the government, academia, and industry, experts who actually worked with chemical warfare (CW) and biological warfare (BW) agents and tested delivery systems in the open environment without endangering the public.[4] With the increasing retirements and deaths of those Cold War professionals, the United States has lost that hands-on expertise and practical attitude employed in addressing the threat of CB weapons in particular.

What has made the issue hazier today is that CBRN hazards are not limited to the battlefield anymore. The Aum Shinrikyo cult's release of sarin, a military nerve agent, in the Tokyo subway in March 1995 represented the first time terrorists had effectively used a CW agent against an unprotected public target. While only 12 people died and fewer than a thousand were actually exposed to the nerve agent, the event shook the confidence of many governments.[5] There were cases of terrorist CBRN incidents before the Aum Shinrikyo incident, but they were few and small in the scope of casualties, and garnered little international attention. The Tokyo incident initiated a national response program in the United States, which included developing the National Guard's WMD Civil Support Teams and the DoD Domestic Preparedness Program. For the most part, these actions were limited, knee-jerk political reactions intended to throw a small amount of money at a very challenging topic to show that "something" was being done. That was the general situation until the arrival of the anthrax-filled letters in October and November 2001.

The potential threat of terrorists using CBRN hazards has been emphasized in the post-September 11 world, with politicians making dramatic speeches stressing the need to prevent terrorists from obtaining and using weapons of mass destruction. The problem is, in the popular imagination the term "WMD" conjures an apocalyptic scourge of laboratory-made, vaccine-resistant plagues, flesh-eating super-toxic chemical agents, and suitcase nuclear devices, quickly developed by terrorists and transported to a major city (or small township), resulting in the deaths of hundreds of thousands of people. The potential effects of terrorist CBRN incidents are often equated to those of military CB weapons, to the point that one would think that the threat of al Qaeda's releasing hydrogen cyanide inside government buildings was equal to the threat of North Korean Scud missiles with VX warheads aimed at South Korean cities. And the people telling these stories to the media are the so-called subject-matter experts! "Here be dragons," indeed. How are we going to address the modern threat of CBRN hazards seriously when these fictions abound?

DEFINING WEAPONS OF MASS DESTRUCTION

According to one source, the first use of the term "weapons of mass destruction" was in a *London Times* description of the German Luftwaffe's attack against the town of Guernica, Spain, in 1937. President Francisco Franco had ordered his ally, Germany, to attack the city in order to defeat the Basque insurgency there. The aerial attack, which lasted for three hours, destroyed the town ("mass destruction") and killed a third of the population ("mass casualties").[6] The term "WMD" was not, however, applied to the development and production of chemical and biological weapons between 1915 and 1945. The United States had had an offensive CW program since 1917, and had initiated an offensive BW program in 1941 in response to concerns about potential Axis capabilities. After World War II, when both the United States and the Soviet Union demonstrated that they had a nuclear weapons capability, the three different weapon systems became lumped together as "unconventional weapons." The United Nations established a commission to deal with atomic energy issues in 1946, tasking the commission to make specific proposals "for the elimination from national armaments of atomic weapons and of all other major weapons adaptable to mass destruction."[7]

In 1947, the UN Commission for Conventional Armaments attempted to define conventional weapons by first defining what weapons of mass destruction were. In August 1948, the Commission adopted a resolution (introduced by the United States and opposed by the Soviet Union and Ukraine) that defined WMDs as "atomic explosive weapons, radioactive material weapons, lethal chemical and biological weapons, and any weapons developed in the future which have characteristics comparable in destructive effect to those of the atomic bomb or other weapons mentioned above." [8] Interestingly enough, this definition deliberately excludes nonlethal chemical and biological warfare agents. But the important (and correct) point of this definition is that it does not exclude devices other than NBC weapons, and it emphasizes the metric of a WMD: its destructive power relative to nuclear weapons.

In 1956 Marshal Georgi Zhukov, then the Soviet deputy minister of defense, told the Twentieth Party Congress that future war would include "various means of mass destruction, such as atomic, thermonuclear, chemical, and biological." [9] This speech popularized the terms "atomic-biological-chemical," or ABC, warfare and "weapons of mass destruction." During and following the Korean conflict, the U.S. military invested heavily in building up the Army's CB warfare infrastructure as a key component of Cold War defense strategy. This included confirming Fort Detrick and the Dugway Proving Ground as permanent installations, constructing a biological warfare production plant at Pine Bluff Arsenal, and producing nerve agent munitions at Rocky Mountain Arsenal. The Chemical Corps went to great lengths to impress upon Congress and the American public the importance of developing CB munitions as part of the "flexible response" posture that was replacing the strategy of massive nuclear retaliation. [10]

In the 1960s and early 1970s, the military used the term "chemical-biological-radiological," or CBR, defense to describe the various defensive countermeasures to be used during any military operation that involved these unconventional weapons. Before 1969, the Chemical Corps had a robust research and development program in both CB weapons and CBR defense programs. While arms control advocates spoke of the need to control the proliferation of WMDs, the U.S. military discussed the development and employment of "unconventional" or "special" weapons. On November 25, 1969, President Richard Nixon announced that the U.S. government would unilaterally renounce its offensive biological weapons program and reaffirmed the U.S. policy of "no first use" of chemical weapons. [11] The U.S. government ratified the Biological Weapons Convention and the Geneva Protocol for the Prohibition of Poisonous Gases in 1975 to demonstrate its resolve to rein in the world's WMD programs. The Soviet Union assumed the United States had taken its biological weapons program underground, and redoubled their efforts to modernize and develop new chemical and biological weapons.

In 1969, the United Nations released a report from an international panel of scientists on the dangers of CB warfare proliferation. The group called for the total elimination of CB weapons stockpiles worldwide. This report is known for its comparison of nuclear, biological, and chemical weapons effects. What is not as well known are the report's assumptions (see Table 1). The UN report assumed that a flight of strategic bombers would carry a particular type of unconventional weapon, and that there would be five thousand unprotected people per square kilometer in the city being attacked.

While many authors have used this table from the UN report to compare the effects of nuclear, biological, and chemical weapons, few have looked at the amount of munitions used in this scenario. The table compares a one-megaton atomic bomb to ten tons of BW agent and fifteen tons of CW agent, in this case employed against unprepared noncombatants in a notional American city. These are pretty significant numbers, and naturally those massive amounts of agent are going to cause mass casualties if used against an unprotected and unwarned population. Talking in the same breath about the potential mass casualty effects of a few pounds or grams of CB warfare agents and these WMD examples seems ludicrous, but it is often done. CB weapons experts note that effective use of CB warfare agents during military combat operations call for a good metric ton of CW agent per square kilometer and between two and eight kilograms of BW agent per square kilometer to achieve significant effects against trained, equipped military forces. In real life target areas aren't populated with people standing outdoors on flat terrain in optimal weather conditions, just waiting to be sprayed with their personal minimum lethal dose of agent.

In January 1973, General Creighton Abrams, the Chief of Staff of the Army, announced that he planned to disestablish the Chemical Corps, as part of his efforts to reform the Army.[12] (He intended to move the chemical specialists into the Ordnance Corps to ensure the Army would maintain a retaliatory chemical weapons capability.) While the Chemical Corps was in the process of being eliminated, military analyses of the 1973 Arab-Israeli conflict revealed that the Soviet Union was furnishing armored vehicles with collective protection systems, as well as protective masks and decon kits, to Egyptian military forces. If the Soviets had equipment that could operate in

TABLE 1-1 *Comparative Estimates of Disabling Effects of NBC Weapons*[13]

Criterion for Estimate	Nuclear (One Megaton Atomic Bomb)	Biological (10 Tons of Tularemia)	Chemical (15 Tons of VX Nerve Agent)
Area affected	Up to 300 sq km	Up to 100,000 sq km	Up to 60 sq km
Time delay before onset of effect	Seconds	Days	Minutes
Damage to structures	Destruction over an area of 100 sq km	None	None
Other effects	Radioactive contamination in an area of 2,500 sq km	Possible epidemic or establishment of new endemic foci of disease	Persistent contamination from a few days to weeks
Possibility of latter use of affected area	3–6 months later	After end of incubation period (1–10 days)	Limited during period of persistence
Maximum effect on man	90 percent deaths	50 percent morbidity; 25 percent deaths if no medical intervention	50 percent deaths
Multi-year investment in substantial R&D production capability	$5–10 billion	$1–5 billion	$1–5 billion

a CB warfare environment, what did that mean in relation to a potential conflict in Europe? While considerable resources had been spent developing defenses against Soviet nuclear and radiological weapons (for instance, the development of radiac devices and hardened electronics), U.S. military CB defense capabilities had severely deteriorated by 1976.

The Secretary of the Army formally stopped the disestablishment of the Chemical Corps in 1976, and Congress significantly increased the budget for military CBR defense measures over the next decade. During this time, Army leadership called for the development of low-yield nuclear weapons, such as 155-mm and 8-inch artillery projectiles, as a tactical deterrent against larger conventional forces. This discussion revived the interest in modernizing chemical munitions as well, causing many military professionals to discuss NBC warfare and NBC defense as new terms, replacing CBR warfare and CBR defense (except in the U.S. Navy). In 1985, the Reagan administration convinced Congress to support the reinitiation of the Army's binary chemical weapons program. Increased funding to the CW and CB defense programs in the 1980s resulted in moderate increases in defense capability for the U.S. military. While the decision to develop binary chemical weapons was controversial (to say the least), the political and military leadership didn't talk about the U.S. military's WMD capability. It was understood that, in line with national policy, the United States would retain nuclear and chemical weapons as a retaliatory capability to deter adversaries from using such weapons against U.S. forces. The 1980s saw a renaissance of new concepts and material developed for NBC defense of military forces, with the philosophy that forces would be required to survive and sustain combat operations despite the presence of NBC weapons and associated effects of persistent contamination on the battlefield. In 1990, the U.S. government decided to stop its binary chemical weapons program and began plans to comply with the Chemical Weapons Convention treaty, which was signed in 1993 and ratified in 1997.

U.S. forces deploying to Operation Desert Shield in August 1990 were not prepared for CB warfare. Through a Herculean effort by the DoD CB defense community, they were prepared for the potential Iraqi use of CB weapons by February 1991. This capability was not put to the test, but it did reveal the critical failure of the U.S. military's ability to face a nonnuclear adversary with CB weapons. This assessment resulted in the development of the Defense

Counterproliferation Initiative, which will be covered in more detail in later chapters. The term "WMD," rarely used in the military community prior to 1990, began to be heard much more frequently. Concurrent with the development of this initiative, the threat of terrorist CBRN incidents emerged with the Aum Shinrikyo incident in Tokyo. Because WMDs had traditionally been thought of in terms of their technical composition—that is, that they were nuclear, biological, or chemical—the amount of agent involved did not matter. Terrorists with one gram of ricin were considered to be working with "WMD material," irrespective of how few people they could actually kill with that amount. This new, potential application of CB warfare agents caused several think tanks, such as RAND and CSIS, to begin using the terms "CBRN material" and "CBRN terrorism" around 1997–98, reflecting the start of discussions that maybe "WMD" wasn't the correct catchall term for NBC weapons and materials if their use did not cause mass casualties or excessive destruction.

MODERN USE OF WMD LANGUAGE

There is an official, legal definition of "WMD" in Title 18 of the U.S. Code: "(a) any destructive device as defined in section 921 of this title; (b) any weapon that is designed or intended to cause death or serious bodily injury through the release, dissemination, or impact of toxic or poisonous chemicals, or their precursors; (c) any weapon involving a disease organism; or (d) any weapon that is designed to release radiation or radioactivity at a level dangerous to human life." [14] That definition could apply to a lot of different substances used in many different ways. The military defines WMD as "weapons that are capable of a high order of destruction and/or of being used in such a manner as to destroy large numbers of people. Weapons of mass destruction can be high explosives or nuclear, biological, chemical, and radiological weapons, but exclude the means of transporting or propelling the weapon where such means is a separable and divisible part of the weapon." [15] This definition identifies a key criterion, that WMDs cause mass casualties, while disassociating the delivery system (artillery, aircraft, and missile launchers) that would be required to disseminate the agents. What exactly constitutes "large numbers of people" is left unanswered.

Using the terms "WMD" and "NBC weapons" allows some people to make the incorrect assessment that nuclear, biological, and chemical weapons should be treated the same because they each have the potential to cause mass casualties. It is convenient for arms control advocates, politicians, and many military leaders to use the term to discuss special weapons employment at the strategic level, no matter the distinctly different weapons effects seen during tactical operations or covert use against individuals. Nuclear weapons are in a category by themselves, considering the massive blast and heat effects that can level cities and the radioactive contamination that lingers for months to years. Even tactical nuclear weapons have a unique "shock and awe" effect that distinguishes them from the much quieter and smaller CB weapons effects. More and more military analysts are coming to the conclusion that there is only one WMD, and that is the nuclear weapon. President George W. Bush and Senator John Kerry both identified nuclear proliferation, and specifically nuclear terrorism, as the primary security threat in their first election debate in 2004. There was no talk about the threat of CB weapons.[16] Interestingly, the U.S. Army has developed high-explosive bombs with yields that approach the level of some tactical nuclear weapons, but these are not referred to as WMDs, despite the obvious parallel in weapons effects.[17]

Some argue that biological weapons are equivalent to nuclear weapons in their mass casualty effects; this is a common overgeneralization created by those that focus on anthrax, smallpox, and plague as the only effective BW threats out there. They ignore the many other BW agents that have been weaponized, with much lower lethal effects (such as brucellosis, tularemia, and glanders) or nonlethal nature (such as SEB toxin, Q fever, and Venezuelan equine encephalitis). Similarly, most people who talk about the "deadly" nature of chemical weapons are describing VX or sarin nerve agents and not nonlethal CW agents such as mustard liquid and agent BZ, an incapacitant developed by the United States in the 1960s. Most chemical weapons have a relatively small area of effect and limited persistency, and act very quickly on unprotected targets—within minutes. Some biological agents have great persistency while others fade in the sunlight; some biological agents are ideal for large-area coverage, while others are used solely for assassinations. All biological agents take days to weeks to take effect. We have seen potential BW threats and hoaxes, but no nation or terrorist group has yet caused mass casualties with biological weapons. Clearly nuclear, biological, and chemical weapons have different capabilities, effects, and characteristics that are not necessarily taken into account in discussions on the subject.

On the other hand, some people speak of chemical and biological effects in the same breath, using the terms "CB weapons" and "CB warfare" interchangeably, which may seem at odds with the discussion above about the need to differentiate the effects of chemical and biological weapons. Chemical and biological weapons do have different scientific properties and different effects on people, but they share weapons employment and defensive countermeasure approaches. CB warfare agents use similar delivery systems such as artillery projectiles, rockets, ballistic missiles, bombs, mines, and aerial spray tanks, all of which can disperse an agent over a large area, surprising unprepared combat forces or noncombatants. While CW agents are not the same as BW agents in terms of speed of effect on victims, amount of agent necessary to cover large land areas, and persistency in the environment, they both provide an unconventional capability of demoralizing, diminishing, or destroying a military force if it is unprepared to defend against the particular physiological characteristics of these agents.[18] Both chemical and biological warfare agents harm people by attacking the skin and respiratory system. As a result, military personnel use protective suits and masks, collective protection systems, and decontaminants to protect themselves from CW and BW agent dissemination. When military forces develop CB defense equipment and doctrine for the battlefield, there is general consideration for how military forces address the employment of CB warfare agents, such as detect, warn, protect, decontaminate. Tactical and operational distinctions between CW and BW agents are noted and understood as the U.S. military develops specific capabilities to counter specific CB warfare agent effects.

While CW and BW agents share certain employment concepts, not all CB warfare threats can be addressed with the same doctrine and equipment. The processes by which the U.S. government responds to terrorist CBRN incidents must be distinct from how the U.S. military addresses the threat of CB warfare agents. The target populations are different (prepared military forces versus unprepared civilians), the period of vulnerability is different (short combat operations versus 24/7 throughout the year), and the threat is different (weaponized agents versus improvised hazards), among other issues. Military forces undertake high risks to get the mission accomplished; emergency responders must take extraordinary measures to protect themselves against exposure to low levels of agent, even as they attempt to rescue victims. Terrorist CBRN hazards do not equate to military NBC weapons effects and therefore require unique operational approaches. But again, the general philosophy of detect, warn, protect, and decontaminate against CBRN hazards is still applicable.

In 1995, U.S. military forces supporting Operation Joint Endeavor (peacekeeping operations in Bosnia) included a contingent of Army chemical soldiers (Chemical Corps specialists) and their specialized reconnaissance vehicles. While the warring factions in Bosnia did not have a capability to employ weaponized CW agents and weapon systems, they were capable of using large quantities of industrial chemicals, such as chlorine and phosgene, against each other or against the peacekeeping force. The Chemical Corps decided to modify the detectors in their recon vehicles to analyze certain industrial chemicals, supporting the medical specialists' role of protecting the force from exposure to low levels of industrial chemicals that might result from accidents or intentional releases. This role has grown over the past decade to become what the four services call protecting against exposure to toxic industrial chemicals (TICs) and toxic industrial materials (TIMs, to include biological organisms and radiological material used by industry). [19] Citing examples such as the 1984 Bhopal accident (where a release of forty tons of methyl isocyanate after midnight killed about two thousand sleeping people and injured sixty thousand), many disaster preparedness specialists in the Air Force and Navy, in addition to the Chemical Corps, believe that future chemical defense specialists must be prepared to protect against the intentional or inadvertent release of industrial hazards as well as against NBC weapons. Two international task forces have developed various lists of industrial chemicals that may present a threat to military personnel on the modern battlefield, and work to develop a similar list of biological or radiological industrial hazards is ongoing. Other countries within NATO have adopted similar strategies to address toxic industrial materials as potential threats to military personnel, joining the U.S. military in addressing TICs and TIMs as threats equivalent to CB warfare agents.

In 1998, the Chemical Manufacturers Association (CMA) estimated that there were over 25,000 commercial facilities worldwide that processed or stocked chemicals reportable under the Chemical Weapons Convention. The global chemical industry uses billions of tons of material, more than

70,000 different chemicals, each year. The Organization for Economic Co-operation and Development (OECD) posts a list of more than 5,200 industrial chemicals produced in quantities greater than 1,000 tons per year. The Environmental Protection Agency (EPA) has a prioritized list of 275 chemicals commonly found at Superfund sites that are determined to pose significant potential threats to human health. The International Task Force 25 group started with a list of 1,164 industrial chemicals, reducing it to 98 toxic inhalation hazards of which 21 were considered "high threats."

Are all these industrial chemicals as dangerous as CB warfare agents? Absolutely not. Pound for pound, these industrial chemicals are not as toxic as CW agents, not by several orders of magnitude. It requires a spill of tens of thousands of gallons, tons of industrial chemicals, to cause a mass casualty event that could be compared with a much smaller release of super-toxic CW agents. In addition to lesser toxicity, the overwhelming majority of industrial chemicals have odors, colors, or other physical characteristics that make them unfit for weaponization, which is why countries developing WMD programs do not routinely use them. The use of industrial chemicals as CW agents during World War I was more a case of immature technologies and concepts, and modern military powers quickly abandoned using industrial chemicals as CW agents after World War II. While an accident or terrorist incident at a chemical production facility might be a major event for domestic emergency responders, it does not constitute a tactic that threatens the lives of military forces per se. At best, there are the four industrial chemicals on the Chemical Weapons Convention list—hydrogen cyanide, cyanogen chloride, phosgene, and chloropicrin—that might be of concern to military forces. Placing the military's need for protection against these industrial chemicals in the same category as protection against military CW agents is foolishness, but the increasing focus of terrorism against military personnel and the hazard poised by improvised CB weapons has increased the desire for a single source of CBRN hazard information, defense, and response. The cost of implementing this approach may, however, outweigh any benefits.

On March 17, 2003, President George W. Bush told the nation that Saddam Hussein had to leave Iraq, stressing a clear and present threat posed by that country's alleged WMD program. The fact that Iraq did not use chemical or biological weapons in Operation Iraqi Freedom came as a great surprise to most political and military analysts, who had predicted Iraq would use CB weapons as a last-gasp measure, if not immediately, against attacking U.S. and British forces. To date, with the possible exception of a small number of old artillery projectiles developed in the 1980s, the United States has found no CB weapon stockpiles in Iraq, nor have any terrorists seeking CB weapons been connected with Saddam's regime. There have been, however, discoveries of what David Kay calls "WMD-related program activities" in his October 2003 report.

This "nonfinding" underscores the fact that the very term "WMD" has lost any definable parameters that would make it useful in public discussions. It has become a punch line for comedians; satirists use the term to criticize the United States' and United Kingdom's political leadership. From being named 2002 "word of the year" by the American Dialect Society, "WMD" is ridiculed as "wielders of mass deception," "weapons of mass disappearance," "weapons of mass delusion," "weapons of mass distortion," and "weapons of mass distraction" (to describe the current administration's actions). We even see the term "weapons of mass disposal" used in connection with U.S. support for destroying Russia's very large chemical weapons stockpile. At best, military academics use a more appropriate term, "weapons of mass disruption," when referring to CB weapons; at worst, we have "worthless, meaningless definitions" to describe these unconventional weapons. Some military experts have even suggested that high-yield explosives, terrorist attacks against commercial chemical production sites and nuclear power plants, and even cyber-attacks can be considered WMDs if the body count is high enough. The term causes more confusion than clarity these days.

Political and military leaders often widely overstate the potential employment and effectiveness of CB weapons by including them in discussions regarding nuclear weapons employment. Paradoxically, others argue that CB weapons lack any effectiveness to be employed as an option against prepared military forces. What has changed? For starters, at the risk of being self-evident, the Cold War is over. Cold War scenarios of massive NBC weapons attacks cannot be duplicated with nations boasting much smaller offensive stockpiles, yet the rhetoric of how one gram of ricin or a few pounds of sarin constitute a "WMD threat" continue to come from the mouths of politicians, military leaders, and media talking heads.

Part of the problem is that today's military and political leadership (as opposed to military CBRN specialists) do not seriously address the operational and tactical threat of CB warfare. The possible use of CB weapons on the battle-field or as terrorist devices is often treated as an abstract, strategic issue for arms control and homeland security experts. This was true when the U.S. military strategy included the option of offensive use of CB weapons, even through the 1980s as the military was developing its binary chemical weapons. As the Chemical Corps was developing CB weapons for the U.S. military, the professional trigger-pullers that would be normally expected to employ these weapons eschewed them. In January 1997, General Norman Schwarzkopf told the Senate Veterans Affairs Committee, "We don't need chemical weapons to fight our future wars. And frankly, by not ratifying that [Chemical Weapons Convention] treaty, we align ourselves with nations like Libya and North Korea, and I'd just as soon not be associated with those thugs in this particular matter." [20] However, it was U.S. defense policy between 1941 and 1990 to consider the deliberate use of chemical weapons.

When government officials or media talking heads refer to WMDs, nine times out of ten what they really mean is nuclear weapons or ballistic missiles, not CB weapons. Take a look at any of the public discussions about Pakistan's, North Korea's, or Libya's WMD programs—most of the time, they were talking about nuclear weapons and not the chemical or biological weapons programs ongoing within those same nations. Developing actual countermea-sures to CB weapons use is either swept into nuclear response options (which clearly are not proportional responses) or just ignored completely. As a result, the use of the term "WMD" has actually hurt the ability of the U.S. govern-ment to develop effective and rational responses to the threat of CB weapons and terrorist CBRN incidents.

Let's be very clear about why the U.S. government stopped its biological weapons program in 1969 and its chemical weapons program in 1990. These were national policy decisions that focused on arms control rather than on the particular military effectiveness of the weapon systems in question. Besides the arms control community's desire to rid the world of war and weapons that can disparately impact noncombatants, President Nixon's National Security Council (NSC) recommended that the United States abandon its biological weapons because, its study stated, these weapons were unreliable and not par-ticularly effective, and there were other ways to deter the adversarial use of BW agents against the United States, specifically through the threat of nuclear weapons. This study's findings ran counter to the very concrete successes of the ongoing U.S. offensive BW program, which had developed several very effective and reliable BW agents and delivery systems. This evidence was ignored by civilian defense policy makers in their efforts to develop a near-term course of action that would give Nixon an arms control success story.

In 1990, the U.S. government stopped its binary chemical weapons program, again not because these weapons were unreliable or ineffective, but because the U.S. government decided to change its national strategy of threatening to retaliate against the use of chemical weapons on U.S. forces with its own chemical weapons. The decision to stop chemical weapons development was made easier by the collapse of the Soviet Union a year earlier and the ongoing talks on developing an international Chemical Weapons Convention treaty. Even up to the start of Operation Desert Storm, U.S. military leaders were seriously considering the use of chemical weapons against Iraq's military if it used chemical weapons against U.S. forces. The age of the munitions in question and the lack of compatible delivery systems influenced the decision against the option to some degree, as did White House qualms about the tactic of threatening to use chemical weapons while the U.S. government was engaged in arms control talks.

Prior to 1969, the U.S. military developed CB weapons as operational capabilities that allowed U.S. forces to achieve a specific military objective (protecting the force from CB warfare) through deterrence and, failing deterrence, by retaliation. After 1992, armed with state-of-the-art smart munitions and overwhelming conventional strength, and lacking a Cold War-like superpower adversary, the United States no longer needed these special weapons. This was a conscious decision by civilian defense policy makers and should not be confused with questionable moral or ethical arguments. Other smaller nations without the technical and financial advantages of the United States or Russia still desire an effective and modern capability to attack and defeat their neighbors and adversaries quickly, given the high cost of military operations. One very effective means of accomplishing that is through the tactical use of small numbers of highly precise CB weapons, not with the massive use of CB weapons as envisioned in the Cold War.

In a strange catch-22 fashion, the U.S. military's overwhelming strength in conventional and nuclear weapons has caused an innate lack of understanding of CB warfare among the combat arms leadership.[21] At best, military and political leaders viewed U.S.-owned CB weapons as a tool for deterring adversarial nations from employing CB weapons against U.S. forces. They were strategic weapons to be rattled like sabers in their scabbards as a threat, not to be used as practical weapon systems. This mind-set, which has become more common since about 1972, has been a large reason for the military's view that CB weapons are "weapons of mass destruction," regardless of the number or types of CB weapons used. It was a short step from this mind-set to relegating CB warfare to the realm of the "unthinkable" strategic warfare options and mass casualty events—at least in the realm of military tactics and training. Yet at the same time, there is relatively little focus on CB weapons as opposed to nuclear weapons when strategic military discussions take place.

Few war games are played out with the honest and realistic employment of CB weapons today, despite the many advances in computer modeling and simulation. One reason is that it's seen as just too hard to realistically capture the effects. Most CB warfare simulations are hazard-prediction models of CB agent dispersion across the battlefield. These models are enormously complex; they attempt to portray the realistic transfer of agent molecules in large concentrations across three-dimensional terrain as affected by constantly changing weather conditions. The models are also verified and validated as very accurate in their displays of weapons effects. What they don't do well is model the actual impact on personnel and equipment or the logistical and time-intensive efforts to decontaminate forces or terrain. Very often these impacts are dumbed down to a table of casualty effects, relating casualties to how many troops have equipment, how well trained they are, and how much agent is used. That is, the good war games do this. Many times, the sheer load of running these dispersion models in terms of time, data, and computing power delay the play of war games to such a degree that the use of CB weapons is cut out of the scenario. This is explained away in the game by assumptions that the adversary has the capability but was deterred by threats of massive retaliation, or that the U.S. troops were so well trained that there were no effects at all as a result of the adversarial use of CB weapons.

Political war games are slightly different, in that the goal is more of an exercise of leadership than any real examination of military or civilian response tactics. Exercises such as TOPOFF (short for "Top Officials") and Dark Winter simulate CB terrorist incidents to examine the decision cycle, specifically the need for policy initiatives, such as a national stockpile for vaccines, or robust federal response teams of CBRN specialists to assist states and local counties. Yet even these exercises rarely require a working knowledge of CB weapons other than the general physical effects of the specific agents involved. They test government officials' ability to coordinate a national response to worst-case terrorist CBRN incidents, but rarely question the technical nature of the threat or the credibility of the scenario. The United States has largely lost the knowledge of how these weapon systems actually work against personnel and equipment or how long their hazards remain effective in the environment, but this fact is somehow overlooked or assumed away.

What we need is a new set of definitions that set apart the Cold War image of massive destruction from today's environment of small nation-states and terrorist employment.

- *Weapons of mass destruction (WMD)* Weapons that are capable of a high order of destruction or of being used in such a manner as to create large numbers of casualties (more than 1,000 people) during a single event or incident.[22] This arms-control term generally refers to the asymmetric threat or offensive programs developed by adversarial nations or nonstate actors to cause mass casualties or a massive effect on military or public essential services. This may include the use of nuclear, biological, or chemical weapons, high-yield explosives, information technology systems, high-energy weapons, or those improvised weapons that can realistically cause mass casualties or mass effects.

- *Nuclear, biological, and chemical (NBC) weapons* Military weapons characterized by their nuclear, biological, or chemical physical properties that can cause immediate casualties and whose threat or use introduces individually diverse and distinct challenges to the planning and conduct of military operations. This term does not include riot control agents, herbicides, industrial chemicals, or radiological materials that are "weaponized" for employment against personnel.

- *Chemical, biological, radiological, and nuclear (CBRN) hazards* Those toxic CBRN hazards that are released in the presence of military forces or civilians, not necessarily in quantities that could cause mass casualties. CBRN hazards include those created from a release other than an attack, toxic industrial chemicals (specifically toxic inhalation hazards), biological diseases with significant effects, and radioactive matter. Also included are any hazards resulting from the deliberate employment of NBC weapons during military operations.

These words are important. Some people may question the need for three terms, but whether that confuses rather than aids the discussion depends on whether people are using the terms accurately. We ought to be able to talk about nations that develop WMD programs for arms control purposes, a broad topic that spans diplomatic, intelligence, military, and economic subject areas. We need to discuss the use of NBC weapons on the battlefield, recognizing that the use of chemical and biological munitions, at least, may not actually create mass casualty incidents (especially amongst prepared combatants). Antiterrorist and homeland security personnel ought to plan for responses to CBRN hazards without exaggerating the threat into a "WMD" situation. Once a sound definition is accepted (and proper use enforced), then rational discussions can actually take place. The question is whether we will be able to effect any differences from the constant state of unpreparedness in which we seem to always find ourselves. History shows that we keep repeating our failures to fully protect military forces from CB weapons and the general public from potential terrorist CBRN incidents.

WHY WE AREN'T GETTING BETTER AT THIS

The irony of developing an effective strategy against WMDs, NBC weapons, CBRN hazards, or whatever we call them, is that the United States has faced this threat many times throughout history, but the hard lessons never seem to stick. Years go by without another WMD incident, leaders move on to other positions, budgets focus on the more immediate threats, equipment becomes outdated, and the capabilities to combat WMDs are diminished. Then another event or incident occurs, and we rediscover our vulnerabilities and relearn the same lessons.

In August 1990, the U.S. military deployed to the Middle East to stop the actions of the Iraqi regime in its efforts to take and retain Kuwait as its "lost province." During the six months leading up to offensive military operations, the U.S. military and political leadership were very concerned that Saddam might order the use of CB weapons. The U.S. military knew that he had a chemical weapons capability, and that he had tried and tested this capability against the Iranian military. It was less understood how developed his biological weapons capability was. What was clear was that the U.S. military was not prepared for CB warfare in August 1990; the majority of forces were poorly trained, ill equipped, and vulnerable. In particular, U.S. forces lacked adequate quantities of chemical and biological agent detectors, modern chemical protective suits and masks, biological vaccines, collective protection systems, and modern decontamination systems and decontaminants. The process for verifying any use of CB weapons by Iraq was inadequate, and the U.S. government's response if Saddam did use CB weapons was unclear. By February 1991, many of those challenges had been at least partially addressed, and the forces' training had considerably improved their capability to survive, if not sustain, combat operations in a CB-contaminated environment.

In June 2002, U.S. military and political leaders again faced the question of how U.S. military forces would fare against the threat of Iraqi CB weapons. While the Iraqi CB weapons stockpile was deemed to be only a tenth of its size at its pre-1991 peak (at best), the topic of Iraq's WMD program and its potential impact on U.S. forces was on everyone's lips. Everyone assumed that Saddam would use his CB weapons to stave off the imminent defeat of his regime. Despite ten years of increased focus on military CB defense, many of the same challenges faced by the military in 1990 had resurfaced. An Army Audit Agency report in the summer of 2002 noted that combat divisions were untrained and unprepared for CB warfare. While forces had adequate numbers of chemical and biological detectors, they were short quantities of modern protective suits. There were only two FDA-licensed biological vaccines, the same two that had been available ten years before. Military forces in the rear areas lacked collective protection shelters, a capability that ranked very low on the list of commanders' priorities for some reason. Military forces were again saddled with the same aging decontamination systems seen in 1990 and had to rely on commercial decontaminants because the military version, DS-2, was being eliminated from military supplies despite the lack of a replacement. The same policy issues of "how clean does formerly contaminated equipment have to be to return to the United States," "how do we retaliate against Iraqi CB weapons use," and "what do we do with contaminated human remains" returned to haunt military planners. As in 1991, the feared use of CB weapons against U.S. forces did not take place, leaving weaknesses unchallenged and issues unanswered even today.

During the 1960s and into the 1970s, civil defense efforts designed to protect the entire U.S. population against a Soviet nuclear strike were very ambitious and very costly. Plans to shelter or move vulnerable population from first strikes, let alone construct an antiballistic missile system, had cost estimates that ran into the billions of dollars per year. While studies demonstrated that these efforts would save millions of Americans, Congress never fully funded the efforts. The expectation was that the U.S. military would have to defeat the Soviet weapons prior to their impact on U.S. soil, and very little was actually accomplished in the area of civil defense preparations. Today the government is planning to protect the entire populace from the effects of terrorist CBRN incidents, pouring billions into arrays of biological detectors, a network of new laboratories, new vaccine and countermeasures research programs, and more training and equipment for emergency responders. The actual effectiveness of these efforts against a terrorist CBRN incident is questionable, and the true cost of protecting all the nation's cities is unaffordable. Still, the government implements a partially effective national biological defense program, without recognizing the parallels in its own past.

In 1997, the DoD was tasked to provide NBC defense training to emergency responders in 120 major cities across the nation. In an unprecedented effort, the U.S. Army Soldier and Biological Chemical Command (SBCCOM) at Aberdeen Proving Ground, Maryland, teamed with experts from the law enforcement and fire departments, developed a training program and an equipment package for responders, and took it on the road for three years. This training package is still used as a free training tool for emergency responders across the nation. In addition, SBCCOM developed a CB hotline for reporting terrorist CBRN incidents and a CB helpline to provide additional information to emergency responders seeking more information. Facing a very skeptical audience and numerous critics, SBCCOM was successful in increasing awareness of the potential effects of terrorist CBRN incidents and how emergency responders could effectively take the measures required to save lives.

In 2003, the Office of the Secretary of Defense (OSD) directed the DoD CB Defense Program to develop a plan to provide CBRN defense equipment to two hundred military installations and facilities within the United States. One billion dollars was diverted from conventional antiterrorism programs to fund the low probability of a terrorist CBRN incident occurring on a military installation. Each installation will receive approximately $3 million of equipment and training, with the remainder going to the contractor installing the equipment and the project office executing the plan. The project office is proposing to place a suite of war-fighting NBC defense equipment onto the two hundred installations, equipment that the antiterrorism proponents cannot staff or afford. Few if any of the lessons identified in the DoD Domestic Preparedness Program are being utilized. Why don't we learn to do what works?

THE BLACK SWAN THEORY

Nassim Taleb, the founder and chairman of Empirica LLC, a research laboratory and financial training house in New York, wrote a treatise titled "The Black Swan: Why Don't We Learn that We Don't Learn?" The black swan metaphor refers to the dangers of deriving general rules from observed facts, and only from those observed facts, a notion called Hume's problem of induction.[23] Hume's theory states that there is nothing in any object, considered in itself, that can afford us a reason for drawing a conclusion beyond it; and that even after the observation of the frequent or constant conjunction of objects, we have no reason to draw any inference concerning any object beyond those of which we have had experience. The example given is most people's mental picture of swans is of white swans because most people have only observed white swans. The fact that there are black swans (*cygnus atratus*, a native of Australia, discovered in the 1790s) doesn't stop people from picturing white, rather than black, swans.

Taleb's point is that, while we may think we have sufficient information to form an opinion on a particular topic, we often underestimate the total sample size of the data required to make a rational decision. We are thus surprised by a "black swan"—an event that we might have anticipated had we known the total realm of possible events.

Taleb's black swan is a random event that meets three criteria: it must have a disproportionately large impact against normal trends; its incidence must have a probability so small as to be incomputable, based on information available prior to its incidence; and, at the given time of the event, there must be no convincing element pointing to an increased likelihood of the event. Because they cannot quantity a black swan event and the odds are against it occurring, people neglect to account for the black swan in risk management practices. In the case of an event with large consequences, the more inconceivable the black swan, the more harm it causes.

Taleb's theory rests on a complicated nest of risk probabilities and social science models, and is not easy reading, but it is very interesting and pertinent to this discussion of the reasons why people routinely resist making preparations for WMD events. Taleb posits that we have no way of knowing what we don't know, but policy makers can't very well say that when they are trying to explain market fluctuations, terrorist incidents, or other unplanned, unexplainable major-consequence events. Still, since we don't know what we don't know, and there will always be the black swans, the question becomes, why don't we learn from the past and build black swans into a risk avoidance mechanism to minimize future occurrences? The answer is, because human behavior just isn't that rational.

Taleb goes into some detail in his research on human behavior and statistics, but his main point seems to be that people take the last few observations of a general trend of events—say the steady climb of the stock market—and assume that the trend is both logical and perpetual. In addition, if the major consequence events strike infrequently (say 5 to 10 years apart), people will believe that these are rare events, unlikely to happen during their observation. People overestimate how much they actually know about a given environment and fail to plan for possible factors outside of their control. They underestimate the probabilities of these rare events occurring again because the cycle of evidence they observe does not show this behavior. If in the history of one person's (or a group's) observation of a general process, nothing of consequence happens to alter that trend, the person (or group) will generalize that there will be no dramatic change in events in the future—and then the black swan shows up.

So what does this thesis have to do with our discussion of weapons of mass destruction? It may explain why WMDs are so feared and yet so little is done to prepare our military and our society for the impact of WMD incidents—people are always discounting that WMD-type events will occur in the first place. Military experts recognize the possibility that NBC weapons could be used in any major combat operation against an adversary with an active WMD program. Certainly there are known but unexpected cases of terrorist intents to obtain and to use CBRN hazards against unprotected public targets. In both cases, because there is no real understanding of why nations or terrorists might use these weapons, people cannot accurately calculate the probability of WMD events other than to say "it's not a question of if, but when." As years go by without a terrorist CBRN incident, people become complacent and resources drop or are diverted to more visible and demanding projects. People assume that, yeah, sure, WMDs are dangerous, but what are the odds that they will be used on my watch?

When there is a threat of an NBC weapons attack or a terrorist CBRN incident actually does occur, there is a great uproar about why the military or the general population was not adequately prepared. Why didn't anyone do anything to prevent the massive consequences of untrained troops or unprepared noncombatants being exposed to these dangers? The accusations fly, scapegoats are identified and punished, promises are made to correct the failures, and then ... nothing. Years go by, no new incidents occur, and everyone says, "well, it can't happen again, and besides, there are other more critical defense programs and more probable dangers out there on which to spend money." The cycle repeats itself. NBC weapons events and CBRN incidents are the black swans of military combat operations. They don't happen often enough for anyone to actively support the development of a long-term, comprehensive defense program. Yet military experts were consistently surprised when U.S. forces were found to be not ready for the possibility of NBC weapons employment and the consequences of their use during critical military operations in 1917, 1941, 1950, 1973, 1990, and 2002.

Today, countries around the world continue to develop NBC weapons, although not necessarily for use against the United States. Nonetheless, this remains a factor in future combat operations. Terrorist groups might be interested, some day, in actually using CBRN hazards. The U.S. government has a choice—they can either continue talking about the need to combat WMD programs while systematically underfunding military CBRN defense capabilities and wasting funds on extravagant but limited efforts, or they can focus on actually improving military response to NBC weapons use and domestic emergency response to terrorist CBRN incidents. It's not as if there is any lack of examples of how to improve CBRN defense efforts. In fact, there are as many examples of how the U.S. government has failed to understand CB weapons effects as there are good ideas of how to successfully build a program that works. The challenge is to convince the military and political leadership to stop making speeches and start listening to new concepts that realistically address the real threat, not the imagined threat, of CBRN hazards and NBC weapons. Right now, the rhetoric doesn't match the reality.

CHAPTER 2

AN EVOLVING MANAGEMENT STRUCTURE

Committee—a group of men who individually can do nothing
but as a group decide that nothing can be done.

—FRED ALLEN, U.S. COMEDIAN

This book will focus on those military capabilities developed to operate on a contaminated battlefield in Iraq and, to a limited extent, respond to terrorist CBRN incidents. To understand why the military has particular CBRN defense equipment used in Operation Iraqi Freedom, we must first understand the defense management structure that developed these items. Traditionally, CBRN defense has been a DoD strength and, specifically, the U.S. Army's area of expertise since 1918. Even as the other services became engaged in CBRN defense, the Army remained the only service that had invested in a full-time professional organization. Following the attempted disestablishment of the Chemical Corps in 1973 and its reinstatement in 1976, the DoD decided to refocus its efforts on building a modern CB defense capability. A DoD directive written in 1976 identified the Army as the DoD Executive Agent to lead research and development of CB defense equipment and chemical munitions.[1] This directive did not create a joint program; the Air Force and Navy were free to work on their own service-unique requirements and procure their own equipment. It also did not address radiological defense.[2]

The Chemical Corps held a number of internal reviews that resulted in a requirements-based roadmap for improved NBC defense capabilities, the fielding of several new chemical defense units throughout the 1980s, and plans to modernize the Army's offensive chemical weapons. The overall NBC defense philosophy was threefold: deter an adversary through diplomatic means and a demonstrated retaliatory capability, defend against the use of NBC weapons in the event that deterrence failed, and retaliate in accordance with the U.S. national strategy.[3] Forces were expected to avoid contamination (using reconnaissance, detection, and identification equipment), protect the force (using protective ensembles, medical countermeasures, and collective protection systems), and restore operations (through decontaminating people, assets, and terrain).[4] The U.S. Army Chemical Research, Development, and Engineering Center (CRDEC) at Edgewood Arsenal, Maryland, created directorates for recon, detection, and identification projects, individual and collective protection projects (protective masks and collective protection systems for vehicles and vans), and decontamination projects, in addition to a munitions directorate and a science and technology directorate.[5] The U.S. Army Natick Research, Development, and Engineering Center in Massachusetts led the development of protective suits and collective protection shelters. The Army Surgeon General established the U.S. Army Medical Research Institute of Infectious Diseases (USAMRIID) in 1969 at Fort Detrick, Maryland, to develop medical defenses against biological warfare. In 1978, the Army redesignated the U.S. Army Nuclear Agency as the U.S. Army Nuclear and Chemical Agency (USANCA) to address CB contamination survivability, in addition to nuclear survivability, of military systems. The former U.S. Army Biomedical Laboratory at Edgewood Arsenal became the U.S. Army Medical Research Institute of Chemical Defense (USAMRICD) in 1981, chartered to develop medical countermeasures to chemical warfare agents.

In 1985, the DoD reaffirmed the Army as its Executive Agent for chemical weapons and CB defense research and development efforts, responsible for Army-unique requirements and joint requirements that involved the other services.[6] It remained each service's responsibility to address its unique requirements and to procure CB defense equipment within their respective budgets. The responsibilities of the Assistant to the Secretary of Defense for Atomic Energy (ATSD [AE]) expanded in 1986 to include coordinating CB defense issues within DoD and with other federal agencies and defending the binary chemical weapons program before Congress. This defense official, who reported directly to the Under Secretary of Defense for Acquisition and Technology (USD [A&T]), delegated day-to-day oversight of the program to a Deputy Assistant to the Secretary of Defense for CB Matters (DATSD [CBM]), a career civil servant position.[7]

Three principal-level committees were formed to execute the directive. The Joint Service Review Group (JSRG) had thirteen voting members from the four services and was chaired by the chief chemical officer in the Army's Deputy Chief of Staff for Operations and Plans. They met quarterly in the Pentagon to review the services' CB defense requirements and identify any potential joint requirements. The Joint Panel for Chemical and Biological Defense (JP-CBD) had members of the four services' development agencies, was chaired by the commanding general of CRDEC, and reported to the Joint Logistics Commanders (a three-star-general officer panel). This group would meet to discuss the services' research and development efforts and to collaborate where common advanced research and procurement goals existed. The Technical Panel on Chemical and Biological Defense (TP/CBD) met under the jurisdiction of the Joint Directors of Laboratories (another three-star-general officer panel) to share information on the service laboratories' basic science and technology efforts. An Army chief scientist from CRDEC chaired this committee. These three groups remained focused primarily on nonmedical programs. The Armed Services Biomedical Research, Evaluation and Management (ASBREM) Committee addressed medical chemical defense, medical biological defense, and medical nuclear defense efforts. The U.S. Army Medical Research Development, Acquisition and Logistics Command was responsible for planning, programming, and budgeting for medical CB defense research requirements for all military departments.[8] The Armed Forces Radiobiology Research Institute (AFRRI), charted by the Defense Nuclear Agency in 1981, would oversee the execution of joint medical nuclear defense research efforts.[9]

The creation of these committees did not in any way promise the successful development of joint initiatives. The only requirement that the services faced within these three groups was to share information about their efforts; there was no oversight or budgetary mechanism to force the consolidation of duplicative efforts into joint programs, and there were a few initial attempts at developing truly joint programs. While the Army executed more than 70 percent of the overall DoD efforts in CB defense, each service jealously guarded its budget and often duplicated each other's CB defense efforts in the rationale that only it could address its own "service-unique" requirements. The result was a critically unprepared military force seen at the beginning of Operation Desert Shield in August 1990.

OPERATION DESERT SHIELD
AND DESERT STORM

On August 2, 1990, as Iraqi military forces were crossing the Kuwaiti border, U.S. military capabilities to conduct NBC defense were inadequate. The U.S. military faced the imminent hostile use of chemical and biological weapons against its deployed forces, and it had neither adequate training nor equipment readiness. A General Accounting Office (GAO) report, issued after the conflict was over, noted serious equipment and training shortfalls across all branches of the military.[10] The Army led a hastily formed working group, called the Joint Service Coordinating Committee for Chemical Defense Equipment (JSCC-CDE), to identify urgent requirements and redistribute critically short CB defense equipment to deploying military forces.

The Iraqi offensive chemical weapons consisted mostly of mustard and sarin-filled 155-mm artillery shells and 122-mm rockets, some aerial bombs, and a small number of SCUD warheads. There was little to no intelligence about Iraq's biological weapons program, since Saddam had not used biological weapons against Iran. No one had a clear estimate on how close Iraq was to developing a nuclear weapon. To cover for its own initial lack of capability, the U.S. government sent strong diplomatic messages to the Iraqi government warning them not to consider the use of CB weapons, while CNN and other news agencies showed military personnel training to use protective suits and masks in the hot desert environment. The U.S. Army should have had a new chemical point detector, a chemical agent standoff detector, an NBC reconnaissance vehicle, a new protective mask, a new decontamination system and decontaminant, and modern collective protection shelters by 1990. These efforts were delayed by various cost/schedule issues and technical obstacles, meaning that troops would be working with older equipment largely developed in the 1970s (and some even earlier). All the chemical protective suits had woodland camouflage patterns, given that the U.S. military had been focused on countering a potential Soviet offensive against forces in Europe. About 20 percent of the protective suits were 1970s era olive-drab chemical protective overgarments that offered only six hours of protection once contaminated, as opposed to the twenty-four hours of protection offered by newer battledress overgarments.

One of the most significant challenges was the lack of a military-hardened, near-real-time biological agent detector. The U.S. and the British militaries were able to field special detection teams armed with several commercial and military prototype air samplers with SMART detection tickets, using antibody-antigen reactions. The sensitivity and specificity of these crude biological warfare detection suites restricted their utility, but they did represent a limited capability to determine whether the Iraqis attacked with biological agents. The slow detection process meant that troops would be exposed to BW agents (if employed), but at the least, medical actions could be taken upon successful and prompt identification. Medical specialists in theater were capable of conducting limited epidemiology surveys of sick troops after exposure and when symptoms manifested themselves. Verification and confirmation of any biological attack had to be performed out of theater (e.g., Europe or the United States), meaning days would pass before the national leadership received the information necessary to plan retaliatory actions.

DoD considered the need to conduct mass burials of contaminated U.S. and allied fatalities in country because of the lack of defense policy, operational concepts, and technologies needed to fully decontaminate human remains prior to shipment home. There were no standards or policies in place to address the return of any large equipment, aircraft, or ships that became contaminated and were subsequently decontaminated in theater. Technical experts at Aberdeen Proving Ground and Dugway Proving Ground raced to develop a rudimentary set of procedures to address these concerns, but the war was over before a solution was developed.

Medical chemical defense products included the Mark I Nerve Agent Antidote Kit (NAAK) and the Convulsant Antidote Nerve Agent (CANA) diazepam auto injector for treatment of nerve agent exposure. Pyridostigmine bromide (PB) tablets, intended for use as a nerve agent pretreatment, were not yet approved by the Food and Drug Administration (FDA) for general use. Although medical chemical defense products were available in sufficient quantities to support Operation Desert Storm, the relatively recent fielding of the diazepam auto injector and the necessity of using PB tablets under an emergency waiver of traditional investigational new drug documentation requirements caused considerable confusion. Medical biological defense products were limited to the FDA-approved anthrax vaccine and two investigational new drugs, a botulinum toxoid and a botulinum antiserum. The two vaccines were available in only limited quantities, which caused a great amount of concern as to who among the nearly five hundred thousand personnel in theater should receive the vaccines.

As the air offensive initiated, special operations forces took to the desert searching for SCUD launchers, while coalition aircraft roamed the airspace, prepared to destroy the same launchers. The intense effort reduced, but did not eliminate, the SCUD attacks. Although Saddam's forces did not employ chemical or biological weapons during that conflict, the six-month period prior to the ground offensive allowed coalition forces to receive a great deal of CB defense equipment, to upgrade their training on the equipment, and to deploy several chemical defense reserve companies to increase their capabilities. Overall, the status of CB defense capabilities in February 1991 had improved markedly over the poor state of readiness seen in August 1990.[11]

The postmortems from Operation Desert Storm resulted in a comprehensive series of assessments in the defense and intelligence communities, all leading to the conclusion that U.S. forces, while they would have survived a chemical attack, were unprepared to defend against the sustained use of chemical or biological weapons. Some commanders decided that what Operation Desert Storm really taught them was, if you threaten the adversary with massive retaliation, you don't have to worry about NBC defense. Military interest in CB defense issues remained low, with an annual military budget that was relatively flatlined between 1989 and 1996.

THE EMERGENCE OF A JOINT PROGRAM

The demonstrated lack of preparedness in Operation Desert Storm led to the establishment of a Joint Program Office for Biological Defense (JPO-BD) under the Army in June 1993. The four services agreed to cooperate toward an improved DoD biological defense capability, recognizing that biological warfare represented a real catastrophic threat to military operations. Congress demanded more substantial actions, fearing that the services would not fund the development and procurement of CB defense equipment as a high priority effort. Congress directed the consolidation of the management and oversight of all DoD CB defense research, development, and acquisition programs under Public Law 103-160.[12] This was a radical change, in that the development and acquisition of all CB defense equipment was removed from the three independent service-run programs and centralized in one OSD-level acquisition program.[13] Again, radiological defense research and development was deliberately left out.

The Army remained as the DoD Executive Agent, coordinating and integrating all service research, development, test and evaluation, and acquisition efforts. The three services' allocated budgets for CB defense equipment were removed from their direct control and rolled up into a single defense budget line, controlled by a single OSD office. The language also decreed that all military CB defense training would be conducted at the U.S. Army Chemical School, and that the DoD would report on the overall CB defense readiness of the armed forces and the ongoing activities of the research, development, and acquisition program every year.[14] On February 26, 1994, Defense Secretary William Perry designated the ATSD (AE) as the single office within OSD responsible for management and oversight of the DoD CB Defense Program and coordination of CB defense policy issues with the Assistant Secretary of Defense for Nuclear Security and Counterproliferation (ASD [NS&CP]), under the Under Secretary of Defense for Policy (USD [P]).[15] The USD (A&T) would be the official oversight for the acquisition program, delegated to the ATSD (AE), whose title would be changed to the Assistant to the Secretary of Defense for Nuclear and Chemical and Biological Defense (ATSD [NCB]).[16]

An OSD-chartered implementation group, chaired by the Army, recommended a more formal committee structure to ensure all services received equal consideration and yet maintained their Title 10 responsibilities to train, equip, and organize their forces. The group developed a plan in April 1994 describing how joint service committees would define NBC defense requirements, prioritize the research, development, and acquisition projects, and manage the service laboratories in the execution of their work. The three service acquisition executives signed the Joint Service Agreement for Nuclear, Biological and Chemical Defense Management on August 2, 1994.[17]

The Joint Service Materiel Group (JSMG), replacing the JP-CBD, would coordinate and integrate the research, development, and acquisition efforts, including basic science and technology efforts, among the service laboratories, in addition to NBC defense logistics and sustainment issues. This group was chaired by the commanding general of the U.S. Army Chemical and Biological Defense Command (CBDCOM), Major General George Friel. Friel was assisted by an executive office made up of a half-dozen Army government civilians and contractors.[18] Voting members included representatives from the four services, to include offices of the Assistant Secretary of the Air Force for Acquisition, Global Power Programs Directorate (SAF/AQP), the Naval Sea Systems Command's Engineering Directorate, the U.S. Marine Corps System Command, and Headquarters Army Materiel Command.[19] Nonvoting members included representatives from the Defense Logistics Agency (DLA), the Joint Staff (J-4, Logistics), the JPO-BD, the Army's Office of the Surgeon General, and U.S. Special Operations Command (SOCOM).[20] The executive office would prepare an annual research, development, and acquisition plan that described and integrated all joint and service efforts through the long term (15–20 years), and an annual logistics support plan that detailed the readiness of the armed services in terms of how much equipment was on hand against overall requirements. The group took the TP/CBD under its purview and renamed it the Joint Science and Technology Panel for Chemical and Biological Defense (JSTPCBD).

The JSMG had no permanent members; the part-time voting and nonvoting action officers (generally field grade officers and equivalent civil servants) met monthly, with the principals (general and flag officers) meeting annually to review the program's progress and budget. The JSMG divided up the CB defense program management among the four services. The Army was to oversee contamination avoidance (minus biological detectors) and the medical CB defense projects, the Air Force would oversee decontamination, the Navy would oversee collective protection and modeling and simulation efforts, and the Marine Corps would oversee individual protection projects. Among the four services, there were eight distinct and separate-milestone decision authorities overseeing the actual development and acquisition of CB defense equipment.[21] While the JSMG chair could recommend particular courses of action, it was up to the four services to vote on issues and the eight milestone-decision authorities to execute the particular projects.

The Joint Service Integration Group (JSIG), replacing the JSRG, would coordinate and integrate the multiservice doctrine and training among the services, in addition to developing and overseeing the documentation and validation of joint requirements for CB defense programs. This group was chaired by the commander of the U.S. Army Chemical School and Center (USACMLS), Brig. Gen. Ralph Wooten. Voting members included representatives from the U.S. Air Force Civil Engineer's Operations and Maintenance Directorate, Deputy Chief of Naval Operations (Resources, Warfare Requirements, and Assessments, N80), U.S. Marine Corps Combat

Development Command, and the Army Chemical School.[22] Nonvoting members included representatives from the Joint Staff (J-5, Strategic Plans and Policy), the U.S. Army Medical Department Center and School, SOCOM and the JPO-BD. This group's main effort (in addition to staffing requirements documents) was an annual modernization plan, which included a list of the long-term, prioritized efforts needed to address near-term and future military requirements.

The JSIG also had no permanent billets, relying on the Army's Chemical School to provide personnel and resources for a secretariat that managed the monthly meetings of the part-time action officers. This secretariat was manned by one lieutenant colonel and one civil servant, and was assisted by a group of contractors. JSIG principals met annually, often with the JSMG principals in a joint meeting in Washington, D.C., to review the annual budget submission. Much of the work on developing multiservice doctrine and training products was done at the Chemical School at Fort McClellan, while the JSIG developed virtual joint subpanels to address NBC defense issues within medical requirements, modeling and simulation requirements, doctrine and training requirements, intelligence requirements, and other issues.

A Joint NBC Defense Board, cochaired by the Vice Chief of Staff of the Army and the Assistant Secretary of the Army for Research, Development and Acquisition (ASA [RDA]), oversaw the two joint committees. One- and two-star generals and flag officers from each of the services' requirements agencies and acquisition commands sat on the board as voting members (totaling eight members, but limited to one vote per service), with the JSMG and JSIG chairs, JPO-BD program manager, and general officer representatives from DLA, the medical community, SOCOM, and the Joint Staff (J-4 and J-5), participating as nonvoting members. These general officers would be the arbitrators in the event that there was a dispute between the services or between the JSMG and JSIG, meeting at least once a year to review and forward the final draft DoD CB Defense Program Objective Memorandum (POM) to the DATSD (CBM). On occasion, special events would cause the board to meet more frequently, although this was rare.

The JSMG and JSIG action officers jointly prepared the draft DoD CB Defense POM for the approval by the Joint NBC Defense Board. The Joint NBC Defense Board secretariat, composed of the chief chemical officer of the Army's Office of the Deputy Chief of Staff for Operations and Plans

(ODCSOPS), his staff and a few contractors, would prepare the draft POM for the board's approval. Following the board's recommendations and approval, this secretariat forwarded the draft POM to the DATSD (CBM). With all of these joint committees, the consistent rule was one service, one vote, with the Army chair as the tiebreaker.

As an OSD-funded budget, the program needed a funds manager, a legal way to get OSD money to the service laboratories for execution. The USD (A&T) decided to use the Ballistic Missile Defense Organization (BMDO) as the conduit. The DATSD (CBM) would tell the Army's acquisition office how to execute the funds appropriated and authorized by Congress, based on its approval of the president's annual budget. The Army would release execution and program status reporting instructions to the service project offices. The BMDO comptroller would pass the funds to the service project offices, and the Army's acquisition office would report to OSD on how well the services executed the defense funds.

The funds were only to be used for that research, development and acquisition and military construction specifically designated to support CB defense programs. The services were not supposed to use the OSD program to procure CB defense equipment normally purchased through operations and maintenance funds. That included consumable items, such as manual chemical detection kits, decontamination supplies, medical items, mask and collective protection filters, and associated training equipment. There were two exceptions to this policy: DoD wanted to replace large stocks of older (and rapidly expiring) battle dress overgarments (BDOs) with the newer joint service lightweight integrated technology (JSLIST) suits, and quickly implement the anthrax vaccine policy across the total force. Having the DoD program take these high-cost burdens on was seen as the best way to quickly increase the services' CB defense readiness, because the services were reluctant to pay for the suits and vaccines themselves.

This new management structure had a few loopholes. One was that the JPO-BD was not subordinate to the joint committees, but rather had its own direct reporting chain through the Army to the USD (A&T) by virtue of the JPO's charter signed by the Deputy Secretary of Defense. The medical community also had a degree of autonomy, in that the ASBREM committee claimed the prerogative to set the overall priority of medical CB defense requirements and to execute the medical CB defense research programs.[23] The

JSTPCBD addressed only nonmedical science and technology efforts, and the Army medical community addressed all medical basic science and technology efforts. Both the JPO-BD and the medical community, however, relied on the funds overseen by the JSMG and the requirements process established by the JSIG, so they had to work with, but not for, the joint committees.

The DoD CB Defense Program's Successes and Challenges

The initial CB Defense Program defense budget for 1996 and 1997 relied on the existing services' funds dedicated to CB defense programs rolling into the OSD program line, resulting in a budget of about $400 million to $500 million per year. More than 50 percent of the funds came from the Army. The DoD CB Defense Program's budget for FY 1998–2003 would see a slight increase in funding, creeping over the $600 million line and edging steadily upward (see Figure 2-1). Overall, this represented less than one half of one percent of the total DoD budget, a percentage that has remained roughly the same even to this date.

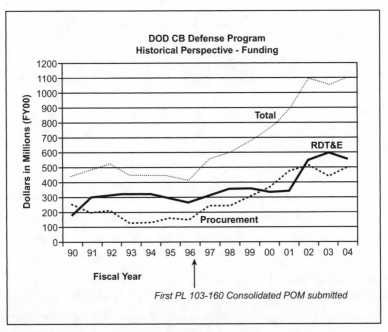

FIGURE 2-1 *DoD CB Defense Program Historical Funding*

About 45 percent of the annual funding was dedicated to procurement efforts, with about 50 percent dedicated to research and development efforts. This allotment would gradually reverse itself as new equipment began fielding. The other 5 percent addressed management (overhead) and counterproliferation support issues. In a model that would set the program's profile for the next decade, the funds for FY 1998–2003 were split about one-third for CB detection efforts, one-third for medical and nonmedical protection, 28 percent for technology base research, about 8 percent for decontamination and collective protection, with the remainder for management overhead projects (see Figure 2-2).[24]

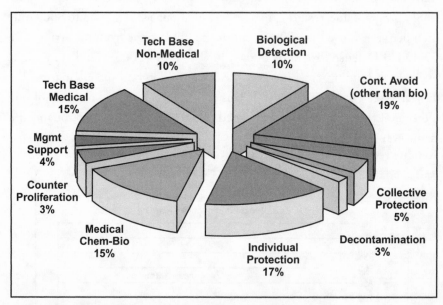

FIGURE 2-2 *DoD CB Defense Program Budget Allocations*

The heavy funding of detection efforts over decontamination or collective protection was mirrored by an emphasis on contamination avoidance (detecting hazardous CB warfare agents as quickly as possible) as the primary CB defense focus. Detectors, especially the biological detectors, were very expensive, because the users demanded smaller, lighter systems that detected and identified more agents with increased reliability and with fewer false alarms. Protective suits and masks were high-priority items; if there were CB warfare agents present, the troops had to survive to complete their missions. More than 90 percent of the medical funding went to biological vaccine development and production of anthrax vaccine, with the remainder allocated to medical chemical defense countermeasures. Decontamination systems and collective protection systems scored very low on the service priority lists, despite the glaring lack of capability in those areas.

In March 1996, the GAO criticized the ability of combat units to survive and sustain combat operations in a CB warfare environment, largely due to shortages of equipment and consumables, insufficient training, and lack of leadership attention.[25] The 1997 Quadrennial Defense Review stated, "the threat or use of chemical and biological weapons . . . is a likely condition of future warfare, including in the early stages of war to disrupt U.S. operations and logistics."[26] Yet at the tactical unit level, the CB defense capability had not visibly improved; it was as if the lessons learned from Operation Desert Storm had been either ignored or forgotten. On the other hand, the DoD CB Defense Program had not had much time to field these new joint capabilities and positively affect the readiness of U.S. military forces (or change the attitude of senior DoD leaders).

The joint program had shown its value at consolidating similar service-unique requirements. The Joint Chemical Agent Detector (JCAD) would consolidate six requirements to create a small, lightweight chemical agent detector to be used on aircraft and ships and for individual needs.[27] The expected fielding date for this new detector was 2003. The new JSLIST suit was to be fielded starting in 1998, and the four services committed to adopting one common aviator protective suit and mask and one common ground protective suit and mask. The anthrax vaccine would be in full production to achieve the goal of immunizing the total force from the number one BW threat. The Joint Vaccine Acquisition Program (JVAP) focused its research on vaccines for smallpox, botulinum toxin, tularemia, plague, SEB toxin, and a next-generation anthrax vaccine. The services would cooperate on the development of a joint NBC reconnaissance vehicle, expected to be fielded in 2001. The medical community wanted its new CB Protective Shelter by 1999, while an advanced integrated collective protection system was planned to be available for military vehicles, vans and shelters by 2000. In the decontamination area, the Modular Decontamination System (MDS) was to be available by 2000, with a new sorbent decontaminant in and a fixed site decontamination system fielded by 2002.

These programs would not be completed on schedule or on cost. This was due to a combination of changing user requirements, overestimates of the maturity of particular technologies, and an increasingly outdated test and evaluation infrastructure. The DoD program suffered from poor integration of the medical and nonmedical CB defense programs, poor threat definitions and risk management, and an inability to relate the importance of CB defense capabilities to other counterproliferation efforts such as counterforce and missile defense programs.[28] One particular problem was that the DoD CB Defense Program continued to operate as a stand-alone entity, rather than as part of the DoD counterproliferation strategy. Most CB defense specialists relied on the fact that the U.S. military needed equipment to protect its forces against the former Soviet Union's NBC weapons. When the Soviet Union went away, so did the main rationale for the program's existence. The failure to integrate the CB defense program into the counterproliferation strategy left it vulnerable to being minimized and ignored by most defense leaders. Because the DoD CB Defense Program failed to make its case effectively to the OSD leadership, it remained underfunded and unable to provide enough equipment to address the requirements of two nearly simultaneous military regional conflicts.

In 1996, OSD conducted a review of its counterproliferation portfolio, out of concern that they were spending too much in the areas of active defense acquisition efforts, especially missile defense. To put things into perspective, for every $1 that was invested in passive defense, about $2 went to counterforce efforts and $7 went to active defense programs. The target was to cut $1 billion from counterproliferation programs between 1998 and 2003. In the final recommendation, this OSD working group recommended a cut of nearly $1 billion out of the six-year DoD CB defense budget, while leaving the counterforce (special operations) and missile defense efforts largely whole. The Joint Staff and service leaders signed off on this assessment and forwarded the results to Deputy Secretary of Defense John White. The DATSD (CBM) pointed out the significant impacts to combat readiness issues to the OSD Program Review Group. White not only disapproved the CB defense cuts, he directed an $800 million increase to the FY 1998–2003 budget.

The Defense Advanced Research Projects Agency (DARPA), which answers to the Director of Defense Research and Engineering (DDR&E), decided to initiate its own BW defense research and development program, in line with its mission of managing and directing selected basic and applied research and development programs that were risky but potentially rewarding. However, DARPA had no intention of allowing the ATSD (NCB) to oversee or manage its budget, because such oversight would hamper its ability to conduct independent and high-risk projects. DARPA sought and received Congressional exemption from the law mandating a single point of contact for DoD CB defense research.[29] It would be up to the Deputy Assistant to the Secretary of Defense for Counterproliferation and CB Defense (DATSD [CP/CBD]), a position filled by Brig. Gen. Walt Busbee (Ret.) between 1997 and 1998, to manage the transition of any useful technology efforts from DARPA and Department of Energy (DoE) national labs into the DoD program.[30]

As a result of the Defense Reform Initiative report released in November 1997, OSD decided to transfer the ATSD (NCB) responsibilities for oversight of nuclear and CB defense matters to the DDR&E, who had oversight over all the DoD science and technology efforts. This action effectively eliminated the ATSD (NCB) position. The report recommended that the program's fund execution process be transferred from BMDO to the Defense Threat and Reduction Agency (DTRA, formerly the Defense Special Weapons Agency). Defense Secretary William Cohen's intent was to move the single focal point for CB defense from OSD to DTRA, given its new mandate to lead DoD effort to combat WMD activities. Congress blocked this new arrangement, but the ATSD (NCB) position remained unfilled after Dr. Harold Smith left.[31]

DTRA proposed a twenty-five-person CB directorate to assist the Deputy Assistant to the Secretary of Defense for Chemical-Biological Defense (DATSD [CBD]) in its oversight role.[32] The CB directorate, headed by a senior executive service civilian and a military deputy, would assist in the day-to-day execution of the program, relieving the DATSD (CBD) of the need to retain a large staff. In addition to supporting the OSD office and managing the CB Defense Program funds, the CB directorate took the chair of the JSTPCBD from the Army.[33] The directorate would have three branches: one for science and technology research, one to address advanced development and procurement areas, and one for funds management of the program. DTRA would also become a milestone decision authority for CB Defense Advanced Concept Technology Demonstrations (ACTDs).

Busbee strongly opposed the creation of DTRA and its CB directorate, proposing instead the creation of a larger DATSD staff to provide the stronger oversight role for which Congress had continuously asked. He thought the work could be done more efficiently and with fewer people at the OSD level. John Hamre, Deputy Secretary of Defense, overruled Busbee's objections and approved the Defense Reform Initiative with all of its recommendations. The DATSD (CBD) position remained, although very short-staffed, to oversee and maintain overall budget authority for the DoD CB Defense Program. Between 1998 and 1999, Colonel John Wade served as the acting DATSD (CBD) with Lieutenant Colonel Stan Lillie as his deputy.

When Dr. Anna Johnson-Winegar became the DATSD (CBD) in 1999, she created an OSD CB Defense Steering Committee, composed of four voting members—the DDR&E (who chaired the group), the DATSD (CBD), the Director of DTRA, and the director of the CB Directorate. This group would be the overarching body to discuss DoD CB defense issues and receive the Joint NBC Defense Board recommendations (see Figure 2-3). Perhaps most important, these four individuals would discuss and make changes to the final DoD CB Defense POM, prior to sending it to the Under Secretary of Defense for Acquisition, Technology, and Logistics (USD [AT&L]) to incorporate it into the DoD budget. The DATSD (CBD) would still develop the program strategy guidance, conduct programmatic reviews, oversee the budget, coordinate international efforts, and interface with Congress, the GAO, and other OSD agencies.

THE NEED TO REFORM THE PROGRAM

In addition to the many organizational changes and challenges going on, there were other reasons why the DoD CB Defense Program needed to change. As top-level debates about adversary nations' WMD programs and counterproliferation policy dominated the literature and symposia, the development of critical CB defense equipment relied primarily upon field grade action officers (not the general officer principals) within the JSMG, the JSIG, and the Joint NBC Defense Board. The lack of involvement by general officers combined with politicization within the joint committees limited the success of the program. These joint committees' action officers were serving their respective services, rather than the priorities voiced by the U.S. military's commanders in chief (CINCs), the Joint Staff, and OSD.[34]

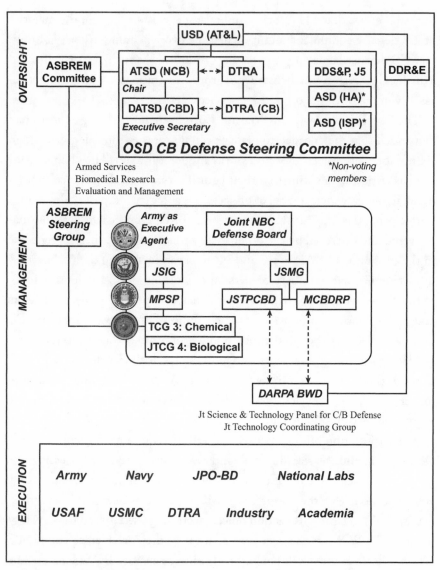

FIGURE 2-3 *DoD CB Defense Program Management Structure, circa 2000*[35]

While the committee approach had ensured the four services' equities and improving cooperation amongst the services, it had eroded the Army's leadership of the program by reducing its vote from the majority stockholder (to use an analogy) to a partner with 25 percent (or less) of the company's shares. Prior to 1994, the U.S. Army directly controlled about 70 percent of what constituted the DoD CB Defense Program. This was largely because it was the only service that had full-time military specialists, it bought the majority of CB defense equipment, and it owned the overwhelming majority of military CB defense laboratory and testing grounds.[36] As such, the program had a distinct leadership and focus toward ground operations, which was not necessarily in line with the other three services' desires.

The Air Force, Navy, and Marine Corps general and flag officers had demanded that they needed to manage equal shares of the defense program (in numbers of projects, not necessarily monetary value). They defined this need as critical to ensuring that their equities were met, although certainly a desire to increase their control of projects was apparent. As part of these committee processes, the Army's action officers often found themselves outmaneuvered and outvoted by the other three services, despite their larger stake in the program. The Air Force and Navy began increasing their laboratory infrastructure and numbers of personnel working on CB defense efforts. While the Marine Corps had no laboratories, it appointed project managers and hired contract support to oversee some of the most important CB defense projects. Although the total number of projects was reduced by consolidating similar requirements into joint efforts, inefficiencies actually grew through the introduction of new staff and agencies and by the demand of longer coordination cycles. New capabilities were not being fielded in line with the overly optimistic schedules being presented.

The JSIG action officers focused on writing requirement documents and working on multiservice doctrine and training rather than assessing the progress (or lack thereof) of the materiel programs. In nearly all cases, they voted in concert with their respective JSMG acquisition colleagues in a partisan fashion.[37] While the JSIG action officers were supposed to lead the development of the POM as the user representatives, they deferred to the JSMG action officers in the development of a business-sensitive POM budget. The JSIG developed several joint priority lists to guide this budget drill, one for nonmedical programs, one for medical programs, and one for technology base efforts, all of which had to be integrated into the budget drill. These lists were more reflective of the services' acquisition desires than the CINCs' CB defense requirements and priorities. Tweaking last year's budget plan, rather than assessing their progress and need for change, was the norm.

These turf wars were not uncommon in other defense acquisition programs. The services have three missile defense programs, for example, overseen by a joint agency, as opposed to one or two joint missile defense programs. The Joint Strike Fighter is the first joint fighter plane program since the F4 jet aircraft was built during the Vietnam conflict. Noted general officers such as Wesley Clark, Anthony Zinni, and Tommy Franks have all commented on the tendency of service chiefs to protect their budgets at all costs, rather than supporting joint operations and developing joint concepts and programs. General Zinni once noted, "We teach our ensigns and second lieutenants to recognize that sister service as the enemy. It wants our money; it wants our force structure; it wants our recruits. So we rope ourselves into a system where we fight each other for money, programs, and weapon systems. We try to out-doctrine each other, by putting pedantic little anal apertures to work in doctrine centers, trying to find ways to ace out the other services and become the dominant service in some way."[38] This attitude starts at the top and is mirrored all the way down, affecting even the relatively small acquisition programs such as the jointly managed CB defense projects.[39]

In July 1999, a federal commission evaluating the government's capability to combat the proliferation of WMDs released its report to Congress. The commission found that the U.S. government was not effectively organized to combat proliferation and lacked a comprehensive approach to achieving this objective.[40] The report called for presidential leadership and a renewed priority on this issue, clear policy guidance on priorities and objectives, a dedicated intelligence system focusing on early warning of threats, an effective interagency process with clear delineation of responsibilities on developing a coordinated program, a broader effort to prepare for the potential use of NBC weapons, and a greater engagement with international allies and potential proliferators. The report graphically demonstrated the large number of government agencies involved in combating WMD proliferation, in addition to the usual DoD agencies addressing CB defense (see Appendix A). It bemoaned the lack of progress in developing CB defense equipment since the Gulf War, and noted that the U.S. government no longer had the intellectual infrastructure for understanding the biological and chemical threats in the same fashion as it did for nuclear threats.

The report noted that USD (P) was not sufficiently engaged in counterproliferation strategy, given the elimination of the Assistant Secretary of Defense for International Security Policy (ASD [ISP]) position (those responsibilities had been assumed by the Assistant Secretary of Defense for Strategy and

Threat Reduction (ASD [S&TR])). The ATSD (NCB)'s absence had resulted in a critical leadership gap, and the Assistant Secretary of Defense for Special Operations and Low Intensity Conflict (ASD [SO/LIC]) was not addressing the possibility of terrorist CBRN threats. The report saw the DoD budget process for counterproliferation programs (to include passive defense) as broken and its threat definition within the requirements process as inadequate. The missile defense program was taking substantially more funds than the CB Defense Program, although most agreed that both efforts were critical. The DoD CB Defense Program lacked the organizational leadership and an integrated planning needed to relate the importance of new CB defense requirements to other emerging counterproliferation requirements.

Questions from Congressional committees and numerous audits by the GAO continued to probe at why DoD's overall CB defense readiness wasn't visibly improving despite the management reforms taken five years earlier. While the DATSD (CBD) testified before Congress as to specific CB defense acquisition issues, there were nine program offices among the four services and DTRA that had acquisition decision authorities responsible for executing the programs. The DATSD (CBD) had difficulty directing improvements in specific programs without the support of these decision authorities, but Congress didn't want to hear that. It was increasingly obvious that no one was developing capabilities to respond to CBRN hazards caused from terrorist incidents. In August 1999, Deputy Secretary of Defense John Hamre directed a review of the DoD CB Defense Program management structure to identify which features of the program arose from approved requirements and the Defense Planning Guidance; to identify how the current process was discouraging the services from using their own funds to procure CB defense equipment; and to identify alternative programming alternatives, including returning the responsibility to develop CB defense equipment to the services.

The joint committees protested that there had been several advances in NBC defense capabilities. Overall funding for CB defense programs had increased, which demonstrated (to them) that their program was increasingly viewed as important. The program had fielded new CB defense equipment to the armed forces (although most of these projects had been initiated and matured prior to the formation of the joint committees). The program had forced the creation of joint programs where multiple, similar requirements existed. Service cooperation had increased, with all four services meeting to discuss all programs and issues with consensus-driven conclusions. The GAO disagreed with this rosy view, noting that the CINCs were not happy with their current CB defense capability, that the JSIG's methodology for determining war-fighter requirements was flawed, and the overall program was still too slow to procure and field new equipment.

By 2000, after two years of production, the number of fielded JSLIST suits was far behind expectations. There would only be enough protective suits between 2003 and 2007—including numbers of older BDOs—to support requirements for little more than one major theater of war. The JSMG had adopted a business strategy for producing the 4.4 million protective suits over a fifteen-year period. While this would minimize any production spikes and inventory issues, it also deliberately pushed the "get well" date for protective suits to 2012 or so. This strategy also conveniently released the services from buying any consumable protective suits with their own funds. Nearly all CB detection programs, to include the joint NBC reconnaissance vehicle, had slipped on cost and schedule issues, adding years to the fielding dates and millions of dollars to what was already the most expensive aspect of the program. The battle management system Joint Warning and Reporting Network (JWARN) was three years behind schedule and was not integrated with the Army's Maneuver Control System or DoD Global Command and Communication System. Schedules for the proposed joint service aviator mask and general-purpose mask programs were slipping and program costs were increasing. The planned joint service protective aircrew chemical ensemble was delayed while action officers argued over the potential that helicopter rotor wash could cause chemical agent to penetrate the suits. The anthrax vaccine production line was beset with critical challenges that prevented the DoD from executing its total force anthrax vaccination program. Rep. Christopher Shays (R-CT) called for the suspension of the mandatory vaccination program in June 2000, in part because BioPort was having problems getting FDA approval of its new manufacturing processes. Dr. Johnson-Winegar nearly cancelled the anthrax vaccine program because of these challenges, but heavy pressure from the Joint Staff and CINCs convinced Defense Secretary Cohen to continue the program.

There were no new medical CB defense countermeasures despite more than a decade of work and many millions of dollars in research funds. Decon programs (including replacements for the ancient M12A1 power-driven decon apparatus and its DS-2 decontaminant) were going nowhere, and collective protection shelters (other than those for medical units) were similarly stalled due to unrealistic requirements and unfounded expectations of immature technologies. The CB defense science and technology program had not transitioned any new technologies to advanced development projects in more than a decade, with the possible exception of a sorbent decontaminant resin. The proposed joint NBC recon system to replace the M93A1 Fox vehicle was not due for several years, due to weight issues and the inability to keep its detector units on track for fielding. Most new equipment designs had come from other countries or directly from industry rather than government labs. In a very real sense, the government labs had become contracting experts and testing agencies rather than true innovators in the field of CB defense research and development.

Each service had its unique pet projects in the budget, even as the program increasingly failed to field new capabilities.[41] Test and evaluation costs continued to increase every year, because the services' test and evaluation agencies demanded the program pay for new testing equipment, additional tests for specific service requirements, and evaluators' salaries. As a result, the DoD CB Defense Program stretched out or shifted procurement schedules to accommodate a broad research effort featuring multiple programs aimed at addressing current and future CB warfare threats. There was not enough money in the DoD CB Defense Program budget to fully outfit the military's two major theater-of-war requirements and simultaneously advance all of its priorities in research and development. OSD knew the CB defense acquisition projects were slipping, the four service chiefs and their staffs knew, even Congress knew, but the risk was deemed acceptable in light of other more urgent defense projects.

In November 1999, the DoD inspector general released a study on the results of protective mask surveillance, noting that of 19,218 masks tested over a two-year period, 10,322 had critical defects. A critical deficiency was defined as one that had "the potential to result in mask leakage and may impact on the protection of the wearer," including dirty or leaking outlet valves, leaks in the external drink tubes, or missing side voicemitter gaskets.[42] The report noted that the commanders had failed to provide adequate training, the field manuals were poorly written, and the masks were awkwardly made and difficult to maintain. The implication was that tens of thousands of service members were in peril due to poorly designed masks and insufficient training. What the DoD inspector general failed to acknowledge was that military leaders at the unit level could have easily repaired the overwhelming majority of the nearly 20,000 critically deficient masks with very little time or effort.

In February 2000, DLA directed the services not to use BDO suits from two specific lots manufactured in 1989 and 1992 by Isratex, Inc. of New York City. Many of the suits from the 1992 lot contained holes and tears that had gone undetected until the DoD inspector general directed a quality inspection of the suits during an investigation into alleged fraud. Apparently, Isratex employees were providing samples of their work that were specifically manufactured to contract specifications during inspections, but the majority of their work was made with different material and substandard assembly.[43] Further investigations led to indictments of the managers and corporate officers of Isratex on conspiracy and fraud charges in October 1998, and sentencing taking place in April and May 2000. In May 2000, DLA directed that all 780,000 BDO suits manufactured by Isratex be designated for training use only, although it was the 173,000 suits manufactured in 1992 that were the suspect. Many of these suits had been distributed to troops in the field, including units in Bosnia and South Korea. This had severe effects on some units, such as the Second Infantry Division, which saw its retail suit inventory plummet from 100 percent to 48 percent. Because these were consumable items held at unit level as well as in warehouses, tracking down the individual Isratex suits would be challenging. Messages went out to all units to verify whether the Isratex lots were present in their inventory, and all four services were able to turn in their Isratex suits and verify that they had searched all of their supplies. About a quarter million of the Isratex suits could not be accounted for; they may have been used up in training exercises or thrown out, but they were not in the supply chain.

These reports on critically flawed protective masks and protective suits caused some degree of concern within Congress. Dr. Johnson-Winegar, as the single focal point for DoD CB defense, became the target of many congressional hearings and questions. In her capacity, she also fielded many congressional questions about BioPort's anthrax vaccine and the Army's chemical demilitarization program. Her ability to affect the maintenance of the protective suit and mask issues was limited, however, as the services stressed their Title 10 responsibilities to oversee the training and equipping of their respective troops. While Dr. Johnson-Winegar attempted to increase the focus on CB defense readiness issues in the services, the service leadership politely ignored what they saw as attempts to influence their prerogatives. It was her office, however, that would suffer Congress's and the media's criticism of military CB defense capabilities.

CHAPTER 3

REFORMING THE DoD CB DEFENSE PROGRAM

*Most new things are not good, and die an early death; but those which
push themselves forward and by slow degrees force themselves on the
attention of mankind are the unconscious productions of human wisdom,
and must have honest consideration, and must not be made the subject
of unreasoning prejudice.*

—THOMAS REED, U.S. POLITICIAN

During the mid-to-late 1990s, the U.S. government's conception of "weapons of mass destruction" was changing, but these changes were not addressed by the DoD CB Defense Program and its joint committee management structure. The 1994 reorganization was undertaken because of the Cold War military acquisition effort's failure to provide necessary capabilities in the Persian Gulf War. However, the reorganization did not address increased concerns over a lack in biodefense adeptness, the maturation of the DoD counterproliferation program, and the requirements of the DoD Domestic Preparedness Program. The DoD CB Defense Program's continued and resolute focus on NBC defense solely within the context of traditional military war-fighting operations was resisting the need to address these external pressures.

On December 7, 1993, Defense Secretary Les Aspin announced the Defense Counterproliferation Initiative at a speech to the National Academy of Sciences. He had five major points to present. First, counterproliferation was a new mission, not a continuation of the Cold War. Second, developing nonnuclear technologies to combat "future Saddams" and counter their ballistic missiles would require a new acquisition approach. Third, the Chairman of the Joint Chiefs of Staff (JCS) was directed to develop a military process to operationally effect this strategy. Fourth, intelligence collection on future adversaries and their WMD programs would have to be a key component. And last, international cooperation was a key factor. Not only should U.S. allies and security partners be concerned about the growing proliferation of NBC weapons, said Aspin, all the world's countries must become involved: success would require a global initiative.[1] When Defense Secretary Aspin left his post shortly after that speech it fell to Deputy Secretary of Defense John Deutch and Assistant Secretary of Defense for Nuclear Security and Counterproliferation Ashton Carter (later the Assistant Secretary of Defense for International Security Policy) to refine this policy.

In response to Aspin's initiative, the DoD created the Counterproliferation Program Review Committee, which included the Departments of State, Defense, and Energy, the Central Intelligence Agency (CIA), the JCS, and the Arms Control Disarmament Agency, to focus on the acquisition efforts related to or directly supporting counterproliferation.[2] Primarily, this included an annual review of programs within the DoD, the Department of Energy (DoE), and the CIA, and an annual, prioritized list of areas of capability enhancements.[3] In 1995, the Chairman of the JCS designated counterproliferation as one of his fourteen joint war-fighting capability assessment (JWCA) teams. The Deterrence and Counterproliferation (Det/CP) JWCA, run under the JCS J-5 directorate (Strategic Plans and Policies), would work with staffs of the combatant commands on counterproliferation issues and to ensure that the CINC's priorities were addressed by DoD acquisition efforts.

The DoD identified four major areas of investment in its 1996 "Proliferation: Threat and Response" report: counterforce, active defense, passive defense, and "measures to counter paramilitary, covert, and terrorist NBC threats," later called consequence management. Counterforce addressed those military capabilities used to choose targets and plan attacks, and to seize, disable, destroy, disrupt, interdict, neutralize, or deny the use of NBC weapons and launch platforms and their supporting command and control, logistics, and reconnaissance assets while minimizing collateral effects. Ideally, DoD forces would defeat these NBC threats prior to the enemy's preparing the weapons systems for use against U.S. forces. SOCOM and the Air Force would play a large role in this area, including planning attacks against hardened and deeply buried targets such as underground command-and-control facilities and WMD production and storage facilities. Active defense involved capabilities that would detect, track, identify, intercept, destroy, and neutralize NBC warheads delivered by airborne launch platforms, ballistic missiles, and cruise missiles, again while minimizing collateral effects. Primarily, this addressed air and missile defense systems that would intercept any launched CB warfare missiles or aircraft armed with CB delivery systems. The Ballistic Missile Defense Organization (today the Missile Defense Agency) oversaw several theater-based missile defense programs, while the Air Force had its Airborne Laser Program, a separate missile defense effort.

Passive defense involved military capabilities that provided protection against NBC weapon effects, including contamination avoidance (reconnaissance, detection, and identification), force protection (individual and collective protection and medical support), and recovery (decontamination). That is, the traditional NBC defense program made up the passive defense pillar of counterproliferation. It would be interesting to know who made the decision to equate NBC defense with passive defense, a new term, instead of using the existing term, but it is easy to see how this term evolved. During the Cold War, the DoD had developed a strategic nuclear defense strategy consisting of counterforce (bombers, submarines, and ballistic missiles aimed at Soviet military bases and launch sites), active defense (interceptors and antimissile defenses), and passive defense (civil defense efforts intended to protect noncombatants). The civil defense efforts included radiological detection, individual and collective protection efforts, decontamination, and medical countermeasures. It must have seemed natural for counterproliferation experts to label NBC defense as "passive" in the 1990s. It was not a label, however, that the DoD CB defense community would embrace. The term *passive defense* had a negative connotation compared with the U.S. military's more action-oriented operational lingo.

DoD nonproliferation and counterproliferation policy, strategy, and associated programs would grow and mature throughout the 1990s. The Clinton administration's nuclear arms strategy changed in November 1997 to permit U.S. nuclear strikes after enemy attacks using CB weapons, a decision that was fiercely debated as disproportional. Indeed, the whole rationale of the counterproliferation policy was to improve U.S. conventional military capabilities to defeat or deter a Saddam-like adversary, ideally increasing the number of proportional, nonnuclear options. In 1998, Secretary Cohen formed the Threat Reduction Advisory Committee (TRAC), a group of civilian and defense experts, whose purpose was to identify threats and develop solutions to counterproliferation strategy.[4] In 1999, the Counterproliferation Mission Support Senior Oversight Group (CP-MSOG) was created to focus on cooperative efforts to improve counterproliferation among the CINCs.

The effectiveness of the strategy's implementation is fiercely debated throughout the defense community. Although the Counterproliferation Review Committee's annual report noted that some of the highest priorities were passive defense programs, the overwhelming majority of funding went to the services' active defense and counterforce programs. For every $1 invested in the passive defense program, $2 went to counterforce and $7 went to active defense. It was clear that the DoD's focus was not on passive defense. The counterproliferation crowd saw the DoD CB Defense Program as small potatoes, and the DoD CB defense community was not interested in participating within the counterproliferation program. In fact, the CB defense community was somewhat afraid of being subsumed by the larger missile defense effort. Overall, the active defense, counterforce, passive defense, and consequence management communities operated more as distinct entities than as a cooperative family of defense systems trying to combat WMD employment.[5]

BIOLOGICAL DEFENSE MATURES

Prior to 1990, there was little discussion in the United States about countermeasures to biological warfare threats, other than within arms control debates and strategy sessions, and as a passing nod in research and development programs. General Colin Powell, as chair of the Joint Chiefs of Staff, lambasted the Army in a classified memorandum for its poor biological defense efforts during the first Gulf War.[6] Efforts during the 1980s focused on developing protective measures against CW threats, which was seen as much more credible than BW threats. The armed forces had protective masks that were designed to filter out biological organisms, but no detectors to warn service members when to put on their masks. Before 1990, fielded military biological defense measures were limited to medical surveillance, vaccines, and treatments. The top researchers at the Army's laboratories at Aberdeen Proving Ground, Maryland, admitted that biological warfare was not seen as an immediate tactical threat and that they felt developing biological detectors was technologically too challenging. There had been at least two active research programs in 1990 to develop a reliable, portable BW detection system, but they were not high priorities. Neither system was fielded in Operation Desert Storm.

Although the DoD did have an anthrax vaccine available and was conducting research on several other vaccines, no one had really thought about the challenge of vaccinating the total force against the major BW agents. It's hard to say why, given concerns about the known scope of the Soviet BW program effort, for instance, the subject of vaccines did not get more attention. Possibly the military leadership felt that biological warfare could be addressed with threats of nuclear retaliation, and that it was not, therefore, a credible tactical challenge like the CW threat. Meanwhile, the Army's CB defense research and development program was still catching up on building defensive measures for the chemical and radiological threats after a long dry spell between 1972 and 1981. It seemed more likely the U.S. military would face a CW or even nuclear threat on the battlefield than a BW threat. That all changed after the first Gulf War.

The Joint Program Office for Biological Defense (JPO-BD, or JPO-Bio) was created following the first Gulf War, after General Colin Powell's blistering assessment in a classified memorandum. An interim plan to fix this deficiency, dated March 1992, failed to reach joint consensus. A Joint Services Committee for Biological Defense, led by the Army's ODCSOPS chemical officer, conducted a study to outline a DoD operational concept for biological defense, addressing the areas of detection, protection, decontamination, and immunization. On June 28, 1993, the USD (A&T) approved the formation of the JPO. This office was initially chaired by an Army colonel (Col. Gene Fuzy) and deliberately stationed in Falls Church, Virginia, in an attempt to break away from what the Air Force, Navy, and Marine Corps felt was undue influence by the "old Army CB defense crowd." [7] This office would have a small number of Air Force and Navy personnel assigned to it, due to its charter to centrally fund and manage all DoD biological detection research and development and vaccine production efforts. A general officer steering committee staffed and approved the charter, defining its roles and organizational structure, prior to final approval by Deputy Secretary of Defense John Deutch on May 19, 1994.

The JPO-BD would manage its own program element budget line, act as the deciding authority for its own programs, and report through the Army acquisition executive to the USD (A&T) with oversight by the ATSD (AE).

Its programs would include vaccine production and procurement, a fixed/mobile platform-based, point biological integrated detection system (BIDS), a long-range biological standoff detection system (LR-BSDS), and the Navy's shipboard interim biological agent detector (IBAD) (some service-unique requirements still remained). The Air Force's experimental biological detector Morning Song, employed in Desert Storm, was not one of the JPO's projects. The JPO-BD's programs would not be considered a major defense acquisition program; although its programs were considered important, the budgetary levels did not put it anywhere near the major programs that were directly overseen by the OSD, such as the Joint Strike Fighter and the Crusader artillery system.

The JPO's decision to develop a mobile biological point detection system resulted in the BIDS program. This was a three-stage evolutionary effort; the first system would be a nondevelopmental item, using commercial biological detection systems mounted in a military high-mobility, multipurpose, wheeled vehicle (HMMWV) platform. The M31 BIDS had five components: an aerosol particle counter/sizer that would indicate the presence of an aerosol associated with a BW attack (having particulates sized between 1-5 microns); a biological sampler to sample the ambient air and concentrate the particle stream to a wet collector; a liquid sampler to transfer the concentrated liquid to sample tubes arranged in a carousel; a bioluminescence analyzer to differentiate bacteria from natural, airborne materials such as pollen and mold spores; and a manual antibody-based detector to monitor the results of specific antigen-antibody reactions. The total cycle time from initial trigger to identification would take less than forty-five minutes, with the BIDS operator conducting tests for up to four BW agents simultaneously. The improved version of the BIDS, the M31A1, would replace the commercial equipment that would quickly be obsolete by industry standards (and therefore not sustainable), increase the number of detected BW agents to eight, and reduce the time of detection to less than thirty minutes. The final version of the BIDS, the M31A2, would use the planned Joint Biological Point Detection System (JBPDS), just starting its research and development. The JBPDS would decrease the time of detection to fifteen minutes and increase the number of BW agents it could detect from eight to ten. The JBPDS was the single biodetector that all four services would use, and included a "man-portable" version for the Marine Corps (*man-portable* being defined as requiring four people to carry), a mobile version for the Army, and a fixed-site version for Air Force bases, with fielding expected to start in 2000.

In 1998, one could sense some undercurrents of dissension within the Pentagon as far as how the DoD CB Defense Program was addressing biological defense in particular. Perhaps this was a result of Saddam Hussein's continued resistance to ongoing UN inspections in Iraq and the U.S. Central Command (CENTCOM) response of Operation Desert Thunder and Desert Fox. Perhaps it was the result of an increasing role of counterproliferation discussions within the OSD, the Joint Staff, and the CINCs. The OSD and the United Kingdom's Ministry of Defense jointly addressed the challenges of biological defense policy and programmatic issues, in the interests of ensuring that both nations would have similar CB defense capabilities and policies in future military operations. Although the two allies' strategies did not mirror each other (for instance, the UK had an optional, not mandatory, vaccination program), the discussions were fruitful. Critics of the DoD CB Defense Program pointed out that much of the doctrine, training, and equipment for BW defense seemed to be too similar to CW defense, with the implication that this approach was somehow flawed. The CINCs were not happy with the capabilities they had for surviving and sustaining combat operations in a CB warfare environment, and they turned to the Joint Staff for assistance. The J5/Nuclear and Counterproliferation Branch, then headed by Capt. Patrick Casey, a Navy submariner, chaired the Det/CP JWCA team and would be directed to review the DoD CB Defense Program and recommend actions to address the CINCs' concerns.

The DoD CB Defense Program had funded that Air Base/Port Biological Detection Advanced Concept Technology Demonstration (ACTD) starting in 1996, which was to field eight sets of SENTEL Corporation's prototype Portal Shield Biological Warfare Agent Detection System, networked to a central command node, four each in U.S. Pacific Command (PACOM) and CENTCOM's areas of responsibility, in 1998. These sensors were deployed during Operation Desert Thunder, and although there were some operational concerns about sensitivity and how quickly the sensors detected BW agents (only four agents, up to forty-five minutes cycle time from sampling to warning), the geographic commands were desperate to get any kind of in-theater biological detection capability at their seaports and air bases. The main concern was that an adversary would use biological agents prior to initiating hostile ground movements, since it took days to weeks for some BW agents to fully manifest their effects. There would be no time to deploy mobile biological detection units from the United States. The Det/CP JWCA, with assistance from IDA, developed an analysis that recommended the DoD procure Portal Shields for an additional fourteen sites between 1999 and 2002, a proposal which was accepted by the Joint Requirements Oversight Council (JROC) and approved by the OSD. The services resented this decision. They did not believe that an adequate concept of employment was in place to support this decision and that maintaining the Portal Shield sites on a full-time basis was too expensive.

In 1998, U.S. European Command (EUCOM) was the sponsor of an ACTD called Joint Biological Remote Early Warning System (JBREWS), designed to test and evaluate a short-range biological standoff detection system (transportable by a ground vehicle) and several sentinel sensors networked into command nodes, essentially an attempt to reduce the warning and detection cycle to allow forces in the field to be warned earlier. If successful, the ACTD would transfer what it had learned to the standoff biological detection project that JPO-BD had underway. The early ACTD results were not favorable, and the DoD CB Defense Program moved to shut down the standoff biological detection effort after only a year of preliminary evaluations. EUCOM assessed JBREWS as not identifying any mature technologies that were ready for transition into a mature program in 2001, and the DoD CB Defense Program immediately diverted the funds for developing a biological standoff detection program to other projects. This action alarmed the CINCs tremendously; five combatant commands had identified biological standoff detection as their top CB defense priority.

The CINCs were concerned about the fact that the Army had fielded only one BIDS company, the 310th Chemical Company, a reserve Army unit stationed in Anniston, Alabama. The Army planned on fielding one active BIDS company in 1999, the 7th Chemical Company. All other BIDS units were to remain in the Army reserves. What this meant to the CINCs was that the Army was prepared to send the one active-duty BIDS company to one major theater of war, and then the reserve unit BIDS company would have to be called up in the event the military had to respond to a second theater of war. So if CENTCOM got the active BIDS company based on priorities, PACOM was going to be put on hold until the reserve BIDS company deployed, and that was not satisfactory to PACOM. In addition, the CINCs were concerned about the continuing shortages of NBC defense equipment being reported by the services and the combat units that would be deploying into their theaters.

In January 1999, the Det/CP JWCA presented its analysis and recommendations on the two issues to the JROC. The JROC agreed that a combination of fixed-site (Portal Shield) and mobile biodetection systems (BIDS) were required to meet CINC requirements. The Joint Staff prepared language for the Secretary of Defense to direct the Army to field a second active-duty BIDS company in the short term. The JROC also designated the DoD CB Defense Program as a special-interest topic. This meant that the DoD CB Defense Program would be expected to brief its POM budget strategy to the JROC annually, outlining how it met the CINCs' requirements.[8] The services in general and the Chemical Corps in particular were less than thrilled with the Joint Staff's "assistance." To them, the Joint Staff was interfering in their role of managing the program. To the Joint Staff and CINCs' staffs, the DoD CB Defense Program was failing to execute its mission effectively.

DOMESTIC PREPAREDNESS—
A NEW INITIATIVE

What was initially called "domestic preparedness" had its roots in what might be called the initial concerns about modern homeland security. The Oklahoma City bombing occurred only a month after the Aum Shinrikyo incident in 1995, adding the issue of large amounts of conventional explosives to the definition of *weapons of mass destruction*. The increasing concerns about terrorist employment of CBRN hazards in potential WMD situations had a ripple effect through the federal government, starting with President Clinton's release of PDD-39 in June 1995 outlining the administration's policy on counterterrorism. The Federal Emergency Management Agency (FEMA) and the Federal Bureau of Investigation (FBI) would formalize PDD-39 by modifying the FEMA Federal Response Plan on February 7, 1997, with a terrorism annex outlining the two agencies' roles prior to, during, and following a terrorist incident.

Although there was no real evidence that the domestic terrorist threat was growing, Congress wanted military assets prepared and in place in the unlikely event that a terrorist CBRN incident did take place within U.S. borders.[9]

This legislation had a particular section (Title XIV), called the Defense Against Weapons of Mass Destruction Act, otherwise known as the Nunn-Lugar-Domenici Act, for the three senators responsible for the language. It had four sections, one on a proposed domestic preparedness program, a second on interdiction of WMD and related materials, the third on control and disposition of WMD and related materials threatening the United States, and the last on coordination of policy and countermeasures against proliferation of WMDs. The immediate significance of this act was the direction that the DoD should carry out a program to provide civilian personnel of federal, state, and local agencies with training and expert advice regarding emergency responses to a use or threatened use of a WMD or related material. The DoD Domestic Preparedness Program would become an effort to train a core of emergency responders at 120 cities, establish a helpline and a hotline for these responders, and develop a military CB emergency response team. The Army was appointed as the executive lead for the effort, with the Secretary of the Army designating Headquarters, Army Materiel Command (HQ AMC) as the lead Army agency. HQ AMC designated the U.S. Army's CBDCOM, (changed to SBCCOM in 1998) to execute the program. The DoD CB Defense Program would not lead, manage, fund, or otherwise influence this effort. Its focus would remain on the military war-fighting mission and would not address this new mission of "domestic preparedness."

The Program Director for Domestic Preparedness at SBCCOM, Jim Warrington, would spend $79 million between 1997 and 1998, $50 million in 1999, and $31.4 million in 2000 during the execution of this program. Between 1997 and 2000, the Army would visit more than a hundred cities and train tens of thousands of emergency responders in what was referred to as "the NBC delta," spending a week to educate a city's emergency responders on what made responding to NBC weapons effects different from responding to more common hazardous materials incidents. Six months later, the DoD trainers would return to host a daylong city exercise for the city. SBCCOM created a CB helpline to assist emergency responders with technical questions and with establishing their local programs. In cooperation with the National Response Center, SBCCOM also developed a 24/7 CB hotline for reporting suspected or actual CBRN terrorist incidents. DHHS was to oversee the creation of medical response teams in major metropolitan areas. FEMA would develop a database called Rapid Response Information System to provide an online source of information on CB agents and similar technical issues.[10]

The Domestic Preparedness Program trained Denver emergency responders in June 1997, in anticipation of the Summit of Eight meeting and Timothy McVeigh's trial, being held at that city. In late August 1997, Philadelphia became the first city to receive the formal "train-the-trainer" course. The city training program was controversial, more because of its success than its failures. FEMA and the National Fire Academy criticized the city training program, possibly resenting DoD involvement in what they considered their domain. The state governments didn't like the DoD dealing directly with the city governments instead of going through them. Amy Smithson of the Henry L. Stimson Center wrote a report criticizing the program as inefficient, wasteful, and ill planned.[11] The criticism was undeserved. In an unprecedented effort, the Domestic Preparedness Program delivered vital training across the country to address a perceived national vulnerability, and many emergency responders were appreciative.[12]

CBDCOM created a CB quick reaction force, later called a CB rapid response team (CB-RRT), using the Army's Tech Escort Unit (TEU) as the core specialists, a fly-away analytical laboratory, and a robust command-and-control center. The TEU had more than 120 military and civilian personnel stationed between Aberdeen Proving Ground, Pine Bluff Arsenal, and Dugway Proving Ground, most of them involved in remediation and transportation of U.S. chemical weapons, but increasingly involved in support to federal agencies during national special security events. The CB-RRT had memorandums of agreement with Army ordnance units, and Navy and Air Force CB response assets, as well as traditional medical CB experts such as USAMRICD and USAMRIID. The Marine Corps' Chemical and Biological Incident Response Force (CBIRF), activated in April 1996 to support detection, decontamination, medical, and security response at a terrorist CBRN incident, was a partner separate from the CB-RRT.[13] Neither the CBIRF nor the CB-RRT would receive funding or support from the DoD CB Defense Program, because these two units were using currently available military and commercial equipment and were not considered war-fighting units.

In September 1998, DoD and the Department of Justice (DoJ) began talks on transferring the Domestic Preparedness Program to the DoJ. Out of a desire to create a one-stop shop for emergency responders, Attorney General Janet Reno proposed the establishment of a national domestic preparedness program under the Office of Justice Programs to assume the responsibilities of working with the cities and states in the area of responding to CBRN terrorist incidents. President Clinton designated the DoJ to assume programming and funding responsibilities as of October 1, 2000. The handover was less than elegant; despite the DoD's superior technical knowledge, the National Domestic Preparedness Office did not want to benefit from the Army's experience, preferring to establish a brand-new office, helpline, and training and exercise program unique to their own perceptions.

The DoE national laboratories (in particular, Sandia and Lawrence Livermore) became interested in obtaining funds to produce CB defense equipment for the military and emergency personnel responding to terrorist events. After the Tokyo subway sarin incident in March 1995, new domestic markets had emerged outside of the once military-only, small target audience of CB defense specialists. The national labs had attempted to support the DoD in developing prototype standoff chemical agent detectors during Operation Desert Shield, and they were interested in keeping their scientists and engineers employed, particularly because work in the traditional fields of nuclear weapons research were scarce after the Cold War ended. Although efforts at the national labs remained relatively small and did not result in any new ideas, they would continue to work independently of DoD research and development projects.

In October 1997, Deputy Secretary of Defense John Hamre asked for an assessment on how to integrate the National Guard and reserves into the Nunn-Lugar-Domenici–sponsored Domestic Preparedness Program. After some discussion, this led to a tasking to the Under Secretary of Defense for Personnel and Readiness (USD [P&R]) to construct a complete model for developing component reserve units into a consequence management response for domestic terrorism incidents involving WMDs. The USD (P&R) turned to Under Secretary of the Army Mike Walker, who created what he called a "tiger team," headed by Brig. Gen. Roger Schultz from the Army's Director of Military Support. In a period of about a month, the team drafted a plan laying out the concepts, model, direction, and funding required to develop a team of National Guard soldiers with the mission of supporting a response to the use of WMDs.

One of the team's findings was that, despite the creation of the CB-RRT and CBIRF, few military elements were focused, trained, and equipped to execute this mission. The report recommended the creation of rapid response assessment teams, one for each state and territory in the United States. Each rapid response assessment team would consist of twenty-two people, including a four-person command cell, three-person reconnaissance cell, four-person medical cell, and others specialized in security, logistics, air liaison, and communications, that could respond within four to eight hours of notification. Additionally, the report recommended developing and equipping Army and Air Force reconnaissance and decontamination elements specifically for domestic response. The report called for the creation of a consequence management program integration office, with a staff of fourteen to oversee and execute the program, including coordinating with the OSD and the national guard, facilitating training exercises, purchasing the equipment, developing budget requirements, and leveraging the Domestic Preparedness Program's efforts.[14]

The initial commitment to which Secretary Cohen would agree was to deploy one team per FEMA region (of which there were ten). The initial teams would be located in Los Alamitos, California; Aurora, Colorado; Peoria, Illinois; Natick, Massachusetts; Saint Roberts, Missouri; Scotia, New York; Fort Indiantown Gap, Pennsylvania; Austin, Texas; and Tacoma, Washington. Each team was projected to cost about $2 million to stand up, not including the training and sustainment costs. After a fifteen-month training period, each team would be evaluated to determine its readiness. In addition, in response to congressional direction, the DoD began plans for the creation of forty-four "light" military support detachments based on the twenty-two-person model to complete the deployment throughout the United States. In October 1998, Congress authorized and funded the creation of ten rapid assessment and initial detection (RAID) teams through the National Defense Authorization Act for FY 1999. The first ten teams were planned to be fully mission-capable by January 2000. Later, DoD officials would view the term *RAID* as too forceful and changed it to WMD civil support teams. Today this effort has grown to fifty-five full teams across the nation, one in each state and territory, and two in California and Texas, and continues to thrive under the National Guard Bureau's watchful gaze.

The 1997 Defense Reform Initiative resulted in the creation of the Consequence Management Program Integration Office (COMPIO) in March 1998 under the Army's Director of Military Support. This office was intended to improve military support for response to incidents involving WMDs, specifically by integrating national guard and reserve component units into the response plan. Neither the DoD CB Defense Program nor the Chemical Corps were chosen to oversee or support the development of these teams, since (similar to the CB-RRT and CBIRF) the teams were using currently available equipment and this was not a war-fighting mission. COMPIO was not successful in coordinating this project, being an ad hoc agency created outside the traditional mainstream of defense acquisition and training and doctrine centers, resulting in its disestablishment in 2001 and transfer of responsibilities to the OSD (for acquisition) and National Guard Bureau (for training and sustainment).

REVIEWING THE PROGRAM

In early January 2000, Deputy Secretary of Defense Hamre decided not to ask Congress to devolve the DoD CB Defense Program to the services, but he did want to see more improvement to the process, especially any effort to encourage greater CINC participation in the development of the CB defense POM. The number of OSD players taking an interest in CB defense had been growing. In October 1999, Secretary Cohen had appointed Pam Berkowsky as the Assistant to the Secretary of Defense for Civil Support, to provide advice and full-time oversight of the use of the WMD civil support teams, and to serve as the focal point for coordinating DoD efforts in preparation for requests from civilian agencies. The OSD director for Program Analysis and Evaluation (PA&E) played an increasingly critical role in reviewing the DoD CB Defense Program budget against the Defense Planning Guidance and in making recommendations on how the DoD CB Defense Program should spend its funds.

The Director for Operational Test and Evaluation (DOT&E) had six CB defense programs on his oversight list, bringing considerable energy on evaluating the ability of these programs to fully meet all desired user requirements. DOT&E representatives joined the joint committees as nonvoting (but influential) participants in their discussions on all CB defense programs. In March 2000, the Army comptroller office zeroed out the Army's test and evaluation budget for CB defense equipment, believing that Public Law 103-160 could be interpreted to mean that the DoD CB Defense Program should pay for all test and evaluation costs for CB defense equipment, and legal counsel agreed. But there were limited test and evaluation funds budgeted within the individual CB defense programs, and the additional testing requirements resulted in increased program costs and schedule slips. The blame had to be shared among excessive enthusiasm on behalf of the services' test and evaluation agencies, an aging and increasingly underfunded test and evaluation infrastructure, overly ambitious user requirements, and the failure of project managers to allocate adequate funds or time for the testing.

In February 2000, the OSD CB Defense Steering Committee grew to include the Joint Staff's J-5 deputy director for strategy and policy as a voting member and the ASD (S&TR) and ASD (HA) as nonvoting members.[15] The J-5 two-star flag officer used his nuclear and counterproliferation branch to lead the development and coordination of DoD CB defense issues with other Joint Staff and OSD members.[16] As part of the management reform effort, the Joint Staff suggested that a Joint Staff flag officer and a SOCOM representative be added as voting members to the Joint NBC Defense Board and that the 1994 Joint Service Agreement should be revised.[17] All four services nonconcurred with the Joint Staff's recommendations, believing that the CINCs' CB defense priorities were best addressed through the services and the current committee process, and that adding CINCs as voting members on the Joint NBC Defense Board was an infringement of the services' Title 10 responsibilities. Hamre directed that the Joint Staff flag officer be added as a voting member, that SOCOM remain a nonvoting member, and CENTCOM, EUCOM, and PACOM representatives be added as nonvoting members to the Joint NBC Defense Board in May 2000.[18] This move was largely symbolic, but it did shake up the services by forcing them to acknowledge that they had failed to address high-priority CINC issues in the past and that they had to make room for the Joint Staff as an active player in future discussions.

The Joint NBC Defense Board directed a joint working group to review the Joint Service Agreement and recommend changes. Col. Stan Lillie, the director for CB defense projects in Dr. Johnson-Winegar's office, led the joint working group through March and April 2000. The group recommended that the DoD program codify the new management structure and practices in a formal DoD directive and instruction, consider the development of a program executive office (PEO) for CB defense programs, better integrate special operations requirements into the program, develop a performance plan in accordance with Government Performance and Results Act, increase multiservice support for the joint committees, and develop a budgetary process to allow the services and SOCOM to add funds to the DoD CB Defense Program for high-priority, short-notice, and unique requirements.[19] The Joint NBC Defense Board acknowledged the need to update DoD regulations, but deferred any actions until the services had further reviewed the idea of a joint PEO for CB defense.

In August 2000, Dr. Johnson-Winegar announced that she would hold off making organizational changes, citing the arrival of the new Bush administration and the lack of an appointed ATSD (NCB). Other changes continued to take place. In December 2000, Deputy Secretary of Defense Rudy deLeon appointed Maj. Gen. Randall West, his former special advisor for anthrax and biological defense affairs in the USD (P&R) office, to the position of senior advisor to the Deputy Secretary of Defense for chemical and biological protection. The general's focus would be limited to addressing the DoD's anthrax vaccination program. The DATSD (CBD) assumed oversight of the WMD civil support team acquisition efforts in February 2001, while the chief of the National Guard Bureau would be the Army user proponent for the teams. Deputy Secretary of Defense Paul Wolfowitz designated the USD (P&R) as the new DoD proponent for the WMD civil support teams in November 2001, until the OSD homeland defense office was established.[20] Army Secretary Tom White, while streamlining the Army's PEO/PM structures, decided to consolidate all Army CB defense management within a single PEO for CB Defense in October 2001, combining the JPO-BD, Product Manager for NBC Defense Systems, the Joint Vaccination Acquisition Program, and Product Manager for Smoke and Obscurants into a single office, headed by Col. (promotable) Steve Reeves (formerly the manager heading the JPO-BD).

No changes of major consequence would happen until after the events of September 11, 2001. The tragic attacks against the World Trade Centers and the Pentagon caused some to believe that future al Qaeda attacks would include the use of CBRN hazards against military and public targets. Congress and the OSD demanded quick action to address vulnerabilities at military installations, equipment shortages within military units, and homeland security overall. People began to look for the appropriate agency to address the many CBRN hazards across a multitude of new and uncharted mission areas. The DoD CB Defense Program was poorly positioned to respond.

BACK TO THE DRAWING BOARD

Congress was getting impatient over the pace of reform within the DoD CB Defense Program. The House Appropriations Committee noted in its markup of the FY 2002 defense budget:

> The Committee believes the current management structure of the [DoD CB Defense Program] is deeply flawed. The multitude of bureaucratic layers and ad hoc organizations that were created for this program have led to bureaucratic infighting among the Services and chronic inaction on important questions pertaining to requirements generation, funding allocations, program execution, and funds management. Given the growing importance of this activity, the Committee believes the Department must make it a priority to redesign and streamline the organizations managing Chemical and Biological Defense in line with proven and established DoD management processes.[21]

Specifically, the Committee recommended establishing a joint program executive officer who would report through the Army Acquisition Executive to the Defense Acquisition Executive; that the services should provide qualified acquisition officers and government civilians to manage programs under the joint PEO; that the Army be designated as the funds manager for the program; and that the Joint Requirements Oversight Council (JROC) process be the basis for establishing, validating, and prioritizing CB defense requirements. The report also directed that DARPA's BW defense program be excluded from this reorganization effort.

On October 19, 2001, Edward "Pete" Aldridge, the USD (AT&L), directed the formation of an OSD-led task force to review the need for a single milestone decision authority for the DoD CB Defense Program, the establishment of a Joint PEO for CB Defense (JPEO-CBD), and other necessary reforms.[22] This was the beginning of a year-long effort to redesign the overall management structure into a more flexible, responsive, and streamlined program. Dr. Johnson-Winegar would lead a general/flag officer and senior executive service task force with participation from the four services, DTRA, DARPA, OSD counterproliferation policy, ASD (HA), and the Joint Staff (J-5).[23] The principals met between November and December to expand and iron out options for the program management, science and technology efforts, and most important, the POM development. During this time, Aldridge directed that the ATSD (NCB) (the newly appointed Dr. Dale Klein) would oversee DTRA's organization.[24][25]

The idea of a JPEO was not new—the GAO, the Defense Science Board, and other defense advocates had all recommended a JPEO to streamline the authority, responsibility, and accountability of the DoD CB Defense Program. The action officers identified five possible options: having the JPEO report directly to the USD (AT&L); having the JPEO report through the Army Acquisition Executive to the USD (AT&L); having the JPEO report through a rotating service acquisition executive to the USD (AT&L); having the JPEO report through DTRA to the USD (AT&L); and creating a new CB defense agency, similar to the Missile Defense Agency, through which the JPEO would report directly to the USD (AT&L). Each option had pros and cons, and much consideration was given to changing the public law that designated the Army as the DoD executive agent.

Lisa Bronson, the Deputy Under Secretary of Defense for Technology Security Policy and Counterproliferation (DUSD [TSP/CP]), and Dr. Johnson-Winegar thought that the Army had not shown adequate leadership of the CB Defense Program and felt that a new management structure should balance Army and civilian roles.[26] They recommended DTRA's CB Directorate retain control of the funds management and "provide executive management oversight" of the CB Defense Program's science and technology program. Although the services owned all the military laboratories conducting CBRN defense basic research efforts, DTRA's CB Directorate felt it could provide the requisite leadership to oversee and transition basic research efforts into DoD CB defense projects, because it had done this when it was the chair of the Joint Science and Technology Board for Chemical and Biological Defense. Others thought that the DTRA CB Directorate could be dismantled and its responsibilities incorporated into other DTRA directorates. Because the DATSD (CBD) OSD office was now fully staffed and a JPEO was being formed, some argued that the Army could manage the program's funds and oversee the science and technology efforts the way it had prior to DTRA's formation. Yet it seemed that the OSD wanted to maintain alternatives to the Army's executive agent role.

The services were not happy with the suggested changes. The Air Force and Marine Corps did not like the idea of giving up any program management control. The Navy was generally supportive but wanted more details on the exact implementation and implications of the changes, such as control and rating of the services' joint acquisition officers. Even the Army, where the JPEO would reside, had strong objections to some specifics of the new management structure. The Army wanted budget reallocation authority over all projects, elimination of OSD withholding authority, a limit to OSD quarterly program reviews to only seven "sentinel" systems, full responsibility for funds management, and increased limitations on DTRA's oversight of the science and technology program (specifically with regard to execution and control over the funds that would go to the service laboratories). There was no question in that Aldridge, the USD (AT&L), wanted a joint PEO to run the program, and he was going to get it. It was just a matter of developing the details, such as managing other service program managers, developing the budget, and effecting policy and interagency coordination.

The OSD had some ongoing internal debates as well. Aldridge had to address persistent recommendations from Dr. William Winkenwerder (the ASD [HA]) that the medical CB defense program should be completely divorced from the nonmedical CB defense program—including requirements generation, research, development and acquisition, and policy—and overseen by his office. Because the ASD (HA) had absolutely no authority or experience with acquisition or requirements generation, the proposition was clearly unworkable, except for one thing: homeland security concerns had created an intense focus on the issue of biological terrorism, which was seen by many to be a health care responsibility; Winkenwerder felt that DoD biodefense capabilities would be similarly improved by an intense (and separate) focus by DoD medical experts.

The Defense Science Board agreed, going so far as to suggest that the DoD should develop a "NORAD-type organization" to oversee and execute all military warfare and homeland defense biological defense efforts.[27] In addition to doubling the bureaucracy of the DoD CB Defense Program and ensuring that the medical and nonmedical CB defense programs would be forever disjointed, these proposals ignored fundamental differences in homeland defense and combat operations requirements. How long would it be before this separate medical biodefense organization would assert its authority over biological detector development or demand separate biodefense protective masks and suits? The impracticality of such a radical reorganization, with its many potential pitfalls and challenges (not the least of which were funding and staffing concerns) finally allowed Aldridge to put these suggestions to rest.

On September 19, 2002, Aldridge signed an acquisition decision memorandum that significantly changed the management of the DoD CB Defense Program by making it a defense special interest topic, rather than a major defense acquisition program. He would remain the ultimate decision authority, but would delegate that authority to the JPEO for specific programs (really, all of them). The JPEO would report through the Army Acquisition Executive to him, with the ATSD (NCB) having responsibility for overall coordination and integration of all activities within the program. DTRA would manage and integrate all CB defense science and technology efforts and continue to perform funding management functions.

Brig. Gen. Steve Reeves, the Army PEO for CB defense, would see his office transformed into the JPEO-CBD, assuming control over all CBRN defense acquisition efforts. The program managers would remain commodity-oriented, and each service would retain its respective program managers largely as had been arranged prior to the reorganization. The Army would provide officers for contamination avoidance and medical programs; the Navy would provide officers for collective protection and information systems; the Marine Corps would provide a civilian for individual protection programs; and the Air Force would provide an officer for decontamination programs. In addition, the JPEO would designate a new (Army) program manager to oversee the acquisition efforts for the WMD civil support teams, the installation protection program, and other special efforts. The JSMG executive office would become an "independent" Army-staffed group named the Program Analysis and Integration Office (PAIO), responsible to DATSD (CBD) for supporting the POM budget development and developing the program's annual reports. No legislative changes were required to the public law that directed the formation of the DoD CB Defense Program.

As the OSD task force was working in November 2001, the USD (AT&L) asked the director of the Joint Staff to direct a joint working group to examine the user requirements process and to determine whether similar reform efforts were required. Army officers held out hopes that the Joint Service Integration Group could be "tweaked" with selected process improvements, but it rapidly became evident that the joint committee was completely dysfunctional and could not be fixed. A new organization was required, and the best option was an office within the Joint Staff. Initially, the services resisted the idea of losing their votes, suggesting a continued committee structure or joint strategic planning cell, but any new organization required authority, responsibility, accountability, and agility to drive and advocate DoD CB defense issues, and that was best done inside the Pentagon. A joint "committee" that was outside the Beltway and outside the decision loop and had no authority to implement its recommendations was of little to no use.

The Joint Staff proposed a new organization of twenty-two people, led by a one-star general or flag officer, to be organized under the JCS J-8's directorate. The JROC subsequently approved the formation of an interim working group to develop the overall plan and charter for the new office by July 2002.[28] The resistance to this new office was not as fierce as that the acquisition task force had faced. Many senior service officers recognized that the Joint Service Integration Group was not adequately resourced, staffed, or empowered to make the necessary decisions required to execute the increasing responsibilities of the program. The joint working group developed an organizational structure for a Joint Requirements Office for CBRN Defense (JRO-CBRND), which would reside under the J-8 Directorate, similar to how the Joint Theater Air and Missile Defense Organization (JTAMDO) had been organized in 1997. The JRO charter was almost a mirror of the original JTAMDO charter, replacing the words "theater air and missile defense" with "CBRN defense." This was deliberate, based on the success of JTAMDO's stand-up and operations, but had to be done almost surreptitiously. The Air Force community had strong feelings about how JTAMDO took control of the theater air and missile defense program, and had no desire to see history repeated.[29]

The JRO would become the single office within the DoD, responsible for the planning, coordinating, and oversight of joint CBRN defense operational requirements, including development of operational concepts and a modernization plan, representing the services and the CINCs in the requirements generation process, leading the development of the CB defense POM, and facilitating the development of joint doctrine and training that would include the sponsor of multiservice doctrine and training. The JRO was to serve as the chairman's focal point, addressing all issues involving CBRN defense within passive defense, consequence management, force protection, and homeland security. It would have four cells: an analysis and demonstration branch for science and technology coordination and experimentation; a material requirements branch to develop capability documents; a mission-area-integration branch to develop concepts and studies; and a doctrine and training branch. The intent was also to consolidate CBRN defense work within the Joint Staff, although the JRO had difficult time convincing the other directorates that it was just leading the development of CBRN defense issues and not taking over the respective policy responsibilities within consequence management and antiterrorism (J-3 areas), logistics or medical defense matters (J-4 areas), or counterproliferation strategy (J-5 area). On July 1, 2002, the JROC approved the JRO-CBRND concept, with all four four-star generals concurring. On September 9, 2002, Gen. Peter Pace (then vice chairman of the JCS) signed the memorandum establishing the JRO-CBRND, which would officially assume its duties on October 1, 2002. Brig. Gen. Stephen Goldfein, an Air Force general officer and the J-8's deputy director for joint war-fighting capability assessments, was the first acting director.[30]

On April 22, 2003, Aldridge signed the implementation plan detailing the responsibilities of the new management structure and its efforts to address DoD CBRN defense requirements across passive defense, consequence management, force protection, and homeland security. The plan detailed the new responsibilities of four primary organizations: the ATSD (NCB), as the oversight office; the JRO, as the user requirements office; the JPEO, as the material developer; and DTRA, as the funds manager and head of science and technology efforts. The Deputy Under Secretary of the Army for Operational Research (DUSA [OR]) became the joint executive agent for DoD CB defense test and evaluation, an area that desperately needed to revitalize its aging infrastructure and streamline its own joint service practices. DTRA's CB Directorate has been renamed the Joint Science and Technology Office. The four services have action officers within the JPEO and JRO, but no longer would joint committees make least-common denominator decisions to guide the DoD CB Defense Program (see Figure 3-1).

There are still shortcomings in the overall program and lots of defense players still heavily involved. Whereas the JPEO is much more streamlined and acquisition decisions can be made much more smoothly, the heavy emphasis on detection programs remains, with decontamination and collective protection systems languishing and few funds to advance those critical shortfalls. The JRO did not get the permanent government civilian slots and

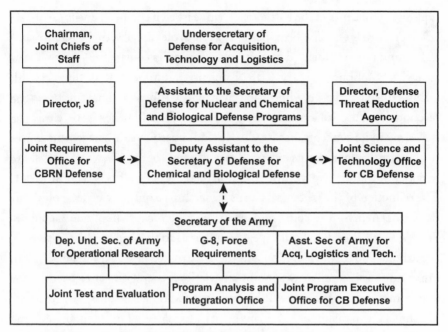

FIGURE 3-1 *Current DoD CB Defense Program Management Structure*

joint military billets it requested in its initial plans, not to mention a full-time general officer to lead the office, so it relies heavily on contractor support. As a result, the JRO has a tough time addressing day-to-day policy challenges and managing the new requirements process for CB defense projects, let alone leading the Joint Staff, services, and CINCs when it comes to emerging CBRN defense issues within consequence management, force protection, and homeland security efforts.

Although the CINCs do have at least one chemical officer or counterproliferation cell in their staff, in all cases these officers are underpowered (they are usually lieutenant colonels or lower ranks) and too understaffed to influence CBRN defense issues within their commands. The CINC staffs' view of the world extends out about two years, and their focus on real-time execution of operations often fails to articulate the need for long-term strategies and policy fixes to OSD and Joint Staff leadership. From a top leadership perspective, the four services have not significantly changed their positions on CBRN defense; the four services have different views on CBRN defense and only reluctantly embrace JRO concepts. The Air Force counterproliferation experts talk about counter-CBRNE (chemical, biological, radiological, nuclear, and high-yield explosives) concepts in the battle space, while its civil engineers focus on installation preparedness. The Navy has only a few professional CBRN defense specialists and remains focused on ship survivability. Its cousin, the Coast Guard, struggles to obtain military CBRN defense equipment as it supports the CINCs during wartime, while using civilian hazardous material equipment to respond to industrial accidents along the coasts. The Marine Corps, closest to the Army in its concepts, has its CBIRF and consequence management expertise but warily maintains its independence. Outside of the Chemical Corps, the majority of the Army pays little attention to addressing CBRN defense issues. The reduction of the Chemical Corps leadership to only one general officer in the entire Army—the commandant of the Chemical School and Center at Fort Leonard Wood—should speak volumes as to the Army leadership's concern about WMD proliferation and the importance of CBRN defense.[31] It is unnerving to see the Army appoint an aviation general officer to become the first commander of the new 20th Support Command (CBRNE), a group which is an expansion of the Army's TEU, to address DoD CBRN defense response needs, at Aberdeen Proving Ground in 2004. This unease is exacerbated by the fact that after eight months as the commander, the aviation general moved on and was replaced by an infantry general officer. The Chemical Corps' rank and file see these trends as well, and grow increasingly nervous about staying in a specialty that is so undervalued by its own leadership.

It may be that the OSD, sensing this lack of senior Army leadership support, was correct to retain DTRA's CB Directorate and its responsibilities in the new management structure. If the Army leadership is not going to commit to the executive agent role, the OSD needs a team that will run the program responsibly. However, the OSD has not benefited the defense community by delaying the development of a new DoD instruction and directive addressing the new management structure, continuing a nebulous and confusing process of different agencies addressing overlapping DoD CBRN defense issues on a day-to-day basis. There is still a great deal of confusion as to who's in charge. The number of OSD and Joint Staff agencies involved in deliberating CBRN defense issues, in addition to the four services, makes it easier to understand Congress's 1994 call for a "single office within OSD" to lead the development of DoD CBRN defense efforts. At best, the landscape remains fluid, with politically charged agencies that strive to lead in their respective areas without a consistent, shared, long-term vision.

As this management structure matures, these organizations face the significant challenge of meeting new CBRN defense requirements in consequence management, antiterrorism, and homeland defense. It remains to be seen whether this management team will attempt to force a war-fighting construct on these new mission areas or if it can creatively adapt to the new national security challenges and develop the appropriate strategies, concepts, and materials so desperately needed. Perhaps even more important, will the political and military leadership adequately back the DoD CB Defense Program in terms of priorities, funds, and involvement to allow military forces to meet the new CBRN defense challenges of the twenty-first century?

CHAPTER 4

9/11 CHANGES LIFE AS WE KNOW IT

Next week there can't be any crisis. My schedule is already full.

—HENRY KISSINGER, U.S. STATESMAN, 1969

It may seem cliché now to state that 9/11 changed everyone's lives. Before September 2001, the press and defense experts were ridiculing Defense Secretary Donald Rumsfeld's transformation ideas as being out of touch; the government considered the need to address CBRN hazards as a low priority; and the four services insisted the DoD CB Defense Program focus solely on war-fighting requirements. After September 2001, Rumsfeld's critics couldn't touch him; government officials, citing the potential threat of terrorist CBRN incidents, sent citizens flocking to hardware stores to buy plastic sheeting and duct tape, and OSD began instituting long-needed reforms to the DoD CB Defense Program.

At the Pentagon on 9/11, Arlington County emergency responders treated patients who were short of breath and teary-eyed, and wondered if these symptoms were indicative of nerve agent poisoning (it was actually smoke inhalation). New York's National Guard WMD Civil Support Team deployed to Ground Zero to assist in the assessment of the damaged buildings and monitor for toxic inhalation hazards and signs of CB warfare agents. The FBI clamped down on flights of cropdusting planes, fearing that terrorists would use them to disperse CB warfare agents over major cities. Several government officials had apprehensions that CBRN hazards would be used against the Pentagon following the use of commercial planes as an improvised weapon of mass destruction. Every CBRN defense issue was in uncharted territory, now that the threat seemed imminent—everyone was making new policies and decisions were based more on emotions than on logic.

On September 14, 2001, President George W. Bush authorized the call-up of thirty-five thousand reserve forces.[1] DoD announced the plan as Operation Noble Eagle. The Air Force began flying continuous air patrols over New York and Washington D.C., with random patrols over other major cities throughout the country. While the Navy and Coast Guard patrolled the shores, the Army called up military police, intelligence specialists, engineers, chemical defense specialists, and others. On September 25, 2001, Defense Secretary Rumsfeld announced that the military phase of the global war on terrorism was to be referred to as Operation Enduring Freedom.[2] Forces had begun deploying to the Middle East. U.S. allies offered their military support and, in some cases, supported patrolling the perimeters of overseas U.S. military installations with joint U.S./allied force protection teams.

Between the two operations, increased preparedness at U.S. military installations, and homeland security issues, there was a concern that the four services and other government agencies were going to dramatically increase their CB defense equipment requisitions. If that happened, the DoD CB Defense program would not be ready. The program procured equipment against the services' warfighting requirements, and there was precious little slack to accommodate requests for CB defense equipment to be used for antiterrorism purposes. At the end of September, the Joint Staff's J-5/ Nuclear and Counterproliferation (Nuc&CP) branch joined in discussions with the Joint Material Prioritization and Allocation Board (JMPAB), and its secretariat. The JMPAB is a general-officer committee chaired by the Joint Staff's J-4 director, with participation from the chief logistics commanders from the four services and DLA. There are occasions when the services compete for jointly-developed items that are managed by one service, for example, Army medical supplies or Air Force Joint Direct Attack Munitions (JDAMs), and the owning service refuses to meet the requesting service's requirements due to shortages created by increased combat usage or production problems. The secretariat runs a forum for the services to voice and justify their requests, and if the issue is not successfully resolved at the colonel/captain level, it goes to the full JMPAB for the director, J-4, to decide.

The J-5/Nuc&CP branch promoted the creation of a CB defense subgroup to the JMPAB as a forum to recommend resolution of service (and other government agency) demands for additional joint CB defense equipment. This subgroup, chaired by the J-5/Nuc&CP branch chief and including representatives of the four services, DLA, J-4, OSD, and other defense agencies, updated the Joint Service Coordinating Committee for Chemical Defense Equipment charter to use as their own (that group had become inactive after 1995), and developed a prioritization plan for CB defense equipment. In short, extenuating circumstances aside, all deploying military forces would have top priority, followed by those DoD organizations directly supporting those deploying military forces. Third would be those DoD organizations or other government agencies supporting homeland security efforts. All DoD forces that were requesting CB defense equipment for installation preparedness would be the fourth priority, and last, any other requests.

The feared flood of requisitions did not occur. There was a concern that the JPO-BD's production line of assay tickets would be insufficient to meet the demands of other government agencies in addition to the military's demands, but production numbers more than met customer requests. DARPA asked for thirty M22 Automatic Chemical Agent Detector/Alarms (ACADAs) and twelve improved Chemical Agent Monitors (CAMs) for their immune building program, but that request was later withdrawn. Col. Tim Madere, chemical officer for the U.S. Army V Corps, wanted to purchase commercial equipment to develop a number of small CB response teams in Europe that would assist in responding to CB terrorist incidents against U.S. military installations and personnel. All other CBRN defense logistics concerns seemed manageable. Part of the relief came in the form services putting up their own emergency funds to procure CB defense equipment, notably additional protective suits and biological Dry Filter Units (DFUs).[3] The JMPAB would continue to meet monthly to review and try to preempt any emerging CBRN defense logistics issues.

In December, it came to light that the Navy had asked the JSLIST project manager to increase its share of protective suits from the DoD CB Defense Program. The program spent about $80 million to $90 million a year to procure approximately 30,000 JSLIST suits a month for the four services. By previous agreement, the Army received 50 percent of the suits paid for by the program, with the Air Force and Navy each receiving 20 percent, and the Marine Corps 10 percent. Any service could buy additional suits for combat operations or for training using its own funds from DLA, which used its contingency funds to procure protective suits for sale to DoD and other federal agencies. The Navy had miscalculated their wartime requirements and, while they had enough protective suits in their inventory to support Operation Enduring Freedom requirements, did not want to have to move suits from one carrier group that was at home station to another carrier group that was outbound to the Persian Gulf.[4] That would be logistically challenging and time consuming, so the Navy declared a high priority for additional suits. The project manager agreed to take suits from the Army and Air Force quotas and redirect them to the Navy.

The Army's reaction was predictable. It appeared to the Army that the project manager had made a unilateral decision to change the distribution plan without consulting the Army or Air Force as to the impact on their efforts. The decision would severely restrict the Army's ability to field JSLIST suits to critical Army reserve units, so they requested that the JMPAB intercede. The Navy's actions were particularly questionable as they had received a loan of several thousand JSLIST and Saratoga suits from the Army and Marine Corps in 2001, but had not repaid the loan prior to their request for additional suits. Upon review, the JMPAB CB Subgroup decided that the Navy did not have a case for increased priority, and that they should not receive more suits than the normal quota. It would fall to a multiservice working group, chaired by the Army chief chemical officer in ODCSOPS, to work out the details of a resolution and examine how the services developed their suit requirements, to be presented to the Joint NBC Defense Board. The requirements analysis was later abandoned.

EARLY HOMELAND SECURITY CONCERNS

In early October 2001, Robert Stevens, a photo editor for the American Media, Inc. in Boca Raton, Florida, was admitted to a local hospital and was diagnosed as having fallen ill with pulmonary anthrax. Already symptomatic, Stevens died on October 5, 2001, and the Centers for Disease Control and Prevention (CDC) and the FBI came to investigate. At first they suspected that the exposure was due to natural causes, but when a second employee demonstrated anthrax symptoms, it became clear that this incident was not accidental. Two letters postmarked from Trenton, New Jersey, had been mailed on September 18 to NBC News and the *New York Post* in New York City. Federal authorities described the anthrax in these two envelopes as crude and unrefined. Employees from CBS and ABC news stations in New

York City reported cases of cutaneous anthrax, although no letters were found. These incidents were followed by anthrax letters sent to Senators Tom Daschle and Patrick Leahy, featuring a grade of anthrax that seemed much more refined, termed "weapons-grade" anthrax. In all, it is believed that eleven people contracted inhalation anthrax, five of whom died from this exposure, and eleven people contracted cutaneous anthrax, none of whom died. The Bush administration openly speculated that al Qaeda might be behind the letters, while others wondered if Iraq or another nation might have been the source. FBI investigations began looking for a disgruntled U.S. citizen, possibly a DoD employee or consultant with access to laboratory equipment and stock to produce the anthrax.[5]

The DoD response to anthrax letters came in three forms: first, emergency response assistance from the Army's TEU and Marine Corps' CBIRF; second, sample analysis by the USAMRIID at Fort Detrick; and third, deployment of biological air samplers throughout Washington, D.C. From their base at Indianhead, Maryland, the CBIRF sent a 100-person force to work under the U.S. Capitol Police. The TEU and CBIRF took samples and supported decontamination operations in the Longworth House Office Building in mid-October and the Dirksen Senate Office Building in early December.[6] The Army's and the CDC's limited laboratory capability was quickly overwhelmed by the flood of suspected anthrax samples from across the nation and from other countries such as the United Kingdom. To complicate matters, scores of hoaxes produced a steady demand for quick analysis and response that was just not there. The CDC laboratories and agencies tested more than 125,000 samples in the weeks following the first reports, the overwhelming majority of which were false alarms, and included everything from crushed Tic Tacs to spilled flour.[7]

DTRA and the JPO-BD procured and deployed biological air samplers throughout the Washington, D.C. metro subway in an effort to monitor any release of biological organisms. Studies during the Cold War had identified that covert dissemination of biological organisms in the subways could be attempted, although the effectiveness of such an attack was unclear. Given the Aum Shinrikyo attacks and the large number of defense employees that traveled on the subway every day, this seemed like a prudent measure. While these samplers would not prevent the subway riders from being exposed, monitoring would decrease the time to deliver medical countermeasures to them. DFUs were placed in key leadership offices and in mailrooms within the Pentagon and nearby military buildings. The Pentagon mail would be transferred to remote facilities for X-ray and thermal treatments to kill anthrax spores, resulting in true "snail-mail," with delays of months for routine delivery.

The CDC oversaw health treatments, and it is estimated that more than 30,000 people in four states and in Washington D.C. took Cipro in the event that they might have inhaled some amount of anthrax. The FDA had approved ciprofloxacin as a postexposure treatment for inhalation anthrax in August 2000, requiring a five hundred milligram dose twice a day for sixty days. The antibiotic was not tested on humans as a general anti-inhalation anthrax treatment or for its safety and effectiveness for children or pregnant women, but given the lethality of inhalation anthrax, the FDA was willing to certify its general use (an interesting counter to critics' views on the FDA's certification of DoD's anthrax vaccine).[8] In addition to pharmacies being mobbed by people wanting stocks of Cipro "just in case," illegitimate sellers appeared on the Internet offering the drug to the public. Later reports would estimate that pharmacies processed prescriptions for 160,000 extra doses of Cipro and 96,000 doses of doxycycline in October 2001 alone, a spike of about 40 percent and 30 percent over use in October 2000, respectively. The military had used ciprofloxacin and doxycycline as pre-treatments in the first Gulf War, but the FDA had been unwilling to certify its use to the general public for that purpose. The military had originally set the post-treatment regime at thirty days, but the FDA doubled the treatment period of the nausea-causing antibiotic as an additional safety measure.

BioPort's anthrax facility was now in the position of facing a much larger customer base than it ever dreamed of. Given the facility had not resumed full production, DoD claimed all previously produced anthrax vaccine in storage. There were far fewer concerns about the safety of the vaccine now; if an infected person took Cipro, it would keep the anthrax under control, but only the vaccine could stop the anthrax fully. Few had considered using the vaccine as a post-treatment, and that was causing some concerns. A report released by the National Research Council's Institute of Medicine noted that the anthrax vaccine was proven safe and effective to use to protect U.S. soldiers, but there were not enough studies to assure its safety for wide use by the (potentially) more sensitive members of the general public. While some of the potentially exposed victims chose not to accept the vaccine due to these concerns, if inhalation anthrax victims stopped taking the Cipro treatments before it fully arrested the anthrax growth, they would have died very quickly and very painfully. As of late February 2002, 192 people had begun receiving the anthrax vaccine.[9]

In November, Dr. Johnson-Winegar met with the three service surgeon generals and a FDA representative to discuss DoD's ability to surge-produce vaccines in support of both military operations and homeland security demands. One of the major obstacles was the FDA's glacially slow review of tested pharmaceuticals for safety and efficacy. Its role as an independent evaluator of drugs is very important, but its ability to address DoD issues was limited due to manpower, budget, and the much larger demands of the commercial pharmaceutical industry. One of the challenges of vaccine development was that while DoD could conduct safety trials within FDA guidelines, it could not fully prove that the vaccines were fully efficacious, as that would entail proving that the vaccines protected human volunteers against weaponized BW agents. These kinds of tests were ethically wrong as well as illegal, and despite conspiracy theories to the contrary, DoD has not worked that way since at least 1975. In 1999, the FDA proposed amending its new drug and biological product regulations to prove the efficacy of new drug and biological products that would be used to reduce or prevent the toxicity of CBRN hazards, specifically when studies would require administering a potentially lethal or permanently disabling toxic substance or organism to a healthy human volunteer. The agency would accept the results of appropriate studies in animal trials, combined with other data and studies, to make a ruling on the effectiveness of these products.[10] This ruling represented a potential leap forward for vaccine development, but would not be effective until July 1, 2002. There were continued difficulties obtaining enough primates to develop the necessary data for the proposed trials.

In mid-December 2001, newspaper articles discussed the fact that scientists at Dugway Proving Ground, Utah, were capable of producing dried anthrax similar to those strains found in letters sent to Senators Daschle and Leahy. The Army had the legal right to produce small amounts of weaponized agent for the purposes of testing defensive equipment. Now the Army was accused of its labs being the source of the biological agent used in the letters. The quality and grade of anthrax, with its extremely small particle size, purity, and ability to easily disperse into the air, made some suspect that a U.S. government worker, familiar with BW agent preparation, might be the source of the anthrax letters.[11] The Army stated that Dugway had indeed shipped a paste form of anthrax to Detrick, where it was irradiated and made harmless before being shipped back to Dugway for testing defense equipment. The FBI soon included interviews of the Dugway scientists, in addition to the Detrick scientists, in their investigations.

Near the end of December 2001, it was revealed that Governor Ridge's Office of Homeland Security had placed $420 million into the DoD CB Defense Program for the purposes of "advancing biological detection technologies." Most of the funds ($300 million) were to promote initial homeland security science and technology efforts with long-term payoffs, with $5 million in military construction funds to break ground for a Biological Counterterrorism Research Institute at Fort Detrick and $115 million for research and development efforts. The DATSD (CBD) placed these funds directly into the program, earmarking them for this purpose. This unilateral action did not go unnoticed or uncommented upon. Gen. John Keane, the Vice Chief of Staff of the Army and chair of the Joint NBC Defense Board, challenged this effort, noting that the four services had no opportunity to review or comment on what exactly this large amount of funding was going to do for homeland security, or even if the DoD CB Defense Program should manage the project. Later in 2002, OSD quietly pulled the funding out of the DoD CB defense budget, citing guidance from Rumsfeld that DoD should not fund or execute homeland security efforts that Governor Ridge's office should be implementing.

Protecting the Pentagon

Immediately after 9/11, the Army Chemical School sent an officer and two sergeants to the Army Operations Center (AOC), then headed by Brig. Gen. Peter Chiarelli (an armor officer), to allow the AOC to address specific CBRN defense issues relating to Army units' deployment to the Middle East. Gen. Chiarelli directed them to develop a brief on CBRN response capabilities available and to recommend how to improve the Army's defensive capabilities. While there were no indications that any terrorist CBRN threat was immediately present or imminent, he shared the concern by Gen. John Keane that the Pentagon needed to be prepared for a terrorist CBRN incident and that the security capabilities had to be tightened. Gen. Keane reportedly walked around the Pentagon itself, checking the outdoor heating, ventilation and air conditioning (HVAC) access points and ensuring that they were locked. The anthrax incidents in October ignited interest in taking measurable steps to improve the Pentagon's CBRN defense capabilities.

Deputy Secretary of Defense Paul Wolfowitz formed a special task force to address the CBRN defense equipment and personnel requirements, short of individual protection, for the protection of the Pentagon's workforce. The working group was headed by DATSD (CBD), and included members of all four services, the Joint Staff, Assistant Secretary of Defense for Homeland Defense (ASD [HD]), OSD counterproliferation policy, and other OSD agencies. Through most of October, this group sketched out a plan to procure military detectors for the purposes of monitoring for CBRN hazards in the Pentagon reservation, including the Pentagon proper and the Naval Annex. Sensor equipment would include military chemical, biological, and radiological detectors. On October 7, 2001, Wolfowitz signed a memorandum authorizing the procurement and fielding of this military equipment to the Pentagon's security force.

On October 26, Wolfowitz approved the OSD working group's CBRN protection and response plan for protecting the Pentagon. This included $5 million for purchasing eight JPBDS, portable biological agent samplers, polymerase chain reaction (PCR) monitors, DFUs, M22 Automatic Chemical Agent Detection Alarm (ACADAs), M21 Remote Standoff Chemical Agent Alarms (RSCAALs), and additional radiacs. The plan also recommended the formation of a dedicated support team, collective protection within critical areas of the Pentagon, enhanced medical surveillance and medical treatment efforts, and a public education strategy. General Keane volunteered to deploy the 7th Chemical Company (BIDS), stationed at Fort Polk, to provide a biodetection capability around the Pentagon. Initially, ten BIDS vehicles surrounded the Pentagon and four were at the Navy Annex, beginning immediate 24/7 monitoring operations near the end of October. After two weeks, the numbers were reduced to five vehicles around the Pentagon and two at the annex.[12] The JPO-BD would field eight JBPDS, coming literally straight off the assembly line by a "low-rate initial production" decision, to replace the BIDS vehicles by mid-December.

General Chiarelli and his chemical officers in the AOC continued to develop a central CB cell that would coordinate an inner ring of defense within the Pentagon and an outer ring of defense, briefing the Army leadership up to General Eric Shinseki, Chief of Staff of the Army. No one had ever done anything like this as an antiterrorism effort: procuring a number of disparate military chemical and biological agent detectors, wiring them to a command cell, and turning over the operations to a security force. Through close coordination with the Pentagon's police force, they developed a plan for action that would address the multiple scenarios examined by the OSD task force. On November 6, the AOC announced the formation of a Biological-Chemical Center, headed by Lt. Col. Doug Norton, an Army chemical officer. This cell would be the starting point for what would be named the Biological-Chemical Joint Operations Cell under the Defense Protective Services (later renamed as the Pentagon Force Protection Agency). Norton continued to refine and improve the command and control process over the next year.

Dr. David Chu, USD (P&R), was given the lead to address the issue of providing individual protection equipment to the Pentagon employees in the event of a biological attack. The OSD task force met to review the costs and benefits of outfitting the entire Pentagon population, including visitors, with protective masks. The Navy, Joint Staff, and OSD counterproliferation policy preferred the concept of half-masks; that is to say, half-faced respirators protecting the mouth and nose but not protecting the eyes, similar to those used by workers painting or laying down insulation. The Marine Corps and Air Force preferred issuing military protective equipment and masks to the entire work force, although this was clearly too costly to consider. Dr. Winkenwerder, ASD (HA), preferred issuing surgical masks that would prevent continued inhalation of biological particles once there had been a detection (an important point), but these masks would not afford protection from chemical hazards.

While the OSD working group was discussing personal protection issues, the OSD counterproliferation policy office chose this time (following the anthrax letter incidents) to encourage the JSIG and Joint Staff to review and change its multiservice and joint doctrine on CBRN defense operations. With the increased discussions of bioterrorism within and outside the DoD, the OSD felt that this was the ideal opportunity to promote a separate and distinct concept for conducting military biological defense operations.

Col. Robert Kadlec, an Air Force officer in the OSD counterproliferation policy office, believed that the services' approach to biological defense was too "detector-centric" and too similar to chemical detection. Instead of the military's existing doctrine of "avoid, protect, decon," he had a parallel concept that called for the forces to "monitor, mitigate, respond." The first step was to monitor the weather, conduct environmental sampling during times of heightened risk, and increase medical surveillance efforts. Mitigation was done through the use of half-masks by the entire population during times of heightened threat conditions. The idea was that, depending on meteorological conditions, people would proactively wear masks throughout the day. If a BW attack did occur, the installation commander could direct exposed people to receive postexposure treatments and, if the agent was contagious, be isolated. The response included emergency actions to contain the contamination, continue medical treatment, and promote rapid restoration of operations. The services and Joint Staff were skeptical about separating biological defense from chemical defense merely because the detectors weren't perfect. The military had combat development centers, at least in theory, to examine new concepts and develop doctrine, and were unused to having OSD challenging their concepts and recommending drastic changes.

There was a fundamental flaw in Kadlec's concept, in that the philosophy of detection, protection, and decontamination was essentially the same as his system of monitoring, mitigating, and responding. Because both chemical and biological agents are delivered by the same types of weapon systems, are very reliant on weather conditions, and affect personnel through their skin and respiratory system, the doctrine of countering their use could (and should) be very similar. Every CB defense specialist knew that biological agents were different than chemical agents, and even within chemical agents, there were differences that demanded special consideration. The tactics, techniques, and procedures involved had to be different, not the doctrine, and indeed, CB specialists understood that the reaction to nerve gas is different than the reaction to anthrax or mustard agent. Kadlec had inadvertently hit on one important issue; that is, installations and facilities with limited funds, facing a year-round threat of terrorism, did need a different concept to defend themselves than combat maneuver units, which faced a (more or less) known threat for short periods of conflict. Changing the bumper sticker from "avoid, protect, decontaminate" to "monitor, mitigate, respond" for all DoD forces was not the answer. His concept did ultimately drive the DoD purchase of emergency masks for the Pentagon's population.

The vexing question that the OSD working group had to answer was, when should the populace be told to don masks or evacuate the building in the event of a suspected terrorist CBRN attack? If the agent was released outside of the Pentagon, perhaps the instruction should be to remain indoors and shelter in place. If the agent was released inside the Pentagon, should the people evacuate? How would one ensure that the people didn't leave the area and spread potentially contagious diseases or persistent chemical agents? How would the Defense Protective Services alert the populace to put on the masks in the first place, if not through indications by the biological detectors surrounding the Pentagon? Should the entire Pentagon population just wear masks all day if the threat condition was high? How many masks would be required for the diverse population of the Pentagon reservation—the thousands of workforce, the visitors, the concession workers rotating in and out of the building daily? Who would maintain and track this program? It should also be noted that this program was only intended for the Pentagon, as a high-value terrorist target. No thought had been given to how to develop a program to protect other military installations or facilities within the United States.[13] Unfortunately, there would be little analysis of these important topics prior to the decision to buy masks for the Pentagon.

SBCCOM had been testing a variety of quick-doff, one-size-fits-all protective masks, under an initiative that originally was intended to develop a disposable, compact military mask for special forces and certain Air Force personnel. The Domestic Preparedness Program had identified a similar need for a disposable protective mask for certain emergency responders (other than hazmat techs) responding to a CBRN terrorist incident: a negative-pressure mask that would have to be National Institute for Occupational Safety and Health (NIOSH)-approved. One of the leading candidates was a mask called the Quick2000®, a one-size-fits-all chemical protective fabric hood with an integrated visor, mouthpiece, rubber neck dam, and external filter cartridge.[14] To use the hood, the wearer attaches a noseclip and inserts a mouthpiece, which is attached to the filter (similar to a scuba respirator), then stretches the neck dam to pull the hood over his or her head.[15] When not in use, the mask stays in a compact, vacuum-sealed package with a four-year shelf life. The cost is approximately $125 each, equivalent to the cost of a military protective mask. While the mask was tested to protect an individual against CB agent particulates, it is not designed for more than 15–30 minutes of use, or for situations involving fire, water, or low oxygen.

In late December, Defense Deputy Secretary Wolfowitz approved the development and implementation of an employee awareness and training effort, which would include protection measures and the immediate issue of surgical masks for Pentagon workers. The Quickmask was chosen for the protection of the general population of the Pentagon personnel as a follow-on effort, with emergency mask boxes positioned throughout the building for visitors. In February 2002, the Pentagon ordered eighty thousand of these disposable emergency masks.[16] The entire DoD work force of approximately twenty-five thousand, including employees and journalists working in forty-six DoD buildings in Washington, D.C., would draw a mask (one training mask and one actual mask that would stay in a sealed package) and take a training class on how to use it. Each Pentagon employee was expected to keep the mask nearby in the office, and in times of increased threat indications, carry the mask around. In June 2002, the U.S. Capital buildings would order twenty thousand of the same masks for their personnel and visitors, given their recent incidents with anthrax letters. The Capitol police had been using them since 1997.[17] Ironically, the Pentagon protection and response concept would use the same "detector-centric" concept of operations that Kadlec had found wanting in the first place.

The actual effectiveness of procuring these tens of thousands of emergency masks and prepositioning many of them in the hallways of the Pentagon and Congress remains highly questionable. The biological detectors couldn't alarm in time for many people to avoid exposure to the BW agents, and if the terrorists used CW agents, chances were that it would be a volatile industrial chemical and affect only a small area of the building. A Navy officer pointed out that a mask made for filtering smoke during a fire would probably be much more useful, given the recent experience of 9/11. For emergency responders that would have to work in and around a potentially contaminated area, a disposable emergency mask that they could keep in their vehicles or pockets did make sense. For people quickly evacuating from a potentially contaminated area, emergency masks didn't make sense, especially given the millions of dollars being spent against a very low probability scenario.

Protecting Military Installations

Simultaneous with the actions to protect the Pentagon, installation commanders across all four services were requesting CB defense gear to prepare their installations for any potential CBRN terrorist incidents. Even had they gotten the military equipment, the installations lacked trained personnel to man the detectors, employ collective protection systems or decontaminate buildings and equipment: and yet the requests came in. The flood of applications was directed to the DoD CB Defense Program. Initially, the OSD comptroller refused to fund these requests (since military CB defense equipment was addressed under an OSD program line) until the DATSD (CBD) could straighten out who was paying for the equipment and who was approving these unconventional requests. The Joint Staff's J-5/Nuc&CP branch, in conjunction with DATSD (CBD) and including representatives from the four services, Joint Staff, and OSD, hosted an intense, week-long joint working group in October 2001 to develop some immediate "back-of-the-envelope" solutions and a common approach to improving DoD installation preparedness for terrorist CBRN incidents.

The group relied heavily on the Army staff and JPO-BD in their development of a concept featuring a network of CB detectors that might be emplaced on an installation and tied into the installation's emergency operations center (EOC).[18] The concept would also add a limited number of suits and masks for essential personnel who might have to work through the hazard's duration (none for the general population) and some medical countermeasures, including a package of vaccines and atropine kits. The group recognized that some level of collective protection systems for certain critical sites (such as the installation EOC and any VIP offices) and decontamination would be required, but it seemed too hard to sketch out even a guesstimate within the time available. There was no examination of terrorist delivery means or likely agents"—only that the threat of greatest impact would be a large quantity of an airborne-delivered lethal chemical or biological warfare agent against the installation. The working group developed three options, ranging between approximately $702 million for 100 bases to $3.05 billion for 530 installations. This did not include the costs accrued each year due to operations and maintenance of the CB defense equipment, which would increase the total costs of the options to between $962 million and $4.3 billion over a five-year budget period (FY03-07).

The JROC general and flag officers balked at the potential costs, and decided to not support the effort further. Proposing billions of dollars to develop an admittedly limited defensive capability against the relatively low probability of a terrorist CBRN incident on all military installations was not seen as realistic, especially given the less-than-rigorous analysis that the group had rushed through and lack of any operational concept other than throwing a bunch of specialized equipment onto a military installation. OSD did not want to give up on the idea quite yet. The offices of the DATSD (CBD) and DUSD (TSP/CP) worked with OSD (PA&E) to bring up the installation protection issue at the Program Review Group, a group chaired by the Director, PA&E, and including OSD principal deputies and assistant secretaries, the services' budgeting chiefs, and the Joint Staff's director for J-8 (Force Structure, Resources and Assessment). The Program Review Group also balked at the proposed costs on November 20, 2001, but directed that a pilot program might be initiated to better develop the concept, capabilities required, and associated costs. On November 27, the Defense Review Board reviewed the installation preparedness efforts, and developed Program Budget Decision (PBD) 289, which created the Joint Service Installation Pilot Project (JSIPP).

JSIPP would use the concept of operations and equipment outlined in the very rough, back-of-the envelope estimates developed by the October joint working group, emplacing CB defense equipment on nine diverse installations (three each for the Army and Air Force, two for the Navy, and one for the Marine Corps). The intent was to run a one-year program starting in fiscal year 2003, with approximately $5 million per base spent on CB defense equipment and $1.5 million spent on emergency responder equipment and training per installation. PBD 289 was released in December 2001, with the ASD (SO/LIC) initiating discussions with the services on which nine installations would receive the equipment. ASD (SO/LIC) lobbied the service staffs to pick one large, one medium, and one small installation within the United States, to allow for a variety of concepts and lessons learned to emerge within a controllable environment.[19] Simultaneously, ASD (SO/LIC) initiated the development of DoD guidelines addressing how installations should develop and train their first responders to handle Chemical, Biological, Radiological, Nuclear, and Explosive (CBRNE) incidents (these guidelines would not be completed until December 2002). The term *CBRNE* was distinct to the antiterrorism community, which, having recognized that high explosives have the potential to cause mass casualties, sought a term to address both the unconventional and conventional terrorist threats. Bureaucratic fights over the terms and intent of these discussions are not uncommon.

Dr. Johnson-Winegar, DATSD (CBD), chose DTRA's CB directorate to manage the JSIPP effort. DTRA outlined a plan to OSD, Joint Staff, and the four services for equipping the nine installations with different levels of CB detection equipment, enhancing installation emergency response capabilities with CB defense equipment and training, collecting data and refining concepts of operation for CB defense of installations, and providing recommendations on personnel, equipment, and logistics support to aid further installation preparedness efforts. The effort would be limited to a focus on detection systems and responder equipment. The services submitted a list of installations that would participate in the project to ASD (SO/LIC) in the summer of 2002.

In April 2002, OSD released its Defense Planning Guidance for FY 2004–2009 (DPG-04). This document is a mix of policy initiatives and directives to conduct various operational assessments and budgetary studies, drafted by OSD policy and coordinated with the service chiefs, combatant commands, Joint Staff, and other defense agencies. The 2002 report largely reiterated the strategies laid out in the Quadrennial Defense Review (QDR) released in September 2001.[20] The DPG would direct the development of a portfolio of capabilities to allow the swift and decisive defeat of adversaries (à la the "1-4-2-1" strategy); a commitment to a rigorous experimentation and transformation culture; and a transformation of the department's planning, programming, and budgeting system.

Of particular interest to the DoD CB defense community were the numerous directives to conduct specific CB defense assessments, probably the most that had ever been seen in such a top-level document. There were three DPG studies in particular, all originating from the OSD counterproliferation policy office. One directed the chairman of the JCS to review the need to develop a new biological defense concept of operations for military installations and forces. A second directed the chairman to develop a plan to improve CBRN defense capabilities at six hundred military installations over the next six years, at a pace of one hundred installations each year. The last study was a Deputy Secretary of Defense direction to assess PACOM operational capabilities for

CBRN defense within fifteen days, and to assess the operational capabilities for DoD forces worldwide within thirty days following the first assessment. The JRO was not officially stood up, but its small interim staff would have to address each study and coordinate the studies within the DoD prior to briefing the chairman and releasing their results.

At a later OSD meeting, a program decision memorandum reduced the size of the CBRN defense installation program to two hundred installations over six years, starting with fifteen installations in 2004 and ramping up to fifty installations by 2009. OSD would take $1 billion from the four services' antiterrorism budgets over a six-year period, which would have been directed toward critical conventional antiterrorism efforts, and direct the DoD CB Defense Program to execute what would become known as the Installation Protection Program. Another $600 million would be provided for installation emergency responder equipment and training, its implementation to be overseen by ASD (HD). Stephen Cambone, the Director of PA&E, instructed that the program address 185 installations within the United States in the first four years, and only fifteen overseas military installations in the latter years.[21] Each service would receive equipment for a certain number of installations each year over the six-year timeframe, corresponding with the level of antiterrorism funds taken out of its respective budget (thus neatly circumventing any arguments over who had the most critical or vulnerable bases and therefore higher priorities). The Army had sixty-two installations that would receive CB defense equipment, the Air Force had sixty-four, the Navy had fifty-nine, the Marine Corps had nine, and three defense agencies would have six installations. In anticipation of taking on this mission, the Army PEO for CB Defense created the Project Manager Guardian office in October 2002, which would oversee the two hundred-installation effort and the development of the WMD Civil Support Team equipment. This office formally stood up in October 2003. The JRO's responsibilities included working with the services to develop a prioritization list, developing a concept of operation for protecting military installations and facilities from terrorist CBRN attacks, and integrating CBRN defense measures into antiterrorism directives.

The antiterrorism crowd had not played a major role in this effort, being pushed out of its lead role and supplanted by counterproliferation policy and CB defense subject-matter experts, because of the perceived technical nature of the threat and their historic inability to integrate responses to CBRN hazards into their program. Their continued lack of participation would result in substantial problems. Little thought had been given to the cost to sustain these antiterrorism initiatives, costs which would be significant. No one had considered the precedent being established for other military installations and facilities lacking the funding and priority to enact similar defenses of their own. The antiterrorism community should have assisted in developing rational procedures to adjust day-to-day operations and resources in accordance to the perceived threat and risk analyses.[22] But the community's failure to do so was an indication of the lack of resonance between it and the CB defense community. The antiterrorism community saw CBRN defense as a low-priority threat in relation to bombings, kidnappings, and other conventional explosive attacks, and often ignored the challenges. At the same time, it was unwilling to let the CB defense community take the lead in developing doctrine and equipment for specific CBRN efforts within antiterrorism.

For most of 2002, DoD CBRN defense support to homeland security was minimal other than maintaining protective forces in the air and on the U.S. coastlines and attending interagency meetings. The expectation was that U.S. Northern Command (NORTHCOM) would be the lead DoD agency in supporting any homeland security efforts, a duty formerly assumed by U.S. Joint Forces Command (JFCOM). Essentially, all the homeland security-related efforts that JFCOM had, including the Joint Task Force for Civil Support, would be turned over to NORTHCOM. That is, after NORTHCOM had hired and organized its staff, developed its plans, and fully stood up as an organization (planned for October 1, 2003). In the meantime, the focus for most, if not all, of the DoD CB defense efforts would be in support of Operation Enduring Freedom.

NEW STRATEGIES AND CONCEPTS

The Bush administration was determined to address the continued proliferation of WMD programs through Defense Secretary Rumsfeld's new defense strategy. The 2001 QDR was published on September 30, just weeks after the 9/11 incident.[23] In a telling statement, the report noted, "The United States . . . will continue to depend on the energy resources of the Middle East, a region in which several states . . . seek to acquire—or have acquired—chemical, biological, radiological, nuclear, and enhanced high explosive (CBRNE) weapons. . . . the rapid proliferation of CBRNE technology gives rise to the danger that future terrorist attacks might involve such weapons." [24] Defense officials may sometimes use the antiterrorism term "CBRNE" when they are actually referring to warfighting CBRN defense issues, and vice versa. In general, military combat operators do not talk about CBRNE weapons, since they primarily address the use of major ordnance systems using high-yield explosives. The Bush administration liked the term "CBRNE" because it emphasized the terrorist threat that the military would attack.

The 2001 QDR proposed to move from a threat-based, two major theater of war construct, to a more flexible and agile transformed force that employed defense capabilities that could be used anywhere in the world across a number of scenarios. The Clinton administration had received harsh criticism of its plan to conduct two nearly simultaneous military operations (Northeast Asia and Southwest Asia), with military analysts noting that the assumptions (splitting the force into two, combat operations lasting 120 days) were not realistic, especially considering the state of defense logistics and transportation. Secretary Rumsfeld's strategy was to build a force that could execute a "1-4-2-1" strategy; that is to say, defend U.S. homeland, deter aggression and coercion forward in four critical areas (what was called smaller scale contingencies), swiftly defeat the efforts of two adversaries in overlapping major conflicts, and decisively defeat the adversary in one of those conflicts (what was called major combat operations, replacing the term major theaters of war)—including the possibility of regime change or occupation. The strategy still focused on Northeast and Southwest Asia, depicting a storyboard where forces held off the adversary's offensive actions in one theater while forces in the second theater defeated a major adversary in short order and then reinforced the first theater to finish off the other adversary. There was little change from the Clinton administration's strategy other than adding unquantifiable homeland security requirements to an overburdened military force and implementing a change of acronyms.

What had the DoD CB defense community excited was the number of times "CBRNE" came up in the document (fourteen times). Notably, of the six critical operational goals listed to provide the focus for DoD's transformation efforts, the first one was "protecting critical bases of operations . . . and defeating CBRNE weapons and their means of delivery." The report noted, "it is possible to identify confidently some of these means [by which future adversaries would threaten the United States], including new techniques of terror; ballistic and cruise missiles; weapons of mass destruction, including advanced biological weapons; and weapons of mass disruption, such as information warfare attacks on critical information infrastructure." [25] The third critical operational goal was "project and sustain U.S. forces in distant anti-access and area-denial environments." Because U.S. forces had to quickly deploy and initiate combat overseas, DoD would "monitor attempts by adversaries ... to attack U.S. forces ... or hold at risk critical ports and airbases with missiles and CBRNE attacks." [26]

The White House had been working on its *National Strategy to Combat Weapons of Mass Destruction* since early in the calendar year. This strategy had begun as a classified National Security Council document, National Security Presidential Directive (NSPD) 17 being circulated to the services, combatant commands, and Joint Staff for review. [27] The NSPD had been developed simultaneously with the development of the Nuclear Posture Review (NPR), which would define the military's strategy to employ nuclear weapons. DoD had delivered the NPR to Congress in late December 2001. One of the first things that struck many was the statement "The United States will continue to make clear that it reserves the right to respond with overwhelming force—including potentially nuclear weapons—to the use of [weapons of mass destruction] against the United States, our forces abroad, and friends and allies."

The NPR discussed a deterrent strategy based on a new triad of nuclear and non-nuclear strike options, active (read missile defense) and passive defenses, and "a revitalized defense infrastructure that will provide new capabilities in a timely fashion to meet emerging threats." [28] The U.S. nuclear stockpile was to provide credible military options to deter a wide range of threats, including WMDs and large-scale conventional military forces. With this strategy, the DoD hoped to reduce its nuclear weapons stockpile to a goal of between 1,700 and 2,200 weapons by using non-nuclear weapons to attack potential WMD targets. This would be a reduction in nuclear munitions by about two-thirds. DoD would also make the case to rearm strategic delivery systems (such as ballistic missiles) with highly accurate, conventional payloads. In the event that traditional deterrence failed, missile defense systems would be developed to counter incoming ballistic missiles. The NPR states that the emplacement of defensive missile systems would be a key factor to reducing the overall requirement for nuclear weapons.

Translating the term "developing a responsive defense infrastructure" equates to the need to rebuild the national laboratories that had shrunk since the end of the Cold War, and to fund the "development and procurement of new capabilities." The NPR argued that, given the potential duration of research and development, a more robust capability was needed to "increase confidence in the deployed forces, eliminate unneeded weapons, and mitigate the risks of technological surprise." That is to say, the DoD needed a strong research base, composed of scientists, engineers, and a capable research program, to ensure that the current nuclear weapons worked safely and reliably, that antiquated weapons were taken out of the inventory, and that DoD knew what other nations' nuclear weapons could do.

The NPR noted that potential future contingencies include military confrontations against U.S. forces or allies, with new, hostile military coalitions in which one or more members possessed a WMD capability. China, North Korea, Iraq, Iran, Syria, and Libya were explicitly named as countries that could be involved in one of these contingencies. In addition to discussing the modernization of the nuclear weapons stockpile, the report discussed DoD's reorganized ballistic missile defense program, supporting the Air Force's Airborne Laser program, an Army ground-based midcourse missile defense system for long-range threats, and a Navy sea-based Aegis missile defense system for short to medium-based threats. While there was little to no discussion about passive defenses such as CBRN defense capabilities, there was mention of the need to develop Agent Defeat Weapon concepts to deny access to, immobilize, neutralize, or destroy chemical or biological agents in storage or production facilities. That is, offensive actions were strongly favored over any defensive options, while recognition was given to the need for a complementary suite of capabilities.

The idea of using nuclear weapons to deter the use of WMDs, particularly nuclear weapons, was not entirely new. Under the Clinton administration, the military had developed its joint doctrine (Joint Publication 3-12, *Doctrine for Nuclear Operations*) to state this intent. It notes that the selective capability of using lower-yield weapons in retaliation, without destabilizing the conflict, would be a useful option to the National Command Authority. The deterrent effect of nuclear weapons would also apply to counter an enemy's overwhelming use of conventional weapons. Following the Aum Shinrikyo incident in March 1995, the Clinton administration reaffirmed the Nuclear Non-Proliferation Treaty (along with Britain, China, Russia, and France) to not attack non-nuclear countries with nuclear weapons in 1995, but there was increasing pressure by Congress and the military to develop a strategy to deter countries from using CB weapons against the United States. President Clinton released PDD-60 (Nuclear Weapons Employment Policy Guidance) in November 1997, reaffirming the continuing need for a robust and flexible nuclear deterrent following the end of the Cold War, especially with the advent of rogue states developing their own WMD programs. Following this release, the Clinton administration leaked to several newspapers that it would now consider using nuclear weapons against attackers who used CB weapons against U.S. forces.[29] The focus of efforts, however, remained on deterring a nuclear weapons threat with a retaliatory capability. The Bush administration's NPR appeared to suggest pre-emptive attacks on chemical and biological weapons storage and production facilities, whether or not the country had nuclear weapons, which seemed to lower the threshold of nuclear weapons use. The Bush administration's National Security Strategy (released in September 2002) points out, however, that the "United States will not use force in all cases to preempt emerging threats, nor should nations use preemption as a pretext for aggression. Yet in an age where the enemies of civilization openly and actively seek the world's most destructive technologies, the United States cannot remain idle while dangers gather."[30]

NSPD-17 came to the Joint Staff as the J-5 directorate was developing and staffing a formal counterproliferation strategy and joint doctrine for counterproliferation. Drafting the strategy had taken considerably longer than anticipated, in part due to the change of political administration and the impact of 9/11 on current military operations. The military strategy of identifying four pillars within counterproliferation, counterforce, active defense, passive defense, and consequence management, was basically solid, despite attempts by the Air Force to usher in last-minute changes based on their own view of counterproliferation.[31] Action officers from U.S. Strategic Command (STRATCOM) and SOCOM had taken the lead on coordinating the strategy, focusing on the active defense and counterforce sections respectively. The Chemical School had been tasked with developing a passive defense construct, and a contractor was working on the consequence management section (JFCOM had refused the task, surprisingly). While the military played a role in non-proliferation programs, the Joint Staff supported the OSD and the State Department leads, and so had little concern over that area. The NSPD-17 largely followed the Joint Staff strategy, but had a few new wrinkles.

Bush's National Security Council had decided to move consequence management into its own distinct area. This idea might have taken place as a result of Secretary Tom Ridge (Office of Homeland Security) co-authoring the report with Dr. Condoleezza Rice, the National Security Advisor. This action of separating consequence management from counterproliferation appears to have been done largely to accommodate the desire to include a response to a perceived threat of terrorist WMD threats to the United States and its populace, under the supposition that the global network of terrorists were seeking these weapons from adversarial states with mature WMD programs. OSD policy and the NSC staff seemed intent upon developing a distinct counterproliferation strategy, different (but not decidedly so) from the past administration's efforts. NSPD-17 was released on September 14, 2002, and translated into an unclassified form for public release in December—the *National Strategy to Combat Weapons of Mass Destruction*.[32]

The National Strategy identifies three main pillars: nonproliferation, counterproliferation, and consequence management. The report's introduction notes that some states possess NBC weapons as "militarily useful weapons of choice" intended to counter U.S. military conventional strengths and to deter the United States from responding to their regional affairs. This statement was counter to the usual arms control talking points that describe NBC weapons as weapons of cowards and immoral tools of war. The strategy starts its discussion with counterproliferation first; this was a departure from past arms control discussions that usually emphasized the more diplomatic efforts of nonproliferation as the first measure to combating WMDs.

Counterproliferation is defined as the full range of operational capabilities to counter the threat and use of WMD by states and terrorists against the United States, its military forces, and its friends and allies. This definition differs from past concepts where counterproliferation focused on military forces to a broader and generic concept that addressed noncombatants as well as combatants. Counterproliferation included the broad topics of interdiction, deterrence, defense and mitigation efforts. In effect, this was the older DoD concept of counterforce, active defense, and passive defense expressed in slightly different terms. Interdiction is easy enough to understand, calling for the capability to prevent the movement of WMD materials, technology, and expertise to hostile states and terrorist organizations. The Bush administration's Proliferation Security Initiative, announced in May 2003, would result in an international effort led by the United States to search planes and ships in international air or waters carrying suspect cargo and to seize illegal weapons or technologies.[33] Deterrence called for a strong declaratory policy of using any and all options (unstated: to include nuclear weapons) to respond to the use of WMDs against the United States, its forces abroad, and friends and allies. Intelligence and surveillance on adversarial countries would enhance this deterrence by ensuring the U.S. government could respond accurately against these threats.

Military and domestic law enforcement agencies need active and passive defense and mitigation measures in the event that deterrence did not succeed. Active defenses included missile defense projects. Passive defense is the traditional CBRN defense effort, with the understanding that these defenses had to be "tailored against the unique characteristics of the various forms of WMD." The strategy includes a paragraph that observes that biological defense had long been based on approaches to chemical defense, "despite fundamental differences between these weapons" and promised to develop new approaches to provide for an effective defense against biological weapons. Finally, following any use of WMDs against U.S. forces, mitigation would include the destruction and dismantlement of any residual WMD capabilities of the hostile state or terrorist network.

Nonproliferation addressed those efforts to dissuade supplier states from cooperating with proliferant states, and inducing proliferant states to end their WMD and missile programs. It includes active diplomacy, participation in multilateral arms control regimes, cooperative threat reduction measures such as the Nunn-Lugar program, controls on nuclear materials, U.S. export controls, and nonproliferation sanctions. However, we must consider the Bush administration's record on pulling out of international treaty discussions such as the Anti-Ballistic Missile treaty, the Biological Weapons Convention verification talks, the Fissile Material Cut-Off Treaty, and other similar international arms control efforts. Notably, this section states that "sanctions have proven inflexible and ineffective," but that the United States would develop policy to better integrate sanctions into an overall combating WMD strategy.

Consequence management included both the response to WMD use within the United States by terrorists or hostile states and the response to WMD use against U.S. forces abroad or friends and allies. The strategy identifies the White House Office of Homeland Security as the lead agency to coordinate all federal efforts to prepare for and mitigate the consequences of a terrorist WMD attack within the United States. The National Security Council's Office of Combating Terrorism would coordinate U.S. efforts to respond to and manage recovery from terrorist WMD incidents outside the United States. There is no mention of how military forces would execute foreign consequence management assistance to coalition allies attacked with NBC weapons, other than the earlier reference to the need to support response efforts overseas.[34]

The overall tone of the strategy strongly emphasized the threat of terrorist WMD incidents, noting that the "current and potential future linkages between terrorist groups and state sponsors of terrorism are particularly dangerous and require priority attention. The full range of counterproliferation, nonproliferation, and consequence management must be brought to bear against the WMD terrorist threat, just as they are against states of greatest proliferation concern." By expanding the "combating WMD" strategy to address domestic terrorist CBRN incidents as well as adversarial state WMD programs targeting U.S. military forces overseas, the strategy effectively genericized a focused counterproliferation strategy into a "one-size-fits-all" approach for combating WMD efforts on the battlefield and within the homeland. It assumed that the key to stopping domestic terrorist CBRN incidents could be effected through nonproliferation and counterproliferation actions against those nations developing, and supposedly supplying terrorists with, NBC weapons. At the end of the day, the White House's *National Strategy to Combat Weapons of Mass Destruction* was neither revolutionary nor innovative. It was a tweak of the Clinton administration's Defense Counterproliferation Initiative, with the addition of OSD policy's penchant for global terrorist networks and a desire to respond to WMD threats to homeland security in the same manner as those faced by troops during combat operations.

OPERATION ENDURING FREEDOM

CENTCOM plans to strike the Taliban and al Qaeda forces in Afghanistan began immediately after the 9/11 attacks. It would be a four-phased operation, starting with setting the conditions and building forces to develop credible military options. In addition to obtaining basing and staging agreements from allies in the region and moving military forces into position, CIA paramilitary forces and special operations forces would prepare to move into Afghanistan. Phase 2 would involve the conduct of initial combat operations and set-up of conditions for continued operations. CENTCOM's air component would concentrate on Taliban and al Qaeda targets with aerial bombing and cruise missile attacks, while special forces teams linked up with the Northern Alliance to support offensive ground actions. Phase 3 would involve the conduct of decisive combat operations throughout the area of responsibility. As the Northern Alliance, supported by special forces teams and coalition air power, routed the Taliban, coalition ground forces, including American soldiers and Marines, would deploy into theater to finish the job. Phase 4 would address actions required to prevent the re-emergence of al Qaeda in Afghanistan and to continue humanitarian assistance. This phase would be the longest; Gen. Tommy Franks, CENTCOM commander, estimated that it would take three to five years to stabilize and rebuild the country.[35]

While the Taliban were not assessed as developing or producing CB weapons, the intelligence community had long assessed al Qaeda's interest in developing CBRN hazards for terrorist attacks. This effort was seen as a modest and small-scale effort, mostly focused on the use of small quantities of toxic inhalation hazards within buildings or biological toxins as assassination tools rather than mass casualty weapons.[36] One possibility was that the Taliban was allowing al Qaeda the opportunity to develop improvised CBRN weapons at dual-use industrial facilities, such as a fertilizer plant in Mazar-e Sharif or the vaccine production facility in Kabul. The 310th Chemical Company (BIDS) deployed to alert U.S. forces in theater to any improvised aerosolized BW attacks. CENTCOM staff, with DTRA support, developed a sensitive site exploitation (SSE) concept to quickly seize and search facilities for any terrorist intelligence of al Qaeda's capabilities and intentions (including evidence of CBRN capability). Sensitive sites included research and development facilities, laboratories, universities, weapons production facilities, and storage sites. Most of these would be commercial dual-use facilities; others would be military sites or private facilities that might hold individuals associated with development of CBRN devices. The Defense Intelligence Agency (DIA) deployed independent CB Intelligence Support Teams (CBIST) to collect intelligence, question individuals, or collect samples for analysis, while the Army's TEU would assess captured sites with their capabilities. CENTCOM estimated at least forty places that had potential for WMD research, assessments of which would begin in late November.

On October 7, 2001, President Bush authorized the first strikes from CENTCOM's air component, sending Tomahawk cruise missiles, land and carrier-based bombers, and carrier-based fighters into the air to destroy air defense radar sites, command and control headquarters, terrorist training camps, Taliban military units, and leadership targets. On October 19, the first special forces units inserted into Afghanistan to link up with CIA elements and Northern Alliance units. In a major operation in the north, Mazar-e Sharif fell to Northern Alliance forces on November 9, 2001. Air Force expeditionary support soon included AC-130 gunships stationed in Uzbekistan and F-15 and A-10 fighter aircraft in Kyrgyzstan, Tajikistan, and Pakistan to support the alliance forces. Other cities quickly fell, with forces liberating Kabul on November 13. Soldiers from the 101st Airborne Division came in to secure U.S. bases in Pakistan, while a brigade from the 10th Mountain Division settled in the Uzbekistan camp.

The Marine's Task Force 58 seized Objective Rhino, a desert airstrip south of Qandahar, as a forward operating base on November 25. The 3rd platoon 310th Chemical Company (BIDS) and 26th Romanian NBC Detachment moved into Kandahar, while the TEU sections and 2nd Platoon of the 310th stayed in Bagram. The United Kingdom had its NBC Detachment and a decon unit in Kabul. In early December, approximately thirteen hundred Marines from the 15th and 26th Marine Expeditionary Unit deployed to Camp Rhino near Kandahar (see OEF Order of Battle for Army chemical units at Appendix B).[37] The first Army combat units deployed to Mazar-e Sharif on December 4, and a few days later, the last major Taliban stronghold in Afghanistan surrendered at Qandahar. Remaining Taliban and al Qaeda forces fled to the mountains in Tora Bora and the Pakistan border. On December 22, 2001, General Franks traveled to Kabul to participate in ceremonies of the installation of an interim government headed by Hamid Karzi.

With regards to CBRN defense, CENTCOM was more concerned with force protection of the installations within its area of operation than the traditional warfighting force-on-force operations. The chemical companies were not as familiar working at fixed bases as opposed to maneuver units. With the many CB defense units in theater, a battalion headquarters to manage these assets would have been useful. CENTCOM activated its Joint Task Force for Consequence Management (JTF-CM) under Marine Forces, CENTCOM (MARCENT), in November to support host nation requests to mitigate terrorist CBRN hazards, composed of U.S., German, and Czech NBC defense units. Initially, the JTF was to facilitate the continuation of combat operations by restoring contaminated areas to pre-incident conditions (battlefield consequence management). Perhaps because of the lack of any identified CBRN threat to the military, the JTF worked out command and control coordination and exercised its forces to identify what it could reasonably promise in forms of consequence management support to the host governments in CENTCOM's theater area of operation (foreign consequence management). In the end, this concept was of limited value other than for political purposes and learning what areas needed to be improved. The JTF-CM's lift requirements were substantial, requiring the redirection of sixty or more aircraft to move the Initial Response Force alone. CENTCOM saw this asset as a one-time use capability, given the relatively limited assets of the joint task force and the extensive time required to manage a CBRN incident and restore an area.

During these initial operations, CENTCOM had conducted more than one hundred SSE missions aimed at discovering evidence of al Qaeda's CBRN research and development, production, or storage efforts.[38] General Franks commented, "We're very systematically going about our way of visiting each one of those [sensitive sites to] perform the analyses ... to assure ourselves that we do not have evidence of WMD."[39] While many documents were found and many chemical compositions were sampled, no stocks of CB warfare agents or other hazardous chemicals or toxins were discovered. These documents demonstrated that al Qaeda had crude methods to develop rudimentary chemical weapons and had a strong interest in biological weapons.[40] However, the White House leaked word of information from a "sensitive and credible source" that al Qaeda had taken possession of a chemical weapon in Iraq in October or November, which an intelligence analyst had speculated to be VX, a persistent nerve agent. There was no definitive, hard evidence of any such event. When the media asked Rumsfeld about the story, he stated he had not heard of it, but that he had seen other information that suggested that could be happening.[41]

Evacuating samples from the suspect sites to U.S. labs was difficult, in part due to the Air Force's unwillingness to ship potential hazardous samples with other personnel or cargo and the cost to dedicate a plane solely to carrying a suspect CB warfare sample, despite how small or how safely wrapped the sample was. An in-theater lab with equivalent capabilities as U.S. laboratories would have helped, or TEU couriers could simply not tell the Air Force flight masters what they were carrying. Between the intelligence community, TEU, and other agencies, CENTCOM worked out a protocol that would allow waivers for shipments of carefully packed "unknown environmental samples" from Afghanistan to the United States. Although this challenge existed during Operation Desert Storm more than ten years earlier, there had been no resolution on defining a policy for promptly evacuating CB samples. Eventually, these protocols would result in smoother sampling analyses when ground operations began in Iraq a year later.

Between January and March 2002, U.S. military and coalition forces continued to seek out and defeat Taliban and al Qaeda forces operating in the mountains. Operation Anaconda involved a ground force of about two thousand soldiers including soldiers from the 10th Mountain Division and 101st Airborne Division, special forces, and coalition units. This task force, strongly supported by air and aviation assets, engaged groups of fighters in caves and tunnels around the Shahikhot valley region between March 1 and March 18, in one of the largest ground battles seen to that date. Eight soldiers were killed in action and eighty-two were wounded, with the enemy deaths estimated in the hundreds. This operation effectively reduced the last al Qaeda sanctuary in Afghanistan. In late August 2002, Afghans turned over sixty-four al Qaeda videotapes to a CNN correspondent, one of which showed young dogs being deliberately gassed within a glass cage in a demonstration on the effectiveness of chemical agents.[42] While inconclusive, experts believed that the three demonstrations on the tape showed that al Qaeda possibly had access to quantities of sarin, hydrogen cyanide, and perhaps chlorine gas, and intended to train its members on how to use these chemicals.[43]

General Franks and his staff in CENTCOM had an especially difficult task between December 2001 and March 2002. In addition to overseeing actions in Afghanistan, on November 27, 2001, Defense Secretary Rumsfeld had directed him to dust off the operational plans for military operations against Iraq. One month later, Franks was briefing Rumsfeld on the high points of the updated plan, with two primary objectives—regime change and WMD removal. These objectives would remain the primary goals in March 2003.[44] On December 28, Franks briefed President Bush on a four-phased operation, similar to the Afghanistan operation. Phase one was preparations; phase two was shaping the battlespace; phase three was decisive operations, and phase four was post-hostility operations. Frank's assumptions began with the estimate that Iraq possessed and would use WMDs, forcing U.S. forces to fight in a toxic environment. While the intelligence community would be expected to identify the locations of these weapons and indications of potential use, Franks was not confident that he could preempt WMD use. Vice President Cheney asked Franks if U.S. forces were properly trained and equipped to face the challenge of CB-armed SCUD missiles landing in their areas. Franks replied that WMD would be the greatest problem that they faced, but CENTCOM's staff work was too immature to provide a good answer as to the force's readiness.[45]

Between January and June 2002, the intelligence community would work full-bore on this issue, as OSD, CENTCOM, EUCOM, the four services and the Joint Staff worked to identify what impact CB weapons would have on military forces and what they would require in the event that Saddam did authorize the use of CB weapons. The only facts they did have was that there had been no inspectors since 1998 and no one knew what weapons Iraq may have developed or where they were located. No one knew what Saddam would do in the event of a regime survival situation, but he had authorized the use of chemical weapons in the past against Iranian forces and Iraqi insurgents. While the president voiced his hopes that a military conflict could be avoided, barring Saddam's voluntarily leaving Iraq, the defense machinery was in full motion to go to war against the Iraqi regime.[46]

CHAPTER 5

THE CASE FOR WAR

How is the world ruled and how do wars start? Diplomats tell lies to
journalists and then believe what they read.

—KARL KRAUS, AUSTRIAN WRITER AND SATIRIST

The Bush administration gave many reasons why the United States should attack Iraq. The administration stated that they wanted to establish a representative democracy in the Middle East that would be emulated by other nations in the area; that Saddam's alleged possession of CB weapons and his pursuit of a nuclear weapons capability were unacceptable; that his alleged connections with terrorist groups (in particular al Qaeda) constituted a threat to the United States; and that his history of war against Kuwait and Iran and the Iraqi regime's horrific pattern of abuses against its own people made him a threat to regional stability. Certainly Saddam Hussein's regime was an oppressive bunch of thugs, and the world is better off without him. The real questions were: was there adequate rationale to support the claim that Saddam had an active and flourishing CB weapons program, that he was actively seeking a nuclear weapons capability, and that he had ties to terrorists that desired these unconventional weapons?

The intelligence agencies of many countries had analyzed Iraq's industrial capabilities and had formulated opinions as to extent and maturity of Saddam's unconventional weapons programs. The military had reason to believe, based on pre-war intelligence estimates, that Iraq had (at the least) a small arsenal of chemical and biological weapons.[1] It was the military's job to anticipate the use of these weapons, plan appropriate countermeasures, and mitigate their effectiveness while defeating Iraqi forces. This chapter examines the intelligence assessments of Saddam's WMD program, conducted during the

Clinton and Bush administrations, that were used to justify going to war to remove Saddam's "weapons of mass destruction." [2]

It is not easy examining intelligence products relating to CB warfare because many people instinctively throw up the classified label to stop any discussions of the potential impact of CB weapons on military forces. Intelligence products are classified due to the need to protect sources and technical means of obtaining such information, or because the release of this information could, in some fashion, be damaging to the national security (and in particular, the armed forces). In the area of CBRN defense, there is a double-edged sword that dangles over defense analysts' heads. Any public discussion about a potential adversary's offensive CB warfare capability might reveal that we understand what they can do on the battlefield, and in general it's not a good thing that they know that we know what they can do. But in the case of CB weapons, in many situations even seasoned intelligence analysts cannot predict with any great resolution the potential damage caused by a particular weapon system. There are too many unknowns:

- How efficiently does the delivery system work?

- Is the adversary well trained in delivering the weapons on target?

- How pure is the agent?

- How long will it persist in the environment (as opposed to a laboratory or storage area)?

- How will the agent affect military personnel who have defensive equipment and are trained to use it effectively?

In large part, this inability to understand and articulate CB weapons effects is due to strict congressional limits on the U.S. military's ability to test CB agents in the open environment (caused by the alleged Dugway sheep incident of 1968, where ranchers claimed that their herds had been exposed to an Army aerial spray trial employing VX nerve agent nearly thirty miles away).[3] Even the latest models and simulations of CB agents focus on hazard dispersion modeling, wherein very little effort is expended on accurately modeling the operational impact of CB agents on personnel and equipment. Ultimately, intelligence estimates regarding the impact of CB weapons use is largely an educated guess; but, as it is a guess based on the best possible analyses of adversarial capabilities, it is carefully guarded information.

Second, discussion of U.S. CBRN defense capabilities is often muted due to the concern that any weaknesses or identified lack of capability would be interpreted as a potential vulnerability of U.S. forces. There are discussions that focus on U.S. military capabilities with regard to defensive equipment and training, which are mostly unclassified, and then there are operational analyses of how specific forces would suffer casualties and loses as a result of the use of CB weapons against them, which are mostly classified. Developing CBRN defense capabilities is not merely a matter of adequate quantities of modern equipment; a military force also requires good doctrine and training, leadership, specialized organizations and personnel, and facilities to support a strong defensive capability. Yet most people would rather discuss the technical aspects of the CBRN defense equipment U.S. forces carry, such as those detectors, protective suits and masks, collective protection systems, decontamination gear, and medical countermeasures required to survive and sustain combat operations. Some authorities assume that even unclassified CBRN defense information on basic equipment and general concepts is too sensitive for public release unless an official government agent has previously printed it as open source material first.[4] This is a great handicap to the ability to openly and honestly dialogue about how the armed forces can best counter the threat of NBC weapons and associated CBRN hazards. Had it not been for the investigation into the Gulf War illnesses in the mid-to-late 1990s, many facts about the U.S. military's CBRN defense capabilities during Operation Desert Storm may have never emerged. As a result, we see a lot of general statements, but few specifics, in predictions about the potential impact of CB warfare on U.S. military forces.

It is increasingly difficult to have a reasoned discussion on this issue. Many details on CB defense are classified in the aftermath of a given conflict due to the excessive concern that open discussion will allow insights as to potential vulnerabilities against CBRN hazards (and therefore could be leveraged by future adversaries). As a result, journalists and some defense critics grab onto a particular issue, such as false alarms from chemical agent detectors or the unknown source of Gulf War illnesses, and blow it up into a story that accuses the military of procuring faulty equipment. These critics often do not take the time to understand the rationale of military equipment development, the tradeoffs in capabilities versus time and cost, and cost/benefit analyses. For instance, the military can accept having some false positive alarms (alarming in the absence of agent) as a tradeoff for having more sensitive detectors, while false negative alarms (not alarming in the presence of agent) are not acceptable in any situation. But we do not see that discussion in the media—technical details are boring, much better to talk about combat units bringing chickens into theater as sentinel CW alarms.[5]

Despite these challenges, it is vital to understand what the U.S. government thought Iraq had in 2003, why the administration thought this was a threat, whether it was reasonable to believe the intelligence analyses, and what policies were developed and what plans were made to counter Iraq's capabilities to employ CB weapons. Nonproliferation and counterproliferation agencies have designed strategies intended to limit and contain the potential damage caused by CB weapons during a combat operation without the United States having to resort to nuclear weapons response. By 2003, these strategies were mature and workable, reducing the threat of CB weapons to a manageable battlefield event, especially from a relatively small and largely ineffective military like Iraq's. Reports following the second Gulf War show that sanctions and inspection regimes had a much larger effect than many neo-conservatives and the administration were willing to admit. Somewhere along the march to war, there was a jump of logic from the initial statement that Iraq was pursuing a WMD program to the assumption that Iraq had a viable offensive CB weapons capability, and then to statements that this capability represented a grave and growing threat to national security. These jumps in logic were not made by the intel community, but by policy makers. If the Bush administration seriously believed that Iraq's WMD program was a threat that constituted going to war, then this was an inherent failure of the administration's policy and its interpretation of intelligence analyses.

AFTER OPERATION DESERT STORM

After the end of Operation Desert Storm, UN inspections made clear that Iraq had a mature CB weapons capability and was working toward a nuclear weapons capability. Military forces and the United Nations Special Commission (UNSCOM) found numerous production facilities containing tons of chemical and biological precursors, thousands of rockets and bombs filled with nerve and mustard agents, thousands of mustard-filled artillery shells, hundreds of tons of mustard agent in containers, and al-Hussein binary chemical missile warheads.[6] There was no question that Iraq had thousands of scientists and engineers dedicated to the research, development, and manufacture of these weapons, a military force that was trained to use them, and a proven capability to employ them. There was no question that Iraq had attacked Iran with chemical weapons in during the 1980s, and that Iraq had used chemical weapons against Shi'ite and Kurdish insurgents and noncombatants. The U.S. government knew about this use during the Iran-Iraq war, and warned Saddam Hussein that he would be removed from power if he used these weapons against U.S. forces during Operations Desert Shield and Desert Storm. By 1991, Iraq had produced 3,859 tons of CW agents, to include 2,850 tons of mustard agent, 795 tons of sarin and cyclosarin, 210 tons of tabun, and nearly 4 tons of VX nerve agent. Of that sum, about 85 percent was weaponized, and Iraq declared later that about 80 percent of that weaponized stockpile had been used during the Iran-Iraq war. The fact that Iraq had developed chemical weapons and had used them on its own people and against Iranian military forces was not enough justification for the U.S. government and its coalition allies to seek a forced regime change in 1991.

Following the war, UNSCOM's task was to verify that Iraq was in line with UN Security Council Resolution 687, calling for the complete elimination of all NBC weapons and missiles, and forbidding Iraq from developing, producing, or possessing any NBC weapons or missiles with a range greater than 150 kilometers. In return, economic sanctions would be lifted once Iraq was in compliance. Rolf Ekeus was the UN-appointed chairman of UNSCOM from June 1991 to June 1997. UNSCOM and the International Atomic Energy Agency (IAEA) had hundreds of inspectors in Iraq between 1991 and 1998 to oversee the destruction of these weapons and the dismantlement of the Iraqi physical infrastructure supporting the WMD program; to verify that Iraq had ended all efforts to pursue these weapons; and to establish a long-term monitoring effort of those facilities. This included visitations and surveillance of about 170 chemical and 86 biological facilities and monitoring the imports of any potential dual-use technologies or equipment into Iraq.[7] UNSCOM ran an incineration facility at Samarra between 1992 and 1994, dedicated to destroying more than 690 tons of chemical agents, more than 3,000 tons of chemical precursors and 426 pieces of production equipment items. In addition, UNSCOM destroyed 38,500 filled and unfilled munitions, 28 SCUD missiles, 11 mobile launchers and 56 fixed sites, 30 filled chemical SCUD warheads and 20 conventional SCUD warheads. The inspectors discovered that the Iraqis had learned to produce, stabilize, and weaponize VX, a nerve agent that had not been found immediately after the war. While the Iraqi government was willing to admit that it had an offensive chemical weapons program, it did not admit to having developed an offensive biological weapons or nuclear weapons program.

In 1995, UNSCOM discovered that Iraq had produced about four tons of VX and had probably imported six hundred tons of precursors to manufacture two hundred tons of VX prior to 1991. Iraq had not admitted to having produced VX, and declared it had not weaponized VX either. Following Hussein Kamel's defection in August 1995, Iraq admitted that it had an offensive biological weapons program and had produced nineteen thousand liters of botulinum, eighty-four hundred liters of anthrax, and two thousand liters of aflatoxin, clostridium, and ricin toxin.[8] It appeared that Iraq had not weaponized much of its biological agents other than about twenty-five al-Hussein missile warheads and about 150 aerial bombs. The inspectors also uncovered and dismantled forty nuclear research facilities in the mid-1990s, including three uranium enrichment facilities and a lab-scale plutonium separation plant. Iraq claimed to have destroyed much of its CB stocks and munitions unilaterally following the Gulf War, although some of these statements could not be proven to the inspectors' desires. The inspectors were able to account for 817 out of 819 SCUDs that Iraq claimed to have destroyed. Many of the inspectors' attempts to travel around the country to particular sites were increasingly obstructed by Iraqi government officials, who gave false or misleading responses to inspectors' questions, directed Iraqi escorts to interfere with inspections, denied access to sensitive sites on grounds of national security, and removed or tampered with evidence at the sites.[9]

Ekeus resigned in June 1997, and Richard Butler was appointed to assume the mission in July. In late October 1997, Iraq barred American UNSCOM personnel from conducting inspections, and on November 13, 1997, it temporarily expelled the American inspectors. In mid-December 1997, Butler visited Iraq with his deputy Charles Duelfer and other UN commissioners to work out the issue of resuming inspections of sensitive sites such as national security sites. He developed an aggressive inspection program that included searching Saddam's presidential palaces, which provoked some displeasure in Iraq. In June 1998, the teams found missile warheads with traces of VX, according to tests conducted at Aberdeen Proving Ground (separate French and Swiss tests did not confirm these test results). This effort became complicated when accusations surfaced that the CIA was using UNSCOM as a vehicle to spy on Iraqi military and political efforts. Iraq announced that they were not going to deal with American inspectors, and increased their interference with the teams. This led to Richard Butler's pulling the UNSCOM teams out of Iraq on December 16, 1998, just prior to President Clinton's authorizing U.S. military attacks against Iraqi WMD program-related facilities.

Saddam had been provoking U.S. forces for some time. In addition to blocking the UNSCOM inspectors, he continued to send military planes into the no-fly zones and threatened to shoot down the U.S. reconnaissance flights traveling over Iraq. In response, CENTCOM put together Operation Desert Thunder, a show of force in which more than thirty-five thousand U.S. and coalition forces were deployed to Kuwait in January 1998 through March 1998. These forces included the 20th Chemical Detachment of the 310th Chemical Company (BIDS). General Tony Zinni, the CENTCOM CINC, and Lt. Gen. Tommy Franks, commanding the Third Army forces, directed a multinational joint task force that included an Army brigade from the 3rd Infantry Division, forces from the First Marine Expeditionary Force, thirty-nine ships, and more than four hundred aircraft. United Nations Secretary General Kofi Annan flew to Baghdad in February in an attempt to negotiate continued inspection visits, which Saddam agreed to allow under a more restrictive memorandum of understanding, ending the crisis. Iraq's continued interference with the teams resulted in a second iteration of force in mid-November, resulting in the deployment of twenty-three hundred military personnel to Kuwait. This caused Iraq to agree to cooperate unconditionally with UNSCOM's inspection teams.

Following the Iraqi capitulation, President Clinton warned the Iraqi leadership that he would use appropriate force if Iraq continued to impede the UNSCOM efforts. Saddam refused to allow the inspectors to have unlimited access until after the UN had lifted its remaining sanctions. CENTCOM began planning Operation Desert Fox, an air power operation that would attack WMD-related facilities, missile delivery production sites, and security sites over a four-day period (December 16–19, 1998). President Clinton wanted to eliminate Iraq's WMD program, but as Gen. Zinni explained, the

U.S. military didn't know enough about the current WMD program since the inspectors had taken down the known physical infrastructure. They could hit missile production facilities, the research and development programs working on new missile fuels, security forces that protected WMD program information and materials, factories making high-quality machinery for the nuclear program, and political targets such as the intelligence headquarters and Ba'ath party headquarters.[10] During Operation Desert Fox, U.S. and British forces attacked thirty-two SAM facilities, twenty command and control facilities, eighteen security facilities, and eleven WMD industrial and production facilities with more than 415 Tomahawk missiles and three hundred air sorties. Defense Secretary Bill Cohen noted that the attacks had avoided chemical production facilities, which, if attacked, might cause collateral damage to nearby noncombatants. President Clinton announced on December 19, "We have inflicted significant damage on Saddam's weapons of mass destruction programs, on the command structures that direct and protect that capability and on his military and security infrastructure."[11] In reality, this operation was not intended to destroy Iraq's WMD program as much as it was to punish Saddam for not cooperating with the UNSCOM inspectors.

When UNSCOM left Iraq in 1998, they were unable to account for all the munitions Iraq had declared. These numbers included six thousand aerial bombs that would have been filled with nerve agents, thought to have been manufactured during the Iran-Iraq war. These bombs could not present a threat in 2003, considering that Iraqi technology had only been able to produce sarin at 60–70 percent purity, and it degraded rapidly once produced. This was one reason why Iraq had moved on to binary mixes of nerve agent. Iraq declared they had lost 550 mustard-filled 155-mm artillery shells shortly after the Gulf War, and disregarded their loss as unimportant. UNSCOM discovered a dozen mustard-filled artillery shells in April 1998, and their purity after seven years in storage still ranged between 94 and 97 percent. These shells would still be viable, but five hundred and fifty mustard-filled shells did not represent an operationally-significant capability in and of themselves. About five hundred R-400 binary sarin-filled bombs could not be accounted for in Iraq's claim that they had unilaterally destroyed 1,550 such bombs. Also unaccounted for were two SCUD missiles, fifteen thousand 122-mm artillery shells, twenty-five thousand 122-mm rockets, and a few hundred tons of VX agent precursor.

As far as what remained of Iraq's BW program, it was difficult to assess exactly what the truth of the matter was. Because Iraq had never fully disclosed what it had in the way of BW-filled warheads and bombs, biological growth media, and total bulk BW agent manufactured, UNSCOM was unable to present a final summary to either declare Iraq as compliant or noncompliant. While UNSCOM had dismantled a number of facilities and set up monitoring devices in others, they could not verify the absence of BW munitions in a full and complete manner. Iraq's final position was that, unless the commission could demonstrate that Iraq did in fact retain NBC weapons, it should declare that Iraq had fully met its obligations under the UN resolution.

The Iraqi nuclear weapons program was completely dismantled, at least to the degree of known Iraqi facilities, equipment, and refined uranium. The IAEA's final report noted that Iraq had intended to have their first nuclear weapon by 1991. By October 1997, the IAEA reported that all known facilities capable of producing uranium, as well as all known fuel fabrication or isotopic enrichment facilities, had been destroyed along with associated equipment, and all known procured uranium compounds were in IAEA custody. All known research and development equipment for weaponizing nuclear weapons had been recovered and destroyed.[12] At the end of the inspections, it appeared that there was no way for Iraq to produce quantities of weapons-grade nuclear material of any practical significance. Yet, the IAEA warned that there was always the chance that Iraq had successfully hidden parts of their program from sight.

Iraq claimed that its entire WMD program had been dismantled, but did not offer full and verifiable documentation for all of its claims. Saddam had little incentive to cooperate as long as the U.S. policy was to remove him from power and to merely suspend sanctions, instead of lifting them entirely, as a result of his cooperation. As Scott Ritter would point out in 2000, while it was impossible to confirm that Iraq had disposed of all of its weapons, certainly Saddam had no capability to wage war with CB weapons. UNSCOM had been able to ensure that the vast majority of Iraq's WMD arsenal, including its physical infrastructure, had been eliminated. Because of their presence, UN inspectors had been able to verify that Iraq was not reconstituting any meaningful capability.[13]

BEFORE SEPTEMBER 2001

The question now moves from what Iraq had in 1998 to what the U.S. government thought Iraq had in 2002. More important, what level of threat did these weapons present to the United States and its interests? In 1997, nations that were suspected of developing, producing, or storing NBC weapons included China, North Korea, India, Pakistan, Iran, Iraq, Libya, Syria, Russia, Ukraine, Kazakhstan, Belarus, and extremist groups such as Aum Shinrikyo. In 2001, the DoD *Proliferation: Threat and Response* report stated that twenty-five nations possessed, or were in the process of acquiring and developing, NBC weapons and the means to deliver them. Secretary Cohen's message specifically listed North Korea, Iran, Iraq, and Libya; within the report, China, Pakistan, India, Syria, Sudan, and Russia were listed. The report also mentioned al Qaeda leader Usama Bin Laden, noting that Bin Laden had made public statements in 1999 defending the right of the Muslim community to pursue the development of NBC weapons capabilities.

The report assessed Iraq as possibly reconstituting its WMD program, given its continued resistance against UN inspections and attempts to purchase dual-use items "under the guise of legitimate civil use since the end of the Gulf War." As for its nuclear weapons program, the report noted that Saddam had sought nuclear weapons and retained the personnel and information to restart such a program. The report restated UNSCOM's findings about the Iraqi BW program, noting the U.S. government's concern that "Baghdad again may have produced some biological warfare agents" in the absence of inspections. Baghdad was rebuilding key portions of its industrial and chemical production infrastructure, including former dual-use CW-associated production facilities destroyed by U.S. bombings. "In 1999, Iraq may have begun installing or repairing dual-use equipment at these or other chemical warfare-related facilities." The report noted Iraq's continued work on short-range ballistic missiles and its unmanned aerial vehicle (UAV) program, notably the L-29 jet trainer aircraft acquired from Eastern Europe that "may be intended for the delivery of chemical or biological agents." While these signs indicated intent to develop a WMD program, they did not indicate that Iraq had a viable military capability to employ these weapons.

The 2001 *Proliferation: Threat and Response* report diplomatically did not address efforts of the other fifteen nations suspected of developing WMD programs, including Cuba, Egypt, Ethiopia, Israel, Myanmar (Burma), Taiwan and Vietnam because they were not suspected proliferators. Neither did the report address those countries that possessed chemical weapons and had not yet destroyed their stockpiles in accordance with the Chemical Weapons Convention treaty (South Korea and the United States).[14] In the intelligence community, there is a great deal of distinction between those states that are known possessors, probable possessors, and possible possessors.[15] It is clear that DoD recognizes that a significant number of countries do possess or may be developing NBC weapons, and that U.S. forces may be deployed to a region where those weapons might be used by those countries during regional conflicts or to deter U.S. forces from interfering in its affairs. So why was Iraq special? As Defense Secretary Rumsfeld would note to Congress in September 2002, "The connection between weapons of mass destruction and global terrorist networks [in Iraq] is the nexus that causes the problem."[16] Yet, there are many countries today that might be suspected of both developing a WMD program and having clear connections to terrorist organizations, of which Iran, Syria, and North Korea immediately come to mind.

The question of to what extent Iraq could rebuild and reconstitute its WMD program in four years (1998–2002) is the real issue. On February 24, 2001, Secretary of State Colin Powell noted, "And frankly [the sanctions] have worked [against Iraq]. He [Saddam] has not developed any significant capability with respect to weapons of mass destruction. He is unable to project conventional power against his neighbors. So in effect, our policies have strengthened the security of the neighbors of Iraq, and these are policies that we are going to keep in place, but we are always willing to review them to make sure that they are being carried out in a way that does not affect the Iraqi people but does affect the Iraqi regime's ambitions and the ability to acquire weapons of mass destruction ..."[17] In May 2001, Powell noted that Saddam Hussein had not been able to rebuild his military or to develop weapons of mass destruction for the last ten years, due to the successful containment policy. This assessment was a solitary position. Political hawks blasted the failure of UN sanctions to limit what they saw as a continued and growing threat in the Middle East, while political doves attacked his statement as support for a policy that was hurting Iraqi women and children more than the Iraqi regime. In July 2001, Condoleezza Rice noted, "Saddam does not control the northern part of his country. We are able to keep his arms away from him. His military forces have not been built."[18]

INTELLIGENCE ANALYSES AFTER 9/11

In October 2001, USD (P) Douglas Feith created an office known as the Policy Counterterrorism Evaluation Group. This office was composed of two people, David Wurmser and F. Michael Maloof. Feith would later explain that the function of this team was to help him read and absorb the intelligence produced by the intelligence community.[19] According to other sources, the purpose of the team was to come up with counters to CIA analyses that had not found credible links between Iraq and al Qaeda. This group completed its work in late August 2002, identifying links between Iraq and al Qaeda in addition to outlining other interconnections between terrorist organizations and state sponsors worldwide.[20] When Feith took these results to the CIA, the CIA discounted the analyses as not credible. Despite this assessment, Feith presented the same brief to the White House and the NSC as credible evidence of a direct Iraq-al Qaeda link, and criticized the CIA's inability to see the obvious.[21]

In August 2002, Feith created an Office of Special Plans (OSP) within the ASD (ISP) Near East and South Asia Affairs section. Its intent was not to collect intelligence, but to conduct policy planning for Iraq as a result of the focus on that country. Headed by Abram Shulsky, this team of less than ten full-time staffers and scores of temporary consultants, including lawyers, congressional staffers and policy experts from conservative think-tanks, would rely on the intelligence estimates developed by the Policy Counterterrorism Evaluation Group, as well as raw intelligence from Iraqi National Congress (INC), Israeli intelligence sources and other U.S. intelligence agencies. Their assessments would be sent to senior aides of the president and vice president, often without vetting by professional intelligence analysts.[22]

Between August 2002 and March 2003, President Bush repeatedly stated that the main reasons for preemptively attacking Iraq were its possession of chemical and biological weapons; Saddam Hussein's intent to use these weapons on either his own people, countries in the region, or the United States; or the possibility that terrorists might obtain these weapons from his regime for use against the United States. These statements were repeated by Vice President Dick Cheney, Secretary of State Colin Powell, National Security Advisor Condoleezza Rice, Defense Secretary Donald Rumsfeld, Defense Deputy Secretary Paul Wolfowitz, and others in an attempt to convince the American public and the world community that Iraq's WMD program represented a *casus belli* to attack Iraq.[23] The media echoed the administration's views and did not question them, as evidenced by the *Washington Post* publishing more than 140 front-page articles focusing on the administration's rhetoric against Iraq during this time. The *New York Times*, *Wall Street Journal*, and other major news outlets had a similar practice. Despite claims by these newspapers that there were more skeptical articles (located in the back pages), one Pentagon correspondent noted the attitude of the editors was "look, we're going to war, why do we even worry about all this contrary stuff?"[24]

On June 20, 2002, Vice President Cheney told a crowd in Detroit, "A regime that hates America and everything we stand for must never be permitted to threaten America with weapons of mass destruction."[25] On August 26, 2002, he told the Veterans of Foreign Wars, "Simply stated, there is no doubt that Saddam Hussein now has weapons of mass destruction." In December, addressing the Denver Air National Guard, he said, "Iraq could decide on any given day to provide biological or chemical weapons to a terrorist group or to individual terrorists. . . . The war on terror will not be won until Iraq is completely and verifiably deprived of weapons of mass destruction." On September 8, 2002, Powell told Fox News, "There is no doubt that he has chemical weapons stocks . . . with respect to biological weapons, we are confident that he has some stocks of those weapons and he is probably continuing to try to develop more." On the same day, Rice stated, "There will always be some uncertainty about how quickly he can acquire nuclear weapons, but we don't want the smoking gun to be a mushroom cloud."[26] On February 24, 2003, she noted, ". . . we're talking about missing anthrax and missing botulinum toxin and missing VX and missing sarin gas. . . . we're talking about biological—mobile biological weapons labs that have—now we have confirmation from several sources, exist that Saddam Hussein continues to hide."[27] In testimony to Congress on September 18, 2002, Rumsfeld stated, "[Saddam's] regime has amassed large clandestine stocks of biological weapons, including anthrax and botulinum toxin and possibly smallpox. His regime has amassed large clandestine stocks of chemical weapons, including VX and sarin and mustard gas. His regime has an active program to acquire and develop nuclear weapons." On October 16, 2002, Wolfowitz remarked at a conference, "We cannot afford to wait until Saddam Hussein or some terrorist supplied by him attacks us with a chemical or biological or, worst of all, a nuclear weapon, to recognize the danger that we face. . . . We must not wait for some terrible event that connects the dots for us."[28]

On September 12, 2002, President Bush addressed the UN General Assembly, and on September 24, Prime Minister Tony Blair talked to the British Parliament on the threat Iraq posed. Both leaders stressed that the fundamental outcome had to be the disarmament of all WMDs from Iraq.[29] At the same time, the State Department and the British government released unclassified assessments of Iraq's WMD program. A DIA assessment, published that same month, discussed aspects of Iraq's chemical weapons program. In October, the CIA published a classified National Intelligence Estimate on Iraq's WMD program, and an unclassified version of the same report for public release. These documents outlined what the Bush administration felt was a mature and growing WMD program.

The State Department's background paper included a short (three-page) summary of unclassified reports on Iraq's attempts to rebuild its WMD program.[30] One of the first items referenced a *New York Times* article describing an Iraqi defector, Adnan Ihsan Saeed al-Haideri, who had given details on renovations of twenty secret WMD facilities in underground wells, private villas, and under the Saddam Hussein Hospital in Baghdad within the last year.[31] In January 2002, many national and international news organizations widely quoted the defector's accounts, with Charles Duelfer agreeing that his descriptions made sense in light of past CB weapons activities in Iraq. In 2004, further media investigations would discover that this defector had been to the CIA and DIA, and that both agencies had rejected him as unreliable. The State Department document described Iraq's rebuilding dual-use production facilities for both chemical and biological weapons production, as well as its continued purchases of precursors and equipment for these plants. It repeated the UNSCOM observations that Iraq had failed to account for stockpiles of chemical agents, hundreds of tons of chemical precursors, and tens of thousands of filled and unfilled munitions.

The document noted that Iraq had only admitted to the weaponization of biological agents after the 1995 defection of a senior Iraqi official, that UNSCOM had concluded that Iraq had actually produced two to four times the amounts of anthrax and botulinum toxin than it had declared, and that Saddam had continued attempts to procure mobile biological weapons laboratories for research and development efforts. The State Department document cited the 2001 DoD *Proliferation: Threat and Response* report in its description of Iraq's conversion of L-29 jet trainer aircraft as a potential UAV. Reports of

Iraq's attempts to modify the L-29 UAV to disperse CB warfare agents had started as early as 1995. British intelligence had suspected that the aircraft had been fitted with underwing spray tanks that could carry three hundred liters of anthrax or nerve agents, with the purpose of spraying large built-up areas.[32] It would be revealed later that the Air Force had estimated that Iraq had discontinued its L-29 UAV program as early as 2001, due to guidance system failings and other design problems.[33]

In the area of nuclear weapons, the document cited a report from the International Institute for Strategic Studies stating that Saddam Hussein could build a nuclear bomb within months if he were able to obtain fissile material. Iraq was seeking to procure thousands of specially designed aluminum tubes as components of enriching centrifuges, and still had the technical expertise and some infrastructure to continue its pursuit of building a nuclear weapon. Finally, the report noted that Iraq continued to build ballistic missiles, including the al-Samoud liquid-propellant short-range missile and the al-Ababil-100 solid-fuel missile. The al-Samoud was a scaled-down Scud that Iraq had been flight-testing since 1997. The al-Ababil 100 was a newer short-range missile. Neither missile had been operationally used, and was unclear whether they had warheads designed for chemical warfare agent fills. Both were supposed to have ranges of less than 150 kilometers, as per UN resolutions, but suspicions were that these missiles exceeded that range. In essence, the State Department document outlining Iraq's WMD program merely repeated the 1998 UNSCOM findings, the 2001 *Proliferation: Threat and Response* report, and a poorly researched article from the *New York Times*.

The DIA's two-page assessment was more circumspect and conservative than the State Department's paper.[34] It did note that Iraq was rebuilding its industrial chemical facilities "under a guise of a civilian need for pesticides, chlorine, and other legitimate chemical products, giving Iraq the potential for a small 'breakout' production capability." The assessment noted that there was no reliable information on whether Iraq was producing or stockpiling chemical weapons, or where Iraq would establish its chemical agent production facilities. While Iraq retained equipment and precursors for mustard agent, the DIA doubted that Iraq could produce large quantities of nerve agents without external aid. DIA lacked any direct information on Iraqi possession of CW agent munitions, but assessed that Iraq "probably possesses CW agent in chemical munitions, . . . [and] bulk chemical stockpiles, primarily containing precursors, but that also could consist of some mustard agent or stabilized VX." DIA felt that Iraq was reconstituting parts of its CW program, but it was not clear that Iraq had a serious offensive CW capability. The declassified DIA assessment did not address the biological warfare or nuclear weapons program, but the paper did suggest that the size, nature, and condition of Iraq's BW stockpiles were unknown and subject to debate. In June 2003, the media would jump on this report as evidence that the intelligence community did not have hard evidence on Iraq's stockpiles.[35]

The CIA developed its National Intelligence Estimate (NIE), titled *Iraq's Continuing Programs for Weapons of Mass Destruction*, over a three-week period in September 2002: a relatively quick piece of work.[36] The NIE was coordinated with the State Department's Bureau of Intelligence and Research (INR), DoE, National Security Agency, National Imagery and Mapping Agency, DIA, and all military intelligence agencies. CIA usually develops these estimates for the president to develop national policy, not in response to Congressional requests. This report was not intended to inform the president about the Iraqi threat, but to convince Congress that there was a credible threat.[37] In October 2002, Congress received the NIE ten days prior to a vote on whether to authorize the use of military force against Iraq. It outlined a number of key judgments not included in the DIA assessment. In addition to noting that Iraq had continued its WMD program, the report stated that, "Baghdad has chemical and biological weapons as well as missiles with ranges in excess of UN restrictions; if left unchecked, it probably will have a nuclear weapon during this decade." If Iraq obtained enough fissile material from external sources, the estimate was that Saddam could have a nuclear weapon within a year. If not, then it might be five to seven years, based on the time to build and operate the necessary facilities and produce a nuclear weapon. Interestingly enough, in 1996 the intelligence community had thought, with key foreign assistance, that Iraq could build a nuclear weapon within "five to seven years."

The CIA document noted Iraq's "aggressive attempts to obtain high-strength aluminum tubes" as evidence of Iraq's attempts to develop an indigenous uranium enrichment capability. The UK assessment also noted Iraq's covert attempts to acquire sixty thousand or more specialized aluminum tubes. On September 8, 2002, the *New York Times* had published a story about Iraq's reputed attempts to obtain high-grade aluminum tubes designed for uranium enriching centrifuges, based on statements from Bush administration officials.[38] However, both the DoE and State Department's INR argued that the tubes were not part of a nuclear weapons program, a position echoed by the IAEA's technical experts. In fact, it was much more likely that these aluminum tubes would be parts of rocket artillery (for instance, the U.S. Army's obsolete 115-mm nerve agent filled rockets were constructed with aluminum tubes). The National Ground Intelligence Center (NGIC), an intelligence agency under DIA that specializes in ground weapon systems, considered the aluminum tubes poor choices for rocket bodies. This fueled speculation that the tubes were therefore associated with the Iraqi nuclear program's gas centrifuges.[39]

The CIA report noted that Iraq had 2.5 tons of enriched uranium (allowable under IAEA oversight) that might make up one or two nuclear weapons, and 550 tons of "yellowcake"—refined uranium ore—and low-enriched uranium, and that, according to a foreign government service, Iraq was planning to buy up to 500 tons of yellowcake from Niger. An Italian journalist had provided government documents purporting to show these transactions to the Italian intelligence services, which in turn forwarded a summary of the information to the British, French, and U.S. governments in 2002. The CIA claims they did not receive the actual documents until February 2003, but accepted the findings of the British intelligence assessment (which allegedly relied on other sources of information) as fact.[40] Other sources have discussed in great depth former Ambassador Joseph Wilson's CIA-sponsored trip to Niger in February 2002 to investigate these purported sales of yellowcake, his assessment that no sales to Iraq had taken place, and the discovery that the Niger documents were forgeries. Despite these findings and the CIA's supposed attempts to withdraw these claims from administration speeches on the topic, the British government continued to claim that Iraq had sought significant quantities of uranium from Africa since 1998; claims that were reiterated by President Bush in his State of the Union speech in January 2003 and Vice President Cheney on *Meet the Press* in September 2003.

The CIA assessed Iraq's BW program as active, with most elements larger and more advanced than they were prior to the Gulf War. In part, this assessment was based on the 1995 discovery of Iraq's past BW program and the assumption that, without inspectors on site, Iraqi scientists were free to resume their work. The CIA believed that Iraq possessed some lethal and incapacitating BW agents, including anthrax, and the ability to produce and weaponize these agents. Chances were even that smallpox and genetically-engineered BW agents were part of this effort. In addition to large-scale, concealed BW agent production facilities, the CIA report noted "Iraq has mobile facilities for producing bacterial and toxin BW agents." The reports of Iraq's development of mobile BW trailers came from four defectors associated with the INC, one of which was code-named "Curveball" and was the brother of a top lieutenant to Ahmed Chalabi, one of the top directors of the INC.[41] This source claimed to be a chemical engineer who had helped design and build mobile laboratories; he told his story to German intelligence, which in turn relayed the information to the DIA, who in turn forwarded almost one hundred reports to the CIA. U.S. military intelligence officers never questioned the defector in person. In 2005, media investigations into the Curveball story revealed that the German intelligence agency had very serious doubts about his credibility and had warned the CIA in the fall of 2002 not to consider Curveball a reliable source.[42] Two other Iraqi defectors stated that they had heard reports of the program but had no direct evidence. A fourth defector, Major Mohammad Harith, corroborated Curveball's assessment that these trailers were intended to test BW agents. According to a classified DoD report, Major Harith was brought to the DIA by R. James Woolsey, a former CIA director and advocate for the INC.[43] The DIA suspected that these reports were coached by Chalabi's INC and discounted the veracity of these testimonies.[44]

According to the CIA, Iraq had begun renewed production of mustard, sarin, cyclosarin, and VX at a more limited capability than in 1990 but probably with improved VX production and storage life. Iraq had hidden its chemical weapons program within its legitimate chemical industry and procured necessary equipment and precursors to restart its chemical weapons program. The CIA estimated that Saddam had probably stocked at least one hundred metric tons and possibly up to five hundred metric tons of CW agents. An Iraqi defector going by the name Ahmed al-Shemri told the New York Times that there were many mobile and secret fixed laboratories throughout the country still producing chemical agents, including a "dusty VX" agent that was extremely persistent and able to penetrate protective clothing. He also testified that Iraq was producing thousands of gallons of anthrax, botulinum toxin, aflatoxin and gas gangrene.[45] The CIA believed that Iraq maintained a few dozen SCUD missiles that could deliver CB agents, and that the new al-Samoud and Ababil-100 exceeded the UN-authorized 150 kilometer range.

The CIA report contained an alarming statement that read, "Baghdad's UAVs could threaten Iraq's neighbors, US forces in the Persian Gulf, *and if brought close to, or into, the United States, the US Homeland*" [italics as in report]. This statement was based on a number of data points, including Iraq's attempts to convert L-29 jet trainer aircraft into UAVs mounted with droptanks that could hold up to two thousand liters of anthrax. The CIA suspected Iraq's UAV program was developing newer, smaller, but more capable airframes that would increase range and payload while their smaller size would make them harder to detect. The Air Force had not agreed with this assessment, noting that the UAVs' size made it more logical that these devices were reconnaissance platforms and not capable of dispersing a significant CB warfare agent payload. There was barely room for more than the camera and flight controls on the approximately seventy-five small UAVs.[46] Finally, the CIA discussed an alleged Iraqi attempt to procure commercially available route planning software and a topographical database to support targeting areas within the United States. Later, CIA analysts would admit that, under further review, it was impossible to determine whether the software had been delivered to Iraq or even if the software could be used for purposes of targeting cities. Several congressmen related that they had been personally briefed that these UAVs could be launched from ships off the Atlantic coast to attack U.S. cities.[47] In a speech he delivered in Cincinnati in October 2002, President Bush used this data when he mentioned the possibility of Iraq using drones filled with germs or chemical weapons against the United States.

The CIA estimate assessed that Saddam would not employ terrorists to attack the United States with conventional or CB weapons unless the survival of the regime was at stake, or as a desperate last chance to exact revenge against the United States as his regime crumbled. These terrorist attacks, more likely using biological than chemical warfare agents, might be conducted by his own special forces or intelligence operatives, or might be conducted by al Qaeda operatives. In closing, the CIA reported with confidence that Iraq was continuing and expanding its WMD program, and that it possessed CB weapons but not a nuclear weapon. There was moderate confidence that Iraq could have a nuclear weapon between 2007 and 2009. What the CIA was not sure about was when Saddam would use WMDs (preemptively or in response to being invaded by U.S. forces), whether he would engage in clandestine attacks against the United States, and if he would share these CB weapons with al Qaeda. There was no doubt in the CIA report's findings, however, that Saddam had these weapons.

In December 1999, the UN Security Council passed resolution 1284 to create the United Nations Monitoring, Verification, and Inspection Commission (UNMOVIC) to replace UNSCOM and to continue the UN mandate to verify the dismantlement of Iraq's WMD program. In return for cooperating, Iraq would see the streamlining and eventual suspension of the remaining economic sanctions. In January 2000, Secretary General Kofi Annan appointed Dr. Hans Blix of Sweden as the chairman of this new group, and Dr. Blix assumed these duties in March. The UNMOVIC team spent most of 2000, 2001, and 2002 developing its operations, obtaining equipment, training its personnel, and briefing the UN Security Council on how it would accomplish its mission. Following President Bush's speech to the UN General Assembly, Iraq agreed to allow the return of UN weapons inspectors to Iraq without conditions. On November 8, the UN Security Council passed Resolution 1441, calling for Iraq to submit a full and complete declaration of all aspects of its WMD program and to allow the return of UN inspectors under the threat of being held in material breach of UN resolutions. In late November, Dr. Blix and the UNMOVIC team arrived in Baghdad to start their inspections.

On December 7, Iraq submitted a formal declaration of all aspects of its past WMD program to UNMOVIC and IAEA in response to UN resolution 1441; the documents comprised more than twelve thousand pages. UNMOVIC's assessment of the declaration was that there was little new information available. Most of the pages were restatements of earlier declarations. Iraq did attempt to better explain its disposal of unaccounted chemical precursors and its new projects in the area of short-range ballistic missile development. Still, there was a great deal that was not explained, and uncovering those issues would be the responsibility of the more than two hundred UNMOVIC inspectors coming from sixty countries. Between December 2002 and the end of February 2003, UNMOVIC would conduct more than 550 inspections covering 350 suspected sites, including ammunition depots, research centers, universities, presidential sites, mobile laboratories, private houses, missile production facilities, military camps, and agricultural sites.

MAKING THE CASE FOR WAR

On January 28, 2003, President Bush presented his State of the Union address. After discussing several domestic initiatives, he declared that the "gravest danger facing America and the world, is outlaw regimes that seek and possess nuclear, chemical, and biological weapons." He described the UN conclusions as stating that Saddam had biological weapons sufficient to produce over twenty-five thousand liters of anthrax and thirty-eight thousand liters of botulinum toxin, with no accounting for the material or its destruction. He noted that U.S. intelligence officials had estimated Saddam had materials to produce as much as five hundred tons of sarin, mustard and VX nerve agent, and upwards of thirty thousand munitions capable of delivering these agents. Three Iraqi defectors had stated that Iraq had several mobile biological weapon labs. In what are now considered the infamous sixteen words of his address, Bush stated, "The British government has learned that Saddam Hussein recently sought significant quantities of uranium from Africa," despite previous efforts by the CIA to get the White House to delete this reference. He also noted that U.S. intelligence sources were told of the attempts to purchase high-strength aluminum tubes suitable for nuclear weapons production. The only purpose for these weapons, Bush said, was "to dominate, intimidate, or attack." Saddam could "provide one of his hidden weapons to terrorists, or help them develop their own." Bush's message to Saddam was to fully disarm his WMD program or face a U.S. coalition that would disarm him.[48]

On February 5, 2003, Secretary of State Colin Powell addressed the UN Security Council on the issue of U.S. intelligence regarding Iraq's weapons of mass destruction in light of resolution 1441. Powell's testimony was convincing and appeared overwhelming, in no small part due to the enormous respect that the man had engendered from the general public, the media, and the international community. In June 2003, he stated that his team had spent four days and nights working with CIA personnel to ensure that what he presented was "solid, credible, representing the views of the United States of America."[49] Powell had initially been provided with a forty-five-page script from the White House that had been put together by Feith's Office of Special Plans and Vice President Cheney's office. Instead of using this script that "was all bullshit," Powell relied heavily on the CIA National Intelligence Estimate.[50]

By the time Powell was preparing to brief the United Nations, CIA analysts had been increasingly pressured by the White House and senior CIA leadership to present Iraq's WMD program as a grave threat, with one CIA director stating, "if Bush wants to go to war, it's your job to give him a reason to do so."[51] In March 2004, Powell admitted that key aspects of those intelligence briefs were wrong.

He began with audiotapes purported to be of Iraqi officials discussing their continued deception of the UN inspectors. He charged the Iraqi government with providing a twelve thousand-page document that was "rich in volume, but poor in information and practically devoid of new evidence," while the Iraqi military was concealing the real documents and computer hard drives from the inspectors. Powell then proceeded to show satellite imagery of chemical weapons storage sites allegedly being decontaminated and scrubbed prior to the arrival of UN inspectors, and Iraqi truck caravans carrying material away from sites. He stressed the Iraqi government's deliberate interference by denying UN inspectors access to scientists and engineers associated with the WMD program.

The case against Iraq's BW program included their denial of having an offensive BW program between 1991 and 1995, UNSCOM estimates that Saddam could have produced twenty-five thousand liters of anthrax rather than the eighty-five hundred liters he declared, and Iraq's continued failure to account for the BW agents, growth media, and munitions. Powell displayed slides showing artists' depictions of Iraqi BW factories "on wheels and on rails," noting that, in a matter of months, they could produce a quantity of BW agent equal to the entire amount Iraq had produced in the years prior to the 1991 Gulf War. The source, Powell noted, was an Iraqi chemical engineer, a defector who had seen twelve technicians die from exposure to BW agents during an agent production run of one of these mobile facilities. Three other Iraqi defectors confirmed the existence of these transportable facilities (essentially repeating the CIA assessment, which was based on INC-supplied defectors). The United States was aware of at least seven of these mobile biological agent factories, numbering at least eighteen trucks. In addition to weaponizing anthrax, Powell stated that Iraq had successfully weaponized botulinum toxin, aflatoxin, and ricin, and had aerial spray tanks that were capable of dispersing BW agent and causing massive death and destruction.

In the area of chemical weapons, Powell repeated the list of unaccounted chemical munitions, to include the 550 mustard-filled artillery shells, 30,000 unfilled munitions, and chemical precursors that could create up to 500 tons of chemical agents. Powell noted Dr. Blix's quip, "Mustard gas is not marmalade. You are supposed to know what you did with it." Iraq had failed to admit that it had weaponized VX, even after being caught with evidence that they had produced four tons of it. Iraq had reconstituted facilities associated with its past chemical weapons program, allegedly for legitimate means. Powell's bottom line was that Saddam had chemical weapons, had used these weapons in the past, and had no compunction about using them again.

Powell noted that Saddam had a cadre of nuclear scientists with the necessary expertise to design and build a bomb. All Iraq needed was the ability to enrich uranium. Powell testified that Saddam had made "repeated covert attempts to acquire high-specification aluminum tubes." While acknowledging that some experts thought the tubes were intended as rocket bodies, "all the experts . . . agree that they can be adapted for centrifuge use." In the area of delivery systems, Powell described an Iraqi test range that was obviously built for firing long-range ballistic missiles. "These are missiles that Iraq wants . . . to deliver chemical, biological, and, if we let him, nuclear warheads," Powell stated. He noted the Iraqi UAV program and the development of spray devices as another effort designed to dispense chemical and biological weapons.

Before closing, Powell made a case that al Qaeda terrorists had strong links with Iraq both in Baghdad and through the Iraqi embassy in Pakistan. In addition to al Qaeda contacts, Baghdad had cooperated with Hamas and the Palestine Islamic Jihad agents. One senior al Qaeda terrorist had described sending militants to Iraq several times between 1997 and 2000 for help in acquiring poisons and gases, a relationship that was described as successful (in July 2004, it would come out that this information came from an al Qaeda commander captured in Pakistan in November 2001 who, when faced with contradictory evidence from other detainees, recanted this claim).[52] Powell noted that, given these terrorist associations, Saddam's history of aggression, and his current capabilities, the United States could not risk leaving Saddam Hussein in possession of weapons of mass destruction. Powell's bottom line was that "today Iraq still poses a threat and Iraq still remains in material breach."

According to testimony by Rice and Tenet, the UNMOVIC inspectors had received briefs from the U.S. intelligence community identifying WMD sites in Iraq.[53] In fact, the CIA would relay information on the location of only about half of their suspected WMD sites to UNMOVIC. UNMOVIC took more than 250 chemical samples and 100 biological samples from suspect Iraqi sites, none of which revealed any undeclared Iraqi CB warfare agents. In February, the Iraqi government agreed to allow aerial surveys over Iraq. They did discover a half-liter of thiodiglycol, a precursor for mustard agent, and about sixteen empty 122-mm chemical rocket warheads that needed to be destroyed. They destroyed fifty liters of mustard agent and fourteen 155-mm artillery shells that Iraq had already declared and that UNSCOM had placed under seal at Muthanna in 1998. Iraqi government officials took UNMOVIC inspectors to a firing range where they had unearthed the destroyed remains of the 157 R-400 aerial bombs that had been filled with biological agents. UNMOVIC's inspections of the al-Samoud missile revealed that it was inherently capable of ranges just greater than 150 kilometers, which meant they had to be dismantled and destroyed. Fifty of the seventy-five Samoud missiles were destroyed in March 2003.

In a presentation to the UN in early March, Blix testified that progress was being made. The UNMOVIC teams were unable to verify if Iraq had any mobile biological laboratories or what the capabilities of Iraq's UAVs were, but given time, they could continue their investigations. Iraq had declared that one converted L-29 plane and several smaller UAVs had been produced, but the team did not have time to determine if the UAVs had the ability to dispense CB warfare agents or if they exceeded a 150-kilometer range. Iraq did describe six different types of mobile laboratory facilities in its possession, but none matched the description of the mobile biological laboratories that Powell had described to the United Nations. On June 5, 2003, Blix presented his thirteenth quarterly report to the UN Security Council, covering the inspection results up to the end of March 2003. While the inspection teams had been unable to find any evidence of a WMD program or significant quantities of banned materials, Blix acknowledged that this did not necessarily mean that these items could not exist. On the other hand, while there remained a long list of unaccounted items, it was not logical or just to jump to the conclusion that "something exists just because it is unaccounted for."[54]

SUMMARY

It appeared that Iraq's WMD program had been severely curtailed by the UN inspections and destruction of their former NBC weapons production and storage facilities. There was no bulk agent found, although it might have been moved and hidden somewhere. Iraq was in the process of trying to maintain what little infrastructure it had in terms of personnel, technical knowledge, and equipment, while developing commercial chemical and biological industries that might have had dual capability for building CB weapons components. With the exception of some older munitions, there appeared to be no stockpiles of CB weapons. There was no nuclear weapons program, and Iraq was manufacturing short-range, conventional ballistic missiles similar to those found in the military of every other nation in the Middle East. The potential for this program to represent a capable military threat to anyone, let alone the U.S. military, seemed remote. The United States had multiple intelligence assets that were unsure about the actual threat that Saddam's WMD program posed. UN inspection teams had been on site for months to ascertain that there were no WMDs in Iraq and that nothing had been produced at the inspected sites for years. Yet the Bush administration had carried out an intense marketing campaign to convince the American public and international community that this WMD program was cause enough to remove Saddam Hussein from power. The media, to a large extent, faithfully repeated the administration's claims and supported the call for war.

Certainly officials from the Clinton administration and foreign governments such as Britain, France, Germany, the Czech Republic, Egypt, and Jordan all thought that Saddam had chemical and biological weapons and the capability to make more. Many of these government officials believed it would be in the world's best interest that Saddam not have these weapons. The difference was that none of these governments believed that the potential threat posed by Iraq's development and stockpiling CB weapons was adequate rationale to force a regime change (even, according to the Downing Street minutes, Britain).[55] It was a containable situation that could be enforced by UN inspections, punitive military actions, and economic sanctions. That's why the U.S. government participated in nonproliferation meetings and joined the international community on arms control talks, at least in theory.

It is understandable that intelligence agencies assumed that Iraq might have had limited amounts of CB weapons and an even more limited capability to employ them in 2002, but this capability could not seriously impact U.S. military operations. Intelligence agencies made the case that Iraq was seeking to rebuild its CB weapons production capability, and that it wanted a nuclear weapon—some day. It was not credible to assume that Iraq was planning to give CB weapons to terrorists in an effort to attack the United States through such intermediaries. Other authors have much more eloquent discussions on Saddam's secular regime and his unwillingness to support radical Islamic terrorist groups (among those, the Presidential 9/11 Commission). I do not believe that Iraq presented an imminent threat, or even a grave threat, to its neighbors, U.S. forces in theater, or the United States or U.S. strategic interests in its pursuit of CB weapons. Saddam wanted CB weapons as a strategic tool to keep Syria, Iran, and Israel at bay, all countries suspected of having similar WMD programs. A much more understandable justification for regime change was that the United States could not allow Saddam to possess nuclear weapons in the volatile Middle East region, although these weapons were years away from actual production. The *New York Times* quoted a "senior administration official" as saying "The closer he gets to a nuclear capability, the more credible is his threat to use chemical or biological weapons. Nuclear weapons are his hole card. The question is not, why [oust Hussein] now? The question is why waiting is better. The closer Hussein gets to a nuclear weapon, the harder he will be to deal with." [56] The Bush administration did not strike Iraq as a preemptive measure to stop Saddam from attacking the United States; instead, the United States was going to strike Iraq to prevent Saddam from causing any mischief. This was a preventive war to stop a future threat, not a preemptive attack to stop an imminent threat.

The Bush administration never claimed that the Iraqi WMD program was an imminent threat to the United States, although the media and many talking heads would interpret the administration's speeches as stating as much. The Iraqi regime was a "great and immediate threat," a "significant threat," a "serious and growing threat," a "threat of unique urgency," a "real and dangerous threat," the "most dangerous threat of our time." [57] But as David Kay would say in October 2004, intent without capabilities is not an imminent threat. As the president implied in his 2003 State of the Union speech, the U.S. government was going to act prior to Iraq's becoming an imminent threat. While the Bush administration would call this a preemptive strike, it was really a preventive step to remove Saddam because they considered it a moral cause that could be done cheaply and quickly; and the U.S. government had the power to do it. The outcome would benefit U.S. interests in terms of regional and domestic security, and besides, it was inevitable that Saddam's ambitions would eventually need to be dealt with.

On March 16, Vice President Cheney was asked on *Meet the Press* "What do you think is the most important rationale for going to war with Iraq?" He replied, ". . . the combination of [Saddam's] development and use of chemical weapons, his development of biological weapons, his pursuit of nuclear weapons."[58] On March 17, the United States announced it would not seek a second UN resolution to authorize the use of force against Iraq. President Bush announced to the nation:

> Intelligence gathered by this and other governments leaves no doubt that the Iraqi regime continues to possess and conceal some of the most lethal weapons ever devised. This regime has already used weapons of mass destruction against Iraq's neighbors and against Iraq's people. The regime has a history of reckless aggression in the Middle East. It has a deep hatred of America and our friends. And it has aided, trained and harbored terrorists, including operatives of al Qaeda. The danger is clear: using chemical, biological or, one day, nuclear weapons, obtained with the help of Iraq, the terrorists could fulfill their stated ambitions and kill thousands or hundreds of thousands of innocent people in our country, or any other. . . . Saddam and his sons must leave Iraq within 48 hours.[59]

On March 18, 2003, the UNMOVIC inspectors withdrew from Iraq. The U.S. military was on the move.

This Biological Integrated Detection Suite (BIDS) is being displayed at Fort McClellan, Alabama. Note the air sampling stacks on the roof. *Courtesy of the author*

The Pentagon had a number of BIDS around its perimeter. This one, with a camouflage net covering it, was parked near the river entrance. Note the air sampling stacks again. *Courtesy of the author*

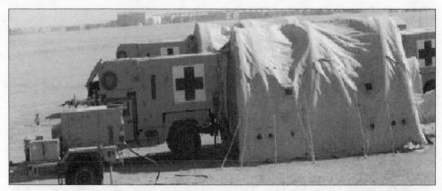

This medical Chemical-Biological Protective Shelter is shown in Kuwait, fully extending its pressurized shelter from the medical HMMWV. *Courtesy of Pine Bluff Arsenal*

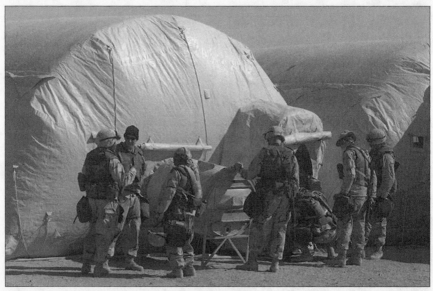

The medical Chemical-Biological Protective Shelter was pressurized to keep vapors out. This view shows the litter airlock that allowed medics to decon their patients prior to their entry. *Courtesy of Pine Bluff Arsenal*

CENTCOM inspectors check out the first "mobile BW laboratory," which turned out to be a hydrogen generator vehicle for an artillery unit. *Courtesy of U.S. Army*

The 101st Airborne Division found this second "mobile BW laboratory," stripped of parts and tires, in Mosul. *Courtesy of Maj. Brian Lynch*

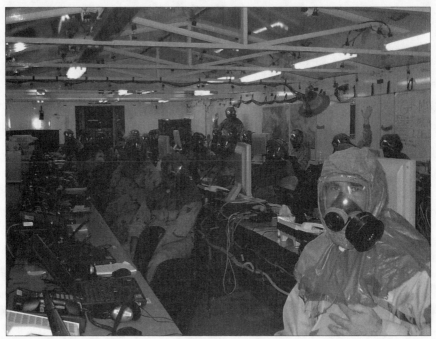

The USCENTCOM operations center at Qatar undergoes a gas drill.
Courtesy of Col. Tom Woloszyn

Maj. Pete Lofy of the 4th Infantry Division inspects Iraqi SA-2 missiles for possible chemical weapons use. *Courtesy of Maj. Pete Lofy*

A 4th Infantry Division Hazard Assessment Team prepares to survey a suspected biological weapons site. *Courtesy of Maj. Pete Lofy*

A 101st Airborne Division soldier uses M8 paper on a stick to check these drums for chemical agent materials. None were found. *Courtesy of Maj. Brian Lynch*

CHAPTER 6

OPERATION IRAQI FREEDOM

Wars spring from unseen and generally insignificant causes, the first outbreak being often but an explosion of anger.

—THUCYDIDES, GREEK HISTORIAN

Defense Secretary Donald Rumsfeld asked Gen. Richard Myers, chairman of the JCS, to provide a quick assessment of CENTCOM's CBRN defense capabilities in January 2002, after Gen. Tommy Franks had indicated his team had not had time to assess the readiness of the U.S. forces that would fight in the upcoming operation. The J-5/Nuc&CP branch developed what is commonly known as a stoplight chart assessment, indicating the red, yellow, or green status of CENTCOM's CBRN defense capabilities for early warning detection, automatic CB detection, protection of its personnel, ability to maintain combat operations, and ability to restore combat operations. This assessment was coordinated with CENTCOM, the four services, DATSD (CBD), ASD (HA), and the OSD counterproliferation policy office. The report was a quick-and-dirty assessment and did not include the use of models or simulations; rather, it was a subjective evaluation based on an understanding of what offensive and defensive capabilities CENTCOM had and what Iraqi forces might do with a stockpile such as the one described in the DIA and CIA intelligence assessments.

Considering the counterforce, active defense, and passive defense capabilities that would be available, the assessment noted that Iraqi chemical attacks would have a limited impact on operations. A biological attack would have a greater impact, especially on unprepared noncombatants. There were some capabilities that could be improved, notably the need for additional JSLIST protective suits, biological vaccinations, and decontamination and collective protection of fixed sites, but overall, Iraq did not present the robust threat that it had in 1990. In the Joint Staff's estimation, use of CB weapons, although a potential threat, would not significantly impact U.S. military operations; at best, it would slow down the initial entry into Iraq but not cause significant disruption. This is the message that Gen. Myers and Vice Chairman Gen. Peter Pace would communicate to Secretary Rumsfeld, to Congress, and to the media throughout 2002 and into 2003.[1] From the OSD counterproliferation policy office perspective, that estimate was too conservative, and the OSD pushed to emphasize a greater threat.

The DoD CB defense community shared the view that the U.S. military force was in much better shape in 2002 than it had been in 1990. Brig. Gen. Steve Reeves would point out in later press briefings that the CB Defense Program had fielded many new items since 1991, and this equipment would offer improved protection to the force. These included a new line of masks (the M40 protective mask for ground forces, the M42 protective mask for vehicle crews, and the M45 aviator mask), a new protective suit (JSLIST), and the M41 Protective Assessment Testing System to check the fit of military masks. There were a number of new chemical detectors (M22 ACADA, M1 CAMs, and M21 RSCAAL) and four new biological detectors (Portal Shield, JBPDS, Navy's interim biological agent detector [IBAD], and the DFUs). The M31/M31A1 BIDS had joined the M93A1 NBC recon system as the Army's newest specialized vehicle, and the Army had fielded three radiation detectors (AN/UDR-13 pocket radiac, AN/VDR-2 radiac set, and the AN/PDR-75 radiac set). JWARN Block I was CB hazard prediction software that could be tied to the military's communication systems. The Army had begun fielding the CB Protective Shelter and Chemically Protected Deployable Medical System (CP DEPMEDS) for its medical units. The M291 skin decon kit had been fielded in 1991, and M295 individual equipment decon kit had been released in 1998 with a new sorbent decon powder.

Although the state of chemical and biological detection and protective suits and masks had visibly improved, decontamination and collective protection system capabilities had actually deteriorated due to the DoD CB Defense Program's inability to field new systems within the last ten years. The Army had been unable to maintain more than 70 percent of its M17 lightweight decon systems, and its M12A1 power-driven decon apparatuses were increasingly hard to maintain due to the lack of spare parts available for the old system. The Modular Decon System, its replacement, was held back from fielding due to technical challenges. Medical countermeasures for CB agents had not significantly advanced; notably, U.S. military forces had only two FDA-licensed biological vaccines (for smallpox and anthrax) available. Although the new CB defense items represented a potential increase in capability, it was unknown how much opportunity the new troops had to train with the new equipment in realistically simulated CB hazard environments. DoD had long tried to determine the operational readiness of its forces in terms of their ability to fight in a CB environment, but it was too difficult to monitor the quality and inclusion of CB defense training for units below division level, and the senior leadership was focused more on conventional war-fighting readiness. It was easy to use CB defense equipment inventory as an indicator of readiness, but that was not a good indicator of actual defensive capability. The Joint Staff had a review process for identifying critical operational problems and focusing on near- and midterm solutions, but they had no way of enforcing changes in the few CBRN defense readiness issues they identified in the process.

One of the major concerns after the first Gulf War was the extent to which the U.S. military would be impacted if the enemy used CB weapons. In 1997, SBCCOM had sponsored a study called "Assessment of the Impact of Chemical and Biological Weapons on Joint Operations in 2010," or "CB 2010." This effort was headed by retired four-star generals John Foss, Wayne Downing, and Frederick Kroesen, along with fifteen other general and flag officers—including Maj. Gen. (Ret.) John Stoner, a Chemical Corps general officer—and a team of supporting contractors. The study used a tabletop exercise to identify policy and military capability issues that might come up during a military deployment in 2010 to combat an Iraqi invasion of Kuwait. This scenario featured CB attacks at air bases and seaports within the United States from which troops would deploy as well as the air bases and seaports in Kuwait where the forces would arrive. The study noted that U.S. forces would encounter serious delays, mispositioning of forces, and severe degradation of their operational tempo, which could result in significantly higher fatalities and casualties (although ultimately, U.S. forces would succeed).

In particular, the study noted that the future threat of CB weapons would be characterized by limited, localized attacks on key units, facilities, and equipment at both U.S. and overseas sites. It noted that the United States, with its emphasis on technical, rather than human, intelligence collection, lacked adequate resources to determine whether Iraq could develop and intended to use CB weapons (particularly limited use.) The U.S. government also lacked a clear deterrence and retaliatory policy that might convince opponents not to use these weapons. Strengthening military facilities, especially ports and air bases, against CB weapons attacks would require additional force structure, training, equipment, and policy development (notably decontamination standards). Failure to address these vulnerabilities would result in a significant drop in ability to bring forces and equipment into major theaters, in addition to any casualties at the sites—a key factor for areas such as the Middle East, which has a limited number of seaports and air bases available for large military operations. At the time, the DoD CB Defense Program was not investing in critical capabilities to decontaminate combat equipment or large-frame planes and cargo ships (both military vehicles and civilian vehicles loaned to the military) to levels that would allow extended military use in theater and the eventual release of formerly contaminated equipment back to the United States. The reliance of U.S. military forces on government civilians and contractors in theater, in addition to coalition forces, could be seriously impacted by any CB weapons attacks, because personnel other than military forces rarely had CB defense equipment.

The decontamination question—notably "how clean is clean"—weighed heavily on the minds of military planners and the CB defense community, although for the most part they were admiring the problem in what many called "paralysis through analysis" rather than developing solutions. In 1997, U.S. Transportation Command (TRANSCOM) asked the Joint Staff to help develop a policy for dealing with contaminated large-frame commercial and military aircraft and ships; that is, how would they be deconned, to what standard, what detectors would be used to certify that they were clean, and to what a degree was it necessary to accommodate civilians reusing the formerly contaminated vehicles. Given the limited numbers of large-frame aircraft and ships supporting military operations across the globe, any number of contaminated vehicles could adversely impact the flow of equipment and personnel into a major theater. That year, the DATSD (CBM), Joint Staff (J-5/Nuc&CP), and Joint Service Integration Group cosponsored a workshop to review the policy, doctrine, resources, logistics, and training required to address decon requirements at fixed sites (air bases, seaports, logistics bases, communication nodes, and hospital bases). The study, "CHEMWAR 2000," identified many challenges around the issue of "how clean is clean." It did not offer many recommendations on how to meet these challenges.

In 1999, the Joint Staff released a memorandum that identified the interim level of acceptable cleanliness if a chemical contamination was to raise no alarms—that is, no agent detected—from any fielded military chemical detector.[2] This did not satisfy TRANSCOM, because, according to these standards, no formerly contaminated aircraft or vehicle could ever be used by civilian crews or allowed to return to the United States (a particular concern of U.S. commercial air companies that leased planes to the military). The question lingered until the summer of 2001, when the Joint Staff's J-5/Nuc&CP branch attempted to reopen the issue. The services agreed to more comprehensive guidelines for identifying CW exposure, but they did not want to address biological contamination standards (too hard, as the efforts to decontaminate the Senate building had shown) and decided to pass on the radiological contamination standards (although they were readily available, the services preferred not to develop a joint standard). In April 2002, the Joint Staff updated its interim policy on CW exposure, but the policy retained its singular focus on using only fielded military detectors to assess the effectiveness of decontamination and did not address postconflict remediation. TRANSCOM's "how clean is clean" questions, originally identified in 1997, remain largely unanswered today.

PHASE 1: PREPARATIONS FOR WAR (JUNE 2002–DECEMBER 2002)

The goals of Phase 1 were to secure regional and international support; degrade the Iraqi regime's ability to resist; establish an air bridge and secure lines of communication into theater; interdict tactical ballistic missiles and WMDs; and alert, deploy, and posture American forces.[3] By April 2002, CENTCOM had drafted its prepare-to-deploy order, identifying V Corps as the lead agent to plan and deploy Army forces into theater under Coalition Forces Land Component Command (CFLCC). The First Marine Expeditionary Force (I MEF) would coordinate the Marine Corp forces that deployed under CFLCC. As operations in Afghanistan were being reduced, plans were developed for a main ground offensive, emerging from Kuwait, with two major supporting operations from special operations forces. In the north, the Joint Special Operations Task Force (JSOTF)-North and Iraqi Kurds would fix Iraqi forces, attack south to isolate Tikrit, and stabilize the area. In the west, JSOTF-West under Task Force-20 and Coalition Forces Air Component Command (CFACC) would conduct a robust and visible SCUD hunt to deny Iraqi forces the ability to engage Jordan, Turkey, or Israel with ballistic missiles. During the fall, EUCOM would be brought into the planning under the Northern Option, intended to facilitate the introduction of coalition forces from Turkey. EUCOM was also responsible for establishing a joint task force for theater missile defense purposes in Israel. U.S. Army Europe (USAREUR) and V Corps would receive the mission to establish a joint rear area coordinator, who in turn would delegate the job to 1st Infantry Division. V Corps and I MEF were given orders to deploy their forward staff headquarters into Kuwait.

As forces began to mobilize, CENTCOM would evaluate its CBRN defense capabilities and increasingly call on the DoD CB Defense Program to remedy some of its deficiencies. In June, the JRO-CBRND conducted a quick assessment of the geographic CINCs' CBRN defense capabilities, breaking the review into eighteen distinct subcapabilities.[4] This exercise allowed CENTCOM to reexamine its immediate list of needs, which had not changed substantially since January. Some policy issues had emerged, such as the need to prioritize anthrax and smallpox vaccines for troops deploying to CENTCOM, to the point of cutting off anthrax vaccine shots for forces in or deploying to PACOM. Needless to say, PACOM was not happy with this decision, since they had an adversary believed to have a mature BW program just across the border from U.S. forces. The OSD counterproliferation policy office, DASTD (CBD), and ASD (HA) participated in the assessment to develop solutions to CENTCOM's prioritized list of requirements.

DATSD (CBD) had the interesting task of determining what they could do within six months to address the material shortfalls identified by CENTCOM, given that they had no immediate source of funding other than research and development dollars and that the majority of industries supporting CB defense could not possibly ramp up quickly enough to meet these shortfalls. Nonetheless, DoD could address some of the issues and recommend funding to execute the others. OSD counterproliferation policy was concerned that Iraq might have *novichok*-type nerve agents, allegedly developed by the Soviet Union in the 1980s and 1990s. These advanced binary nerve agents supposedly had different chemical compositions than those specified in the Chemical Weapons Convention, and were said to be more persistent and more lethal than VX.[5] Although intelligence sources did not address Iraq's possession of these agents, OSD counterproliferation policy warned that DoD could not rely on the accuracy of U.S. intelligence products and that the development of CB warfare agents had always surprised defense experts.[6] The services and Joint Staff focused on defensive measures against traditional CW agents (such as sarin and mustard) as the more credible threat. OSD counterproliferation policy strongly advocated that CENTCOM acquire a limited capability to detect nontraditional agents, through procurement of either prototype detectors or foreign detectors that used viable technologies.[7]

ASD (HA) pushed for CENTCOM to procure and stockpile pentavalent botulinum toxid medicines in theater. The common wisdom regarding botulinum toxin was that it was not an effective agent for large-area coverage and therefore was more appropriate for covert operations. Nonetheless, ASD (HA) felt compelled, against the intelligence analyses and advice from the defense acquisition community, to help CENTCOM prepare for this threat by pushing for the production of an investigational new drug treatment: pentavalent botulinum toxoid. The Joint Staff's assessment provided the necessary vehicle to drive their policy and funding recommendations. In January 2003, Col. Erik Henchal, commander of MRIID, reiterated the critical need for botulinum toxoid to the press as an example of the "serious holes in [U.S. military] defenses."[8]

CENTCOM held an NBC defense symposium in early July 2002, at which they analyzed their efforts to exploit sites in Afghanistan where they had expected to find weaponized CBRN hazards. They had continued to search for capabilities that could be fielded quickly, in particular a replacement for the decontamination solution DS-2. In January, the Joint Staff had asked the CINCs whether they wanted an interim replacement for the liquid-based DS-2 decontaminant based on a Sandia National Labs product called DF-100. This was a foam-based decontaminant, the idea being that it would cover more area with less product than a liquid-based decontaminant and not require as much water to rinse off. In addition, the product would be less caustic and more environmentally friendly than DS-2. The Marine Corps program manager for the Joint Service Family of Decontamination Systems had thought they could accelerate its testing and deliver an immediate capability to the field, even if the formula fell short of answering all the military's objective requirements.[9] PACOM and CENTCOM backed the concept and immediately wanted to know where the interim decontaminant was. In June, CENTCOM sent the Joint Staff an operational needs statement, a short paper documenting an urgent need with a cover memo signed by its deputy CINC. In addition, CENTCOM sent the Joint Staff a draft needs statement for a proposed decon applicator to decontaminate large areas and heavy equipment. CENTCOM actually had a particular piece of equipment in mind: a modified aircraft deicer called the GL-1800 vehicle, produced by Global Ground Support. In August, Global and Modec demonstrated the decon applicator truck and a decon foam to General Franks at CENTCOM headquarters in Tampa, Florida, with positive results, and they expected the general's interest to help speed the request through the DoD CB Defense Program. Similar demonstrations at Fort Leonard Wood had earned the Chemical School's endorsement.

On August 13, the Joint Staff validated the CENTCOM request for an interim decontaminant, which would give DATSD (CBD) what it needed to seek funding and permission to accelerate a new decontaminant to the field. The Marine Corps Systems Command would lead an abbreviated operational testing at Fort Leonard Wood and begin negotiations with two manufacturers, Modec Inc., of Denver, Colorado, and Enviro Foam Technologies, of Huntsville, Alabama, that could manufacture DF-200, a formula similar to what was generically referred to as *Sandia foam*.[10] One company had its formula in a two-part mixture; the second had a three-part mixture. In both cases, the DF-200 had to be mixed prior to preparation, which, although unwieldy, promised a short-term solution to replacing the very caustic and ancient DS-2 decontaminant stocks.

Col. Karl Semancik of the DATSD (CBD) office began holding meetings between the Marine Corps program manager and representatives from the office of the DOT&E, the Joint Staff, and the Army, to discuss a plan to conduct the operational testing for the interim decon DF-200. A small group of Marines at Fort Leonard Wood would conduct limited operational testing in October and November, under the supervision of the Army test and evaluation agents, with a proposed December start date for production and fielding. Simultaneously, scientists at Dugway Proving Ground were to test the decontaminant against CW agents. They would also test protective suits and chemical detectors to determine whether the interim decontaminant interfered with their performance. Assuming the operational testing and evaluation went well, the war-fighters would get a limited supply in time for operations in the spring. The challenge was that the military would not be allowed to use a foam version of DF-200. The DOT&E argued that they could not approve an operational test of a foam decontaminant, because there were no approved applicators or procedures for using it. If the military preferred a liquid version of the DF-200, they could use the standard military applicators (or mops and buckets), which had approved procedures. The Marines thought this would not be a major challenge. At the end of October, the USD (AT&L) signed off on approval for CENTCOM (and only CENTCOM) to use the DF-200 liquid as an interim decontaminant, following procedures developed during the operational testing.

In early September, the Joint Staff became involved in discussions over a CFLCC message to the Army staff supporting the resolution of a new decontamination issue; that is, the Army medical community felt that it could not decontaminate human remains to a level of cleanliness that would permit transportation back to the United States for burial. In fact, the Army had developed and published a set of tactics, techniques, and procedures for handling chemically contaminated remains in the early 1990s and had published these procedures in a joint publication for mortuary affairs.[11] But would these procedures work for biological decontamination? This issue was really an attempt by the Army medical community to get the DoD CB Defense Program to buy currently available medical and decontamination equipment for specific mortuary affairs units and to test DF-200 on human skin samples to determine its efficacy. This was a particularly contentious issue, in part because the DoD CB Defense Program was not in the business of buying fielded equipment for a military unit on the sole basis that its parent service thought a CB defense mission was important. If the Army felt it was important, they could easily dedicate funds to this effort, but they wanted Joint Staff validation before seeking OSD funds. Some CB defense funds were made available to MRICD to test DF-200's efficacy on human skin samples.

On October 2, the CENTCOM operational needs statement requesting an interim decon applicator, signed by General Franks, arrived at the Joint Staff. The needs statement was specifically written to describe the GL-1800 system, down to its two onboard tanks, capability to decontaminate elevated surfaces and structures, and mobile capability. CENTCOM wanted thirty-two systems, enough to outfit two Army chemical decon companies. There remained some concern about the GL-1800 applicator's ability to use a liquid form of DF-200 vice its designed foam state, but CENTCOM's strong push for this particular system overrode initial concerns. Another issue was finding the funds to procure the systems, get past DOT&E requirements, and then ship them in time into theater. On October 24, the vice director of the Joint Staff signed off on a memorandum to validate CENTCOM's request for the GL-1800 systems. CENTCOM's surgeon general had also pressed for accelerating the fielding of CB protective shelters and CP DEPMEDS for medical units deploying to CENTCOM.

Meanwhile, things were warming up in Congress. On October 1, 2002, Representative Chris Shays (R-CT), as the chair of the House Subcommittee on National Security, Veteran Affairs, and International Relations under the Committee on Government Reform, chaired a hearing on the armed forces' CB defense readiness, which would include witness testimony from Dr. Johnson-Winegar, Brig. Gen. Stephen Goldfein (JRO), Maj. Gen. William Bond (Army G-3), Mike Parker (SBCCOM), and George Allen (DLA). Also testifying were members from the DoD Office of the Inspector General and the GAO. The main focus was the DoD Inspector General and GAO's critical reviews of the readiness of military protective masks and protective suits (notably, the Isratex issue). The main concern presented was DoD's inability to account for about a quarter million of the Isratex suits, and the GAO had reported the sale of several protective suits on the Internet. Spirited questioning from Rep. Dennis Kucinich (D-IL), the ranking minority member, and others probed whether U.S. forces were at risk of being unprotected in a CB conflict as a result of these problems. In large part, the representatives depicted the DoD efforts as a failure to protect the force, contrary to General Myers' statements in September that the force was ready.

The GAO alleged that DoD had not clearly located, identified, and destroyed 250,000 Isratex suits of the approximately 780,000 suits in the overall inventory (of which only 173,000, the 1992 lot, were suspect). The issue was accountability, not whether military units were actually issuing these suits for deployment. DLA had stopped storing any protective suits for war reserves. They had purchased quantities of JSLIST suits for sale to DoD and other federal agencies, but had no BDOs in their inventory. The Air Force inventory check had ascertained that they had no Isratex suits, a quick process as they had centralized their CB defense stocks in warehouses. The Marine

Corps had no BDOs, having given their stocks to the Navy in lieu of using only Saratoga and JSLIST suits. The Navy had checked their few stocks of BDOs and had no Isratex suits, which left the Army. The Army had about 25 percent of their BDOs distributed down to unit level, all the better to deploy to the field quickly with their full protective ensemble. The other 75 percent was located in prepositioned supplies overseas. The Army had identified and turned in nearly half of their 480,000 Isratex suits.

The Army and Air Force used BDOs for training exercises, and, once removed from their packages, these suits had no identifying markings to show what lot they had come from. The services used about 400,000 BDOs annually for training purposes. All commanders verified that they had turned in all unopened packages identified as coming from an Isratex production lot. Although the Army could not verify that 100 percent of the Isratex suits had been found and turned in, they could verify that any soldiers deploying with an unopened BDO bag would have a good protective suit and not an Isratex-manufactured suit.

In sum, there were about 3 million BDOs not manufactured by Isratex and 1.5 million JSLIST suits in DoD. The four services and DLA had made a complete sweep of their inventories, and any Isratex suit that could not be accounted for had most likely been used in training or been disposed of. The challenge was accounting for all these suits within the military's complex logistics system: the four services did not routinely track the distribution and storage of consumable items. Unlike durable end items like chemical detectors and protective masks, protective suits were discarded after use. It took time to check all existing supplies against the Isratex lot numbers. As for the GAO's observation that about 430 protective suits were being sold on the Internet, the DoD response should have been, "so what?" Was the GAO really arguing that the actions of a few individuals selling used protective suits to hunters and military enthusiasts represented a serious drain on the military's preparedness, considering the tens of thousands of JSLIST suits being produced every month? There was a very, very low risk of any defective Isratex suits actually showing up on the battlefield, but the politicians' accusations against the leadership of the DoD CB Defense Program made for great posturing and show.

Rep. Shays wanted someone within DoD, preferably either DLA's director, the DATSD (CBD), or the service chiefs, to step up and own the problem.

DLA headquarters was not going to assume responsibility for suits owned and stored by the services. Dr. Johnson-Winegar, DATSD (CBD), pointed out that her responsibility was research and development, not suits controlled by the services. It was appropriately a command responsibility of the services. Yet in closed session before Shays, Dr. Johnson-Winegar agreed to direct the services to use only JSLIST suits in the CENTCOM area of responsibility. She was not empowered to make this statement as it represented an infringement on the services' Title 10 responsibilities, but she was willing to act as the designated OSD focal point for CB defense to address the problem. As we will see later, this statement would come back to haunt her. The next day, October 2, Shays sent a memorandum to Secretary Rumsfeld, restating concerns over the adequacy of supplies of protective suits and the Isratex issue.

Also in October, the NSC deputies were meeting to discuss the DoD smallpox vaccination policy, acceleration of the anthrax vaccination program, and the ability of DoD to assist coalition allies and neighboring countries in the Middle East with quantities of vaccines. A DoD task force, including members from ASD (HA), OSD counterproliferation policy, DATSD (CBD), the Joint Staff (J-4, J-5, and J-8), the Army PEO-CBD, the Army medical community, the Department of Health and Human Services (DHHS), the State Department, and others met to assess DoD capabilities, expected requirements, and ability to help allies and friends in the region. Simultaneously, the group had to consider requirements for responding to any terrorist incidents within the United States. Immunizing Middle East-bound military service members with anthrax and smallpox vaccines was executable; putting aside vaccines for international allies and for domestic use would strain the program's resources. BioPort's production line had not had enough time to produce lots of anthrax vaccine sufficient to address the military requirements let alone new unforeseen requirements, due to the delays in obtaining FDA approvals. Nonetheless, OSD policy was adamant that a certain minimum number of doses had to be set aside for use by international allies in the region, and it was up to the acquisition community to figure out how to accomplish this. One way to do this, perhaps the only way, was to stop vaccinations for all DoD personnel not deploying in support of Operation Iraqi Freedom.[12]

In November, the Army had noted that the availability of its decontamination applicators was below acceptable limits because of shortages of operational systems, lack of funds for rebuilding currently deadlined systems, and the failure of the M21/M22 modular decon system to be fielded on time. The Army was critically short of working M17A3 lightweight decon systems, which had been neglected by combat units and were in a general poor state of repair. Sixty systems were held in war stocks at Pine Bluff Arsenal and were eventually released just weeks prior to the beginning of Operation Iraqi Freedom. Similarly, the aging M12A1 power-driven decon systems, which were supposed to be replaced by the M21/M22 Modular Decon System, were critically short due to downed systems. SBCCOM was funding a rebuilding effort with the M12A1 systems at Pine Bluff, with fifty-six systems due to be fielded to five Army chemical companies, three of which would be deploying to the Middle East. The Army had three options to augment the lightweight decon system shortages: accelerate the rebuild program, buy commercial decon systems, or field the M22 high-pressure washers of the Modular Decon System. More than two hundred Modular Decon Systems produced for final production testing and evaluation were sitting (and would remain) at Pine Bluff Arsenal because of Chemical School concerns about safety issues and the system's ability to conduct large terrain decontamination missions. The rebuild program would field some new systems, but not enough to significantly address the shortfall. The Army PEO's recommendation was to buy 125 commercial decon systems, of which there were at least a half dozen potential contenders, along with continuing Pine Bluff Arsenal's rebuilds of the existing military systems.

On November 12, the media reported that Iraq had ordered more than a million atropine autoinjectors from the world markets. This caused a great deal of discussion, even though Iraq had submitted the contract through the UN as required and atropine was not on the list of products that Iraq was barred from importing. The State Department immediately ruminated that the large purchase of atropine, more than what would be required for normal humanitarian requirements, was of concern since "that could indicate preparations to use chemical weapons by preparing to protect their own forces from the consequences of such use." [13] It was not clear whether any country had delivered the atropine to Iraq.

In early November, results of an SBCCOM assessment cast doubt on the ability of BDO protective suits to fully protect individuals to the same degree as JSLIST suits. This assessment examined BDO test results developed at Dugway Proving Ground in 1990 against current test methodologies and results derived from JSLIST suit tests. Initial statistical analyses seemed to indicate that the BDO suits would not be effective for more than a few days, even if not contaminated with liquid agent. The BDOs were supposed to be effective if worn for up to twenty-two to thirty days, depending on field conditions. Because these suits represented two-thirds of the DoD inventory, and with services planning on four suits per military service member, this was a problem. Or was it? One of the major flaws of this study was that there was no substantiating physical evidence. There had been no funding to conduct chemical agent tests to compare the two materials side-by-side. The services had continuously tested random BDO lots over the previous fifteen years, ensuring that the suits had retained the protective qualities promised by their manufacturers. Despite the potential shortcomings of the study, SBCCOM sent the results to the OSD and the Joint Staff. The DATSD (CBD) and the JRO felt compelled to act on this information, fearing that the worst-case scenario—that the BDOs' protective capability being less than fully adequate—would turn out true. About 95 percent of the protective suits in CENTCOM and in Europe were BDOs, in part due to the desire to field and expend the millions of older BDOs prior to using the newer (and fewer) JSLIST suits. When General Myers was informed about the issue, he immediately directed the director of J-4 (Logistics) to freeze any further distribution of JSLIST suits until a practical solution could be developed. The Army's commanding general of Forces Command (FORSCOM) also demanded that all deploying soldiers receive JSLIST suits.

An Army demonstration at the Pentagon had not improved anyone's impression of the protective suits. On November 12, a soldier wearing a JSLIST suit, rubber gloves, and boots, fainted during a press briefing under the hot lights. The sergeant was quickly revived and led out, but it was evident that the other soldiers in the room, similarly dressed, were very uncomfortable. The media openly speculated on the effect Iraqi desert heat would have on troops similarly dressed and with much less experience than these chemical specialists. They would soon find out, as reporters from many news outlets reported to Fort Benning in December for a combat-preparedness training course that would include the wear and use of the protective suit and mask.

On November 14, Rep. Shays sent a second memo discussing the previous October hearing and asking for an update on Dr. Johnson-Winegar's statement that CENTCOM forces would only use JSLIST or Saratoga suits. In addition, numerous representatives and senators had sent memorandums of concern over the readiness of U.S. forces for CB warfare. In a hearing later that month, Shay's subcommittee grilled the DoD CB Defense Program leadership on the issue of sixty-seven thousand defective gaskets for M40 protective masks supplied to DLA in 2000 by two manufacturers. The Army claimed that neither manufacturer was at fault, as they had made the part in accordance with government drawings. Although this problem was easily addressed through a recall of the spare part, coming on top of the previous protective mask and protective suit issues, it represented another mark against the DoD CB Defense Program's credibility.[14]

The larger issue was what to do with the BDOs, if indeed they were only good for a few days or even a few weeks' protection. When a staffer on Shay's subcommittee had leaked the news about the BDO test results to the media (an action resulting in no visible retribution), DoD developed a plan to address the potential challenge.[15] First, production of JSLIST suits would be surged from seventy-nine thousand per month to ninety thousand per month by December.[16] Every military service member in or deploying to CENTCOM would receive two JSLIST suits each, and the BDOs would be used as training suits and backups to the first two JSLIST suits in the event that additional chemical weapons attacks required their use. This plan was feasible if the services diverted most of their JSLIST suits to forces deploying to CENTCOM. PACOM felt its troops were getting the short end of the stick and refused to release their war contingency suits for redistribution (and rightly so, considering they were also in a high-threat environment). Everyone preferred JSLIST suits because they were less bulky (and therefore perceived as adding less heat stress), had a forty-five-day protective factor (not exposed to agent) as opposed to thirty days, and did not get the troops "dirty" by contact with activated charcoal, as the BDOs did.[17] The BDO suits were fine for anything short of massive chemical weapons attacks, but the inference that they might be somehow tainted, no matter that the basis of the decision was derived from a purely statistical analysis, drove the emphasis to produce and deploy more JSLIST suits.[18]

The Army PEO-CBD was working hard to complete its fielding of Portal Shield systems to CENTCOM. Of the twelve sites intended for Southwest Asia, three were not yet operational, although the equipment was manufactured and ready to go. The Portal Shields were scheduled to be emplaced and ready by the end of December. In late November, CENTCOM sent an operational needs statement requesting additional biological detectors, ideally the newer JBPDS, at five sites within the CENTCOM area of responsibility that were not covered by Portal Shields or the BIDS platoons. This was a huge demand on the program, because it would imperil the Army's ability to field a second reserve BIDS company (the 375th Chemical Company) in 2004. CENTCOM eventually agreed to accept seven JBPDS and a number of DFUs that would be emplaced at Camp Arifjan in Kuwait, a large Army supply base south of Kuwait City. The Navy was receiving 500 DFUs for its ships and buildings, and another 350 DFUs were on their way to EUCOM.[19] About 140 DFUs would find their way to CENTCOM.

On November 18, Deputy Secretary of Defense Wolfowitz chaired a senior readiness operational council meeting on immediate CB defense issues.[20] OSD policy led the discussion, using the Joint Staff's assessment of CENTCOM's CB defense capability as background, while DATSD (CBD) offered possible acquisition actions. The Joint Staff, the OSD, and the services had spent much of October refining the recommendations to address the CENTCOM priorities that had been developed in June. Much of the discussion focused on industry's ability to produce enough protective suits to address CENTCOM's requirements within a few months. The meeting resulted in the approval of more than $200 million for protective suits (allowing production of about a million suits) and approximately $100 million for funds to support the procurement of decontamination applicators (to include the GL-1800 and the Army's commercial alternatives), accelerating the fielding of medical collective protection systems, and additional chemical and biological detectors.

There was one catch—following the meeting, the OSD comptroller announced that he could not find a way to execute the spending. That is to say, he had no instructions on whose budget(s) to cut to allow for these procurement actions to take place. Everything was high priority and important. Although Wolfowitz had authorized these specific CB defense actions, the comptroller had to work the details into the FY03 defense supplemental budget request that would be sent to Congress for approval prior to any actual production and delivery of equipment to the troops. DLA needed to have funds prior to directing industry to surge produce the suits, and three months was not very much time.

On December 4, DATSD (CBD) received the news that the interim decontaminant DF-200 had failed its operational testing, in part because it acted more like a foam after mixing, and the testing guidelines had specified its use as a liquid. Although the formula was designed to be foam, the DoD test and evaluation agencies were willing to rule against its use if it failed to act like a liquid. On December 9, ASD (HA) submitted a memorandum to DATSD (CBD) urging the prompt release of a medical pretreatment Skin Exposure Reduction Paste Against CW Agents (SERPACWA), so named because the FDA thought "topical skin protectant" was misleading, because the product didn't fully protect the skin from all hazards. This lotion would provide protection from liquid agents for about four to six hours after application, and would lessen the need for immediate skin decontamination after exposure. The lotion was expected to cover the areas where agent might penetrate the chemical ensemble, such as closures between the gloves and jacket, and between the boots and pants. It had been planned for release in 2000 but had been delayed until late 2003 for fielding to the military. As a consumable medical item, SERPACWA could be procured by any service using its own funds, but the Army wanted the DoD program to spend $5 million on an early release of the lotion, a request which the JRO would validate.

On December 19, CENTCOM queried the JRO on the status of an Army request for validating an aerial radiological and chemical survey UAV, a system that had never been tested or even developed. This request had to be rejected.[21] On December 20, the FDA announced that they would accept a new drug application from DoD on the use of pyridiostigmine bromide (PB) tablets, specifically for exposure to soman nerve agent, based on its new animal efficacy rule. The DoD had used PB tablets in the first Gulf War with some controversy, and its approval had been held up since 1991 by FDA requirements.

On November 20, General Franks designated the Third U.S. Army as the CFLCC for Operation Iraqi Freedom, as it had been for Operation Enduring Freedom in Afghanistan. The Third Army would deploy to Camp Doha, Kuwait, with Lt. Gen. David McKiernan assuming command as CFLCC commander. Forces began to flow more rapidly into theater, with I MEF arriving in Kuwait in late November. The 3rd Infantry Division's 2nd Brigade Combat Team was already in Kuwait, having deployed in September 2002 for Desert Spring operations (maintaining an operationally ready combat brigade in Kuwait). The Division Tactical Command Post deployed in November. In December, the remainder of 3rd Infantry Division, including its 92nd Chemical Company, began its deployment from Fort Stewart, Georgia, with arrivals through January. The soldiers would fly into Kuwait to fall in on prepositioned heavy brigade equipment sets. The 4th Infantry Division would load its personnel and equipment at Beaumont, Texas, and travel through the Mediterranean to Turkey, with the intent of creating a second front in northern Iraq. The deployment group Task Force Ironhorse included the 2nd Chemical Battalion and chemical companies from Fort Hood and Fort Lewis.

The 83rd Chemical Battalion, an active duty chemical battalion stationed at Fort Polk, Louisiana, received its orders to deploy to Camp Arifjan, Kuwait, on December 22. Its advance party would leave for Kuwait on January 9, joining the 310th Chemical Company headquarters and one BIDS platoon already in theater, with another BIDS platoon in Afghanistan. The Air Force would deploy a number of their Biological Augmentation Teams (BATs), two-man teams with deployable laboratory analysis capability, and civil engineering teams that provided limited recon, detection and decon to its major airbases in the Middle East. The Navy had developed protocols for biological sample analysis within its naval task forces. Also deployed, under prior OEF orders, were one NBC recon platoon from the 51st Chemical Company and one decon platoon from the 101st Chemical Company. These chemical units were focused on protecting the force from NBC weapons; another, more specialized force was being developed to seize and exploit WMD sites.

WMD exploitation and elimination became a hot topic in the summer of 2002; notably, the idea that a small task force could work with combat units to quickly capture, document, and ensure the destruction of WMD production, storage, research and development facilities, and other WMD infrastructure. In Afghanistan, CENTCOM had responded to what units had originally thought was fifty drums of phosgene, which turned out to be decontaminants. The question arose as to who was supposed to deal with these materials. The Army's chemical demilitarization experts said it wasn't their job, DTRA's liaison officer said it wasn't their responsibility, and TEU was not equipped for eliminating large chemical stocks. In preparation for Iraq, the OSD felt that they would have to deal with a similar issue on a much larger scale.

The OSD counterproliferation policy office led a working group of analysts at the National Defense University in July and August 2002 to develop a concept for WMD elimination. This was an attempt not merely to secure Iraq's WMD capability to protect the force, but also to meet a major national objective of the war. The group identified a framework of finding, securing, characterizing, exploiting, eliminating, and verifying WMD sites. They had intel data suggesting the size of Iraq's arsenal, but lacked information on exactly where the weapons were and how much existed at specific storage and production sites. Separately, other DoD offices were addressing the issue of identifying and apprehending Iraqi personnel associated with the WMD program.

The controversy was over how and when military forces should eliminate WMD materials. CENTCOM ideally wanted air strikes to eliminate WMD sites before the initiation of ground conflict (assuming they had good intelligence); otherwise, it was assumed that they'd be cleaned up after the conflict ended. If the ground units overran the sites and had to secure them or move the materials to a safer location, they would lose critical combat power. A CENTCOM staffer noted that the mission would cause "combat suck" away from the main operation, and there were few combat forces with which to execute this resource-intensive mission. OSD policy insisted on exploiting those sites while in a "non-permissive" combat environment. The British allies cautioned against plans to destroy CB munitions in place, fearing potential arms control treaty violations. There was no dedicated military force currently organized or equipped to conduct sensitive site exploitation (SSE) missions, so OSD policy tasked the Army to develop a structure and to support the development of such a group. This concept would build upon the site exploitations executed in Afghanistan. Army Training and Doctrine Command (TRADOC) chose the 75th Field Artillery Brigade headquarters to lead what would be known as the 75th Exploitation Task Force (XTF). OSD policy tasked all defense agencies to identify their WMD and arms control experts, as DTRA developed an organizational framework that would deploy the personnel and equipment.

Although the Army's two reserve chemical brigade headquarters would have been more appropriate, they were not ready to deploy and the 75th Brigade headquarters was. The 75th Brigade headquarters had been readying for deployment since October, with the idea that their mission was going to be supporting the 4th Infantry Division in its attack on Iraq from the north. In December, Col. Richard McPhee, the commander of the headquarters, was alerted to his brigade's new role as base of operations for command and control for a number of teams searching for evidence of Iraq's WMD program. His unit would oversee a disparate group of military specialists including the Army's TEU, USANCA, the 52nd Ordnance Group (Explosive Ordnance Disposal [EOD]), DTRA, and government civilian CB subject-matter experts from Aberdeen Proving Ground and the Navy. Their initial list of over six hundred sensitive sites to exploit would come from the intelligence community and information from Iraqi defectors.

The 75th XTF would field four site survey teams, two that would be embedded in V Corps and two that would be embedded in I MEF.[22] The role of these small units was to secure the site, conduct initial assessments at the location, and report the preliminary findings to the headquarters. Based on the reports, the headquarters would deploy one of its Mobile Exploitation Teams (MET) to the site. Each site survey team was to include subject-matter experts from DTRA; EOD technicians; NBC reconnaissance specialists; and a support element. Based on its initial assessments, the team would recommend sites for further exploitation by the MET. The MET elements would collect evidence, perform computer and document exploitation, and interrogate captured personnel. The Army's TEU members, as part of the team, would collect CB warfare agent samples, render safe munitions, and evacuate samples and materials to a laboratory or collection center for further evaluation and exploitation. There were two METs, Alpha and Bravo, initially planned to be staffed with fifty personnel, with the possibility of developing two additional METs later in the operation. The METs expected that they would be exploiting small, secured, well-defined sites, with missions lasting less than forty-eight hours.[23] SOCOM's Task Force-20 was searching for WMD sites in western Iraq, while DIA once again deployed its CB Intelligence Support Teams.[24] There was no question as to the DoD's intent to seize WMDs and ensure Iraq's WMD program was eliminated once and for all. The challenge was finding the NBC weapons in the first place.

PHASE 2: SHAPING THE BATTLESPACE (JANUARY 2003–MARCH 2003)

The goals of Phase 2 were to posture coalition forces to conduct sustained combat operations, begin initial operations to degrade Iraqi command-and-control and security forces, and seize key pieces of terrain. The U.S. government would continue diplomatic measures and develop theater missile defense and counter-WMD operations. In January 2003, the 101st Airborne Division was alerted to deploy, beginning its movement into theater on February 6. Final division units would arrive in theater in early March. The 2nd Brigade,

82nd Airborne Division began its deployment to Kuwait. The Third Army and V Corps deployed their forward command posts and joined the 3rd Infantry Division, I MEF, and CENTCOM's forward command posts. The 4th Infantry Division was held up in ships off of Turkey, while the 2nd and 3rd Armored Cavalry Regiments began to deploy as well. As forces continued to flow into theater, the soldiers moved out to training areas to practice force-on-force exercises, live fires, urban combat training, and operations in a chemically contaminated environment. This training would continue practically up to the start of offensive operations.

On the medical side, the Army was fielding a new multichambered antidote kit in January called Antidote Treatment Nerve Agent Autoinjector (ATNAA), which replaced the two-component Mark 1 Nerve Agent Antidote Kits.[25][26] Each autoinjector held 2.1 milligrams of atropine and 600 milligrams of pralidoxime chloride, the idea being that the individual would use a single autoinjector instead of two, in the event of nerve agent exposure. The Army had originally submitted the device for FDA approval in December 1999, but the FDA had questions on the components and labeling language that delayed its fielding by two years.

President Bush had announced a nationwide smallpox vaccination policy in December to address the larger issue of a potential bioterrorism incident in the United States. This announcement also heralded the DoD vaccination effort for military and civilian personnel operating in high threat locations, including those deploying to Kuwait. The challenge was negotiating between DHHS and DoD as to how many anthrax and smallpox vaccine doses DoD would get for combat forces, how many doses DHHS needed for its homeland security requirements, and how many doses OSD policy felt should be put aside for coalition allies and friendly nations in the Gulf. More than a hundred thousand service members would receive the smallpox vaccination by early April, with a small number suffering side effects and a few showing serious reactions.[27] One National Guardsman died from a heart attack following a smallpox vaccination in March 2003, causing DoD to suspend giving smallpox vaccinations to people with a history of heart disease.

At the end of January, General Reeves sent a memorandum to the JRO asking the Joint Staff to reconsider the CENTCOM operational needs statement for an interim, power-driven decon applicator, and that they consider alternatives to the GL-1800 applicator. His concern was that limiting competition constrained his ability to identify a safe and effective capability that could use the DF-200 solution, in addition to possible legal issues concerning the federal acquisition regulations. Needless to say, Global Ground Support was not happy that the decontamination funds approved at the November Senior Readiness Operational Council had not been dedicated to procuring its system, and its representative had been very vocal at the DATSD (CBD) office. In February, Rep. Dennis Moore (D-KS) and Sen. Sam Brownback (R-KS) would send letters of concern to the OSD asking about the hold-up of procuring the GL-1800 systems (Global Ground Support headquarters was based in Olathe, Kansas). The PEO-CBD decided to go with the Falcon Fixed Site Decon System, built by Intelagard, instead of the Global GL-1800 system. The thirty-two Falcon systems did make it to a warehouse in the Gulf in late April 2003 but were never deployed to the field.

On February 20, Mr. Walt Hollis, the Deputy Under Secretary of the Army for Operational Research (overseeing Army test and evaluation efforts) released a memorandum stating that the military utility of DF-200 had significant operational limitations. The Air Force operational test and evaluation agency failed the interim decontaminant because it kept foaming when it was supposed to be a liquid, but the Army recognized that it could still be used—within limitations and strict guidelines. The Army's recommendation was that only forces in CENTCOM should use the interim decontaminant, and only if other commercial alternatives (such as high-test hypochlorite bleach) were not available. This announcement was practically too late for many combat forces that had already deployed to Kuwait and had purchased the DF-200 solution in bulk. The demand for DF-200 had far exceeded the supply, with some military units ordering the formulation directly from the manufacturers. There were other problems associated with the new decontaminant. It had not been tested on different vehicle surfaces—helicopters and fixed-wing planes, for instance. These concerns, plus the lack of production and continued freeze on DS-2 stocks, meant that many units would be using commercial rather than military decontaminants. The 3rd Infantry Division purchased 7,500 pounds of bleach prior to departing for the Middle East and 6,800 pounds of calcium hypochlorite in Kuwait. Every battalion had a minimum of 100 pounds of bleach; the decon platoons had 300 to 600 pounds of bleach.

In mid-February, DoD announced that it had decided to retain its current policy on the handling of contaminated human remains. In September, the Armed Forces Epidemiology Board had met to discuss the policy issue based on a request from the ASD (HA) and military surgeon generals. Cases of chemical or radiological contamination were easily addressed by current decontamination practices, but ensuring that human remains were clean of BW agents would be hard to verify. The difficulty lay in how to handle human remains that might be contaminated with anthrax or smallpox. Bringing contaminated human remains back to the United States was risky; what if a contaminated body were exhumed? Was there an exposure issue for relatives who wished open-casket viewing? Initial discussions focused on the possibility of permanent internment in the Middle East or cremating the bodies prior to their return to the United States. Neither option was politically acceptable, in part because viewing the body assured U.S. families that it was indeed their relative who had been killed.[28]

The State Department refused to plan for the possibility of dealing with contaminated human remains until the event actually happened. In mid-March, Dr. Winkenwerder (ASD [HA]) told reporters, "There are no plans for cremation, or incineration, or deep-pit burial, or anything of that sort. It is our policy that all such service members [killed by biological agents] would be transported back to the United States."[29] At the end of March, Wolfowitz released a memorandum establishing the DoD policy on contaminated human remains: Under a joint doctrine developed after the first Gulf War, all remains would return to the United States after decontamination. Human remains that were contaminated with contagious BW agents or anthrax that resisted decontamination would be temporarily interred until safe handling procedures and materials could be identified.

This issue was still vexing TRANSCOM. They had conducted several demonstrations at Brooks Air Force Base in March using body bags to evaluate potential challenges of shipping formerly contaminated remains. Although the remains would be deconned, to be safe, the bodies would be returned in double body bags. In all cases, the body bags burst open when the altitude chamber was decompressed to simulate flight at 35,000 feet, meaning the plane's crew could be exposed to the BW agent. If human remains could not be guaranteed free of BW agents, the remains would have to be either temporarily interned (until completely decontaminated) or sent home by ship, rather than by air. In a related issue, EUCOM had to work with European allies on the issue of planes containing potentially contaminated human remains and equipment flying through their airspace. There still was no plan for decontaminating large-frame aircraft to EPA-accepted levels. Small fighter planes would not be an issue, but any formerly contaminated large-frame aircraft would have to be either grounded or kept in theater until confirmed safe.

In early February, an article by a Bloomberg news correspondent identified the results of an Army Audit Agency report dated July 2002. This audit, conducted between November 2000 and February 2002, addressed the unit and individual training on CB defense equipment at Fort Lewis, Washington (including one brigade from the 25th Infantry Division) and Fort Hood, Texas (including the 4th Infantry Division and 1st Cavalry Division). The inspectors examined nineteen nonchemical units and six chemical units. Although the chemical specialists were generally competent, those assigned to nonchemical units had been given so many unrelated tasks, they had little time to maintain their technical skills or assist the unit in training. Soldiers without chemical training had trouble operating chemical detectors, with nearly 40 percent failing to operate an M8 or M22 chemical detector and 25 percent failing to operate the M1 Chemical Agent Monitor. Twelve percent of the detectors were not mission capable. Two of ten decon apparatuses examined would not work, and the operators noted that other decon apparatus were inoperable because they could not obtain repair parts. Nearly 40 percent of the protective masks inspected failed preventive maintenance checks, although many of these masks could be repaired at the unit level. Combined with a shaky record of individual NBC defense training, let alone integrating NBC defense tasks into higher-level unit training and exercises, the report demonstrated a lack of attention to CB defense readiness at the command level.

The CBS show *60 Minutes* decided to examine the DoD CB Defense Program a month prior to the start of the ground offensive. On February 16, Mike Wallace conducted an interview with Dr. Johnson-Winegar, with additional comments from Rep. Chris Shays and Col. (Ret.) David Hackworth, a well-known and outspoken military analyst. The *60 Minutes* crew had originally requested time with Mr. Aldridge or Dr. Klein, both of whom declined and directed the DATSD (CBD) to participate in the interview. This interview was a real hatchet job and a great example of the perils of allowing the media to cut and splice the interviewee's comments as they see fit, especially if the full transcript (released by DoD two days later) is compared against what was actually shown on television.[30] Dr. Johnson-Winegar did not fare well; she looked defensive and seemed not to want to answer Mike Wallace's questions about troop readiness, training, and operations in the field, and accounting for the Isratex BDO suits. One reason she had difficulty answering these questions was that these were all command issues appropriate for the services leaders, and not the responsibility of the OSD acquisition office. However, public law had identified her office as the single OSD point of contact for CB defense, so the expectation was that she had all the right answers.

Alternating between being "a bully" (his own words) and a flatterer, Wallace attacked and distorted the DoD CB Defense Program's record of developing military CB defense capabilities. He interrupted Winegar-Johnson's discussion on JSLIST suits, demanding to know on what bases the military was training with protective suits (this training was routinely done at the lowest levels across the force). He misrepresented the GAO report, insinuating that military units had no control over suit distribution and accusing the DoD of deliberately withholding bad news about CB defense training and capabilities from the public. He misstated information about medical collective protection shelters and medical training, rebuffing Winegar-Johnson's attempts to respond. Wallace raised the issues of the "defective" protective mask—identified by the DoD Inspector General in 1999—and the defective gaskets at DLA as examples of dishonesty or DoD leadership was not being honest in its assessments that the force was ready for CB warfare.[31] He accused her of not responding to a late November letter sent by Rep. Jan Schakowsky (D-IL) that had questioned DoD CB defense readiness, when in fact an official DoD memorandum had been sent to the congresswoman in early January. The interviews with Shays and Hackworth reinforced the perception that NBC meant "No Body Cares" in DoD. This kind of attack journalism, intent on scoring points rather than on discussing facts, is why so few CB defense experts, civil service or military, will talk openly to the media. It is just too common for journalists to clip interviews and create sensationalistic sound bites.[32]

Despite Dr. Johnson-Winegar's attempts to show that the DoD leadership took the issue of CB defense very seriously, that U.S. forces had the best equipment available, and that DoD understood the issues of CB warfare agents well, the nuance of the 60 Minutes report was that DoD was just not doing enough despite the threat posed by Saddam Hussein.[33] This was in spite of statements by military analysts such as Gen. Barry McCaffrey (Ret.), who stated in November that "every fighter wing, every Navy ship at sea, every Army battalion is fully equipped to fight in a chemical environment," an assessment echoed by Lt. Col. Stephen Twitty, commanding the 3-15th Infantry Battalion within the 3rd Infantry Division.[34] Forces in Kuwait, at the least, were serious about refreshing their training on NBC defense. The chemical defense specialists assigned to military units took the time to set up and conduct training for individual skills needed to survive a CB weapons attack.[35] CENTCOM's chemical officer, Lt. Col. Tom Woloszyn, hosted an NBC defense conference in February for all the chemical officers in theater to share information on capabilities and protocols. Pine Bluff Arsenal's production lines had been in full gear, manufacturing nearly twenty-one thousand M291 decon kits and forty-four hundred M295 decon kits for CENTCOM. Their technicians had refurbished more than twenty-two thousand protective masks, eighty M12A1 power-driven decon apparatuses, sixty-seven CB Protective Shelters, and seven CP DEPMEDS shelters, all of which would be used in Operation Iraqi Freedom.

Around the end of February, the media picked up on another great story meant to inspire lack of confidence in DoD's CB defense capabilities. Although the use of M22 ACADAs had reduced the number of false alarms (as opposed to the numerous false alarms experienced with the use of M8A1 detectors in 1990–91), the new detector had not eliminated the issue entirely. The Marines in Kuwait had initiated Operation Kuwaiti Field Chicken (KFC), which used caged chickens as gas sentries, similar to the concept of coalmine canaries. There were a few problems with this less-than-ingenious solution; first, no one really knew if nerve agents would affect the chickens that much earlier than humans. Second, the chickens, not used to the environmental changes of hot days and cold nights in the desert, tended to die quickly of natural causes. Great solution for dinner, bad substitute for chemical alarms.[36] This was not indicative of the general CBRN defense readiness of the military force in Kuwait, but might hint at the average soldier's confidence in his or her equipment.

The M22 ACADA was a notable improvement over the M8A1 detector, but Army reserve units deploying to the Middle East would still have several thousand M8A1 detectors in their inventory. In addition, the Air Force was pushing for more chemical detection capability. CFACC had sent a request to the Joint Staff for approval to buy one hundred lightweight ChemSentry detectors directly from the manufacturer. ChemSentry had been the lead product to develop into the JCAD, the Air Force-led joint service project that was supposed to have fielded the new detector in 2000. The JRO approved this request for the ChemSentry detectors after a personal call from a three-star Air Force general from Wright-Patterson Air Force Base. This decision would be controversial in that the ChemSentry, as a commercial item, had not been tested to determine its ability to actually do what its manufacturer claimed.[37] Dr. Klein, the ATSD (NCB), would release a memorandum to the services in February telling them that they would not receive approval to use commercial hardware for CB defense requirements without JRO validation of the request and rigorous testing to ensure that the product would in fact protect the forces. After the conflict, the Air Force recalled all of the Chem-Sentries used in Iraq and Afghanistan after a DoD audit charged that the units were rushed into use despite poor test results. The DoD Inspector General's office noted that the ChemSentry had not met critical requirements and did not add significant military capability over fielded systems at the time of the request.[38]

Maj. Gen. John Doesburg (commanding general, SBCCOM), joined Brig. Gen. Steve Reeves and Col. Tom Spoehr (commander, 3rd Brigade, Fort Leonard Wood) on March 3 at the Pentagon for a question-and-answer session with reporters on the state of DoD CB defense. General Reeves noted that the new chemical detector had a significantly lower false alarm rate but did not eliminate all false alarms. Generals Doesburg and Reeves addressed the issue of the protective suits, with Reeves noting the important numbers were "three and zero. We checked three times, and there are zero defective suits in our contingency stocks." Doesburg noted that the JSLIST suits were good for forty-five days out of the wrapper, and twenty-four hours if contaminated with liquid agent. Gen. Doesburg addressed the nature of CB agents and Iraqi capabilities with the reporters, while Gen. Reeves discussed the capabilities of the nineteen new CB defense systems fielded to the force since 1991, some of which were on display at the press briefing. He also outlined, in layman's terms, why the Marine use of "sentinel chickens" was not really a good idea. Col. Spoehr discussed the Chemical School's training program and the role of the fifteen thousand Army specialists in protecting the force, ending the discussion with an invitation to the media to come visit the Chemical Defense Training Facility.[39] Unlike the *60 Minutes* interview, this press session focused on the current readiness of the force rather than slanders and allegations against the DoD CB defense capability.

The 83rd Chemical Battalion's subordinate units and their equipment arrived in Kuwait in early February, joining the 59th Chemical Company, which was supporting the 3rd Infantry Division. As more chemical units arrived, V Corps took two decon platoons from the 59th Chemical to establish fixed decon sites in Kuwait. The 83rd's mission would include reconnaissance, biological surveillance, and decontamination support in the Kuwait area, with a focus on the air bases, seaports, and deployment camps. This would include two BIDS platoons of the 7th Chemical Company and the 68th Chemical Company from Fort Hood, and the remainder of the 51st Chemical Company. The 68th Chemical Company, which arrived in theater a week after the 83rd, would be responsible for decontaminating Kuwaiti air bases and seaports if they were attacked by Iraqi missiles.[40] Two more 7th Chemical BIDS platoons were on the way, with a fifth BIDS platoon remaining in the United States to meet homeland security requirements. Two of the 310th Chemical Company's BIDS platoons were already in Kuwait, one platoon was in Afghanistan, another platoon remained active in the United States as an asset for Joint Task Force Civil Support (JTF-CS), and a fifth platoon was preparing for deployment. By mid-March, seven BIDS platoons would be task-organized under CFLCC; in addition, one 310th BIDS platoon deployed to Israel and the last of 7th Chemical's BIDS platoon deployed to Jordan.[41]

By early March, about one hundred and seventy thousand troops were on the ground in Kuwait and other Middle East countries. The 413th Chemical Detachment had joined I MEF to support their operations center in terms of hazard assessments and logistical support. Also joining the Marines were a recon platoon from the 51st Chemical Company, three platoons and the company headquarters from 101st Chemical Company, and a BIDS platoon from the 7th Chemical Company. The Marines wanted one of the 101st platoons to be dedicated as a patient decon capability; although this was not a standard chemical defense role (the medics should have established this as part of their procedures), the chemical company agreed—that's what the war-fighter wanted, that's what he got. The 468th Chemical Battalion would join the

Marines in early April as a reserve headquarters unit assisting the coordination and support of those Army chemical defense assets attached to I MEF, including the 323rd Chemical Company (a reserve company that would not join the Marines until after Baghdad fell, due to their equipment arriving by ship). The 2nd Chemical Battalion, an active duty battalion from Fort Hood, would arrive with the 4th Infantry Division in early April, along with the 11th, 44th, and 46th Chemical Companies.[42] The 450th Chemical Battalion, a reserve headquarters unit originally intended to support CFLCC maneuver operations, would arrive at the end of April along with two additional reserve chemical companies (the 314th and 371st).

CENTCOM's JTF-CM increased its size from Czech and German NBC defense units to include the addition of a Ukrainian NBC defense battalion, a Slovak chemical company, and Polish and Bulgarian chemical defense forces. In all, the task force was composed of about five hundred personnel, including recon, decon, and medical support specialists. Brig. Gen. Craig Boddington (select) led the task force under MARCENT command and control. The JTF-CM headquarters in Kuwait addressed consequence management throughout CENTCOM, including Jordan, Qatar, Saudi Arabia, Oman, and Afghanistan. As traditional military units, these forces were heavy and relatively immobile, and lacked hospital, security, transportation and logistical support, relying on U.S. forces for much of these capabilities. The Marines had the view that this joint task force was similar to a CBIRF unit and a one-shot deal at best. It would not have been able to handle two large-scale incidents at once. The JTF-CM was a hodgepodge of mixed capabilities, but it addressed a key aspect of counterproliferation strategy, and it addressed the concerns of the Gulf Cooperative Council (and specifically the Kuwaiti government) that CENTCOM would help their governments recover from any Iraqi CB warfare attacks against their civilian populace.

Although the possibility of deploying the 4th Infantry Division through Turkey existed, USAREUR planners suddenly realized that they had not considered the possibility of Iraqi CB weapons attacks against seaports and air bases from which U.S. forces would be deploying. In response to urgent EUCOM calls for action, the Army committed to deploying a reserve chemical battalion to support that front. Unfortunately, no Army reserve chemical battalions were prepared to deploy. At best, the Army could send one chemical company to support CBRN defense operations in Turkey in time for deployment operations in that timeframe. The National Security Council was similarly concerned that there was no JTF-CM for Turkey, in the event that the Turkish government might call for U.S. government assistance in responding to Iraqi CB weapons attacks. Their staff leaned on DoD to provide forces for this function, but the forces were not available and the priority was to support combat operations, not military assistance to Turkey's government for an event that might not occur.

The counterproliferation pillars were being set up for the main battle. Along with the CB defense specialists, missile defense, active defense, and counterforce units were moving in. The 32nd Air and Missile Defense Command from Fort Bliss, Texas, provided the Army's component for joint theater air and missile defense. Several Patriot missile battalions would deploy into theater to provide missile defense not just in Kuwait and Iraq, but also covered Jordan, Turkey, Qatar, Bahrain, Saudi Arabia, and Israel. The Air Force had deployed fifty-eight Passive Attack Weapon bombs to the Persian Gulf. These bombs were designed to penetrate the roof of storehouses and fire up to twenty-four hundred steel rods into containers of chemical agents or precursors, the contents of which would harmlessly evaporate or decompose. Pine Bluff Arsenal had developed a prototype white phosphorus bomb for the Air Force designed to incinerate CB warfare agents inside their storage bunkers. These measures would avoid the effects of conventional explosives that might force the chemical agents into the atmosphere.[43] According to a former high-level intelligence official, special operations forces from JSOTF-West had entered western Iraq in mid-March, prior to the ground offensive, to investigate sites identified by Chalabi's INC defectors as suspected CB weapons storage depots or SCUD missile sites. "They came up with nothing," the official said. "Never found a single SCUD."[44]

CHAPTER 7

WHO LOST THE WMDs?

*History teaches that war begins when governments believe
the price of aggression is cheap.*

—RONALD REAGAN, PRESIDENT OF THE UNITED STATES

At the onset of the ground offensive, every military and civilian leader within DoD fully expected that Iraq would use CB weapons against the CENTCOM forces. Rumsfeld commented, "The task here is to change the regime and find the weapons of mass destruction and put in place a government for the Iraqi people that are [sic] representative of them."[1] Bush administration officials publicly warned Iraq's government against authorizing the use of CB weapons. Air Force planes showered propaganda leaflets down on Iraqi forces and cities as others broadcast messages over the radio. "There is no doubt that the regime of Saddam Hussein possesses weapons of mass destruction," said General Franks on the third day of the war.[2] Maj. Gen. David Petraeus, commanding the 101st Airborne Division, saw the odds of American troops being "slimed" with chemicals as fifty-fifty, with the likelihood that Saddam possessed chemical munitions at 80–90 percent.[3] Maj. Gen. Buford Blount, commanding the 3rd Infantry Division, took this threat very seriously and frequently discussed potential chemical strike locations, mitigation options, and the status of chemical defense equipment with his staff. But as Marine Corps commandant Gen. Michael Hagee stated, "I believe we are as prepared as technology can make us today . . . . We have the best equipment that technology and science can provide us right now."[4]

V Corps planners staged a war game in which Saddam used CB agents against the coalition force. There were four major points of concern. If he did not preemptively use CB agents against the steadily growing force in Kuwait, suspicions were that the first use of agent would be as Marine forces crossed the Euphrates River at An Nasiriyah. The second suspected target point was LSA Bushmaster, a very large logistics base developed near An Najaf in preparation for the final push to Baghdad. The third point was at the Karbala Gap, an operationally significant choke point that V Corps forces would have to negotiate on their approach to Baghdad. Last was the second crossing of the Euphrates River by the 3rd Infantry Division at Objective Peach, a major bridge southwest of Baghdad about halfway between Karbala and Baghdad, which would support the main push to the Iraqi capital.[5]

Yet there would remain the skeptics, both former UNSCOM arms control inspectors and military analysts, who predicted that U.S. military forces would not find any evidence of WMDs. The rationale included the possibility that Iraq kept its CB weapons program small and mobile, Saddam's intent being to keep the program "warm" (active but not producing large quantities) and hidden from inspectors rather than fielding an offensive capability. Even if Iraq had small quantities of CB weapons, most were designed to be delivered by aerial platforms, and the Iraqi Air Force had practically ceased to exist. Any covert use of anthrax or smallpox would be a failure, since U.S. military personnel were immunized against those agents. Although any old stocks of nerve agent predating 1995 would be largely useless, there was the issue of the unaccounted for 550 artillery shells filled with mustard agent that might be used against a cluster of American troops. That was, of course, assuming that Iraq could actually deploy any ground systems against the fast moving armored forces. Finally, world opinion was largely on Hussein's side as far as his denial that Iraq had any existing WMD program, and UN inspections had accounted for practically all of the prior program's infrastructure, munitions, and agents.[6]

This time the U.S. military was gunning for Baghdad. That meant that they were facing a regime survival scenario, and every soldier, sailor, airman, and Marine expected the Iraqi forces to use any means possible, including CB warfare agents, to stave off this threat. The issue of chemical protection was on everyone's mind—for the overwhelming majority, it would be their first time using the new CBRN defense equipment. Wearing the suits and masks instilled fear, even claustrophobia, by isolating the person from his or her colleagues on the battlefield. Since everyone wearing full protective gear looked the same, it was nearly impossible to identify the leaders. There were also suspicions that the detectors were not going to alarm in time for effective protective actions.

Those troops that had been in the Chemical School's Chemical Defense Training Facility understood that the equipment worked in the presence of live agent, and it was up to them to express this confidence to the troops.

This confidence was shaken when units in Kuwait examined their JSLIST bags. There was a separate bag for the trousers and the jacket, so each service member had two bags to carry. A small amount of the JSLIST bags had been mislabeled, resulting in a few people having two tops or two bottoms. At the same time, troops were afraid to open their suit bags, because this would initiate the forty-five-day life span of the suit.[7] Fortunately, the mislabeled bags were limited to about a dozen cases, due to the efforts of many individuals conducting inspections of the protective suit stockpiles. When the authorization was given to open the bags and begin wearing the suits days prior to the start of ground operations, it was a great relief for thousands of personnel who were able to ensure that they had one top and one bottom in their correct sizes. In general, contractors were showing up in theater with their own protective gear, and did not expect their host units to provide suits. Although every military unit would have two suits per individual, other precautions were made. For instance, the 3rd Infantry Division used 10 percent of its suit inventory to prepare emergency "push packages," containing the JSLIST suit, boots, gloves, and filters. These packages would be used if a frontline unit was short protective suits.

PHASE 3—DECISIVE OFFENSIVE OPERATIONS (MARCH–APRIL 03)

CENTCOM would begin conventional combat operations, including the air campaign, preparatory ground operations, and the attack to secure Baghdad and remove Saddam Hussein's regime from power on March 19, 2003. Combat operations began at 1015 Eastern Standard Time, with forty tomahawks and 2000-lb bombs dropping on "targets of opportunity" and ground forces preparing for combat. On March 20, the ground forces breached the berms between Kuwait and Iraq and advanced toward Baghdad wearing protective clothing, boots, gloves, and masks. The 3rd Infantry Division drove 140 kilometers to secure objectives in and around Tallil Air Base outside of An Nasiriyah. British armored forces drove toward Basra and the southern oil fields in the Fao Peninsula as the 1st Battalion 7th Marines moved to capture the large Rumaila oil fields prior to any sabotage efforts. The 3rd Infantry Division had planned a smoke and obscurants mission to cover their breach of the ten-kilometer deep obstacle belt, but the Marines had requested that the mission not take place so as to improve the chances of surprising Iraqi forces.

Coincidently, on March 19, the DoD CB Defense Program leadership, including Dr. Klein (OSD), General Goldfein (JRO), General Reeves (PEO), Dr. Anthony Tether (DARPA), and Dr. Stephen Younger (DTRA), was testifying in front of the House Armed Services Committee's Subcommittee on Terrorism, Unconventional Threats and Capabilities on DoD's organization, policy and programs to counter the threat of WMDs. This subcommittee, chaired by Rep. Jim Saxton (R-NJ), led an uncontroversial discussion of the armed forces' readiness for CB warfare and measures being taken to improve homeland response to terrorist CBRN incidents. Klein led a short review of CB defense support to the installation protection effort in addition to the more recent successes of the program, followed by a brief statement from General Goldfein, outlining his role in the JRO. Dr. Tether discussed DARPA's BW defense research, highlighting the ideal products that might emerge to support a response to domestic BW terrorism. General Reeves recapped the PEO's management structure maintaining equipment that was the "result of the substantial Congressional support we received since Desert Storm." Dr. Younger outlined his agency's broad role in countering WMD threats through a number of efforts, including arms control, cooperative threat reduction, offensive and defensive technology development, CBRN defense, and combat support to the CINCs. Unlike Shay's grilling meetings in October and November, this subcommittee saluted the work of the program's leaders.

The 3rd Infantry Division secured Tallil and the roads into An Nasiriyah in the early hours of March 22 and continued northwest toward As Samawah, one kilometer up Highway 8. In addition to becoming an important logistics site for future operations, Tallil represented one of the first SSE sites to be investigated. No chemical munitions were discovered at the air base. The I MEF and Task Force Tarawa (which would later rescue the survivors of the 507th Maintenance Company, ambushed at An Nasiriyah) would cross the Euphrates at An Nasiriyah and feint to the south before turning west toward Baghdad. Further northwest, 3rd Infantry Division forces continued to fight around As Samawah through March 29.

Iraq countered with five ballistic missile attacks around noon on March 20. Two Ababil-100 missiles were fired from al Basra inbound to Kuwait, aimed at the 101st Tactical Assembly area Thunder and Camp Doha. Both were intercepted by Patriot missiles. Of the three other missiles fired, one was intercepted by a Patriot and the other two fell harmlessly into the Arabian Gulf and Kuwaiti desert. The alerts caused all ground forces in Kuwait to mask up until the missiles were destroyed and it was clear that they had not been armed with chemical warheads. That observation did not reduce the stress that Saddam might still use CB-armed missiles against the large ground movements into Iraq. Iraqi forces would launch another twelve missiles against U.S. forces in Kuwait, including Ababil-100s, al-Samouds, and old Soviet Frog rockets, between March 21 and April 3. Of these, Patriot missiles intercepted six missiles.[8] The other six were not intercepted because they were not a threat to military or civilian targets.[9] Patriot missile batteries also destroyed a British Tornado and a Navy FA-18 Hornet, and locked onto an F-16 Falcon, possibly because destroying potential Iraqi airborne CB delivery systems was a higher priority than positively identifying the incoming system as hostile.[10] In all, Iraq would fire seventeen ballistic missiles against the coalition forces. None of them were SCUD missiles, and none of them carried a CB warhead. As each missile landed, Fox vehicles from the 51st Chemical Company inspected the impact sites to verify the presence or absence of CB warfare agents.

On March 21, elements of the 181st Chemical Company began to arrive, augmenting the 68th Chemical Company's decon responsibilities in southern Kuwait. A few days later, troops discovered a potential chemical factory disguised by sand at Najaf; this was later discounted as a false alarm. On CBS's *Early Show*, Generals Doesburg and Reeves were interviewed about military CB defense preparations and the fears that there still could be an attack coming. Major General Doesburg commented, "I personally think that the chances are high that we're going to find something. At this point we should not breathe a sigh of relief, even though Saddam has not used any of these weapons so far."[11]

What the Army would call "the mother of all sandstorms" hit forces in Iraq between March 25 and 27, concurrent with dwindling supplies supporting the 3rd Infantry Division and an increasingly vulnerable supply line. The 3rd Infantry Division was entering into battle against paramilitary and regular forces around Najaf on March 25. The 173rd Infantry Brigade jumped into Bashur with 965 paratroopers to link up with Kurdish forces on March 26, securing a key airfield that would support the landing of 1200 additional soldiers and vehicles from Aviano Air Base in Italy. The 101st and 82nd Airborne Divisions combat elements began to move forward on March 24 to clear the line of advance between Kuwait and Najaf and allow the 3rd Infantry Division to continue north. Each brigade of the 101st and 82nd divisions would have a decon platoon assigned to them throughout the ground offensive. The 101st Division started its deep aviation attacks against Iraqi mechanized divisions that were moving south of Baghdad toward the coalition. Lieutenant General McKiernan also called for the deployment of the 2nd Armored Cavalry Regiment on March 30 to support reconnaissance and security missions along the supply route. The 82nd's combat brigade would clear As Samawah on March 31, and the 101st's two brigades would clear out Najaf between March 30 and April 4.

CHEMICAL AND BIOLOGICAL WEAPONS SEARCHES CONTINUE

The process by which military forces would seize and exploit sensitive sites was very tightly defined. Based on a pre-war intelligence list (which included INC defector information), CENTCOM prioritized the sites, which included WMD sites, Iraqi leadership targets, U.S. soldiers missing in action (MIAs), and other intelligence. It did not include storage sites for conventional munitions or high explosives. As the ground offensive continued, the CENTCOM staff refined and updated this list. CFLCC tasked one of the ground maneuver units through V Corps or the I MEF to seize and secure specific sites as the forces moved north. V Corps worked exploitation into their near term planning, in that the headquarters identified what sites were coming up, who was responsible for coordinating with the 75th XTF, and which units were responsible for securing each site. Planners from V Corps, CFLCC, and CENTCOM updated the list as though maintaining a joint fire table; that is to say, they kept information current on a table that tracked daily operations for their subordinate units. Using this system, they could see which sites were coming up and ensure that these units were prepared to secure them. This was an important and highly visible mission, and Lieutenant General Wallace emphasized to his commanders that it was to be a top priority.

The 75th XTF deployed a CBIST in support of a special operations mission to Khurmal, a town north of Halabjah on the Iranian border. Intelligence sources had believed that al Qaeda terrorist leader Abu Musab Zarqawi had set up a chemical laboratory there, producing ricin toxin and industrial chemicals such as chlorine and hydrogen cyanide for terrorist operations in Europe. After several dozen Tomahawk missiles and precision air strikes hit the suspected training camp early in the campaign, the troops combed the site for evidence. The team found no CB agent material or munitions, but they did find three instructions on manufacturing procedures for chlorine and one for ricin toxin.[12]

On March 25, Marines securing a hospital in Nasiriyah discovered crates containing more than three thousand protective suits along with Iraqi ammunition and military uniforms. The 75th XTF searched ammunition dumps near the port city of Umm Qasr based on intelligence tips that banned weapons would be found there. These were not found in Umm Qasr or at a suspected chemical weapons plant near Najaf.[13] On March 29, they found another three hundred protective suits and protective masks, atropine injectors, two chemical decontamination vehicles, and decontamination devices. They also found huge stocks of conventional ammunition, but no weapons of mass destruction. Near Basra on the same day, British troops found a stash of protective suits and masks, nerve gas simulators, and a Geiger counter.[14] They had found more than one hundred protective masks and suits in a command post in the Rumaila oil field the week prior. U.S. and U.K. government officials and other military analysts were quick to leap on these findings as evidence that Iraq had plans to use such weapons.[15]

On March 28, JSTARS identified ten Iraqi tankers moving south from Baghdad, suspected to have left from the Latifiyah Phosgene and solid propellant production facility. There was no way to confirm exactly what the tankers held, but intelligence suspected that they could be filled with industrial phosgene. The Air Force attacked and destroyed the tankers ten kilometers north of the 1st Brigade Combat Team, 3rd Infantry Division. The brigade assumed full chemical protective posture to guard against the possibility of any downwind hazard, and waited for the 92nd Chemical Company's chemical recon platoon to arrive to confirm an all clear indication. It ended up that there was neither phosgene nor any other industrial chemical identified in the wreckage of the tankers.

On March 29, the 101st Airborne called two Fox vehicles from the 51st Chemical Company forward to investigate suspected exposure to CW agents at a military training complex at Al Hindi, an area south of Karbala. Soldiers had discovered hundreds of protective masks and suits, along with large numbers of weapons and conventional munitions. More than a dozen soldiers from the 2nd Brigade, 101st Airborne Division, had become sick following their occupation of the military complex. Their symptoms included vomiting, dizziness, and skin blotches. Suspecting exposure to chemical agents, the soldiers searched for and found about ten twenty-five-gallon barrels and three fifty-five-gallon barrels of unknown origin located in an underground bunker next to an agricultural warehouse at the same location. They tested positive for nerve agents, but people were walking around the area unprotected without showing symptoms of nerve agent poisoning. The exposed soldiers, a reporter, a CNN cameraman, and two Iraqi prisoners of war walked to a personnel decontamination point, set up by the 63rd Chemical Company, to be hosed down with a solution of water and bleach.[16]

The initial Fox readings read positive for nerve and mustard agents, causing a flurry of media attention as the troops at Aberdeen Proving Ground awaited laboratory confirmation of the samples. This event resulted in personal visits by Col. Joe Anderson, the 2nd Brigade commander, Brig. Gen. Ben Freakley, the 101st assistant division commander, and Major General Petraeus. The 75th XTF sent a team whose findings were indeterminate, so they sent samples to the 520th Theater Area Medical Laboratory in Kuwait, which determined that the chemicals were toxic organophosphate pesticides and not nerve agents. These findings were also confirmed by U.S. labs.[17]

The exploitation of sensitive sites quickly grew beyond the ability of the 75th XTF to execute with its own resources. The initial plan was to secure and assess all WMD sites as quickly as possible; disable the weapons and stop production at any facilities; exploit the intelligence sources; and destroy the munitions after the conflict. Early intelligence estimates had identified more than six hundred sites; continued intelligence sources, in addition to ground forces stumbling over suspicious sites, increased the number to more than nine hundred. CENTCOM received an average of three reports a day from the field about suspected WMD sites, although none had yielded any rewards. OSD counterproliferation policy personnel were hounding the Joint Chief's J-5/ Nuc&CP branch and CENTCOM staff daily for updates on site exploitations and findings. In addition to lacking a practiced concept of operations, the 75th XTF lacked the required personnel—the METs numbered only about twenty-five due to a shortage of technical personnel and linguists, and the site survey teams traveling with the maneuver forces numbered about fifteen. Working in a nonpermissive environment meant that they would face increasing security concerns as they ventured further into Iraq.

This mission, while politically significant, diverted operational resources from ongoing combat operations. Every commander understood that it was important to secure these sites, and had to provide NBC reconnaissance, decontamination teams, medical response, engineers, and military police to assist the SSE teams. The divisions also had to divert scarce transportation assets to the theater-level specialized teams to enable them to move samples and documents from the sites to the rear area and back to the United States. The 75th XTF had anticipated using helicopters, but aviation assets were at a premium and often not available. The increased number of sites, the quick pace of forces northward, and the large size of the military complexes combined to make the WMD exploitation mission much more logistically and operationally demanding than had been anticipated. Anyone knowledgeable about the exploits of the Army's TEU operating in Iraq during Operation Desert Storm would have anticipated these challenges.[18]

The 3rd Infantry Division was responsible for planning, targeting, executing, and reporting on 137 sensitive site exploitations. This was conducted with three site survey teams and MET Alpha (with two missions by MET Bravo). The 92nd Chemical Company also assisted in operations. The 101st Airborne Division used personnel and equipment out of its division chemical cell as its site survey team, visiting forty-five suspect sites. The division site survey teams made initial assessments of suspected WMD sites, reported their findings to higher headquarters, and made recommendations on further exploitation. For planning purposes, the divisions had been told to expect one SSE mission every forty-eight hours. This timeframe soon dropped to one every twenty-four hours, and then one every twelve hours. Each initial survey took several hours to a day to complete.

The METs followed the V Corps movement up through Iraq. They had been expecting their exploitation missions to last twenty-four to forty-eight hours, but some of the sites were large industrial parks, and took days to weeks to assess. In addition to collecting evidence, the METs and their supporting forces had to fight off the looters. Although finding and destroying the Iraqi WMD program was a major strategic objective, by the end of April coalition forces had not found any CB weapons or evidence of a WMD program. When it was clear that there were no stockpiles, the 75th XTF began focusing on identifying and apprehending people and documents associated with Iraq's former WMD program. MET Alpha had the controversial distinction of working directly with INC dissidents to continue its work.

Back in the United States, Rumsfeld was telling the media that he was sure there were WMDs in Iraq, but that coalition forces had not yet secured the areas where the weapons had been dispersed. "We know where [the WMDs] are. They're in the area around Tikrit and Baghdad and east, west, south and north somewhat." [19] The coalition forces would remain wary about the potential threat as well. The BIDS units began moving into Iraq behind the combat forces. The 7th Chemical Company, one of its BIDS platoons, and other chemical defense assets moved into Tallil air base to conduct twenty-four-hour CB warfare agent surveillance starting around April 2 (Figure 7-1).

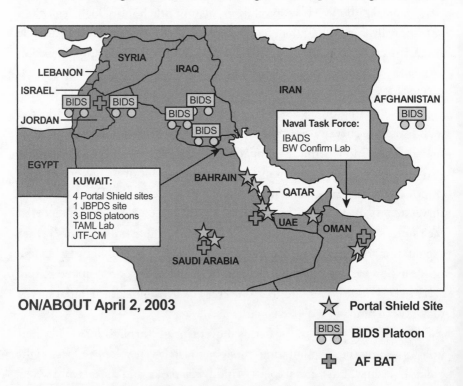

ON/ABOUT April 2, 2003

☆ **Portal Shield Site**

[BIDS] **BIDS Platoon**

✚ **AF BAT**

FIGURE 7-1 *Location of Primary Biological Detector Assets*

The 5th BIDS platoon of 7th Chemical would collocate with the 11th Attack Helicopter Regiment as that unit moved north. The 59th Chemical and its two platoons in Kuwait would move forward to cover V Corps' rear area, eventually stopping at a logistics support area just south of Baghdad.

THE MARCH INTO BAGHDAD

The operational pause had allowed 3rd Infantry Division time to organize and prepare to pass through the Karbala Gap and west of Baghdad. Between March 30–31, V Corps executed a series of limited tactical operations against Iraqi forces south of the Karbala Gap, in part to divert Iraqi attention from the intended river crossing and the move toward Baghdad. The push through Karbala was the best operational maneuver option for the mechanized force to approach Baghdad, because it avoided urban areas, rivers, and the soft agricultural lands along the Euphrates River. However, the gap narrowed to eighteen hundred meters wide with two access roads to the city of Karbala on the east and the Barh al-Milh Lake on the west, presenting an opportunity for defenders to pound any forces negotiating the gap. Simultaneously, Marine forces seized the town of Kut, and continued to move toward the east side of Baghdad.

The concern was that Iraqi forces would target the 3rd Infantry Division and I MEF with both conventional and chemical munitions attacks as these forces took Karbala and Kut. If Iraqi forces used BM-21's and chemical-filled rockets, U.S. forces could be saturated with nerve agent. Lt. Col. David Velazquez, the 3rd Infantry Division's chemical officer, planned to position decon sites to the north and south of the gap. Both recon and decon platoons would support the movement of any forces passing through the gap. Because of operational losses of two M12A1 decon systems, the division was forced to take the lightweight M17 decon systems from the battalions to augment the decon sites. Initial smoke and obscurant plans included the use of M58 smoke generators, smoke pots, and artillery-delivered smoke to conceal the crossing of the Karbala Gap, but the logistics supply line had been so overextended that they could not get enough fog oil to the preplanned cache sites. The priority was on moving ammunition forward, so the deliberate smoke operation was cancelled. Instead, division artillery assets created a limited smoke screen.

CENTCOM's ground forces entered the Red Zone, a figurative circle around Baghdad one hundred miles in diameter, expecting a last-gasp CB weapons attack. Captured Iraqi soldiers and electronic intercepts of Iraqi military communications indicated that Saddam had authorized the Medina Division to take chemical weapons for possible use against forces approaching Baghdad. U.S. military officers suggested that Iraqi artillery systems might be well hidden enough to avoid attack, and use chemical agents to stunt the U.S. offensive.[20] Military analysts in Washington D.C. opined that Iraq would use persistent chemical agents as defensive barriers around the city. CENTCOM spokesman Brig. Gen. Vince Brooks commented, "We don't think the fighting is over yet. And so there are still options available to the regime, including the use of weapons of mass destruction." Rumsfeld would not specify any specific plans for retaliation. "We've allowed as how we thought they'd best not use those weapons, and I don't want to go beyond that," he said in a Pentagon press brief.[21] Loren Thomspon of the Lexington Institute warned, "I'm certain they have [WMDs] and I'm certain they are actively considering using them at this moment."[22] Military forces wore their protective suits and boots around the clock, keeping their rubber gloves and protective masks ready at their sides. CFLCC targeted any suspected Iraqi artillery or missile system they could locate as well as potential firing locations. The expected chemical weapons attacks at the Karbala Gap and within the Red Zone did not materialize, and the forces continued on.

The 2nd Armored Cavalry Regiment arrived in Kuwait on April 4, joining the 4th Infantry Division that had begun offloading its equipment on March 25. The 2nd Chemical Battalion brought a heavy decon company, the 44th Chemical Company, and a mechanized smoke generator company, the 46th Chemical Company, from Fort Hood. These two chemical companies, plus the 11th Chemical Company (decon), would initially be attached to the 4th Infantry Division. Each of the three maneuver brigades in the 4th Infantry Division would receive a smoke generator platoon, but none would conduct any smoke missions. The 44th Chemical had two decon platoons and two Fox recon platoons. It would be attached to the lead brigade, with a decon platoon, a Fox recon squad, and two smoke generator platoons. The other decon platoon and a Fox recon platoon would remain with 2nd Chemical Battalion, which was supporting V Corps.[23] Fox squads would be attached to the 3rd Brigade, 4th Infantry Division, and to the 46th Chemical Company. After preparing for combat, the units moved out toward Baghdad. False alarms from chemical detectors and incoming missile alarms sounding at the Kuwaiti desert camps continued, causing forces to don their protective suits and masks despite the 85°–100° heat.[24] The 2nd Armored Cavalry Regiment joined the 82nd Airborne Division at As Samawah on April 8, and the 4th Infantry moved toward Baghdad to start combat operations in northern Iraq in mid-April. The 172nd Chemical Company (Mechanized Smoke), out of Fort Riley, Kansas, arrived in Kuwait on April 8. They would remain in Kuwait for nearly a year, supporting the rear area security mission around the various Army bases.

Further north, Major General Petraeus, noting the lack of any chemical attacks against the 3rd Infantry Division despite their incursions into Baghdad, authorized the 101st Airborne Division personnel to reduce its protective posture, allowing them to shed their JSLIST suits for the first time in weeks.[25] On the evening of April 7, a mechanized task force 1-63rd Armor, 1st Infantry Division, deployed from Germany to join the 173rd Infantry Brigade at Kirkuk to assist in engaging and defeating Iraqi units in the north. Two days prior, the third BIDS platoon of the 310th Chemical Company had deployed from Afghanistan to support the 173rd conducting biological surveillance operations. The Kurdish forces were concerned that Saddam might use CB warfare agents against them as he did at Halabjah in 1988.

On April 2, the 3-69th Armor Battalion, commanded by Lt. Col. Ernest "Rock" Marcone, would be the first 3rd Infantry Division asset across the Euphrates River at bridges north of Karbala. It would be a contested crossing, and the bridges had been prepared for demolition. The Iraqi defenders attempted to blow the bridge, but only a part of the northern span was damaged. The 5th platoon, 92nd Chemical Company provided smoke support to cover the task force's movement over the river. The 6th platoon, 68th Chemical Company, was also conducting a smoke operation nearby. Artillery smoke against the far side of the bridge had no effect due to the unstable weather conditions. The platoon set up their M58 smoke generators northwest of the bridge and began pumping smoke in the late afternoon. As a forty-minute haze dropped across the bridge, Bradley vehicles and Abrams tanks from the 3-69th Armor Battalion crossed the bridge and engaged the Iraqi defenders, and engineers moved to repair the bridge. On April 3, the 3rd Infantry Division initiated its attack on the Baghdad International Airport, advancing across the tarmac with two Fox vehicles in the lead. An NBC defense team, led by the 181st Chemical Company and including a BIDS platoon from the 7th Chemical Company, immediately moved to the airport to support operations. Two days later, the division began its first "thunder run" into downtown Baghdad. Despite numerous counterattacks by Iraqi irregulars and remnants of the Iraqi divisions, the coalition forces drove steadily into the capital. On April 10, the 3rd Infantry Division effectively bisected the city with two brigade combat teams. Later that same day, Army and Marine forces met north of Baghdad and completed the isolation of the city. The campaign progressed rapidly upon the fall of Baghdad and the general collapse of organized resistance. Kirkuk, Mosul, and Tikrit fell to coalition forces within the next week.

On April 4, 3rd Infantry Division forces took the Al QaQaa Government Enterprise, a massive nine-square mile industrial complex associated with Iraq's nuclear weapons program located about thirty kilometers south of Baghdad. Among the more than one thousand bunkers and buildings, they found TNT, detonation cord, and thousands of small boxes, each holding three vials of white powder, along with documents in Arabic that dealt with how to engage in chemical warfare, and nerve agent antidote kits.[26] Iraq had rebuilt a phosgene production plant there as well, which might have had a role in an Iraqi CW program. Initial speculation was that these vials of white powder were decontamination kits, but later testing revealed this powder to be explosives (possibly the missing RDX and HMX explosives announced in October 2004). U.S. troops overran Salman Pak, the former BW research and development facility, on April 6. Neither the camp nor the facility yielded evidence to substantiate the intelligence claims made before the war. On April 7, a Reuter news report noted the discovery of twenty medium range missiles allegedly equipped containing chemical warheads with nerve and mustard, near Baghdad. To all intents and purposes, these missiles appeared to be Soviet BM-21 122-mm rockets. Defense Secretary Rumsfeld said it might take days to resolve positive confirmation of the warheads' compositions. While the samples were going to Fort Detrick, CENTCOM had no comment on the results of interim testing, but General Brooks did comment, "Initial reports were 'yes, it could potentially be [banned weapons].' "We do not know enough at this point to say [the report] should be discounted or that we have found some weapons of mass destruction for use." [27] The results later confirmed that these were merely rockets with conventional high explosive warheads. On April 14, an unidentified Iraqi scientist told coalition forces that he knew where the WMDs were, but the lead only uncovered industrial chemicals.

The 75th XTF, with support from the 101st Airborne Division, sent a large team into a massive ammunition manufacturing and storage plant near Karbala, finding eleven twenty-foot by twenty-foot metal containers of laboratory chemicals, canisters of radioactive cesium isotopes, dual use biological equipment, and thousands of documents buried among the fifty buildings in the complex. Some considered this proof of a covert Iraqi WMD program, but it was not clear for what purpose this equipment had actually been used. Despite weeks of searching, no evidence of actual weapons was found.[28] They had less luck in Baghdad, when on April 26, a team investigating an alleged chemical munitions workshop suffered two dead and five wounded when the warehouse exploded in flames. There were no munitions or equipment found, leading some to suspect that the warehouse had been deliberately booby trapped and set up for the exploitation teams. On April 27, 4th Infantry Division soldiers found fourteen fifty-five-gallon drums near trucks and missiles north of Tikrit. Their chemical specialists noted positive readings for mustard agent and sarin, using their CAMs. The next day, sensitive site team #4 inspected their find with more sophisticated equipment and declared that the drums did not hold CW agents, but appeared to contain liquid rocket fuel. The Iraqis used a combination of fuming nitric acid and jet fuel for their liquid-fueled rockets, a mixture that caused numerous false positives with the M22 ACADAs and CAMs. The manual M256A1 detector kits were the only reliable means of detection in this case.

On April 25, the 2nd Brigade of the 101st Airborne Division reported heavy looting in central Mosul, and that the Iraqi citizens might have been exposed to chemicals there. Upon investigating, it appeared that the Iraqi citizens had raided several agricultural warehouses to steal 230 fifty-five-gallon drums that once held acids, pesticides, and herbicides. They wanted the drums to hold gasoline for their personal use. In their haste, they dumped nearly eleven thousand gallons of chemicals inside the warehouse and onto the city streets, creating a thick goop that covered the pavement. Although there were children vomiting in the streets and scores of dead animals prevalent in the area, the residents refused to leave due to the fear that their houses would be looted. Because this represented an immediate health risk to the populace, the

101st created a remediation task force including a platoon from the 63rd Chemical Company, engineers, medics, public affairs personnel, and interpreters. The chemical company used its decontamination apparatuses and three hundred gallons of DF-200 to coat the spill, including an area within two storage buildings. Engineers then brought in 120 tons of dirt to cap the contamination. This six-hour mission was accomplished in full military protective gear, and the team used their CAMs to monitor the level of organophosphates (which demonstratively dropped following the completion of the remediation mission). The attached medics evaluated that the hazard had been significantly reduced, and other engineer units would determine the need for further remediation.

On April 21, Lt. Gen. Jay Garner (Ret.) arrived in Baghdad as the head of the U.S.-led interim administration to oversee the beginning of reconstruction efforts—he would be replaced by Paul Bremer on May 11. On May 1, President Bush announced from the deck of the U.S. aircraft carrier *Abraham Lincoln* that "major combat operations in Iraq have ended." By July, many of the chemical units had received their redeployment orders to return to the United States. However, the search for Iraq's WMDs had barely begun.

PHASE 4—POST HOSTILITIES

The final phase of combat operations included the gradual transition from combat to stability and support operations (SASO), including humanitarian assistance and reconstruction. The 75th XTF moved into Baghdad to continue its search for WMD program efforts. The teams had searched about one hundred of the nine hundred sites originally identified by the intelligence community, and the envisioned stocks of CB munitions had not materialized. Searching for individual sites across Iraq was clearly not working; the resources required to secure and exploit the sites, including EOD and chemical specialists, linguists, and intelligence and security personnel continued to drain CENTCOM forces. Many of the Army's chemical defense units began preparations to deploy back to the United States. The remaining chemical defense companies supported post-conflict operations by acting as fire-fighting details and executing other nontraditional security missions such as convoy security and guarding ammunition supply points.

On May 2, U.S. forces nabbed Abdul Tawab Mullah Hwaish, number sixteen and the ten of hearts in CENTCOM's "most wanted" deck of cards. As the minister of military industrialization, he was thought to have extensive knowledge of Iraq's secret weapons programs. He joined Jaffar Dhai Jaffar, the founder and lead scientist of Iraq's nuclear weapons program, already in U.S. custody. Dr. Huda Salih Mahdi Ammash, alias "Mrs. Anthrax" and the five of hearts, was considered to be the lead government civilian overseeing the Iraqi BW program. She surrendered to coalition forces on May 4. Dr. Rihab Rashid Taha, alias "Dr. Germ" was taken into custody about a week later. She was considered to be Iraq's top BW scientist. Special operations forces had raided her house in mid-April, hoping to find her and evidence of Iraq's BW program. She admitted that she had produced BW agents, but only as part of a defensive program. General Ali Hassan al-Majid al-Tikriti, alias "Chemical Ali," was captured on August 21 by British forces. This man was the king of spades in the "most wanted" deck, having been linked to the gassing of Iraqi civilians at Halabjah as well as leading the crackdown on Kurdish dissidents after the first Gulf War. Military and civilian interrogators would grill these individuals and other Iraqi regime members on the whereabouts of Iraq's former WMD program, to little avail. All would claim that the Iraq's WMD program was nonexistent.

The big catch for CENTCOM was the purported discovery of the mobile Iraqi BW laboratories that Secretary Powell had talked about in February. On April 19, Kurdish forces near Mosul turned over a specialized tractor-trailer to U.S. special forces, the design, equipment, and layout of which was very similar to the descriptions that Powell had presented to the United Nations. In late April, U.S. forces discovered a mobile laboratory truck that could have been used to support either BW or legitimate toxicology research. In early May, the 101st Airborne Division found a second mobile BW trailer at the Al Kindi rocket and research development facility in Mosul. The first mobile trailer appeared functional, but the second had been stripped of equipment and its tires, and was obviously not operational. In both cases, no actual BW agents or munitions were found. The description of equipment bolted down within the trucks and the thought that bleach had been used to clean out their interiors led U.S. forces to suspect that this was the missing link to Iraq's BW program. Stephen Cambone (now the Under Secretary of Defense for Intelligence—USD [I]) and Vice Adm. Lowell Jacoby (Director, DIA) announced the finds to the media on May 7.[29] In an interview with Polish television on May 29, President Bush announced, "We found the weapons of mass destruction. We found biological laboratories. . . . They're illegal. They're against the United Nation's resolutions, and we've so far discovered two. And we'll find more weapons as time goes on. . . . we found them."[30]

Except that this announcement was a bit premature—the vehicles were not mobile BW labs. Although the official DoD position would remain that the only consistent, logical purpose for these vehicles was to produce BW agents, the vehicles were in fact nearly identical to U.S. military vehicles (AN/TMQ-42 trailers) used to produce hydrogen to fill weather balloons for meteorological predictions supporting artillery units. The canvas tarps covering the sides were designed to let excess heat and gas escape, and would hardly allow for the optimal production of BW agents within the trailer. There were no vacuum pumps or autoclaves in the trailers, equipment normally associated with BW production. Both British and U.S. State Department intelligence analysts agreed in June that the vehicles had been misidentified, but the DIA and CIA maintained the capability was a convenient cover for their real purpose.[31]

On May 7, Stephen Cambone and Admiral Jacoby announced at a Pentagon news briefing that Maj. Gen. Keith Dayton, operations director at the DIA, would head the Iraq Survey Group (ISG), a new organization to take over the 75th XTF's search for WMDs. Judith Miller's constant reporting on the activities of the 75th XTF had exposed the poor efficacy of its operations to OSD senior leaders, and they wanted to see more progress immediately. Planning for this new organization had begun almost as soon as the ground offensive had started, with Charles Duelfer and other civilian inspectors deploying to Kuwait at the end of March. In addition, the ISG would interrogate individuals and collect documents and media related to terrorism, war crimes, POW and MIA issues, and other potential crimes related to Hussein's regime. In doing so, the ISG would consolidate all intelligence collection efforts in theater and analyze and develop intelligence elements within Iraq, coordinating with intelligence communities in the United States. The group would consist of about fourteen hundred personnel, including investigators, translators, intelligence, and special weapons experts from the United States, Australia, and Britain, reporting through CENTCOM to the Secretary of Defense.[32] Rather pointedly, the Bush administration refused any UN offers to support the inspections. The ISG would set up an analytical intelligence center in Qatar and a forward operating base in Baghdad.

Dr. David Kay, the former UNSCOM chief nuclear weapons inspector, would lead the WMD exploitation effort and would report to George Tenet (many of the WMD team members came from the intelligence agency). His appointment was announced on June 11, 2003. Kay had been in Iraq reporting as an NBC news advisor in May, and had the opportunity to see firsthand how the 75th XTF had done. In his words, the 75th was "badly led, badly managed, totally unsuccessful, and chaotic. So the administration needed to walk away from that, and it needed to walk away with someone who had a clue as to how to do it." [33] The 455th Chemical Brigade would form the headquarters to support teams searching for CB weapons information and stockpiles, moving to set up headquarters in Baghdad in June, along with the 450th Chemical Battalion, the 314th Chemical Company, the Army's TEU, DTRA, and others. The 450th would take over garrison operations from the 75th XTF and run "Camp Slayer," named after their motto "Dragon Slayers." Because of the lack of NBC defense duties, the 450th's personnel would serve as force protection for the camp and convoys traveling on the main supply routes, provide security for the ISG teams searching for WMD evidence at sites, and log and process captured documents. The 75th XTF headquarters and troops that had been in the survey teams would return home to the United States about two weeks after the ISG began its operations in June.

On May 13, troops investigated a number of fifty-five-gallon drums at Al Taji, north of Baghdad, which had tested as chemical agents by local use of M256A1 kits and CAMs. Al Taji had been the former site of several chemical weapons ammunition bunkers. Twenty-two 4th Infantry Division soldiers were exposed to an unknown industrial chemical leaking from a fifty-five-gallon drum found in a warehouse. They were decontaminated and evacuated to a combat support hospital, but none were seriously injured. Further analysis from an NBC recon vehicle proved that the industrial chemical was not a warfare agent. Two days later, two soldiers attempting to disarm an improvised explosive device, a rigged 155-mm projectile, showed low-level chemical agent exposure symptoms when the round detonated prior to the team rendering it inoperable. The ISG examined the round and declared that it had probably held a binary version of nerve agent. Because of the age and configuration of the shell, its actual effects had been muted.[34] CENTCOM also confirmed that the 75th XTF had found a mustard-filled mortar shell about two weeks prior, but the agent was found to be inert. While some speculated that Iraqi insurgents were deliberately selecting chemical munitions from the former regime's stockpile, no other shells were found. These unmarked shells represented forgotten remnants of Saddam's pre-1990 CW program, although the ISG failed to qualify their findings with any suppositions.

In mid-May, V Corps sent USANCA's Nuclear Disarmament Team of eleven soldiers to Iraq's Tuwaitha Nuclear Research Center to assess the quantity and condition of nuclear material stored there. Initial indications were that local Iraqis had pilfered the former nuclear facility prior to coalition forces securing it. Near the end of June, U.S. forces found three hundred bags of castor beans labeled "urea"—a fertilizer compound—in a former brake fluid plant. Although these beans could be used to make ricin toxin, they were also used to make castor oil and fertilizer. Other analysts noted that Iraq had tried to weaponize ricin, but the attempts were not successful.

At a Pentagon news briefing on May 30, Cambone reiterated the administration's belief that there were chemical and biological weapons in Iraq when the war started.[35] In early June, both President Bush and Prime Minister Blair refuted accusations that the available intelligence did not support their administrations' claims about Iraq's WMD program. Blair said, "I stand absolutely 100 percent behind the evidence, based on intelligence, that we presented to people. . . . I have no doubt at all, as I said to you earlier, that the assessments that were made by the British intelligence services will turn out to be correct."[36] On June 5, President Bush told troops in Qatar "No terrorist network will gain weapons of mass destruction from the Iraqi regime, because the Iraqi regime is no more."[37] On this same trip, he had asked Paul Bremer, "Are you in charge of finding WMD?" Neither Bremer nor General Franks would own up to that mission. Finally, someone told Bush that he thought it was Cambone's job to lead the WMD search. "Who?" Bush asked.[38] Doing the talk show circuit on June 8, both Rice and Powell expressed confidence that Iraq's WMD program would be uncovered. Powell told Fox News, "I'm sure more evidence and more proof will come forward as we go down this road,"[39] a phrase repeated by Rumsfeld and his staff to the press.

Lt. Gen. John Abizaid commented that the ISG would have better luck finding the Iraqi stockpiles examining captured documents and interviewing captured Iraqi officials. Were the ISG to find any CB weapon stockpiles or even evidence that such production was imminent, the administration could have validated its claims that a preemptive war was necessary. Despite more than four months of effort, nothing would emerge to justify the pre-war WMD claims. Condoleezza Rice and other members of the Bush administration spent much of the summer defending their views that the trailers were indeed capable of manufacturing BW agents; that Iraq had sought uranium "yellow cake" from Niger; that the aluminum tubes sought by Iraq were capable of being used in uranium enrichment centrifuges; and that terrorists had actively collaborated with the Iraqi regime. Leaders of the House intelligence committee claimed that, if any judgment errors had been made, it was the result of the U.S. intelligence community's use of largely outdated, circumstantial, and uncertain information.[40] On July 11, George Tenet publicly apologized for allowing the statement on Iraq's alleged seeking of yellow cake from Niger remain in the president's State of the Union address in January. At the same time, he also noted that he had tried to correct administration statements in the state of the union address without success.

On September 9, 2003, both Powell and Rice refuted the media's claim that, according to the DIA report, there was no reliable information proving the existence of Iraq's CW program. Powell noted that the report stated in the next sentence that chemical weapons had been dispersed to units, while Rice told CBS' *Face the Nation* that the sentence in question had been taken out of context. "There is a bit of revisionist history going on here," she said. "The truth of the matter is that repeated directors of central intelligence, repeated reports by intelligence agencies around the world, repeated reports by UN inspectors asking hard questions of Saddam Hussein, and tremendous efforts by this regime to conceal and hide what it was doing clearly give a picture of a regime that had weapons of mass destruction and was determined to conceal them." Admiral Jacoby acknowledged that DIA had no hard evidence of Iraqi chemical weapons but believed that Iraq had a program to produce them, as the report stated.[41]

David Kay met with Congress on October 2 to tell the legislators that the ISG had found no NBC weapon stockpiles in Iraq. His first words emphasized that this was an interim report, and that it was far too early to reach definitive conclusions about the true state of Iraq's WMD program. Although the group found no weapons, he could not state that WMDs did or did not exist before the war. What the ISG had found was dozens of "WMD-related program activities" and significant amounts of equipment that had been concealed from UN inspectors. There was no evidence that

Iraq had actually attempted to build nuclear weapons or produce fissile material after 1998, when the inspectors had left the country. Although Iraq had the resources to restart its program, there was no evidence of any efforts to actually do so.

In the BW program area, the ISG had found a collection of vials holding reference strains that should have been declared to the United Nations. One of the samples was a strain of botulinum that could have been the source for a BW agent production line. Interviews with Iraqi scientists seemed to demonstrate that they had conducted BW research along with overt research on nonpathogenic organisms. Officially, the ISG was not willing to rule out the possibility that the two trailers identified as mobile BW laboratories were, in fact, definitely used for that purpose. The group was still conducting interviews with Iraqi officials reportedly involved in that effort. No BW munitions or stockpiles had been found, nor, for that matter, any CW munitions.

While interviews with Iraqi officials indicated that Saddam had been interested in restarting his CW program, evidence suggested that Operation Desert Fox (conducted in 1998) and the years of UN sanctions had effectively eliminated Iraq's ability to develop, produce, or fill new CW munitions. It was possible that Saddam had hidden chemical weapons after the first Gulf War amongst the many conventional ammunition dumps; Kay estimated that they had only searched ten of the 130 ammunition storage points within Iraq. Each storage point could exceed fifty square miles and hold upwards of six-hundred thousand tons of artillery shells, rockets, bombs, and other ammunition. So although no chemical munitions had been found, it was not to say that authoritatively, there were none.

The ISG had had more luck in the area of delivery systems, noting that the long-range ballistic missile effort that UNMOVIC had noted in January 2003 was a clear breach of UN restrictions following the 1991 Gulf War. Work on converting SA-2 surface-to-air missiles to surface-to-surface missiles had begun in early 2003, which would have given Iraq a capability to launch missiles with a range of 250 kilometers. In addition to the al-Samoud missile, Iraq had been working on increasing the range of their missiles to over 400 kilometers. While no SCUDs or SCUD rocket fuel had been discovered, the ISG did find a robust UAV program effort. It was unclear if any missile or UAV had been designed to disperse CB warfare agents.[42]

The administration's reaction was predictable; they had already begun stressing Iraq's former aspirations to develop WMDs, as opposed to actually having the weapons themselves. Powell pointed to Iraq's complicity in the massacre of civilians at Halabjah in 1988 as evidence of Saddam's motivations and capabilities. The idea that Saddam might someday use weapons of mass destruction or that terrorists might acquire such weapons was ample justification to remove his regime. This was in contrast to the previously held belief that he did own these weapons and terrorists were actively seeking to get these weapons from him. Wolfowitz preferred to stress the evil, dictatorial nature of the Iraqi regime.[43] Vice President Cheney would continue to emphasize, in speeches between October and December, that the biggest threat of all was the possibility of terrorists acquiring chemical, biological, and nuclear weapons.[44]

In early January 2004, the ISG released the Joint Captured Material Exploitation Center to return back to the United States, freeing up about four hundred people and reducing their strength to about a thousand personnel. In the second week of January, Danish troops found thirty-six 120-mm mortar shells that were believed to hold some kind of liquid chemical agent, possibly mustard agent. The shells had been buried in a dried-up marsh in southeast Iraq near Qurnah, north of Basra, and were probably excess ordnance from the 1980s war between the two countries. Test results released a week later confirmed that the shells held no CW agent. By March, ISG reports indicated the belief that Iraq's WMD program had effectively ended in 1994, if not earlier.

David Kay formally resigned from the ISG in late January 2004, having announced his intent to leave the group in mid-December. Charles Duelfer, who had served as the deputy executive chairman of UNSCOM, took his place. In testimony to the Senate Armed Services Committee on January 28, Kay said in reference to Iraq's WMD program, "Let me begin by saying, we were almost all wrong, and I certainly include myself here . . . it is highly unlikely that there were large stockpiles of deployed militarized chemical and biological weapons there."[45] Kay blamed the results on a general failure of human and technical intelligence collection and analysis. On the talk show circuit that weekend, Condoleezza Rice defended the effort to invade Iraq based on the impression that Saddam represented a "gathering threat" that the U.S. government could not afford to leave in power.

These statements reiterated President Bush's 2004 State of the Union address, where he referenced Kay's report as identifying "dozens of weapons of mass destruction-related program activities and significant amounts of equipment." Bush noted that, had the U.S. government failed to act, Iraq's WMD program would have continued, and a world without Saddam Hussein was a better and safer place. While true, it remains troubling that the main justification for the war had been existing, not potential, CB weapons, and there had been a number of preparations based on that assumption. Since May 2004, the ISG's finds were limited to pre-1991 manufactured forty-one Sakr-18 and eight Buraq CW rockets, none of which could be effectively launched due to their poor physical state. Of the forty-one Sakr rockets, Iraqi civilians had poured petroleum and a pesticide into five of them (hoping to gain monetary rewards from the coalition forces for turning in "chemical" weapons), and the remainder were empty. In the ISG's final report in March 2005, Charles Duelfer noted that, while he could not rule out the possibility that WMDs were evacuated to Syria before the war, it was "unlikely that an official transfer of WMD material from Iraq to Syria took place." Now, the U.S. military has to address the fact that Iraq had no CB weapons to use against its forces, let alone a capability to produce them.

There are two valid points of view, with a number of postulations, as to what happened to the WMD intelligence. Either Saddam had a WMD program in place or in development, or he didn't have a WMD program but wanted one. If he had a program in place, as the Bush administration believed, Saddam either (1) moved the weapons and material to Syria; (2) hid them so well that no one can find the (relatively) small stockpiles; or (3) destroyed the weapons and materials between December 1998 and March 2003; and (4) continued to destroy evidence of WMD-program related efforts as coalition forces invaded his country and took Baghdad. All of these theories have been suggested by the Bush administration and its supporters. According to some public polls in 2005, up to a third of the American populace still believed that Saddam had WMDs as the U.S. forces invaded Iraq, despite the complete lack of evidence to support that presumption.[46]

The ISG's findings suggest that Saddam didn't have a WMD program after the end of the first Gulf War. The Iraqi scientist "Dr. Germ" detailed how her staff carted off anthrax and dumped the chemically deactivated agent near a presidential palace in July 1991, on orders to destroy all bioweapons agents immediately.[47] This leads us to question why Saddam didn't just admit it and let the inspectors have free reign. One argument was that he needed the perception of owning a WMD program as a matter of prestige among other Arab nations, despite the continuing economic sanctions and UN inspections. It is reasonable that he felt the need to brandish a WMD program as a strategic counter to Israel's, Syria's, and especially Iran's programs. It was a convenient bluff, and he may have thought that the UN inspectors would have gathered enough contrary evidence to deter a U.S. invasion, especially in the presence of Iran's growing nuclear weapons program. Another possibility is that he needed the threat of WMDs as a stick to keep the Shi'ite and Kurdish populations in line, and if he admitted that he had no such weapons, these internal adversaries would become emboldened. It was probably an untenable position for him to admit that he had no WMD program and had allowed four to seven years of unnecessary sanctions and inspections to continue, resulting in hardships on his loyal subjects and military units.[48]

Moving On

In an address to the National Defense University in March 2003, Paul Wolfowitz told the audience: "As short as this campaign was, I think it made abundantly clear what few fully understood before—that chemical and biological defenses are classic examples of what we came to call low-density/high-demand assets. Or, as Secretary Rumsfeld said, 'That's just another euphemism for something we didn't buy enough of.' They are highly specialized capabilities that are called upon to meet many mission needs worldwide at the same time. As we look to the future, it is clear that the chem-bio defense mission is not going to go away. We must ensure sufficient forces to undertake the mission at home and abroad."[49] However, when DoD budget discussions held a year later raised the possibility of increasing the FY 2006–2011 DoD CB defense POM budget by $3.5 billion to address critical capability gaps and inability to fully meet the 1-4-2-1 defense strategy, the answer was mixed. Although OSD had agreed to fund $2.1 billion in overall increases, the majority of the funding went to basic research, building a new biodefense campus at Fort Detrick, modernizing DoD's aging CB defense test and evaluation infrastructure, and basic lab research. No funds went to procuring currently fielded equipment, because the emphasis in Rumsfeld's transformation agenda was on developing new capabilities. It appeared that DoD had not believed that they needed to prepare for CB defense as much as they had to develop missile defense efforts and threaten massive retaliation if attacked by such weapons. Once again, rhetoric was not matching reality.

In testimony to the Senate Armed Services Committee in February 2004, Rumsfeld noted that it was the consensus of the intelligence community, the Clinton and Bush administrations, Congress, and several countries that Saddam was pursuing weapons of mass destruction. So where were they? He theorized that:

- it could be that the WMDs had never existed in the first place, that Saddam's scientists had fooled him or that Saddam had bluffed his neighbors, but that was "unlikely."

- it could be that the WMDs had existed, but that Saddam had moved them to another country. Syria was high on some people's lists.

- the WMDs existed up to the time of the invasion, and the weapons were dispersed and hidden throughout Iraq (in which case the ISG might find them).

- perhaps the WMDs existed but were destroyed just prior to the conflict, or that there were only small amounts of CB warfare agents with a dual-purpose industrial surge capability to rapidly produce more (although had this been the case, the ISG should have found evidence of this capability).[50]

Given the stakes of initiating a preventive war, the intelligence supporting this action should have been more solid. The comparison of policy officials discussing their confidence about Saddam's WMD program to post-war comments casts doubts on similar administration comments about North Korea, Syria, and Iran.

The ISG continued to toil through thousands of documents, numerous interviews with Iraqi scientists, and many trips to facilities and suspect storage sites. In October 2004, more than a year and a half after Dr. Kay's initial interim report, the ISG has not discovered any WMD program-related activities or munitions stockpiles to add to those that had been discovered in the first few months. While the DoD had done its best to prepare for a CB warfare environment, investing hundreds of millions of dollars into crash efforts to ensure the U.S. military was fully protected, it turned out that there was nothing to protect against. Did that mean that future forces should neglect passive defense capabilities and rely on threats of massive retaliation and missile defense systems? Probably not, but the lack of WMD findings in Iraq did little to provide evidence to support requests for billions of dollars for CBRN defense equipment. Whether DoD adequately prepares for future conflicts that may include CB weapons is now questionable in light of the lessons learned from this conflict.

President Bush talked to the National Defense University in February 2004 to discuss his views on the future of U.S. efforts to combat WMD proliferation. He talked about the challenges of addressing Iran's and North Korea's nuclear weapons programs, A.Q. Khan's efforts in Pakistan to export nuclear technology and equipment to potentially hostile countries, and Libya's announcement that it was going to dismantle its nuclear and chemical weapons program (after more than a decade of diplomatic efforts). He discussed the international Proliferation Security Initiative and its goals to interdict shipments of WMD and missile-related equipment and technology that were being delivered to adversarial countries, either by air or by sea. The initiative had been announced in May 2003, prior to a G8 summit meeting; eleven nations had initially signed up to support the effort. Since then, the cooperating countries have held numerous exercises to prepare for such interdiction efforts, which would have to rely on intelligence analysis for direction on which ships and aircraft were carrying such material.

The president also called for countries to criminalize proliferation, increase export controls, and enact better security for sensitive materials within their borders. An extension of this was increased efforts to dismantle, destroy, and secure weapons and materials remaining in the former Soviet WMD arsenal. President Bush had obtained an agreement from the G8 summit members to support these programs, with $20 billion over ten years, half of which would be supplied by the United States. He called for increased efforts to field civilian nuclear reactors that would not be used to create fissile material suitable for nuclear weapons, and increased IAEA capability to verify that nations were complying with their treaty obligations. His remarks, focusing on the threat of nuclear weapons and terrorist desire for weapons of mass destruction, did not address the vexing issue of how to deal with future nonnuclear adversaries that have small stockpiles of CB weapons in their arsenal; not enough to threaten national security, but enough to cause problems for regional combat operations. That challenge remains for the DoD to address.

CHAPTER 8

LESSONS LEARNED

*It should be the duty of every soldier to reflect on the experiences of the past,
in the endeavor to discover improvements, in his particular
sphere of action, which are practicable in the immediate future.*

—B. H. LIDDELL HART, BRITISH MILITARY STRATEGIST

T he counterproliferation community should see Operation Iraqi Freedom as a major success, considering the robust efforts conducted by special operations forces searching for WMD sites and the improved active defense efforts of Air Force pilots and Army missile defense units. Although untested, the improved passive defense capabilities in the combat forces and the potential capabilities within the JTF-CM demonstrated that the U.S. military understood and applied all four pillars of its counterproliferation strategy; counterforce, active defense, passive defense, and consequence management. Perhaps the one failing of the new strategy was that the four pillars still didn't interact very well. Each area had its own peculiar stovepipe of communication. The special operations task force reported directly to CENTCOM but not the other counterproliferation forces. The active defense units did not directly communicate with the passive defense units that would have responded to Iraqi CB strikes even if their weapons had been intercepted by missile defenses. The consequence management task force was committed to a number of tasks other than CB defense and required far too much augmentation from U.S. forces to be considered completely effective. But overall, the counterproliferation actions in 2003 were much improved over the improvised attempts to counter Iraq's use of CB weapons in 1991.

One of the major lessons of this conflict stems from the continued failure of combat units to train and sustain their personnel for CB warfare conditions. For instance, a number of military units deployed without checking their protective masks or having them validated with the unit's M41 protective assessment test system. As had happened in the fall of 1990, the chemical defense officers and NCOs within the combat units had to retrain their personnel on both individual and collective NBC defense skills. Troops intent on personal survival can quickly absorb and retain individual skills; the ability of combat units to survive and sustain combat operations in the presence of CB warfare agents is not so easily developed or retained. Had CB warfare occurred, it is likely that many individuals would have survived, but the tempo of combat operations would have been dramatically decreased, allowing Iraqi forces respite at the least and opportunities for counterattacks at worst. Some military units did not have even one set of protective clothing, boots, and gloves per individual and necessary spare parts and extra filters for their masks. Many consumable items, such as individual decon kits and manual chemical detector kits, had expired while in storage, which went unnoticed until the unit deployed. This basic leadership failure was a factor in CB defense preparedness.

Even some chemical defense companies, having been assured that supplies of decontaminants would be available in theater, had to work frantically once the troops were in Kuwait to get adequate decon supplies prior to the start of operations. This was a challenge even for combat units such as the 3rd Infantry Division, which (flagged as the 24th Infantry Division in 1991) had been one of the best-prepared units during Operation Desert Storm. This time, the 101st Airborne Division had the honor of best prepared, having inspected their equipment and loaded up with adequate amounts of protective suits and decontaminants prior to shipping out. These remain command issues that no amount of Chemical Corps leadership can resolve; only when the combat leaders decide that this is an important enough issue to monitor will military readiness for CBRN hazards be improved.

It is difficult to accurately assess the quality of CBRN defense capabilities during Operation Iraqi Freedom, given that combat lasted only three weeks and that no CB warfare took place. It would be inaccurate to suggest that aggressive, proactive efforts such as diplomatic threats of retaliation, counterforce/active defense efforts, and fast-moving coalition forces were responsible for the lack of CB warfare (as some did in 1991), given that Iraq had no unconventional weapons to employ against coalition forces. Although Iraq's lack of offensive CB weapons capability should not diminish the value of

CBRN defense, not all commanders are willing to sacrifice the resources and time to maintain readiness. It is difficult to assert that the U.S. military has the best CB defense equipment in the world when those capabilities have never really been tested. We can only guess how chemical defense units and CB defense equipment might have worked, and what challenges remain on the issues of CBRN defense equipment, concepts, and policy. It would be unfortunate for people to assume that the state of CBRN defense is adequate merely because U.S. forces have twice avoided being tested in Iraq.

In any assessment of CBRN defense capabilities, it should not be forgotten that DoD has a solid program with more than eighty years' experience in this field. Within its funding constraints, DoD has maintained a large laboratory infrastructure with CBRN research, development, test, and evaluation capabilities unmatched in the world. While DoD has been slow in fielding equipment, its overall record does have a good history of solid, fielded successes.[1] No other government agency has experience evaluating current and future CB warfare threat agents. Its CBRN specialty units are unmatched in their ability to respond rapidly to crises and operations all over the world, but as with any government program, there are areas that need improvement.

CBRN WARFARE AGENTS WITHIN THE THEATER AREA OF OPERATIONS

Prior to 1990, the Army had addressed all requirements for reconnaissance, detection, and identification under one general heading: contamination avoidance. As discussed earlier, this is a very large and technically complex area, in part because it addresses a number of distinct capabilities for different military purposes: standoff (or early warning) detection, automatic detection, and reconnaissance and surveillance efforts. Manual CBR monitors used by individual soldiers are discussed here under individual protection efforts, because that equipment is fundamentally a component of personal protection. Standoff detection is a relatively new capability, given the technical difficulty of developing equipment that can detect low concentrations of agent at great distances. Standoff detection today represents the greatest potential in avoiding contamination.

Early warning biological systems have been and remain one of the CINCs' top CBRN defense priorities. Faced with the image of large BW clouds moving toward their positions, commanders want to protect their personnel from exposure prior to the cloud's arrival ("detect to warn"), rather than having a biological monitor alarm fifteen to thirty minutes after the cloud passes ("detect to treat"). As opposed to efforts in 1990 to field prototype biological standoff detectors to CENTCOM, there were no biological standoff detectors developed or fielded for Operations Enduring Freedom and Iraqi Freedom. The JBREWS ACTD had shown the pros and cons of developing a biological standoff detection capability, and at the time there were definitely more cons than pros because there was no existing standoff capability. DoD did have nearly two full companies of BIDS vehicles (plus all the Portal Shields, JBPDS, and DFUs in theater) that would alert commanders in time to start medical measures prior to taking casualties, and that was considered adequate.

In the area of chemical standoff detection, only the M93A1 NBC recon systems had the M21 RSCAALs as an early warning capability. Because of the lack of any CW attacks, it is uncertain how useful these systems would have been in alerting the maneuver force to the presence of CW agent vapor or aerosols (the M21 system could not detect agent on the ground). Chemical standoff detection can assist in determining whether the enemy is contaminating terrain to deny use to friendly forces (such as the critical choke point at the Karbala Gap). It is believed that today's adversaries possessing less robust stockpiles than the former Soviet Union had would rather use chemical weapons to degrade or cause immediate casualties to unprepared U.S. forces than to contaminate key terrain. This observation along with concerns about the cost of the expensive detectors halted plans to field them as early warning devices for on-the-move forces. Its near-term replacement, the Joint Service Lightweight Standoff Chemical Agent Detector (JSLSCAD), should have been present for duty, but test and evaluation issues and industry troubles with the manufacture and stocking of critical parts delayed its fielding by a few years.

Although the services had discussed the need for radiological standoff detection, they had no effective technology. At the end of the Cold War, the urgency of such a requirement was extremely low. The technology is still discussed as a way to detect low-level radiological contamination from a distance (ideally using a helicopter platform) that might result from nuclear explosions, dirty bombs, or even expended depleted uranium rounds. As an interim capability, DoD could easily mount radiac monitors into UAVs or on helicopter pods and fly the systems over the battlefield, searching for radiological contamination, but no one has been excited enough about the concept to advocate (and fund) this capability.

The expense of developing and fielding standoff detectors that can measure operationally effective levels of CBRN hazards (rather than gross levels) will ensure that any future procurement of these systems remains low. Standoff detectors that can cover large tracts of area, providing relevant hazard information quickly to the commander, are more desirable because the U.S. military will be increasingly required to operate on large areas of terrain with fewer forces (making on-site point detection not as practical for information collection). Because of the low density of standoff detection systems and the desire to protect early entry forces in particular, the goal is to develop disparate sensors, such as artillery fire control radar and meteorological radar, into early warning systems. The science is still being developed, but the intent is to network input from multiple sensors that ordinarily would not be used for CB detection into the military's CBRN defense warning and reporting network.[2] While these disparate sensors may not identify specific agents or hazard levels, they may, if proven reliable, provide personnel enough information to take initial protective actions and avoid exposure.

SITUATIONAL AWARENESS OF UNIT BATTLE SPACES

Automatic detectors allow a combat unit to continuously monitor their immediate area for CBRN hazards. Chemical and radiological automatic detectors are sensitive enough to discover hazards below incapacitating levels, allowing forces to quickly don masks or seek shelter. There are no tactical biological detectors due to the technological challenges of detecting levels below infectious doses prior to individuals being exposed. An important point is that these detectors operate to protect troops from acute exposure to life-threatening levels of weaponized agents—they should not be confused with OSHA/NIOSH standards for emergency responders, which strive to protect individuals from chronic exposure to low-level CBRN hazards over a lifetime.

Although many forces deployed with M22 ACADAs, a few thousand older M8A1 chemical detectors were taken into theater (primarily by reserve units). Had the next-generation detector JCAD fielded on time, the armed services would have had three or four automatic chemical agent detectors performing the same function. The Army never fielded its full requirement of M8A1 detectors in the mid-1980s, because modernizing the older M8 detectors was an interim measure while the M22 ACADA was being developed. Fielding of the M22 ACADA was about ten years late, which mean the Army had both older (and less reliable) M8s as well as the newer M8A1 detectors when the ACADA started fielding in the mid-1990s. The Joint Service Materiel Group made a business decision not to field the ACADAs to the Army's full requirement because the new JCAD fielding date was right around the corner. Because the Army needed more than two hundred and twenty thousand units, fielding would take over a decade to complete. The JCAD project kept slipping its schedule, and the Army tended to use JCAD procurement funds to buy more ACADAs for its force. The Army (and CB Defense Program) should have purged out all the older M8A1 detectors, bought enough ACADAs for the force, and delayed JCAD until the technology was mature enough to meet users' requirements.

At twenty-five pounds, including the battery, the ACADA is a heavy piece of equipment to lug around. On the other hand, the JCAD weighs two pounds and measures about forty cubic inches. Of course, military personnel want the size/weight/power reduction to have absolutely no impact on the JCAD's detection capacity. Ideally it should also cost about a tenth of what the M22 ACADA costs: These expectations delayed the military's acquisition of JCAD from 2000 to 2005. Battery shortages for the M22 ACADAs were common, a repeat of the battery shortages seen in 1991, which forced troops to limit the use of detectors to key periods of the day or simply not use them at all. The BA-5590 was a common battery for the GPS and radios, which made it an increasingly valuable (and scarce) commodity. Many vehicles lacked mounting brackets for the M22 ACADAs, which meant they could not be easily used during offensive movements or slaved to the engine batteries. The reason for this was that mounting brackets cost $1,800 each, and the troops lacked information about their installation and use on military vehicles, making this an instant low priority for units budgeting their scarce operations and maintenance funds.

Even though the newer ACADA detector featured a lower false-alarm rate, soldiers complained that too many false alarms reduced their confidence in the system (not that sentinel chickens were the right answer). Military personnel were trained to leap into action upon hearing the alarm. Unfortunately, in assessing the accuracy of an alarm (especially prior to the start of offensive operations), they did not look for other indications of chemical weapons use, such as munitions impacting the area, hostile aircraft, or signs and symptoms of CW agent exposure. As a result, soldiers spent more time in protective suits and masks than they would have preferred.

The false alarm issue is not a new one. Military leaders have observed that, in theory, the more sensitive the chemical alarms are, the more time military personnel would have to don protective gear and avoid incapacitating levels of CW agents. But equally, the more sensitive the detector, the greater the chance the detector will react to an interfering agent or to an instrument failure (this is known as a false positive indication). The detector may not alarm at all in the presence of a very low agent concentration, a technical inability of the detector to see that particular agent, or instrument failure, such as low power or a broken valve. False negative alarms can get people killed, as opposed to false positive alarms, which are just inconvenient. Of the three desired parameters for new detectors (lower unit costs, lower false positive alarms, and increased sensitivity), the military can achieve only two. With the high density of chemical alarms in the field (about forty thousand or so in the Army alone), the Army chose low cost and high sensitivity as the two most important features. If the Army chose to go with low cost and low false alarms (resulting in low sensitivity), or high sensitivity and low false alarms (resulting in very expensive detectors), the industry would be producing them next year. However, the first option could cause additional casualties due to low agent exposure or not enough time to mask, while the second option would result in the military not buying enough detectors for all of its combat units. Until the combat arms users decide that reliability is more important than high sensitivity or cost, false positive alarms will continue to be around.

The PEO-CBD modified nine M22 ACADAs to detect four nontraditional agents in compliance with OSD pressure to ensure a capability in case Iraq had developed *novichok* type agents. These ACADAs were given to the 75th XTF during their search of sensitive sites. Unsurprisingly, no nontraditional (or traditional) CW agents were discovered. OSD counterproliferation policy continues to champion the need to field detectors for nontraditional agents immediately, believing that "it is not a matter of if, but when" such agents are used against U.S. forces by some adversary in a future conflict. Continuing research and development on new CB warfare agents and developing appropriate CBRN defense countermeasures remains a high priority for the military, but it takes much time and money—and spending attention on future, potential CB warfare threats leaves less attention available for addressing current and known CB warfare threats, against many of which the U.S. military still lacks a full defensive capability.

Some combat units wanted their chemical specialists to detect and confirm the presence of industrial chemicals such as phosgene, hydrogen sulfide, or other chemicals found in unmarked fifty-five-gallon drums in urban areas. In particular, units were told that hydrogen sulfide created from oil-well fires was an immediate operational hazard. Interestingly enough, the CENTCOM J2 WMD section was tasked to deal with the hydrogen sulfide issue, which, on second look, was not as great a threat as had been feared. With support from a chemical officer, that office obtained toxicology information and plotted plume models against all the oil wells in Iraq. Lt. Gen. William Wallace, V Corps commander, discussed an example where ground forces had come upon a cyanide-contaminated water supply on the way to Najaf. It was unclear whether this was an intentional or accidental contamination, but (in his words) someone had to deal with it, and he thought it was the responsibility of his chemical specialists.

Although chemical specialists could confirm that unknown chemicals were not CW agents, commanders were pressing them to detect and identify industrial chemicals discovered in warehouses. The 4th Infantry Division commander told his division chemical officer that the Chemical Corps was no good if it could not detect and identify industrial chemicals at hazardous material sites. Whether this was a knee-jerk reaction to the hunt for WMDs or just a desire to limit exposure to these health hazards is not entirely clear. It is possible that this commander incorrectly assumed that chemical specialists address all chemical hazards, warfare and industrial. The PEO-CBD supplied some chemical units with Draeger chemical monitoring kits for manual identification of industrial chemicals. Many chemical specialists believe that retaining an industrial chemical identification capability in the Fox recon vehicle is necessary. A computer chip designed to add industrial chemical identification to the recon vehicle's mass spectrometer (used in Bosnia) had never been operationally tested but was installed in some Fox vehicles during Operations Enduring Freedom and Iraqi Freedom. The challenge is that chemical specialists in general can't do much more than cite the OHSA and emergency response guidance on these hazards. There is (and remains) a shortage of practical operational knowledge and policy on how to properly identify toxic industrial hazards, and more important, how to realistically assess the hazard and inform the commander of his/her options in light of ongoing combat operations. Military equipment is not designed to protect individuals from many industrial chemicals. Chemical officers with whom I have talked sincerely believe this is an important operational gap that must be addressed in the near future. The question is whether this a Chemical Corps CBRN defense issue, an Engineer Corps environmental remediation issue, or a Medical Corps force health protection issue. This issue needs a leader to clarify the tactical perspectives.

The commanders' desire for chemical specialists to identify industrial chemicals seems to demonstrate a misunderstanding of the role of CB warfare specialists. It changes the chemical specialist's job from supporting operational issues to acting as a technical specialist on both CW and industrial compounds. Although industrial chemicals might make military personnel sick as a result of short-term exposure, this is a secondary concern compared to military-grade CW agents that will kill people very quickly. If the chemical is not weaponized and is in a sealed drum or spilled inside of a warehouse, it is not life-threatening, does not imperil the mission, and requires no immediate action. That is, the chemical is not a weaponized threat, on which CB warfare specialists focus, and appropriately so. At the very least, events seen during Operation Iraqi Freedom do not make the case that all soldiers, sailors, airmen, and Marines other than chemical specialists should have chemical detectors that sense low levels of industrial chemicals, that they should all have protective suits that resist industrial chemical penetration, or that they need decontamination kits for industrial chemical contamination. At best, they might benefit from masks that can protect them against short-term exposure to low and moderate levels of certain toxic inhalation hazards.

Making chemical specialists into experts on all industrial hazards would strain resources and funds, and could eventually dilute the necessary support commanders need. Other are more appropriately trained and equipped to handle postconflict identification and remediation of industrial hazards and chronic exposure to low levels of industrial chemicals: medical personnel, engineers, and civilian contractors. NBC reconnaissance specialists or an in-theater laboratory could adequately address this issue. But we should not try to add the capability to detect multiple industrial chemical hazards to every unit's automatic chemical detector, because fielding new detectors is costly and time-consuming and results in questionable benefits. Instead, we need to better develop the distinction between medical analysis of low-level industrial and environmental safety hazards and immediate operational hazards caused by the intentional weaponization of industrial chemicals. General Reeves calls this discussion a debate over the "OSHA line of death," but it is and remains an important issue among the medical, engineer, and chemical defense communities. The Chemical Corps is proceeding to develop a field manual outlining procedures for executing SSE support, environmental reconnaissance, and hazardous operations missions. It is unclear whether these critical operational issues have been resolved to allow the Chemical Corps to be effective in this area.

The service CBRN defense representatives envision the need for tactical biological detection systems the size of the M22 ACADAs that would detect BW agents and take liquid samples at the site of attack for further analysis. The DFUs emplaced throughout EUCOM, CENTCOM, and Washington D.C., were a step in this direction. In this instance Colonel Kadlec's concerns about a "detector-centric" BW defense concept were valid. In identifying this requirement, the services have failed to address the significant technical challenges that exist in trying to create an automatic, sensitive, and reliable detector for multiple BW agents that would have a low instance of false alarms and could be carried by an individual. The resulting panic from one false positive alarm in one unit would be concern enough, let alone the potential hundreds or thousands of false alarms in a theater. People react differently to the threat of BW agents than to the threat of CW agents, and that has to be taken into account.

The desire for every tactical unit to have a capability to take BW samples for future analysis is inherently flawed for two reasons. Advocates for a tactical biodetector stress the need to collect a sample as close to the release as possible to support medical diagnosis and treatment decisions, but that is a mission currently conducted by the JBPDS and BIDS platoons. Adding a sampler and collector, plus vials for transportation, will instantly increase the size and weight (and cost) of the detector. Advocates for tactical biodetectors should consider the challenge of an in-theater lab trying to analyze thousands of BW samples each day (considering the planned density of tactical biological detectors envisioned). Additionally, only specialized units are trained on sample transfer techniques and the chain-of-custody issues that will stand up as proof of offensive BW agent use in international court. There is currently no DoD or civilian laboratory infrastructure that could handle this huge influx of samples, nor is one planned.

The services fail to understand that the tactical commander does not need to know what the exact BW agent is, just that he is under attack by one. The decision to implement appropriate medical countermeasures will come from headquarters, relying on more sensitive JBPDS and BIDS units and other information. It's hard to understand the fixation with tactical level biological detection, other than (as critics have noted) the desire to develop a biological defense concept that mirrors chemical defense. The services and the JRO have not done the analysis to identify the costs and benefits of this concept. Fortunately, the lack of a clear operational concept and a sound acquisition plan to field a tactical biological detector has muted funding for this poorly thought-out requirement.

There was never a real concern about Iraq using a nuclear weapon—the intelligence community said Iraq probably didn't have one (and we trusted the credibility of the intelligence community)—but it should be noted that the Army and Marine Corps had fairly modern and efficient radiac meters in their inventories. In addition to tactical contamination detection, the services had to consider the (partly political) concern about potential contamination from depleted uranium munitions.[3] The Air Force had a similar, but more expensive, version of the Army's AN/VDR-2 in its ADM-300-series radiac. The Air Force and Navy had been discussing the possibility of a joint multi-function radiac project, but prior to 2006, there was no real impetus for this. The services are considering the initiation of joint radiac programs under the new management structure, but the priority remains very low as compared to chemical or biological detection.

RECONNAISSANCE AND SURVEILLANCE

The Army and Marine Corps have two specialized units for CBRN hazard reconnaissance and surveillance missions. Because of the technical nature of

CBRN hazards and the operational complexity of reconnaissance missions, these units are trained specifically for this combat role. Reconnaissance includes missions undertaken to obtain information about the activities and resources of an enemy, or to secure data concerning the meteorological, hydrographic, or geographic characteristics of a particular area. This is distinct from the task of surveillance, which involves observing an aerospace, surface, or subsurface area, place, person, or thing, by visual, aural, electronic, photographic, or other means.[4] In recon missions, information is sought on the parameters of a particular threat within a specific area (where is it), while in surveillance, a known area is monitored for any changes in the status of a threat (is it there). Some may not agree that BIDS platoons are in fact assets better suited to mobile recon and surveillance than an automatic detector such as the M22 ACADA. However, the BIDS vehicle represents a specific low density, high demand asset that requires very special training and careful allocation to be effective.

The M93A1 NBC Fox reconnaissance vehicle performed well on several missions where it confirmed the absence of chemical when an M22 ACADA or other detection device had identified an agent (thus saving units from prolonged use of protective suits). Some commanders and even chemical officers used the vehicle as a mobile laboratory to assess the findings at sensitive sites. The small, colored NBC markers in the Fox vehicle, designed to mark the boundary of contaminated areas, were inadequate: many friendly forces rolled past markers without seeing them (they were noted as inadequate in 1991 as well). Tires for the Fox vehicle were in short supply because the horrific road conditions and battlefield debris caused numerous blowouts. CENTCOM was unable to get contract maintenance personnel for the Fox vehicle into theater until nearly all hostilities had ended, because initial maintenance support contracts did not permit contractors to enter Iraq with the troops. The PEO-CBD deployed a maintenance team in late April to provide forward contractor logistics support out of Kuwait. These maintenance and spare parts challenges could have been major, had combat operations lasted longer than three weeks. The Army and Marine Corps had not fully integrated the spare parts or necessary repair training into its normal maintenance practices, because the Fox vehicle was a German military system meant as an interim solution until fielding of the joint NBC recon system (which should have been fielded between 2003 and 2005). The Army intends to procure NBC recon vehicles with a common Army vehicle chassis (a HMMWV version and a Stryker version), but had to maintain these vehicles in the meantime. The Marine Corps has opted for a light armored vehicle (LAV) chassis for their future NBC recon vehicle.

There were nine BIDS platoons in CENTCOM's area of operation (including Israel), providing a greater and more sophisticated surveillance role than the dozen biodetection teams hastily deployed in January 1991. The BIDS vehicles performed well monitoring the battle space for BW agent use, although sand particles caused significant problems with the BIDS subcomponents. During operations in Afghanistan and Iraq, the operators saw small concentrations of BW organisms, but no spikes that would indicate a deliberate BW attack. The commercial systems in the vehicles demanded constant contractor support, which was more available than their counterparts in the Fox vehicles because the BIDS contract logistics support extended to the platoon level and deployed forward with each platoon. The BIDS vehicles were supposed to get the new JBPDS, but due to delays in that program, that modernization had not occurred. The main challenge was largely how the combat force viewed the use of BIDS platoons. Although these systems were intended for large-area detection and monitoring, Pentagon security wanted the BIDS to screen mail packages for anthrax. This was not an ideal use of these multimillion dollar systems, to say the least, and demonstrates a fundamental lack of understanding or appreciation of BIDS capabilities.

There were four JBPDS and 140 Portal Shields present at several fixed sites, in addition to the dozen or so IBADS on the Navy ships. These provided an extensive "detect to treat" surveillance network throughout the theater, which was acceptable because the military was immunized against anthrax and smallpox. A number of in-theater laboratories would provide definitive analysis of any clinical or environmental biological samples, allowing the medical experts to recommend specific treatment. As long as the force could detect a deliberately deployed BW agent, military leaders would have time to institute medical countermeasures. The civilians in nearby villages and cities would not have been so lucky, however; even if they were warned, it is unlikely that the hospitals in the Gulf Coast states would have been able to manage the consequences of a large-scale BW attack. CENTCOM worked out a thorough sample evacuation plan to move suspected BW agent samples to laboratories in the United Kingdom and United States, which were prepared to verify whether Iraq had employed BW agents against the force. The Air Force has still not developed protocols that will allow air transportation of suspect CB warfare agent samples without dedicating the aircraft to that sole purpose—which considerably complicates the task of confirmatory sampling by laboratories outside of CENTCOM's theater.

The Navy had purchased five hundred DFUs for more than one hundred ships, and developed protocols for sampling and analysis. If they wanted to field the DFUs without a validated concept of operations, the services had to promise to use these air samplers as monitors for terrorist use of BW agents against installations, as opposed to use by maneuver forces during combat. But perhaps an installation is not that different than a large ship such as an aircraft carrier. In addition, many chemical specialists were issued biological sampling kits with instructions not to conduct sampling missions unless directed. There was a concern that many would use the kits as an "all clear" detection kit similar to the M256A1, rather than as a sampling tool. There was a good chance of false positives if the sampling procedures were not carefully followed.

It is difficult to assess the real success of these biological detection and sampling systems other than to say that there was an elaborate and well-thought-out plan of employment to monitor for the presence of BW agents across the entire battle space. False positives were identified and resolved daily, although this was not publicized. There may be security concerns that do not permit discussion of the actual performance of these systems, but in general, they allowed an extensive and verifiable network that, although expensive, played an invaluable role at the operational level of war. Policy issues such as whether to impose quarantines within the theater for exposed personnel (both military, civilian, and host nation) were debated but not completely resolved prior to the end of the conflict.

CRITICAL INFORMATION FOR CURRENT OPERATIONS

The idea of CB defense having an information and decision support system was perhaps the one new, untested capability since the first Gulf War. That previous conflict saw the Defense Nuclear Agency implement a jury-rigged effort using secure faxes and stand-alone computers in the United States and

Southwest Asia to establish a hazard prediction capability for CENTCOM forces. This time, units had JWARN Block I, a stand-alone hazard prediction software package that could be run by chemical officers in theater. It was lauded as an invaluable tool at the division level for planning and execution, but it had significant limitations, such as its inability to send its graphics output directly to other military communication systems. Units were forced to email their graphics to other tactical forces as a result, but this was better than using fax machines, as had been done in 1991. JWARN was a step in the right direction, but still needs to be integrated at the lower levels with more user-friendly functions and networked throughout the joint force. Considering the state of software design today, this capability should have been mature much earlier than 2003, but differing communications equipment and protocols between the four services and a lack of funding considerably complicated its design and release.

Currently, DoD has three validated CB warfare models for hazard prediction.

- DTRA's Hazard Prediction and Assessment Capability (HPAC) is used to model potential dispersion of CB agents where the U.S. military uses conventional forces to attack a storage or production site holding CB weapons, and an agent release might result.

- The Navy's Vapor-Liquid-Solid Tracking (VLSTRACK) is used to model the deliberate employment of CB weapons.

- The Army's D2Puff model is used to predict the hazard dispersion of chemical accidents or incidents at the Army's chemical stockpile sites.

These models are very detailed and sophisticated, developed using actual test data on CB weapons trials conducted during the Cold War; they are the best available given current technology and knowledge of CB weapons effects. The old manual method, using the NATO-standard ATP-45 template, essentially draws a triangle of certain dimensions on a map that will allow a 90 percent chance of including all agent drift: it's not precise, but it's quick and cheap. While CENTCOM's maneuver forces used VLSTRACK to determine the possible hazard footprint of employed CB warfare agents, the JTF-CM used HPAC to predict the potential hazard to civilians in Kuwait.

A drawback of the current software is that DoD could not send the results of its hazard prediction analysis to a coalition ally during a military combat operation or allow an ally to use this software. The U.S. military needs one software package that all forces can use for all situations, with the ability to ship data and analysis to its coalition allies. In developing a new software model, there are some rather large hurdles. The DATSD (CBD) is the sole DoD point of contact charged by the USD (AT&L) to decide whether particular software can be used to model CB weapons incidents. Any new software model or simulation must be subjected to a vigorous validation and verification process; in the case of CB warfare models, this is much more difficult because the DoD is unable to verify that the model replicates CB weapons use without actually dispersing agent in the open environment outside of its laboratories. Congress has to approve any open-air CB warfare testing based on the president's request for such tests, and any such request would be tantamount to political suicide, so the DoD leadership would rather not ask. Open-air tests could be safely conducted, but the uproar from critics, activists, and conspiracy theorists would make any attempts politically untenable. Still, these data are crucial to validate the models.

DoD does plan to improve its battle management capability with better hazard prediction software and by integrating CBRN detectors into the major command and control systems, but the products are years away. Part of the challenge has been at the higher levels of the services and DoD, because the four services have yet to agree on common command and control system architectures that would allow joint software and hardware solutions to take place. Although there is one high-level communications architecture, called Global Command and Control System, each service has its own communications and software for operational and tactical forces. A solution may have to be imposed from the top down. In addition, this area is not well funded within the DoD CB Defense Program. Because it is a relative newcomer, there were no additional funds added for battlefield management systems when JWARN and its software programs began. A final product that can demonstrate a mature, networked capability is several years away, unless the programs' priorities are raised and funding is identified to accelerate the effort.

ENHANCE PERSONNEL SURVIVABILITY

For individual service members, being able to survive a CB warfare attack is a top priority. Many reduce the concept of individual protection to an expendable protective suit, gloves, and boots, and nonexpendable protective masks, but this definition fails to account for other critical life support equipment, including the skin and individual equipment decon kits, medical CB defense countermeasures, and manual CBR monitors that personnel carry. Aviators have understood the need to address life-support equipment as a distinct capability for decades; it is about time that CBRN defense specialists acknowledge this distinction as well, instead of lumping manual CBRN monitors with automatic and standoff detectors, and addressing skin and individual equipment decon kits with large equipment and terrain decon systems.

The industrial base to produce JSLIST suits was tripled from its preconflict status between January and March 2003, with more than sixteen hundred requisitions for special-order JSLIST suits. One lesson DoD had learned was that it needed to accelerate production in crisis situations, and contracts that it needed that allowed for just that contingency. Although the production lines were in place, there was still the issue of funding and staffing the lines, which accounts for DoD's inability to ramp up in the summer of 2002. Overall comments on JSLIST suits were positive, with many calling them a significant improvement over the BDO. Personnel working in the desert applauded the perceived lighter nature of the suit, combined with its new carbon sphere technology that didn't blacken the skin as the BDOs had. The JSLIST suit's outer fabric durability was less than satisfactory—many infantry soldiers tore their suits in the performance of day-to-day activities. The suit also seemed to absorb fuel products much more easily than the BDOs had, forcing troops to shed their protective suits while conducting refueling or maintenance operations (or to wear wet-weather gear over the suit, which was really uncomfortable).

Some service members, notably those crewmembers in tanks and aircraft, had been hoping for a flame-retardant uniform—a uniform chock-full of carbon particles would burn spectacularly if set aflame—but the aviator/armor crew flame-resistant suit was still being tested and evaluated. As a result, crewmembers had to wear a JSLIST suit and Nomex heat-resistant coveralls over the suit, which was not ideal in high temperatures. Army aviators in general did not like the JSLIST and its integrated hood, which was not compatible with their specialized helmets. The special operations forces had a JSLIST suit designed without an integrated hood to allow for increased freedom of movement, but perhaps there were not enough to issue to the aviators. Many soldiers bemoaned the lack of an "NBC bag" to carry their protective suits, boots and gloves. Some units used MRE boxes or duffel bags to hold the bulky suits, which had to be carried around constantly in preparation for any chemical attacks. The older BDOs had a protective bag for storage, but the square, vacuum-packed JSLIST suit did not fit in the bag. Rather than redesign and reissue the bag, the Army had stopped producing them altogether.

The JSLIST challenges were more procedural than technology-oriented. Units had failed to properly size their personnel before deploying, and, interestingly enough, the size quotas used by DLA in their procurement activities no longer matched the profiles of today's military personnel—many former "medium" personnel needed larger suits, and so on.[5] Despite multiple directives requiring soldiers to train in JSLIST suits prior to arriving in theater, many units had failed to do so. In addition, many contractors assigned to combat forces arrived without any individual protection, forcing the combat units to issue them spare protective masks and suits, already in short supply. In 1990, there had been a rigid process to train and equip contractors with appropriate protective equipment. This time around, the system had failed to provide similar training. The issues of personnel needing larger suits and contractors needing protective equipment added significant stress to the logistics pipeline.

The M40 masks performed well, and were supplied to all ground forces and many noncombatants. The PEO-CBD processed more than five hundred requests for special-sized individuals, with faces either too large or too small for the normal sizes. The Air Force and Navy, which had the MCU-2/P mask for its general purpose airmen and sailors, had some trouble maintaining their aging mid-1980s masks. All four services had service-unique masks for their fixed wing and rotary wing aviators. There are two masks in the works to correct this: a general-purpose mask for all DoD forces fielding around 2007, and a common aviator mask for all DoD pilots and aviators that may be ready in 2008 or 2009. The Marine Corps liked the mask voice amplifiers in particular, desiring that all combat leaders should be fitted with such devices. The protective mask carrier took a few shots for not having sufficient room to hold an extra filter, diazepam and ATNAA autopens, and mask technical manual. Others complained about the bulk of the mask carrier.

The FDA had approved the general use of PB tablets as a pretreatment for nerve agents on February 5, 2003. While this ruling cut close to the start of operations, it did allow CENTCOM to preposition stocks of these tablets within the theater of operations prior to the end of March. As this new drug was being fielded, the PEO-CBD ensured that information sheets on its usage and potential effects were available to all service members. CENTCOM received more than one hundred thousand ATNAA treatments, partly because it worked closely with the FDA to expedite initial production of the devices. The SERPACWA lotion was fielded in small numbers to the Army, but, like many of medical CB defense countermeasures, it is difficult to say how well it worked given the lack of any challenges.

The FDA approved the use of Reactive Skin Decon Lotion on March 5, 2003, as an improved skin decontaminant for military, not public, use. This lotion had been developed and in use by the Canadian military for some years, while the U.S. Army conducted its own test and evaluation. As an item that would be applied to the skin, it required FDA safety and efficacy reviews, even though it was not an antidote or drug per se (an issue that stopped the sorbent decon powder used in the M295 equipment decon kit from being used for skin decontamination). No lotion was actually fielded to CENTCOM during March and April, and the formula has changed since 2003 because of undesirable interactions with other solutions. Expectations are that the lotion will not be more effective than the M291 decon kit that it will replace, which may extend the time of fielding as scientists and engineers attempt to improve it. Expected fielding for this new lotion is not earlier than 2006.

In general, the improved CAM and M256A1 detector kits worked well when used in conjunction with each other—one technology checking the other. Used alone, CAMs could show false positives. The CAMs were used by the survey teams to assess the presence of CW agents, and when challenged with industrial chemicals such as fuming nitric acid, the CAMS and ACADAs were unreliable and the M256A1 kits would give inconclusive or contradictory readings (a review of the first Gulf War lessons would have identified this problem). The survey teams' reliance on military field detectors to the near total exclusion of examining other evidence at the site demonstrated poor understanding of site exploitation. The manual M256A1 detector kit holds twelve samplers that are more sensitive and reliable than the ACADAs, which is why military personnel use them when an automatic alarm goes off. The only downside is that it takes fifteen to twenty minutes to use one expendable sampler. This is old technology, dating back to the 1980s, but it is cheap and reliable, which means every soldier or squad can have one.

Some in the Chemical Corps have suggested replacing the M256A1 kits with JCADs, but it seems a little ridiculous to replace every squad's expendable, fifty-dollar manual detector kit with a five-thousand-dollar automatic detector just because they can't wait fifteen minutes.

The Army has a new pocket radiac that replaced its Cold War-era dosimeters. The other three services have not decided to replace their Cold War-era versions. As mentioned earlier, the Air Force and Navy see individual dosimeters as medical health equipment useful for operating around nuclear weapons and nuclear reactors, as opposed to tactical radiological contamination. All ground forces continue to rely on M8 and M9 paper—colorimetric paper strips that detect liquid chemical agents—as a first-level and very inexpensive method for detecting immediate, life-threatening hazards. There is constant discussion about the idea of a CB dosimeter that would offer a similar total-dose assessment as radiological hazards, but the operational concepts, technical hurdles, and cost issues remain unresolved.

MAINTAINING OPERATIONAL TEMPO OF MANEUVER FORCES

Maneuver forces rely on collective protection systems and operational decontamination systems to sustain combat operations on battlefields contaminated with CBRN agents, and to continue fighting despite the presence of agent. As a unit comes under fire, military personnel, their equipment, and their vehicles cannot simply stop and go into bunker mode when hit by NBC weapons. Poorly trained units may do exactly that, waiting for the CB warfare agent effects to dissipate so they can resume unprotected operations. If they do stop and bunker down, the enemy has the advantage and, if trained to operate through contaminated areas, will defeat those forces (as Iraq's military successfully did against Iran's military in the 1980s). Although combat effectiveness may be considerably reduced, U.S. forces are expected to "fight dirty" until their units can attempt remediation and restore full combat capability.

All M1A1 Abrams tanks have overpressure systems and ventilated face pieces for the crews that enable them to fight without their performance being degraded by hot and encumbering protective suits. The Bradley fighting vehicles have ventilated face pieces for crew members, but the infantry squads in the rear have to wear their full protective ensembles. The Fox recon system, some armored hospital HMMWVs, and artillery command vehicles have collective protection systems built into their vehicles. The Army and Marine Corps received sixty-four CB Protective Shelters, which allowed their medical ambulances to operate tactical field operations in forward areas in the presence of CB warfare agents for up to thirty-six hours. These shelters were also popular due to their ability to guard against the desert environment, causing some military units to consider procuring them for the command-and-control centers. The PEO-CBD sent government and contractor teams to southwest Asia to accelerate the system's fielding and use in theater. There were no reports of collective protection filter shortages for military vehicles, as had been seen in 1990.

The PEO-CBD fielded over one hundred and twenty thousand M100 sorbent decon systems, which replaced the M11 and M13 decon apparatuses, as a step toward reducing the Army's dependence on DS-2 for immediate decontamination of crew and individual equipment. One challenge was that many units had not received any information on how to use the new sorbent decon. Even with fairly substantial sums of money available, there was not enough available sorbent decon to equip all units to their full requirements prior to combat operations. This was another general failure of combat units to appreciate the complexities of the military's logistics system of ordering and storing consumable items such as decontaminants and collective protection filters. Because the peacetime consumption of decontaminants was so low, the production and storage of decontaminants in the warehouses was similarly very low. Everyone expected modern logistics processes to solve all their problems, but the small firms producing decontaminants at low production rates could not ramp up within the time frame of the deploying forces.

The rebuild program had fixed a number of lightweight decon systems, and the procurement of 125 commercial decon systems had allowed the military to maintain a limited decontamination capability that would enable their operating forces to continue operations, even if still contaminated with low levels of agent. Using commercial systems had its disadvantages, especially when the force was given these systems at the last minute. The commercial Karcher systems were heavier than the M17 decon systems and did not use JP8 fuel, which meant that forces had to deliver and maintain multiple fuels. The operators using these Karchers lacked the operational and logistical training to maintain the systems in the field, but did the best they could under the circumstances. These attempts were a band-aid to the failure to procure a modern decon system that had the capability to use modern decontaminants and keep combat systems relatively free of contamination.

SUSTAINING OPERATIONS AT FIXED SITES

Keeping repair, restoration, and refit operations going in the rear area is very important, given the logistically demanding requirements of the U.S. military. The key to sustaining operations and restoring full operational capability to combat units, including addressing the movement and use of formerly contaminated equipment and supplies, lies in the operation of thorough decontamination and collective protection shelters. If combat units can't get the ammunition, food, replacement troops, and medical support to replenish and continue combat operations, the conflict will be over very quickly. Medically diagnosing and treating patients exposed to CB warfare agents over the long term is another restoration issue, which in this instance was not put to the test.

Numerous studies have assessed the vulnerability of fixed sites in combat areas, including command-and-control centers, rear-area (fixed) hospitals, logistics bases, seaports, and air bases. However, most studies merely admire the problems. They note that fixed sites are vulnerable, but given the complexity of operations and mix of different military and civilian personnel at fixed sites, evaluating their vulnerabilities and developing sound solutions is very difficult. Few, if any, analytical studies have actually attempted to quantify the impact of CB warfare agents on fixed sites to the point where military forces can identify how many collective protection shelters and how much decontaminant is needed to restore a site after such attacks. In part, the anticipated high costs of addressing these vulnerabilities (in terms of both manpower and equipment) hinder the solution.

Surprisingly, prior to the conflict CENTCOM had not requested additional collective protection shelters for their fixed sites. Had Iraq had the capability to attack air bases and sea ports in Kuwait and Qatar with CB warfare agents, there is no doubt that these sites would have been put out of commission for days or weeks, until the civilians working at these sites could be convinced that it was safe to come back to work. V Corps had tasked specific chemical decontamination companies to support the decontamination of seaports and air bases in Kuwait, but given the lack of DS-2 stocks and inexperience in decontaminating such large complexes, decon companies may not have been able to restore the sites to the degree where the flow of personnel and equipment could have resumed preincident conditions.

The military's expeditionary medical hospitals have long championed the need for collective protection capabilities and were in the process of fielding this capability in 2002. The Air Force fielded five chemically protected expeditionary medical support facilities in southwest Asia that would have provided "shirtsleeve working environments" in the event of a CB weapons attack. The Army and Marine Corps received six CP DEPMEDS for its field hospitals, which performed well. The air-conditioned tents served as the initial triage area for some of the first wounded during hostilities, and they stood up well to the sand storms that wrecked havoc on so many other tents.

The shortage of M12A1 systems was partially addressed by Pine Bluff's rebuild program and the procurement of commercial Karcher systems, as described previously. The Army's decontamination companies are fairly well manned and have the equipment and doctrine to restore equipment back to a condition where unprotected military personnel could resume use of the systems. This capability might not meet OSHA standards back in the United States, but the capability to continue military operations was present.[6] The challenge was, given the absence of DS-2 decontaminant, that they had to rely on DF-200 or high-test hypochlorite bleach.

The PEO-CBD had decided to use Intelagard's Falcon Fixed Site Decon System to address CENTCOM's request for large-scale terrain decontamination capability, instead of procuring the Global GL-1800 system. The Falcon decon system was specifically designed for large-area decontamination using liquids or foams, unlike the Global candidate, which was a modification of an Air Force de-icing machine. By the time the military had made the decision to go with the Falcon, the conflict was over. The requirement for a military fixed-site decontamination system still exists, but it may not be filled through normal DoD acquisition efforts until 2010. It's embarrassing that the military has let this capability be degraded when the technologies involved are so simple—pumps and spray devices, really. The greater challenge has been identifying a magic "pixie dust" decontaminant that is just as good as DS-2, nonaqueous, and harmless to the environment and human skin. That search continues today, even as the aging DS-2 stocks, the only existing solution, are being destroyed.

SBCCOM had frozen the release of any DS-2 stocks from the consolidated stocks at Seneca Army Depot. This was not a new issue. It was known in the late 1990s that these stocks were deteriorating and that the Army needed to destroy them yet the Army had not chosen a new decontaminant. Because DS-2 was the prime decontaminant used to reduce immediate levels of contamination on vehicles in addition to fully restoring units to full, uncontaminated status, this issue directly impacted the Army's ability to sustain combat operations in CB warfare environments. The failure of DF-200 to pass test and evaluation certification as an interim decontaminant, combined with poor communication to the field on its procurement and use, only compounded the challenge. Some forces had procured thousands of gallons of DF-200 with their own unit funds, without protocol or training. There were no applicators for the DF-200 other than mops and buckets, making the U.S. forces a subject of mockery to the Czech, German, and British specialists and their state-of-the-art decon equipment. While the Marines liked the five-gallon decon containers, the Army maneuver units, who had much more stringent requirements for operational decon, did not like to carry around so many small containers. Many Army units had to purchase high-test hypochlorite in the United States and in the Middle East to fill the gaps in this capability, just as they did in 1990.

To return to full, preincident operations at a military fixed site, CENTCOM's military units would have had to stockpile and use considerable amounts of decontaminants, personnel, and water. The Army and Marine Corps had dedicated assets to address thorough decontamination. The Air Force has a concept that suggests their bases don't have to worry about decontamination, because of some doubt about the validity of the Army's test data on the persistency of chemical agents (developed between 1940 and 1970), and the enemy's ability to knock out the entire air base, considering the accuracy of ballistic missiles and available active defense measures. The Navy was not concerned about being hit at sea with CW agents, given relatively small areas of effect and a big ocean in which to maneuver. BW agent contamination would have been a different issue if Iraq had had any anthrax stocks and planes to use against the coalition forces. Many reasoned that if BW agents been used that the rules of the game would have dramatically shifted, and planning retaliatory nuclear strikes would overwhelm any immediate concerns about BW agent contamination.

The other huge challenge in this area is the eternal question of "how clean is clean?" or as some say, "how clean is safe?" DS-2 allowed the military to avoid that question because it was just so damn efficient, eliminating nearly all CB warfare agent present (but ruthlessly degrading rubber, plastic, canvas, electronics, and everything else in the process). Everyone's default answer to "how clean is clean?" is always "as low as reasonably achievable." Ideally, this level is zero, but realistic considerations must allow some level of risk. On the battlefield, this was never really questioned; no one was looking for a quantifiable standard. With the issues of returning formerly contaminated equipment and human remains back to the United States and the extremely low safety standards of Army chemical surety operations, inquiries began as to what the standard was and if the battlefield standard was different than the standard for returning formerly contaminated equipment and personnel to the United States. The answers were too intimidating, and few wanted to push for a near-term, achievable solution, despite the close calls of two Gulf Wars featuring CB warfare conditions.

The development of a cleanliness policy, so to speak, is not as difficult as one would expect. There are reams of data available on chemical and nuclear hazards, but little for biological hazards. Given the lack of any CB weapons events that have actually forced anyone to adopt a realistic standard, no one wants to be the one to draw a line where the military can say "how clean is clean?". In part, it is fear that they will pick the wrong number. More likely, it is because they just don't want the responsibility. DHS has the mandate to develop CBRN defense standards for responding to domestic terrorist incidents, but the task of developing a decon standard has been kicked upstairs to the White House's Office of Science and Technology Programs. This is not because developing the answer is tough, but because the authority, coming from the very top of government, would be seen as impeachable. The only concern is that developing domestic standards won't help the military; if the military is burdened with OSHA-like decon standards, either its forces won't get the missions done or there will be a lot of military equipment and human remains left behind until natural weathering and time eliminates the exposed CW agent threat. This and other difficult policy questions are addressed in the next chapter.

CHAPTER 9

CBRN DEFENSE POLICY

*In the same way as a man who has not mastered a foreign language
sometimes fails to express himself correctly, so statesmen often issue orders
that defeat the purpose they are meant to serve. Time and again this has
happened, which demonstrates that a certain grasp of military affairs is
vital for those in charge of general policy.*

—CARL VON CLAUSEWITZ

D iscussions about WMDs tend to focus on technical issues such as weapon systems, destructive capabilities, offensive measures, and defensive equipment. What are often ignored are the defense policy aspects of combating WMD programs and developing CBRN defense capabilities; that is to say, developing policies to articulate official guidance and to instruct the services on the execution of military strategy specific to CBRN defense. These are tough issues, requiring technical subject-matter expertise, political acumen, common sense, and a willingness to take a controversial position in the absence of perfect data collection.

The Bush administration's issuance of its national strategy to combat WMD programs impacted the entire department from top to bottom, and continues to drive important reforms in the area of combating WMD. The lesser CBRN defense policy issues that do not receive such visibility include executing the anthrax and smallpox vaccine programs, justifying the need for live agent testing, developing decontamination cleanliness standards, identifying the cause of Gulf War illnesses, and sustaining the WMD Civil Support Teams. Many chemical officers will ask, "So what? Why should we be concerned about policy issues being decided at levels so high above us?" The history of the CBRN defense program is complicated and convoluted and requires close review to appreciate how today's defense officials address critical issues that drive specific CBRN defense topics. If the Army in general and the Chemical Corps in particular does not actively participate with others (e.g., OSD, the services, DHS) in developing CBRN defense policy, their leadership will have to live with the consequences. Unfortunately, many Army leaders (outside the Chemical Corps) do not get involved in CBRN policy development until things reach a crisis point, often leading to rushed, emotional, and poorly-developed decisions. Because military defense is a public policy issue, CBRN defense issues within counterproliferation, military antiterrorism, and homeland security programs must be approached as such. We must appreciate the machinations of Congress, the public, and the media in their views and prejudices of the CBRN defense program to understand the complexities of developing policy that will assist our military forces.

There are four fundamental groups involved in policy issues: those that develop policy goals and objectives (rationalists), those that execute particular assignments within policy areas (technicians), those that adjust policy to fit near-term desired outcomes (incrementalists), and those that don't trust the government's policy (activists). In CBRN defense, the OSD acquisition, personnel, and policy offices are the rationalists, the project managers and military specialists are the technicians, congresspeople are the incrementalists, and the many public activists and think tanks are the reformists. OSD and other military staff policy offices are accused of not understanding the human or technical nature of CBRN defense. Often they are reacting to the changes imposed on them by Congress caused by some recent CBRN defense topic that hit the news. Congressional members focus on near-term issues and rarely, if ever, address the overall well-being of the program. As a result, they may not provide required long-term improvements in CBRN defense other than to fund it in accordance with other defense priorities. While the project managers and military CBRN specialists are confident in their narrow technical analyses, they are often less competent when addressing top-level policy or executive decisions (and when they try, the policy and decisions often fall short). Meanwhile, activist groups who lack complete information but are always willing to make blanket accusations, charge the Department with abuses such as using military service members as guinea pigs in its vaccine program. Understanding that these four general groups exist and interact on nearly all defense policy issues allows us to better understand how issues evolve within the U.S. military.

The media's role is controversial because of its tremendous power in determining what issues the nation's citizens see. Every day, millions of Americans read newspapers or watch the evening news to try to learn about current events. Unfortunately, the media has a motive to sensationalize issues rather than to educate the public and its political representatives. It is up to the news executives and editors to tell the public what issues and events are newsworthy, but ultimately this is a business, not a public service. If it bleeds, it leads, because that's what sells. Politicians, public affairs officials, and special interest groups implicitly understand this fact and use it to obtain favorable coverage. The Army does not always address military issues in a public policy aspect, and, as a result, will often communicate its intent and goals in cold military terms, which diminishes the public's sympathy. This is particularly true in CBRN defense issues, where the media resurrects the ghost of Dugway's 1968 "sheep kill" incident to dismiss DoD CBRN defense statements, or highlight those few individuals who refuse to take anthrax vaccination shots because they don't trust the DoD to administer an FDA-approved vaccine. At the other extreme, we see instances of the media repeating the government's information on adversarial nations' WMD programs and the U.S. military's CB defense measures without any form of proper analysis.[1] One might compare CNN's "Operation Tailwind," where the media accused DoD of alleged nerve gas use during the Vietnam War, to the media's failure to compare the high cost of missile defense against the low cost of CBRN defense equipment.

This is the public environment within which the DoD CB Defense Program must operate. The challenges of developing and executing CBRN defense acquisition and policy objectives are not insignificant, and failure to address them successfully will result in continued equipment shortfalls and capability gaps. Good policy fails to form when Congress or OSD tries to direct specific technical or acquisition-related CBRN defense actions without understanding the implications on combat operations, cost, and schedule. Good policy fails to form when the Chemical Corps or JPEO-CBD tries to lead development of DoD CBRN defense policy without considering other defense policies and Congressional sensitivities. Technical experts should support policy development, and defense policy offices should support acquisition, doctrine, and training development, but each has to know its limitations.

We need USD (P) to lead policy issues, USD (AT&L) to lead acquisition issues, and the Chemical School to lead multiservice doctrine and training issues. Everyone else needs to work with and support the lead agent.[2]

UNDERSTANDING THE THREAT

As far as CW threat agents, DoD generally focuses on what are termed the *traditional agents*. These can be categorized as first generation (World War I agents, including mustard and lewisite agents), second generation (post-World War II nerve agents, including tabun, sarin, and soman), and third generation (Cold War nerve agents, to include VX and other V-class agents). Although these agents have been around for decades, scientists continue to research their properties in an attempt to better understand their effects on personnel, animals, and the environment. Research data developed before and during the Cold War are unearthed and examined with great scrutiny. Within the last decade, Army scientists have reevaluated the lethal dose concentrations for the traditional agents and determined, in some cases, that the lethal dose appears to be lower than had been thought. Because chemical agent detectors are already set to detect agent concentrations below the lethal dose, there is no immediate impact on military readiness or operations. However, it is important to understand the technical properties of CB warfare agents and radiological effects if we are to improve CBRN defense capabilities. Scientists and doctors still do not fully understand the physical properties by which mustard agent damages human skin, but they do understand the signs and symptoms that arise as a result of exposure and how one might protect against these properties.

Two major research issues have arisen from this study of traditional CW agents. Addressing concerns about Gulf War illness, Congress directed the Army to investigate the effects of single exposures of CW agents and the adequacy of military equipment to protect service members from low exposures. This research is particularly difficult, because researchers must use data and animal models to approximate the potential effects on humans. It is a matter of congressional law that DoD cannot perform any human experimentation with CB warfare agents, even on volunteers. This research continues with support from the Department of Veteran Affairs. A similar effort within the Army's Center for Health Promotion and Preventive Medicine has developed a technical guide outlining a set of short-term exposure limits for CW agents for commanders whose troops are exposed to nonlethal concentrations.

The other research issue is the question of how CW agents act in the environment; that is to say, how long does sarin persist as a lethal hazard if a particular concentration is deposited on concrete, steel, asphalt, or grass during a summer day? There is a great deal of debate within DoD as to whether the Army's Cold War data on agent persistence is accurate, or if more recent research suggesting that agent persistence is much less than thought (and therefore decontamination is not a big issue), reflects the truth. What makes this debate more challenging is that Congress has placed severe limits on DoD's ability to test CB warfare agents in the open environment. These limits arose as a result of the Dugway 1968 "sheep kill" incident, and were imposed as a political nod to concerned constituents rather than the result of any actual danger to off-post communities. Be that as it may, this issue of "Agent Fate" must be addressed, and if Congress were serious about its desires to assist the DoD in developing modern and effective CBRN defense capabilities, they would lift this sanction. There is no question that DoD could safely execute outdoor testing of CB warfare agents without any peril to the public today, and it is a capability that is desperately needed. For this to happen, the public and Congress would need to trust that the agency conducting the tests could do so safely. That is the real challenge.

The "traditional" BW agents comprise a much shorter list, which most experts could easily rattle off, although it probably would not do to publish it here. The CDC has a list of biological organisms that have special handling guidelines because of their potential impact on personnel and animals, about half of which could be weaponized. About half of those weaponizable agents are the top concerns of the Department. In general, weaponized forms of natural (but laboratory-grown) bacteria, viruses, and some toxins for the use of large area exposure of troops are considered traditional BW agents. Anthrax, smallpox, plague, tularemia, botulinum toxin, and ricin are some of the better known traditional BW agents. There is a great deal of medical research on the effects of BW agents, but not as much known about the weaponization of these agents or their persistence in the outdoor environment. Even following the anthrax letters from October 2001, there were few who could actually identify what they saw as "weaponized" grade anthrax.

There is a similar debate emerging with involvement of Department of Homeland Security (DHS) and DHHS in biodefense efforts, regarding development of biological vaccines and other medical countermeasures. Many civilian scientists and public health officials believe that the focus on traditional BW agents is too limiting, and ought to be on broader defenses against all potentially lethal biological organisms, regardless of their origin. After all, many people die every year from cholera, malaria, and even flu, and very few (if any) die every year from anthrax, smallpox, or plague. This is a valid point of debate for homeland security policy, but not for military defense policy. The budget is only so large, and (within DoD) we must prioritize threats that can directly impact U.S. military readiness and operations. This point is often lost in debates about CBRN defense, emphasizing the need to discuss counter- proliferation priorities separately from antiterrorism and homeland security concerns.

There is a great deal of concern within the Department about the threat of emerging CW agents, also called nontraditional agents, and genetically engineered BW agents. For the past decade in particular, the concern is that knowledge held by former Soviet researchers was being dispersed to other countries interested in developing WMD programs. The current debate lies in esoteric discussions of what agents these countries actually possess, and if they would employ these agents against U.S. forces if given the chance. Some parties argue that you cannot trust the intelligence community to accurately warn the Department in time for U.S. forces to implement the necessary CBRN defense measures, so there needs to be rapid development of defensive measures prior to any actionable intelligence that new agents are being weaponized and stored by adversarial nations. On the other hand, there are those who argue that enough has not been done to develop adequate defensive measures against the traditional agents, and there is only so much money allocated (less than one half of one percent of the DoD budget) to research and develop these measures. So should the DoD focus on developing adequate defensive capabilities for traditional agents or researching areas of potential future threats? Obviously there has to be a balance, and the OSD offices debate loudly about what that balance should be. Thus we saw the rapid prototyping of detectors for particular nontraditional agents in Iraq in 2003. Better safe than sorry? Or better to be fully prepared for today's threats?

These debates on what agents are threats, how they act in the environment, and what capabilities are required by military forces drive the need for live agent testing in the open environment. If you propose this idea to a DoD official, nine times out of ten you would get peals of laughter or looks of scorn as to the total political impossibility of convincing Congress that this is necessary. The exception is the DOT&E and the GAO—they have been articulating the need for live agent testing for no other reason than to allow the DoD to authoritatively state, "yes, we know the equipment will work during a battle because we tested it with real CB warfare agent in a realistic environment." How can we have confidence in the ability of equipment that has only been tested in a laboratory? Using chemical and biological simulants can go a long way to testing and verifying the equipment capabilities, but there is only so much that simulations will provide. There is nothing more effective than live weapons tests for understanding the adequacy of defensive gear. Anyone familiar with the checkered history of the Bradley infantry fighting vehicle's development can attest to this point.

The other point in favor of live agent testing is the need to better understand the effects of CB warfare delivery systems. Few U.S. experts have developed and tested offensive CB weapons, and practical knowledge of adversarial weapon systems is not extensive. Our data on offensive CB warfare delivery systems developed by the U.S. military is decades old, and other nations' weapons programs have certainly advanced far past what we could have done in the 1970s. There have been many advances in missile and UAV delivery systems but we have only models and simulations to guess as to their effectiveness. It is not just the CBRN defense community that needs to understand weapons effects; the missile defense and special forces communities need this information to understand how to counter these weapons. Yet any time that the U.S. military takes steps in that direction (case in point, DTRA's Project Bacchus in the late 1990s), the arms control community screams that such attempts are a violation of international treaty (despite lacking any evidence of actual intent to produce a CB warfare stockpile).[3] How can the military understand how to defend against the massive use of NBC weapons if it does not understand how the delivery systems work? Politically, this is the third rail of CBRN defense, but it represents an important policy issue that requires resolution.

WMD Intelligence

One year after the end of major combat operations, USD (P) Doug Feith gave a speech to the American Enterprise Institute on the Iraq war.[4] Here are some of his thoughts on the failure to find WMD stockpiles in Iraq:

- "The strategic rationale for the war didn't actually hinge on classified information concerning chemical and biological stockpiles. Rather, it depended on assessments about the nature of the Saddam Hussein regime and its activities.

- The danger was too great that Saddam might give the fruits of his WMD programs to terrorists for use against the United States. This danger did not hinge on whether Saddam was actually stockpiling chemical or biological weapons.

- Reasonable people did and do dispute whether that rationale justified the coalition's military action. But I think no one can properly assert that the failure, so far, to find Iraqi WMD stockpiles undermines the reasons for the war."

More than two years after the occupation of Iraq, after numerous Iraqi scientists have been interviewed, hundreds of ammunition dumps searched, and thousands of documents translated and read, nothing has surfaced to indicate that Saddam's WMD program presented a "grave and growing threat" to the United States. At best, Iraq had retained its nuclear scientists and equipment, but had not taken any significant steps to reconstitute a nuclear weapons program. Iraq's BW program was dormant. Its scientists worked on open, possibly related, research efforts in a string of laboratories and facilities capable of producing BW agents, but no agents were found. Many former CW production sites had not been in operation since the first Gulf War, let alone when the UNSCOM team left Iraq in 1998. Yes, there were civilian chemical production sites that might have been retooled and capable of producing CW agents, but only if there were any precursors to create CW agents or munitions to fill, of which there were none. Iraq had undoubtedly been rebuilding its ballistic missile program beyond what the UN resolutions prescribed. Then again, practically every country in the Middle East and Asia is interested in ballistic missiles (for instance, Yemen's purchase of conventional SCUD missiles from North Korea in 2003).

The debate over the actual rationale for going to war against Iraq will no doubt continue. There are really two pertinent issues for us: how the WMD intel was developed and how the WMD intel was used by policy and decision makers. Understanding these points is important for a number of reasons. The Robb-Silberman Commission focused on how the intelligence community developed its findings, completing its report in March 2005.[5] This report savaged the intelligence community, stating that there had been "poor intelligence collection, an analytical process that was driven by assumptions and inferences rather than data, inadequate validation and vetting of dubious intelligence sources, and numerous other breakdowns." In short, the commission felt that the intelligence community failed at its basic job. A major aspect of this failure, the report noted, was that in the absence of reliable data on Iraq's programs, the intel analysts chose to assume that Iraq probably possessed CB weapons and was seeking to rebuild its nuclear weapons program, based on its history prior to the 1991 Gulf War and its failure to account for all of its WMD program-related materials. Most analysts required hard evidence that Iraq did not have WMDs to change this assumption, and some may have disregarded evidence that did not support their premise.

The report goes into detail as to the missteps on each example—the aluminum tubes alleged to be part of the nuclear weapons program, the Iraqi defectors' reports of mobile biological research labs, the UAVs that could allegedly disperse BW agents. The report puts the burden on the intel analysts for failing to articulate the strength of their intelligence in the many summaries delivered to the Bush administration's senior policy makers. Although the report did not address the issue of how policy makers used this data, the commission believed that there was no political pressure on the analysts to produce inaccurate reports on the status of Iraq's WMD program.

Some believe that the intelligence community was politically influenced to modify its assessments to supporting what the policy makers wanted to hear, or that the policy makers "cherry-picked" what intelligence they wanted to publicize, using creative omission to create a story that the average American would accept. Numerous leaks and innuendo from within the CIA and other sources suggest the intelligence collection was not flawed, but the operational analysis by top-level officials was. As Kenneth Pollard wrote in his January 2004 article "Spies, Lies, and Weapons," the truth may be a little of all of these things. When UNSCOM left Iraq in 1998, the intelligence community had to rely on technical data collection and past assumptions to estimate what Iraq could have developed in four years' time. Although the intelligence community presented their assumptions and estimates, the Office of the Vice President and OSD policy had a different view of the state of Iraq's WMD program and Iraq's connections to terrorist organizations. The latter version was publicly promoted by the administration and echoed by the media. The question remains, was the Bush administration's real motive to create a democratic climate in the Middle East by toppling Saddam's regime, using the potential development of NBC weapons and possibility of terrorists obtaining these weapons as its rationale? The Downing Street minutes, leaked to the press in May 2005, seem to suggest that the British government saw the issue of Saddam's WMD program as insufficient evidence for regime change, while the Bush administration was eager to press on regardless.[6] The focus here, however, is on the intelligence community and the information it produced.

Reorganizing the intelligence community is probably not the answer, nor is increased congressional oversight. Previous intelligence has focused nearly exclusively on nuclear weapons. We must devote more resources to collecting information and correctly analyzing an adversary's offensive capability and intent to develop and use chemical and biological weapons. The U.S. intelligence community may be good at data collection, but it's the operational analysis that is suspect. Without credible expertise in understanding how CB warfare agents act in the environment, and without understanding the motivations of adversarial nations and terrorist organizations in developing and employing these weapons, it will remain extremely difficult to determine the potential effects on U.S. military operations. The result of aggressively prodding the intelligence community to deliver a "yes or no" answer is frighteningly clear. Intelligence analysts don't usually say "yes" or "no" to the question of whether U.S. interests and military forces are in peril. They say, "maybe—possibly—probably, but we're not sure. It depends on the assumptions and confidence in the intelligence assessments."

The tools for analyzing a country's procurement of material and equipment, production, and storage of NBC weapons are already in place—it is a question of allocating the time, personnel, and funding to increase these limited efforts and to fine-tune the analysis. Where the U.S. government is failing is that it has few good tools for evaluating the effects of CB weapons on protected and trained troops, unprotected noncombatants, and equipment.

Current models and simulations describe in great detail where the agent will land, and in what concentration, but it is inherent on analysts to determine the potential effects on exposed personnel. This estimate is usually based on lethal dose calculations, which do not take into account the effects of the environment on the agent's persistence and lethality or the benefits of seeking shelter. It is not always possible to understand the motivations and intents of countries that develop WMD programs, but we can conduct a better intelligence assessment than what was done in 2002 and 2003. The Bush administration accepted seventy of the seventy-four recommendations of the Robb-Silberman commission, one of them being to create a National Counterproliferation Center to better analyze and produce reports on WMD programs. It remains to be seen if the implementation of the commission's recommendations will result in better intelligence assessments.

RETALIATING IN RESPONSE TO WMDS

Did the U.S. government have a plan for retaliating against Iraqi forces if Saddam had in fact authorized use of CB weapons against the coalition (and if he in fact had the weapons to use)? It is unclear whether there was a decided retaliatory policy or not. In Rick Atkinson's book, he quotes Major General Petraeus as stating, "No one knows what will happen if the Iraqis use chemicals. It's not at all clear that he has the capacity to use them effectively. It's not that simple, and the intel on where they are seems shaky. I don't believe that the national command authority will decide on a course of action until they're forced to make that decision." [7] Secretary Rumsfeld would not elaborate on a retaliatory policy when questioned by the media, despite statements by the Bush administration that it would consider the use of nuclear weapons to respond to the threat or use of CB weapons. Gen. Myers commented in April 2003, "There were certainly some things that—where we think our psychological operations had a big impact on them, or we said 'Don't do this, or you're going to bear the responsibility.'" [8]

This ambiguity was not a new concept; the first Bush and Clinton administrations used what is known as *calculated ambiguity* to warn potential adversaries that they could expect an "overwhelming and devastating" response if they used chemical or biological weapons against U.S. forces. The advantage of using calculated ambiguity as the nation's retaliation policy was that it threatened nuclear weapons use but didn't specify the details or outline the results of such an action. The flexibility to choose a conventional or nuclear response keeps the adversaries guessing and the military's options open. On the other hand, this ambiguity leaves a sense of uncertainty in the minds of the people who have to plan and implement any retaliatory policies.[9]

There are two sides to this debate. The military hawks will say that, in the face of actual use of any CB weapons, the U.S. military has the moral right and obligation to respond with nuclear weapons. Usually they don't discriminate about the size, type, or impact of WMD used against U.S. forces—a WMD is a WMD whether it is nuke, chem, or bio weapon, so a U.S. WMD can be used in response. When pressed, they may feel a tinge uncomfortable about responding to small-scale chemical weapons attacks with nuclear weapons, but there is no question about our response to the use of anthrax or smallpox against U.S. forces or unprotected personnel—nuke 'em back to the Stone Age. The military doves question the rationale of using nuclear weapons in retaliation to a CB weapons event that may not match the casualty count of a nuke, particularly if the adversary is a nonnuclear country. Using nuclear weapons in response to a nonnuclear event could set a terrible precedent that might encourage nuclear weapons proliferation and preemptive use by other countries. With the advent of smart munitions, a massive conventional response would be entirely as effective, but there are questions as to whether these smart munitions can penetrate hard and deeply buried targets that may shelter NBC weapons production facilities or storage bunkers.

It is important to have a clear retaliation policy, and current national security policy supports this belief. Yet when it comes time to actually plan and execute necessary actions, the political and military leaders cannot decide on appropriate responses. This disconnect between policy and strategy may result in our military being unprepared to respond when ordered to retaliate, and emotions rather than logic could rule the day. The development of new nuclear weapons is and will continue to be a source of national and international debate. I don't think it will ever be acceptable to nuke a CB weapons site, despite any good intentions to destroy hard and deeply buried targets. If the U.S. government wants to deter adversaries from considering CB weapons use, there are other options, including nonproliferation, counterforce, active defense, and passive defense measures, that do not involve dubious threats of nuclear weapons use. That is not to say that nuclear weapons use should be ruled out, but the response should appropriately match the scale of the attack.

Threatening to use nuclear weapons against a terrorist group that has access to CBRN hazards is clearly untenable. If the number of casualties is too low, say less than three hundred (to use the cases of the Marine barracks in Beirut, Oklahoma City bombing, or Pan Am Flight 103 incident), it would be hard to justify a nuclear response, even if the terrorist group has clear connections to a nation-state. If more than five thousand American military personnel died as a result of an adversarial nation using CB weapons in a single attack against U.S. forces, perhaps a nuclear attack would be an appropriate response. But the U.S. government had better be sure that it can prove without a doubt that this adversary deliberately used a CB weapon or was about to use a CB weapon against U.S. forces prior to issuing a nuclear weapons release. Call it a "global test," if you will. Lacking solid actionable intelligence that stands up to the international community, the possibility of other nations following the precedent of the U.S. military's use of nuclear weapons is frightening. This aspect of national security has not been fully laid out and examined, even now, four years after the events of 9/11.

WMD EXPLOITATION AND ELIMINATION

At a National Defense University (NDU) conference in May 2003, Deputy Secretary of Defense Wolfowitz stated,

> The elimination capability that we put together in the months before Operation Iraqi Freedom will need to be retained, enhanced, and institutionalized. Accomplishing this will be an integral part of the effort to re-balance and re-allocate our force structure that I referenced earlier. In future conflicts, we should not end up playing "pickup games" when we are trying to put together forces for eliminating weapons of mass destruction in the aftermath of a conflict. We must ensure that there are sufficient forces in peacetime, adequately trained, organized, and equipped for that mission. As with all other aspects of our WMD defense capabilities, the enduring elimination challenge will not be just a matter of ensuring a sufficient number of people outfitted with the appropriate equipment, but also ensuring that those well-equipped personnel have the proper concepts, doctrine, and training to use those capabilities effectively to accomplish their mission.[10]

OSD leadership clearly believes that WMD interdiction and elimination are permanent missions for the future. The initial concept of a WMD exploitation task force was certainly rushed, and it was executed by an ad hoc organization developed in a very compressed timeframe without careful consideration of the real scope, logistics, and operational issues involved. To begin with, the selection of an artillery brigade headquarters was, in hindsight, unwise. This is not to question the professionalism of the soldiers who executed this demanding and unprecedented mission, but rather to question the Army and OSD leadership about why technical specialists were not chosen to form the command and control headquarters. OSD policy advocated that a WMD exploitation task force should move with operational units at the start of ground operations, and if a chemical brigade headquarters was not ready (probably the 415th Chemical Brigade headquarters, a reserve unit), any brigade headquarters would do.[11] Perhaps the effort might have been more successful had the WMD professionals been allowed to come in after the conflict, rather than rushing an improvised task force into theater, but OSD policy felt that this had to be done in a nonpermissive environment, rather than post-conflict, to ensure that no WMD material was lost or unaccounted for. If military leadership deems a mission important enough to demand such an effort, it should support careful planning and development of a force structure and capabilities for its execution. Past examples of the military leadership's concern over resolving these CB warfare issues have not been encouraging.

As it turned out, the WMD exploitation was hampered by the failure of pre-conflict intelligence, a lack of logistics support, and a lack of practiced operational concepts in theater. Most of the sites on the intelligence list were either misidentified locations or dead ends. In many instances, WMD-related information was coming down through intelligence channels to the military command without any technical interpretation. There was literally no concept or doctrine development on how to do the mission, no prior training for the teams, and little time to practice the procedure for securing a site, holding it, and processing any potential intelligence and materials found. The chemical units supporting the site exploitation were not prepared for this new mission. They expected to identify traditional CW agents used on the battlefield, not industrial chemicals stored in fifty-five-gallon drums. There was little thoughtful analysis from the battalion or brigade chemical staffs on the alleged "finds" that later turned out to be false alarms or misidentified material.

There was a general lack of understanding about enemy missile capabilities, with soldiers reporting anything bigger than an anti-tank launcher as a surface-to-surface missile capable of delivering CB agents. Many sites that held surface-to-air missiles were misidentified as potential chemical munitions, adding to the work burden. Sites that might have panned out were looted before they could be secured. Intelligence that might have led to information about WMD research and development, production, or storage was either deliberately destroyed or inadvertently carried off by locals. Ultimately, teams found no evidence of any WMDs, although, as Dr. Kay reported, they did discover some "WMD program-related material."

In February 2004, the NDU Counterproliferation Center, believing that WMD elimination would be a likely requirement for future contingencies, emphasized the need for a standing peacetime military organization led by a general officer with dedicated, prepared assets. This unit should be capable of operating in any phase of combat, and the mission must be integrated into the strategic planning process, contingency planning process, and the budget development process. OSD policy inserted language into the 2004 Defense Planning Guidance directing the chairman of the JCS to identify a DoD executive agent for WMD interdiction and WMD elimination within thirty days of the tasking. Once identified, the executive agents would have to develop a permanent force, concepts, and equipment to execute the mission. Unsurprisingly, the task to identify these two willing parties took a bit longer than thirty days (and was closer to 120 days).

Initially, it was thought that SOCOM would be the executive agent for WMD interdiction, and the Army was to accept responsibility as executive agent for WMD elimination, defined as "the systematic control, removal, or destruction of a hostile nation's or organization's capability to research, develop, test, produce, store, transfer, disperse, deploy, or employ nuclear, radiological, chemical or biological weapons, including programs, infrastructure, and technical expertise." This is a big mission. DTRA was considered for this mission, but they were more suited to be a support agency than a lead agency. JFCOM was another option, but had little support from the services (especially the Army, who would have had to provide the majority of personnel and equipment). The Chemical Corps wanted the mission, but the Army G3 was concerned that WMD elimination was "bigger" than the Chemical Corps (and was coming from OSD without resources). The Army's grudging acceptance of the mission concerned OSD enough for Secretary Rumsfeld to decide that STRATCOM should be the executive agent to integrate and synchronize all combating WMD efforts, overseeing both SOCOM's and the Army's efforts.[12]

The Army created a CBRNE Command at Aberdeen Proving Ground in October 2003, reflagging the Technical Escort Unit as a chemical battalion and including other military units such as the 52nd EOD Group, the Chemical and Biological Rapid Response Team (CB-RRT), and other Army specialists in this field.[13] It was flagged as the 20th Support Command (CBRNE), commanded by an aviation general officer, reporting directly to U.S. Army Forces Command. This unit's mission is to deploy teams to conduct CBRNE crisis response, consequence management, elimination, and remediation operations in support of combatant commanders, DoD installations, and the homeland. Other Army assets, such as USANCA, USAMRIID, and the U.S. Army Center for Health Promotion and Preventative Medicine (CHPPM), might be tasked to support their operations, and JFCOM could task the Air Force, Navy, Marine Corps, and DTRA for CBRN subject-matter experts. In essence, this is an attempt by the Army to create a unit that can go one better than the CBIRF, by addressing any military or terrorist scenario involving the use of WMDs. The Army is creating a second TEU battalion to allow coverage of both east and west coasts. NORTHCOM's JTF-CS will provide the overall coordination between federal, state, and local agencies in response to any terrorist CBRN incidents. Although technical expertise is a core capability, any WMD elimination task force will require an intelligence, surveillance, reconnaissance (ISR) function as well as an inherent security, transportation, and medical capability. It is not just about dealing with CBRN hazards, it's about going after a potentially hostile country's WMD program, and that end must remain in the focus.

The real question is whether WMD elimination requires a permanent force, equipment, and policy. Is the expectation that the United States will forcibly interdict and eliminate WMD programs in nations other than Iraq? One colleague suggested that President Bush was very serious about WMD interdiction (witness the emphasis on his Proliferation Security Initiative) and helping countries like Libya get rid of their CB weapons stockpiles. There are terrorists with WMD capabilities (some believe), and it may be that Iran and North Korea ask the United States to assist in disposing of their weapons. Then again, they may be forced to get rid of them. Given that these interdiction and arms control efforts are taking place, and if there are CB weapons stockpiles out there, DoD will require a WMD elimination capability. If this is a valid future mission, the Army (and hopefully the Chemical Corps) needs to develop appropriate doctrine and train its leaders in how to execute a nontraditional CBRN defense mission. If the DoD effort to interdict and eliminate Iraq's WMD program was an aberration and not an expected future mission, then the Army (and Chemical Corps) needs to focus its scarce resources on more appropriate mission areas.

EXECUTING THE DOD VACCINE PROGRAM

What could be more controversial than DoD's anthrax and smallpox vaccination program (other than the intelligence assessments in 2002)? Even when faced with clear evidence in 1991 that Iraq had a very real capability to weaponize and use anthrax against unprotected U.S. forces, it took seven years for DoD to develop a vaccine production capability and to decide to vaccinate the total force against these threats. Because there are no detectors in the world that can detect and identify a BW agent before troops are exposed to potential lethal levels, it made sense that the military would want a medical countermeasure. Except for one thing—as DoD vaccinated thousands, then tens of thousands, and now hundreds of thousands of service members, the number of people suffering from side effects increased (much less than one percent of those vaccinated)—and they started complaining to the press. One potential side effect of the current smallpox vaccine—death—really raised the stakes.

From a military policy standpoint, there is no real debate here. Anthrax, smallpox, and pneumatic plague are serious threats. There are a number of other BW agents that are not as lethal, but that could severely impact the military's ability to conduct operations and win on the battlefield. Vaccines generally work for the overwhelming majority of the populace. From a strictly medical viewpoint, there are particular biological organisms that can cause severe illness or death, and there are specific medical countermeasures that, if applied promptly and correctly, will assist the patient in recovering. Case closed. In fact, future medical concepts envision microorganism-sized "bioscavengers" that could be injected into service members, constantly circulating and attacking CB warfare threats that penetrate the skin. Nice idea, subject to the many concerns one might have to having an active "scavenger" injected into one's bloodstream. All this seems perfectly logical, until disgruntled or scared service members declare that they should not be subjected to medical countermeasures that in their opinion might hurt rather than aid them. The lack of evidence of any BW agents in Iraq fueled objections to vaccines that might have harmful, long-term side effects. When faced with the idea of a court martial for disobeying direct and lawful orders, these service members decided to take their case to the courts and the media. This creates the challenge of justifying the use of these particular vaccines and the policy of total force vaccination.

Most of the top DoD leadership (with the exception of Defense Secretary Cohen and perhaps a few others) initially questioned the total force vaccination policy. Instinctively, they didn't like the idea of 100 percent of the troops taking shots, because they understood that a small percentage would have side effects that would be detrimental to overall morale. On the other hand, the options were few, given that pulmonary anthrax was a quickly lethal BW agent with persistent effects and large area coverage. They could (1) not take the vaccination and threaten nuclear retaliation against any adversary that used anthrax against them; (2) keep large stocks of anthrax vaccine in theater and start treatments upon exposure; (3) vaccinate only those personnel in high-risk theaters for more than thirty days, or (4) vaccinate everyone in the force. Option one had its pros, but the use of nukes wouldn't be allowed without unquestionable proof of a deliberate BW attack. Option 2 had massive logistics challenges and would disrupt combat operations, because vaccination had to occur within twenty-four to forty-eight hours from the time of exposure. Plus, it takes a minimum of two to four shots for 85 percent effectiveness over one year, and six shots for near to 100 percent immunity. Option 3 was more probable, but exposed travelers into and out of the theater to risk, and imposed additional requirements on the reinforcements to that theater if an attack was initiated. Plus there was still the issue of multiple shots for the newly vaccinated. That left option 4, which had the least impact on military operations but posed a huge public relations challenge.

Right now, the DoD medical community is on the defensive. Following allegations that vaccines might have caused Gulf War illnesses after 1993, the medical community adopted a more complex tracking process to identify and report adverse reactions in the population. This practice was not fully in place by the time U.S. forces were in Bosnia, which raised more questions about whether the U.S. military was adequately tracking pre- and post-vaccination health assessments of service members deploying to combat operations. When BioPort bought out the private Michigan vaccine facility and modernized it to allow for manufacturing the FDA-approved anthrax vaccine in much larger lots than before (due to the total force vaccination policy), the FDA did a complete review and report on the facility and its ability to safely prepare and ship the vaccine. The FDA's findings identified areas that needed improvement, which critics instantly jumped upon as evidence that the DoD program was unfit. The recent (2004–2005) federal court cases in Washington, D.C. have called into question the validity of the FDA licensure (again), despite many independent reviews and millions of service members and civilians that have received the vaccine without long-term side effects. The smallpox vaccine has been less controversial only because it was designed for natural outbreaks of the disease, which (for now) is exactly how the weaponized agent works. If the DoD starts a mandatory total force program for smallpox, similar problems will arise.

To successfully get this program back on track, DoD needs a true public policy approach that de-emphasizes the technical aspects of the program and emphasizes the impact on military operations from these specific threats, the options available to decision makers, and the many safety and efficacy measures taken to develop and administer the vaccines. They've been working hard on a next-generation anthrax vaccine that will reduce or eliminate many of the current vaccine's challenges. In a sense, DoD is already doing this for the general public and the service members. In addition, DoD should have a congressional outreach strategy that continuously updates key congresspeople on measures being taken to improve the process. But the concept of vaccination, as a principle, is not going away as long as there is a legitimate BW threat that imperils service members.

What makes this program more challenging is the new input by DHS and DHHS through Project BioShield, President Bush's ambitious multibillion-dollar effort to include the pharmaceutical industries in developing countermeasures for personnel involved in bioterrorism incidents. DoD has the most experience in developing, testing, and manufacturing vaccines, but DHS and DHHS have the lead (and the money) now. Interagency cooperation has improved; for instance, a new DoD-DHHS biodefense facility is being constructed at Fort Detrick, Maryland, for the coordination of federal government medical biodefense efforts.[14] In addition, many biologists and public health officials want to focus on biological diseases other than the traditional BW agent list, such as malaria, cholera, and influenza. They would rather see a broader public health approach than a specific terrorist/military BW agent approach. Obviously, when we combine natural disease outbreaks with potential weaponized BW agents, the list becomes long very quickly, and there aren't enough funds or time to address them all. That's why we need to retain separate but complementary focuses on military biological defense measures and homeland security biological defense measures. The policy implications of implementing vaccination measures must be specific to the mission.

Last, OSD policy offices dealing with counterproliferation, antiterrorism, and homeland security need to ensure they are developing policy on medical aspects of the programs with assistance from medical experts—not the other way around. In executing policy, yes, you need medics to translate defense policy into specific instructions and processes. But keeping in mind the four players in public policy, it is a mistake to let technicians develop top-level policy, just as it is to let top-level policy leaders try to direct and execute the technical aspects of specific medical programs. Too often, however, nonmedical defense experts defer to medical experts because of the technical and scientific aspects of vaccination. That's a mistake. Policy is policy.

TOXIC INDUSTRIAL CHEMICALS AS WMDS

The threat issue leads us back to the alleged danger of toxic industrial chemicals and toxic industrial materials (TICs/TIMs). I don't believe more than a few toxic inhalation hazards are weaponizable threats to U.S. military forces (as opposed to the thousands of general chemical hazards to unprotected noncombatants). No one has developed lists of potential biological industrial hazards or radiological industrial hazards distinct from warfare threats, which makes me constantly question why people use the term TIM. I get no logical responses from my DoD colleagues other than "we're working on those lists," so I guess that, since people recognize nuclear, biological, and chemical weapons, they decided that there must be toxic industrial biologicals and radiologicals, as well as TICs. Other than 1984 Bhopal's chemical spill and the alleged use of industrial chemicals during the Bosnian conflict, there has been little credible analysis of industrial hazards as immediate operational threats to the military. Terrorists or similar indigenous forces might be desperate enough to rig a tanker filled with industrial chemicals or to attack a chemical plant in an attempt to cause mayhem, but is this really a weaponized threat that, because of its questionable potential to disrupt and stop military operations, requires a unique military solution in the form of new equipment and doctrine? Is the potential threat equal to that of traditional CB warfare agents? I don't think so. But if it is, we need to decide exactly which toxic industrial hazards are the real threats, and which protective capabilities we require. The military should not rely on OSHA/NIOSH standards, but due to the current concern about terrorist CBRN incidents and the need to assist civilian emergency responders, that's exactly where the program is inexorably drifting.[15]

Why is this a contentious issue? Low-level exposure to toxic chemicals is a chronic health risk to unprotected individuals; I understand that. As such, this is a medical occupational health issue and should be treated accordingly. If people are exposed to a large dose of industrial chemicals, usually the color, odor, or unpleasant symptoms associated with the hazard will cause them to move away from the source without incurring immediate lethal effects. Emergency responders handle this situation every day across the United States without mass casualty events and without calling on the military CB defense specialists for assistance. At best, military forces can wear their protective masks and escape any ill effects from clouds of inhalation hazards released against their positions.

If military CBRN defense specialists believe toxic chemicals are a general WMD-type threat to all military personnel, they will seek to address this concern by incorporating industrial chemical detection into all their CW detectors, adding protection against industrial chemicals with their general purpose military masks and suits, and trying to clean up industrial chemical spills with their decon systems. This would not be a bad thing except that the consequences of dealing with occupational safety hazards and life-threatening, super-toxic CW agents are so different. Breathing in a small amount of nerve agent will kill an individual within minutes, rendering a combat unit unable to complete its mission. A few soldiers throwing up around an agricultural warehouse because of a few poorly-sealed drums of pesticides is not a mission-stopping issue. Is the U.S. military truly prepared to imperil the success of a combat mission because their small-unit leaders are concerned about what might happen to Sergeant Joe Smith's health thirty years from now as a result of a short-term and non-lethal exposure to industrial chemicals? While good leaders are concerned about the health of their soldiers, sailors, airmen and Marines, mission accomplishment has always been the top priority in the high-risk job of protecting the nation. Understanding the battlefield hazards to which military personnel are exposed is important in that it allows us to take care of them during and after the conflict is over. That is the job of the medical community, not CBRN defense experts.

Many technical questions also remain unanswered. Which chemicals are the really dangerous ones, and what is the standard for protecting military personnel as opposed to industry workers? Should the military adopt low, safe-sided occupational safety levels or high-risk, minimum protection (but less burdensome) levels, and who sets the high-risk levels? What are the costs and benefits of trying to develop new, small chemical detectors that identify multiple industrial chemicals and super-toxic CW agents? What is the commander supposed to do if the detectors start alarming to low levels of arsine, for instance? Do we protect against corrosive acids as well as harmful gases, which would require impermeable protective suits? Should military protective suits be able to resist corrosive sulfuric acid spills? Should military specialists be in charge of decontaminating large industrial spills in overseas locations, or is this a job for civilian responders or contractors? There is a huge void in analytics, policy, and cost/benefit analysis that should be addressed before military CB defense specialists adopt the job of hazardous material handlers. Toxic industrial chemicals are not WMDs, but some people are prone to think so. This notion unnecessarily elevates the importance of industrial chemicals and complicates the discussion.

Some officers have told me that there is a middle ground. We could develop general purpose military masks to filter out some small number of toxic inhalation hazards and create a new set of detectors specifically for those hazards, while keeping general purpose CB detectors, protective suits, collective protection systems (but with NIOSH filters), and decontamination systems aimed at the traditional CB warfare threat. Then we could give specialized equipment to NBC reconnaissance specialists and in-theater laboratories to conduct more thorough analyses, while the Engineer Corps retains the important mission of environmental remediation. It could work, but this requires policy direction—direction which has been absent for too long.

HOW CLEAN IS CLEAN?

I have a personal interest in this arcane issue, because I was the action officer that facilitated the development of an interim DoD "cleanliness" policy memorandum that was approved in April 2002.[16] This memorandum was a step toward resolving how to handle CW contamination of forces and equipment in a military theater of combat, but it fell short in a number of areas. It did not establish quantifiable levels for CW agents, but relied on a "no alarm" condition by any currently fielded military detector as evidence of acceptable military risk. Although different military detectors have different detection levels, resulting in troubling inconsistencies, the four services would not accept any other answer. Trying to use more sophisticated detectors and procedures would require specialists and cost resources that the services were unwilling to support. As a result, the policy did not discuss inter-theater travel by formerly contaminated large aircraft or ships or the issue of those assets returning to the United States during or following the end of conflict. It did not address biological or radiological contamination, although there was plenty of data for low-level radiological contamination limits. The lack of comprehensive data on BW agents and the controversy over decontaminating the buildings affected by the recent anthrax letter incidents caused a complete lack of desire to deal with the issue of resolving post-conflict BW contamination.

Such "paralysis through analysis" is ridiculous, and I am never quiet about saying so. People confront me and say, "okay, so what's your solution?" I do have an approach. It is executable, but demands two key elements—a willingness by some organization with authority to lead and a willingness for the military community to accept operational risk in CBRN hazard exposure. These are two rare commodities. There are reams of data on chemical, biological, and radiological health effects available to anyone who wishes to collate them. It's a matter of drawing a line and stating, here is what we consider "safe" for military operations, and here is what we consider "safe" for the general population. There must be at least two quantitative measures. The military inherently adopts risk as a tradeoff for mission accomplishment; it seems that the only place the military leadership shies away from increased risk (compared to emergency responders in the United States) is with its views on CBRN defense. Second, we must ask what we would do today. The unwillingness to identify low-risk exposure levels is partly due to the fantasy that evolving technology will eventually allow the military to measure hazard exposure below OSHA/NIOSH standards with handheld monitors. And until that happens, no one wants to commit to any low-risk exposure levels. There is an unspoken desire to avoid any connection with potential Gulf War illness claims or face tough questioning as to why the military doesn't adopt OSHA-like exposure standards. Well, this technology is not coming anytime soon. DHS is working with several organizations to develop CBRN hazard exposure standards for emergency responders, but that work may be years away. And (similar to my discussion on TICs) do we really want military personnel to adopt OSHA/NIOSH-type standards that can hinder military performance?

We need an interim DoD decontamination standard that applies to warfighting units on the battlefield, far forward of noncombatants; a standard that permits military personnel to continue operations while significantly reducing acute life-threatening exposure but not necessarily chronic low-level exposure. I hate to use the NIOSH term, but the immediately dangerous to life or health (IDLH) standard for chemical warfare agents could be the level to which all military equipment needs to be decontaminated. For military and civilian personnel who support the movement of personnel and material into and out of theater, there could be a second, more rigorous standard for formerly contaminated equipment moving from forward areas to the clean, rear areas. Call this standard the *worker exposure level* for personnel who understand that a marked piece of equipment was decontaminated and may present some low-level agent exposure risk. This standard is needed not only for the protection of U.S. military and DoD civilian personnel, but also to allow for the transit of equipment and personnel through host-nation ports and air bases and over their territory. There needs to be a decontamination standard for formerly contaminated equipment and personnel returning to the United States for general release. This standard is not simply to protect noncombatants who are unfamiliar with the risks of low-level CBRN hazard exposure. It is also necessary for remediation efforts after the conflict and after any domestic terrorist CBRN incidents. This is clearly DHS's and EPA's realm, but DoD needs to be involved to ensure that an executable plan could be implemented today—not five to ten years from now. Eventually, we need an international standard to ensure the success of multinational military actions, but that's a future objective.

Given these three scenarios—battlefield, rear area/transit, and post-conflict/return to the United States—we need to develop quantitative measures for each class of hazard. For chemical and radiological hazards, this is relatively simple. There are data to support nearly anyone's level of risk, but this should not be the call of the forward military commander. We need a standard, based on both technological merit and potential impact on operations that applies to all military and DoD civilians throughout the world. Many military CBRN defense experts shy away from quantifiable measures and merely want to use the lack of any alarm from military field detectors as the qualitative measure—this is an academically lazy cop-out and needs to be avoided. Once a quantitative limit is set (such as IDLH for chemical agents), we establish a bar at which all future detectors must work, and perhaps we can get the number of false alarms down in the process. For biological hazards, there is more risk, because it takes such a small amount of agent to infect a person and detectors are not sensitive enough to BW agents to allow personnel to avoid exposure. There may be some BW agents to which we cannot set a quantitative battlefield exposure limit that will ensure personnel do not become casualties. For other BW agents, this isn't necessarily a problem. That's why we need an interim policy to address the best we can hope to achieve for today, and why we must continue to focus on a specific quantitative physiological measure.

For rear area/transit through countries, the standard does have to be higher, but it should not be NIOSH standards. The hazardous materials emergency responder has to use equipment that will safeguard his or her health for an entire lifetime of low-level exposures. No one should expect that military personnel will face a lifetime of low-level CBRN hazard exposure (at least not from the deliberate use of NBC weapons). The intent is to allow military and civilian personnel to work unprotected near and around formerly contaminated equipment and personnel (or human remains). To do this will require more sensitive equipment than military detectors intended for combat operations; specifically specialists and laboratory equipment. This requires more time to screen and validate the level of decontamination, which means added operational expenses to the services; something that the services are trying desperately to avoid by insisting on using fielded military detectors as the standard. That won't work.

Here's the rationale for why specialists will work. First, the Cold War is over—assuming the DoD counterproliferation strategy works, there aren't going to be hundreds of major weapon systems slimed with tons of CBRN hazards. There will be a limited and manageable number of major equipment and personnel that can't be left in theater to screen. Second, not doing so may critically impact the military's ability to move critical equipment and personnel into and out of theater during combat operations in a timely manner. The few air and sea transportation assets will not absorb many losses before the impact on logistics is felt on the front lines. Blindly ignoring the problem until it hits us in the face, as the U.S. military has done for the past few decades, is not an acceptable solution.

For post-conflict and post-incident remediation and return of formerly contaminated equipment and personnel to the United States, we can't get around the EPA's insistence on NIOSH-type standards. That's not necessarily bad. The U.S. public should demand a certain degree of surety that returning equipment and personnel are safe from contamination. DHS will have a difficult time establishing decontamination standards that are safe, reasonable, and achievable. Again, well researched chemical and nuclear hazard data exist. It's always the question of residual biological hazards. There is a solution—it requires that a group develop agent-specific hazard data and protocols to form qualitative measures. Bacterium such as anthrax will always be challenging due to its persistency and lethality, and some contagious viruses will always demand extremely strict measures to avoid an epidemic. Many BW agents are not very persistent, and some are very short-lived. We cannot afford to get hung up on the substantial threats of anthrax and smallpox in the effort to develop common sense protocols to address the general threat of low-level BW agent contamination. The answer cannot be "zero" or "as low as reasonably achievable." The costs of cleaning the postal offices after the October 2001 attacks were astronomical. In many cases, it may be more cost-effective to destroy the contaminated equipment rather than clean it up and return it to the United States. It may be that temporary internment of equipment and human remains and quarantine provisions have to be part of the post-conflict/post-incident remediation effort.

Many have addressed this issue, and this discussion has gone on since 1997. We let the technical nature of CBRN hazards and lack of comprehensive data get in the way of risk management and common sense. It is hard work, and it lacks visibility and priority similar to other WMD topics of discussion. It is long overdue for DoD to come to grips with this issue and adopt an interim standard that can be researched and adjusted over time. Waiting for all the low-level exposure data and magical technical fixes to address this problem is not the answer.

Summary

As I mentioned at the beginning of this chapter, it is easy to focus on the technical aspects of the CBRN defense program. It is easy to count pieces of equipment, describe their technical qualifications, and train troops or emergency responders on what to do if these hazards are present. Addressing the defense policy aspects are hard, and are made harder because of the complete lack of any real experience gained from operations in a CBRN-hazard environment. On the policy aspects, we are all guessing to one degree or another because there are no actual cases of U.S. troops dealing with these weapons on the battlefield since World War I. Even the success or failures of deterrence is relative without understanding how NBC weapons and CBRN hazards are really used in wartime or terrorist incidents. The tendency to lump all CBRN defense policy aspects of counterproliferation, antiterrorism, and homeland security into the general category of combating WMDs is unwise, because each scenario has different assumptions, vulnerable populations, acceptable risks, and consequences in the decision-making process.

These policy discussions influence the funding, development, and distribution of doctrine, material, and organizational units that, as a whole, represent those necessary capabilities for dealing with NBC weapons and CBRN hazards. If we are to successfully build capabilities for all potential CBRN defense scenarios, it is necessary to understand that combating WMDs is more complex than just dealing with the technological challenges of the individual threat agents. We cannot afford to lump all combating WMD issues into one pile and expect to effectively address the unique areas of counterproliferation, antiterrorism, and homeland security. Thomas Barnett, in his book *The Pentagon's New Map*, calls the focus of subject-matter experts into one specific area "vertical thinking." He calls for the capability for "horizontal thinking," or the ability to view the execution of war in the broader context of everything else. It's very much like that with CBRN defense policies. If we do not address CBRN defense issues in the operational contexts of counter-proliferation, antiterrorism, and homeland security, we face the very real danger of being mired into further "paralysis through analysis" that focuses only on the specific threats, and not the desired capabilities.

CHAPTER 10

IMPROVING CBRN DEFENSE CAPABILITIES

When a subject is highly controversial one cannot hope to tell the truth.
One can only show how one came to hold whatever opinion one does hold.
One can only give one's audience the chance of drawing their own conclusions as
they observe the limitations, the prejudices, the idiosyncrasies of the speaker.

—VIRGINIA WOOLF, BRITISH NOVELIST

During the Worldwide Chemical Conference at Fort Leonard Wood, Missouri, in October 2004, Lt. Gen. William Wallace discussed how the V Corps handled the perceived CB warfare threat during Operation Iraqi Freedom. He stated that there was no question in anyone's mind prior to March 2003 about Saddam's intent to use chemical weapons. As to whether Saddam actually had a WMD capability, General Wallace asked the attendees whether it really made a difference. Because Saddam had the capability to weaponize CB agents and had a history of using them, General Wallace said, it was prudent to "take him off the street."

But of course, it does matter whether or not Saddam had CB weapons. For a moment, forget the fact that Saddam was a bad guy. Ignore the fact that the Bush administration's stated reasons for the war relied on the presence of CB weapons. Ignore the implication that instead of using our resources to go after al Qaeda, Iran, Syria, North Korea, or Sudan, the military was used to force regime change on a troublesome nation that lacked a capable military force and had no designs against the United States.[1] Although most military analysts thought Saddam had CB weapons in 2003, many knew (or should have known) that this meant nothing if he did not have a trained military force capable of employing CB weapons. The fact that he did not have an effective military force and was not even thinking about supplying terrorist groups with CB warfare agents meant there would be little to no impact from CB weapons on U.S. forces. Because no CB weapons have been found in Iraq, military and civilian leaders now wonder whether the U.S. military, lacking a peer-type competitor, really needs to be fully prepared for CB weapons use. At the same time, they continue talking about combating WMD efforts in Iran and North Korea, but the focus in those countries is clearly on nuclear, not CB, weapons.

The employment of U.S. intelligence capabilities, CB defense technology and doctrine, and numerous counterproliferation and antiterrorism policy initiatives relied heavily on the assumption that these weapons existed and that they represented a clear and present threat to U.S. forces and interests. The issue of "missing" CB weapon stockpiles has ensured that anyone trying to promote a serious initiative on CB weapons proliferation or CBRN defense would be dismissed or marginalized. There are other, more important defense priorities than solving the known capability gaps and policy challenges in CBRN defense. Concerns about terrorist plots to detonate nuclear and biological weapons in U.S. cities may direct funds to DHS, but they do not address existing DoD military shortfalls. As long as the U.S. military continues its nearly ninety-year streak of not being attacked with CB weapons, the lesson seems to be that a heavy-handed diplomatic effort, combined with aggressive overt and covert interdiction missions and a massive retaliatory capability, will do just fine in lieu of CBRN defense capabilities.

I started this book talking about dragons as an analogy to the way people misperceive weapons of mass destruction as dangerous, horrible devices. Many people use the term "WMD" to deliberately paint a picture of fear— fear that some group or some nation is developing insidious, invisible super-weapons that can kill thousands to millions with little skill or effort. Fear that terrorists, even now, are brewing up nerve agents and smallpox in home labs within the United States, waiting to unleash hell in America's shopping malls. Fear that countries across the world are developing sophisticated, large-scale WMD programs in hardened and deeply buried laboratories with the intent of slaughtering massive numbers of Americans. The public, fed by the imagination of Hollywood movie producers and fiction authors as well as the media and politicians, sees WMDs as causing major disaster events, equivalent to city-busting nuclear weapons that may wipe out huge numbers of unsuspecting and unprotected people.

On the other side, military and political leaders remain strangely untouched by these prophecies of doom, thinking perhaps that there is ample time to address critical CBRN defense shortfalls. These people may fail to address CBRN defense seriously because military analysts and politicians often say "WMD" when they really mean "nuclear weapons," and therefore ignore the issue of smaller scale, less lethal CB weapons. Politicians use their positions in congressional committees to demand that DoD officials explain their actions in executing the DoD CB Defense Program, even as they fund pet CBRN defense projects for their constituents and ignore known, critical CBRN defense equipment shortfalls. During war games and exercises, our military leaders often ignore CB weapons effects because addressing worst-case CB scenarios causes operational delays and logistics nightmares that distract from a tidy mission execution.

Little to no thought is given to examining the impact of CB weapons use on the modern battlefield. Attempts to improve CBRN defense in the near term can be stifled by debates among the many government and private agencies involved, calls for additional studies, and arguments over who is in charge and who will pay. While some identify WMDs as the ultimate threat, others apply their energy and funds to more immediate and solvable defense issues. That mindset must not be allowed to continue. Where the United States could once view NBC weapons solely as a strategic deterrence issue between the two major superpowers, an increasing proliferation of CB weapons worldwide means that, wherever it deploys forces, the U.S. military faces the threat that CB weapons might be used.

Nations using NBC weapons and terrorists using CBRN hazards do present credible military threats. The DoD CB defense community, however, lacks the ability to convince the powerful defense advocates who fund and execute conventional military acquisition programs to fully address those threats. Senior military and political leadership understand the implications of high-consequence, low-probability CB warfare events, and they are backing the low probability side by funding only a minimal CBRN defense capability. They discount black swan events because they're hoping these events won't happen on their watch, and, for the most part so far, they've been correct. As a result, DoD remains mired between miniscule funding of CBRN defense during peace time and dealing with frantic money-slinging whenever a crisis looms. We need to demonstrate that a rational solution exists other than throwing billions of dollars blindly at futuristic technologies and envisioning worst-case scenarios that will probably never occur. We need a new, transformational approach to CBRN defense that ensures U.S. military forces will be ready when the next black swan event occurs.

The way forward involves putting the threat into proper perspective; developing necessary threat and vulnerability assessments and cost-benefit analyses with rational studies; and implementing comprehensive solutions that address the realistic threat of CBRN hazards in the context of how the military operates. This is not a technical challenge as much as it is a policy and doctrinal challenge, where OSD and Congress must apply the requisite leadership, DoD execute the focused studies and prioritize appropriate funds, and the CINCs identify those critical shortfalls that address immediate and realistic threats. We need effective policies to guide the development of distinct CBRN defense strategies that can be executed for counterproliferation, antiterrorism, and homeland security. We will not be successful if we stick with the tired phrase "weapons of mass destruction." For the good of our military and the country, this Cold War phrase needs to go. Political speechwriters and Cold Warriors will probably not let us abandon this phrase, but at the least, the definition needs to be changed and it needs to be used in the right context.

DECONSTRUCTING WMDS

Recently, Maj. Gen. Robert Scales (Ret.), discussing past military trends and future transformation needs at a book signing hosted by the Association of the United States Army, mentioned that the threat of CB weapons would not dramatically impact the success of U.S. forces in future military operations.[2] When Gen. Gordon Sullivan (Ret.), the former Army chief of staff, asked Scales, "Are you deconstructing the threat of WMDs?" Scales elaborated that chemical and biological warfare isn't that great a threat to today's military; rather, it was nuclear weapons that pose the threat. Similarly, in the summer of 2003 Gen. Barry McCaffrey (Ret.) told an audience that our military forces can manage the effects of CB warfare, but high explosives still kill soldiers every time (and a lot more frequently). He felt that biological warfare was the least likely threat, while chemical warfare was the most likely, and military installations were at risk of terrorist CW attacks in particular. What worried him was the U.S. ability to deter and, failing that, respond to a small nuclear weapon going off in an American city. At a luncheon in January 2005, former National Security Administrator Brent Scowcroft called for the United States to "disaggregate weapons of mass destruction," if for no other purpose than to focus on the larger threat of nuclear proliferation.[3] This is exactly what military leaders and analysts need to do—deconstruct the myth of "weapons of mass destruction." Most military and political leaders understand that there is a difference between nuclear, biological, and chemical weapons, but they haven't been offered a way out when someone says, "We're worried about WMDs. What can we do?"

The Bush administration's strategy to combat WMDs is not a step in the right direction if we wish to deconstruct this myth. Although the intent to discourage terrorist CBRN incidents may be sincere, the desire to improve CBRN defense can't compete with concerns about cyber terrorism, defending critical infrastructure, or funding traditional major defense acquisition programs. Jonathan Tucker and other analysts have long argued that terrorist groups are unlikely to move toward increased use of CBRN hazards as long as conventional explosives can effectively get the attention of governments and the media. Intelligence analysts seem to assume that the growth of a global economy, continuing advances in chemistry and biotechnology, and increased educational opportunities for people living in adversarial nations will automatically result in a corresponding increase in the probability of terrorist use of sophisticated NBC weapons (as opposed to improvised CBRN devices). Thus we hear the warning repeated every year: "in the next five to ten years, it's coming. . . . It's not a question of if, but when. . . ." The protection of military forces from NBC weapons should not be combined with homeland security concerns, as the Bush administration's strategy would have it. We need to decouple the mission of counterproliferation against NBC weapons from that of responding to terrorist CBRN incidents. We need to tailor policy approaches and build capabilities appropriate to the specific missions and their unique characteristics.

For years, the DoD CB Defense Program focused on developing equipment that would enable military forces to survive and sustain operations in a CBRN-contaminated environment. The military has specific risks and assumptions in a war, and its CBRN defense capabilities must reflect that. The administration's use of the term *WMD* perpetuates the myth that nuclear, biological, and chemical weapons are all equally devastating, whether used by terrorists or military forces. When the military talks about countering a country's WMD program with nuclear-tipped ballistic missiles, it does not encourage the development of CB defense capabilities for tactical operations. Similarly, discussions about terrorist WMD capabilities in terms of an apocalyptic cult's desire to take out a city's population with fifty pounds of anthrax or smallpox or a nuclear device doesn't motivate the states to develop credible emergency preparedness and response capabilities for small-scale releases of CBRN hazards. If we are to develop a solution to a perceived threat, the nature of that threat must be clear, and it cannot be clear if we continue using the term *WMD*.

The NDU Center for Counterproliferation Research changed its name in mid-September 2004 to become the Center for the Study of Weapons of Mass Destruction (WMD Center). The rationale behind this decision was that the center had expanded its scope of activities to include research, education, and outreach, including homeland defense and security, counterproliferation operations, nuclear deterrence, and WMD elimination. This lines up nicely with the Bush administration's strategy. With the adoption of its new title, the center seems to be endorsing the idea that terrorist CBRN incidents will always be mass casualty events, and that WMDs are strictly defined as nuclear, biological, or chemical weapons events, irrespective of actual number of munitions, amount of agent, or number of casualties. This is at odds with Dr. John Reichart's (director of the WMD Center) 2002 thesis that the military had to view nuclear, biological, and chemical weapons as implicitly different. Although the view of CBRN hazards has grown outside of the traditional counterproliferation sector, equating terrorist CBRN incidents with a nation's military NBC weapons capability is not an effective way to improve CBRN defense.

In early November 2004, defense officials announced that the Defense Science Board would undertake a summer study on defenses against WMDs, broadly exploring where there may be gaps or misplaced priorities in the nation's ability to protect against NBC weapons. The board was asked to develop a national enterprise architecture for WMD defenses—one that could adapt to shifting priorities—against the entire spectrum of threats. The article announcing this study noted that in the first presidential debate, President Bush and Senator John Kerry in 2004 agreed that the proliferation of nuclear weapons, particularly involving terrorist groups, constituted the single greatest security threat to the nation.[4] The Defense Science Board completed its study in August 2005, although the results will probably not be available to the public due to sensitivities of their contents. The Board studied a broad range of scenarios, observing that nuclear terrorism was a distinct class of its own when measured against CBR threats. Because intelligence assessments of terrorist WMD capabilities are so uncertain, the Board concluded that the U.S. government might never see a terrorist CBRN incident coming. At the same time, proactive measures are required to lessen the chance of a successful attack. If an attack happened and those measures were unsuccessful, then the government would have to mitigate and recover from the incident. There are tables of data behind these seemingly obvious statements, but the important point is that the Defense Science Board inadvertently proved that the black swan theory applies to combating WMD efforts.

The DoD is currently developing a National Military Strategy to Combat WMD, which outlines how it intends to execute nonproliferation, counterproliferation, and consequence management. The Defense Science Board also recognized the ad hoc development of this military strategy, noting that it did not adequately address the complexities of combating terrorist use of WMDs. In fact, considerable debate continues as to whether the National Military Strategy for the War on Terrorism or one to combat WMD should address the threat of terrorist WMDs (or both). Similarly, the CINCs must determine how to modify their conceptual plans for combating WMD and combating terrorism, resolving if the former is for nation-state WMD programs and the latter will address how to address terrorist WMD threats. The confusion over who is in charge of policy and who is in charge of executing the efforts becomes very clear. We need to deconflict the two areas, but first we need to establish a common definition such as proposed in Chapter 1:

> **Weapons of mass destruction (WMD).** Weapons that are capable of a high order of destruction or of being used in such a manner as to create large numbers of casualties (more than one thousand people) during a single event or incident. This arms-control term generally refers to the asymmetric threat or offensive programs developed by adversarial nations or nonstate actors to cause mass casualties or a massive effect on military or public essential services. This may include the use of nuclear, biological, or chemical weapons, high-yield explosives, information technology systems, high-energy weapons, or those improvised weapons that can realistically cause mass casualties or mass effects.

This definition may be problematic in that past events, such as the World War II strategic bombing of Dresden and Tokyo, might be considered WMD events, and the development of certain conventional munitions such as the Air Force's twenty-one-thousand-pound Massive Ordnance Aerial Bomb might be categorized as a WMD. But the definition does accurately attribute a particular weapons effect—that is, a single incident that can cause mass casualties—as opposed to limiting the discussion to nuclear, biological, and chemical weapons, irrespective of quantity or outcome. Scholars and military analysts who intend to address NBC weapons use during military operations, distinct from terrorist use of CBRN hazards, can then have rational discussions without the histrionics, emotional arguments, and other baggage the phrase "weapons of mass destruction" entails. On the other hand, if they use the term WMD and mean "nuclear weapons," they ought to say "nuclear weapons" —it will just make it so much easier on our CBRN defense specialists.

A JOINT ENABLING CONCEPT FOR CBRN DEFENSE

There is no question that future adversaries will continue to develop NBC weapons—more likely for use against their neighbors than against U.S. forces—irrespective of existing arms control treaties. As long as U.S. military counterforce and active defense efforts cannot guarantee perfect protection against NBC weapons, U.S. forces will need a robust CBRN defense capability and the strong effort to protect the general public will continue. Military installations and facilities have peculiar populations and resource constraints that make their protection concepts distinct from the general approach used by state and local emergency responders. These multiple and competing priorities make it imperative that common technologies and expertise be leveraged against these very different mission areas. Unfortunately, no one in the defense leadership is likely to pay serious attention to CBRN defense until an incident erupts.

To develop an effective approach to these issues, we must understand the priorities of government decision makers and the way in which CBRN defense issues are addressed in national strategies and policies. Within the Beltway, no one (outside of the DoD CBRN defense community) is talking seriously about CBRN defense as a top defense priority. Defense leaders do, however, say that countering the proliferation of WMDs is a top priority, as are antiterrorism efforts at military installations and supporting state and local responders in preparing for and responding to terrorist CBRN incidents. All three topics include CBRN defense as a subcomponent, but not as a central issue. This point cannot be overemphasized. To be successful, DoD CBRN defense specialists need to understand and talk about counterproliferation, antiterrorism, and homeland security. Technological discussions will occur later, when the decision makers want to understand how particular CBRN defense capabilities will enhance their respective approaches and what the cost of implementing these new approaches will be.

The fact that defense officials do not view CBRN defense as a top priority does not mean that we should stop using the term "CBRN defense." The technologies and concepts developed in response to military requirements for CBRN defense have direct applications to homeland security and antiterrorism efforts; but the specific equipment and tactical procedures used need to be adjusted from military specifications to fit antiterrorism requirements and policies in their role to protect noncombatant populations and essential services. *CBRN defense* should be a generic term used to describe a particular response to a specific unconventional weapon system used against military or civilian personnel, irrespective of scenario. We have to stop thinking of CBRN defense as an entity in and of itself, and accept that it is an enabling concept within the larger scope of protection, subservient to the higher requirements of counterproliferation, antiterrorism, and homeland security. That is why we need this new definition:

Chemical, biological, radiological, and nuclear (CBRN) hazards. Those toxic CBRN hazards that are released in the presence of military forces or civilians, not necessarily in quantities that could cause mass casualties. CBRN hazards include those created from a release other than an attack, toxic industrial chemicals (specifically toxic inhalation hazards), biological diseases with significant effects, and radioactive matter. Also included are any hazards resulting from the deliberate employment of NBC weapons during military operations.

When the JROC authorized the establishment of the JRO-CBRN Defense interim office in the summer of 2002, a group of analysts developed a general

CBRN defense concept to capture this new approach (see Figure 10-1). The need for this framework should become apparent. Many others continue to resist this interpretation because it does not allow CBRN defense to be "special," and that contradicts their concept of reality. For many years, people inside the DoD CB defense community have believed that CBRN defense is its own reason for being, and the fact that acquisition funding for CBRN defense has never been seriously cut since 1981 affirms their belief. This Cold War attitude also ensures that its funding and relative importance will also never significantly increase.

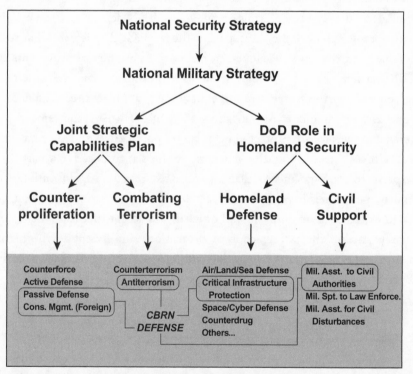

FIGURE 10-1 *CBRN Defense Construct for the Twenty-First Century*

Under Secretary Rumsfeld's directive to transform the DoD's future warfighting capabilities, the Joint Staff developed a common frame of reference to define and develop future joint force concepts, capabilities, requirements, and forces. Lt. Gen. James E. Cartwright, the director for force structure, resources, and assessment (J-8), led the development of a Joint Operations Concept as a framework that would fundamentally alter the basis of all defense research and development efforts. Traditionally, one of the four military services identifies the requirements for equipment and forces that it believes are necessary for military operations; develops and acquires service-unique defense equipment; and tries to integrate these capabilities with their sister services in the execution of joint military operations. Very often, that integration was not effective, as noted when Army, Navy, and Air Force elements had different communication systems that could not talk to each other, or weapons ordnance that was not interchangeable with other services' weapon platforms. This new concept proposed top-down identification of capability gaps and solutions that would establish joint requirements at the onset so that the services could acquire common equipment. That is to say, all future military equipment must be designed from the start to be jointly interoperable. Because this approach largely strips the services of their independence in training, equipping, and sustaining their forces, it was not warmly received. The concept was complex and featured a new set of terms and approaches. Although it made sense to create a fully joint acquisition effort, the shift from requirements-based acquisition to capability-based acquisition was a major change.[5]

Secretary Rumsfeld approved the Joint Operations Concept in November 2003. Its purpose is to describe how commanders (ten to twenty years in the future) will accomplish strategic objectives through the conduct of military operations. The document identifies four immediate joint operating concepts—military combat operations (traditional war-fighting against another nation), homeland security, strategic deterrence (actions taken to discourage aggression by potential adversaries), and stability operations (military operations during peacetime). Against these four operating concepts, there should be a set of functional tools by which the commander executes his or her plans. These joint functional concepts include force application (the shooters), protection (defense), battlespace awareness (data collection), command and control (decision-making), focused logistics (supply), and net-centric operations (communications). Everything that the military develops as a future capability is supposed to fall under one of these functional areas, with applications in major combat operations, strategic deterrence, stability operations, or homeland security. To implement this plan, the Joint Staff identified leads for each functional area, creating six functional capability boards (FCBs), each chaired by a general/flag officer and including representatives from the four services, combatant commands, and OSD agencies. These FCBs meet frequently to review relevant issues and desired joint capabilities under their domain, and to recommend actions to the JROC and OSD on respective defense policy and acquisition actions.

The Protection FCB has oversight on air and missile defense, maritime defense, combating WMD (counterproliferation), force protection (combating terrorism), force health protection (medical), critical infrastructure protection, information operations defense, and a collection of minor areas such as rear area security, noncombatant evacuation operations, counterdrug operations, personnel recovery, and improvised explosive devices. Each of the components illustrates a common set of characteristics that would be executed in any of the four operating concepts (major combat operations, strategic deterrence, homeland security, and stability operations). That is, each protection capability element must explain how commanders will **detect**, monitor, and track adversary actions; **assess** the capabilities arrayed against their force; decide on a course of action and **warn** military and civil authorities in preparation of an attack; **defend** the force through both active and passive measures; and finally, **recover** in a minimum amount of time under all military operations. Developing a joint construct of how forces are to protect themselves against various threats as they are executing military operations creates a common framework by which all services and CINCs are expected to develop joint protection capabilities and to field jointly interoperable defensive equipment. This joint construct is explained in the JROC-approved Protection Joint Functional Concept, dated February 2004.

The functional concept is the Joint Staff's first attempt at defining what "protection" means and how DoD should develop a true joint protection capability, but it is a flawed document. The challenge was that the four services had already developed fully articulated service-unique strategies for many of these "protection" mission areas, and the Joint Staff had to identify joint protection architecture that accommodated these established areas. The current Protection Joint Functional Concept does a poor job of articulating how these components fit under an overarching concept. This may be because entrenched defense programs do not want to give up control of their respective specialty areas, or the document's authors lacked the ability and knowledge to coherently articulate a grand strategy (or both).[6] The theater air and missile defense and combating WMD sections are the only two that outline mature joint concepts.

The combating WMD section tries to address all CBRN defense activities under the four operating concepts but ignores any discussion of counterforce, active defense, or consequence management. Similarly, there is no discussion about how CBRN defense is to be executed outside of its traditional passive defense construct. Either the document's authors expected subject-matter experts from antiterrorism and homeland defense to address CBRN defense within their sections (which is a hopeless endeavor), or they just couldn't describe how the national strategy addressed those mission areas.[7] Instead, they repeated the words of the National Strategy to Combat WMD, which does not offer clear details either.

The DoD CBRN defense community and the theater air and missile defense community had advantages over the other mission areas, in that they had already established joint doctrine and joint acquisition efforts. As the JRO began standing up in 2002, there was an opportunity to change the joint doctrine concept of contamination avoidance, protection, and restoration, which was seen as applying primarily to major combat operations and was very structured—the force tried to avoid contamination first, protected itself when it could not avoid the contamination, and then restored the force with decontamination assets. This doctrine, in general, still works well for combat operations.

In 1999, the Chemical School's commandant, Maj. Gen. Ralph Wooten, championed a new construct called sense, shape, shield, and sustain, the four-S (4S) concept:

- *Sense CBRN hazards.* The capability to continuously provide information about the CBRN situation at a time and place by detecting, identifying, and quantifying CBRN hazards in air, in water, on land, on personnel, and in equipment or facilities. This capability includes detecting, identifying, and quantifying those CBRN hazards in all physical states (solid, liquid, gas).

- *Shape the operating environment.* The capability to characterize the CBRN hazard to the commander—develop a clear understanding of the current and predicted CBRN situation; collect, query, and assimilate information from sensors, intelligence, medical, etc., in near-real time to inform personnel and provide actual and potential impacts of CBRN hazards; provide the ability to conduct operational risk management and the ability to plan and execute CBRN defense operations.

■ *Shield the force.* The capability to shield the force from harm caused by CBRN hazards by preventing or reducing individual and collective exposures, applying medical prophylaxis to prevent or mitigate negative physiological effects, and protecting critical equipment.

■ *Sustain combat operations.* The capability to conduct decontamination and medical actions that enable the quick restoration of combat power, maintain/recover essential functions that are free from the effects of CBRN hazards, and facilitate the return to pre-incident operational capability as soon as possible.

In this approach, the commander could maintain awareness of what was going on within the battle, share information on the hazard with neighboring forces, protect forces that needed to be shielded while unthreatened forces remained unmasked, restore contaminated forces to their full capacity, and sustain combat operations. These were simultaneous operations, rather than the sequential steps promoted in the old concept. The 4Ss align (quite unintentionally) with the Protection Functional Capability's activities of detect (sense), assess and warn (shape), defend (shield), and recover (sustain). Because the 4S concept loses the strict "military combat" connotation, it is applicable (with some changes in interpretation) to antiterrorism, consequence management, and homeland defense.

The Air Force, Navy, and Marine Corps stonewalled the 4Ss in 1999. A good number of military analysts still don't quite feel comfortable with it today, but the JROC and OSD did approve this strategy in the summer of 2003, and that tends to end a lot of arguments. Proponents for a distinct and separate biodefense strategy are not comfortable with this concept because it does not distinguish chemical from biological defense. While the 4S concept has its advantages, one major disadvantage is how the user community has forced the 4S concept into technological niches. That is to say, all detection devices are addressed under *sense*, all information management systems (including medical surveillance) are part of *shape*, all individual protection (including medical pretreatments) and collective protection systems are addressed under *shield*, and all decontamination systems and medical diagnosis and treatments are included under *sustain*. The medical community is uncomfortable with this, but they do retain a distinct acquisition commodity area under the JPEO (and that's where the money-based decisions are made).

This is an artificial and unnecessary constraint for a capabilities-based defense acquisition program, because individuals require decon kits and manual CBR monitors as survival (shield) capabilities, and fixed sites need both heavy decon systems and collective protection shelters to sustain their capabilities. Keeping these categories in acquisition, instead of operational, terms is comforting to the old-school CB defense specialists, so that's the way it is for now. We must, however, rid ourselves of the fixation on technology and equipment in the CBRN defense arena. It has to be development of people, concepts, and things—in that order.

Table 10-1 illustrates how the 4S concept could work across the four major areas of passive defense, consequence management, antiterrorism, and homeland security.[8] The wording in the homeland defense column, in particular, is pure conjuncture. DoD has been reluctant to voice an official position on support to new homeland defense initiatives other than those that have been resourced and directed by Congress. This reluctance should not be confused with DoD's clear role in defending the United States from external attacks. Congress has designated funding for purposes other than direct DoD military operations such as the WMD Civil Support Teams, and the dialogues and temporary personnel details between DoD and DHS demonstrate their ability to co-develop national CBRN defense capabilities.

Aside from how DoD addresses congressionally-mandated programs and works with DHS, there is no national architecture other than what was announced as President's Bush's biodefense strategy for the Twenty-First century.[9] It boasts four pillars: surveillance and detection (active warning and attribution), threat awareness (BW-related intelligence, assessments, and future threat anticipation), prevention and protection (proactive prevention and critical infrastructure protection), and response and recovery (response planning, medical countermeasures, mass casualty care, decontamination, and risk communication). Basically, it is the 4S concept with embellished wording. Although it's unclear whether there is any relationship, it is apparent that the construct does work at the top level. Again, it's the details within each S principle that makes the concept work for these unique mission areas.

TABLE 10-1   *How CBRN Defense Works Across Mission Areas*

Passive Defense	Consequence Management (Domestic and Foreign)	Antiterrorism (Installation Preparedness)	Homeland Defense
Sense			
View CBRN warfare agents in theater of operations (standoff CBRN detection and NBC reconnaissance)	Survey and monitor the extent of CBRN hazards (standoff detection and NBC reconnaissance)	Survey and monitor the extent of CBRN hazards (standoff detection and NBC reconnaissance)	Support a national biodefense surveillance effort (medical surveillance)
Enhance situational awareness in immediate area (automatic point CBRN detection and medical surveillance)	Identify unknown hazards to safeguard personnel (automatic point detection and medical epidemiology)	Detect and identify immediate hazards to safeguard personnel (automatic point detection and medical surveillance)	Maintain awareness at critical military and civilian sites (automatic point detection)
Shape			
Provide near-real-time and predictive hazard information to commanders (integrated early warning, battlespace analysis, battlespace management)	Provide near-real-time and post-event hazard information to responders (hazard prediction and integration with civil information systems)	Provide near-real-time and post-event hazard information to decision makers and threatened populace (hazard prediction, mass alert capability, integration with civil information systems)	Provide near-real-time and post-event hazard information to regional/national agencies (hazard prediction and integration with civil information systems)

TABLE 10-1 *How CBRN Defense Works Across Mission Areas (continued)*

Passive Defense	Consequence Management (Domestic and Foreign)	Antiterrorism (Installation Preparedness)	Homeland Defense
Shield			
Enhance general personal survivability against CBRN agent exposure (manual CBR monitors, protective ensembles, medical prophylaxes, individual decon kits)	Ensure protection of emergency responders to OHSA standards (manual CBR monitors, protective ensembles, medical prophylaxes, individual decon kits)	Protect general population with appropriate protection (protective ensembles, fixed collective protection systems, personnel/patient decon, medical treatments)	Support development of national medical countermeasure stockpile (med prophylaxes, medical diagnosis and treatment)
Maintain ground/air/sea operational tempo thru survivability (vehicle collective protection, operational decon, NBC contamination survivability)	Maintain essential public services through selective protection of critical nodes (mobile/transportable collective protection shelters, operational decon)	Initiate response with installation emergency responders (mobile/transportable collective protection shelters, operational decon, medical diagnosis and treatment, emergency response gear)	Support civilian initiatives at federal, state, and local levels (collective protection systems, operational decon, and emergency response gear)

TABLE 10-1 *How CBRN Defense Works Across Mission Areas (continued)*

Passive Defense	Consequence Management (Domestic and Foreign)	Antiterrorism (Installation Preparedness)	Homeland Defense
Sustain			
Sustain operations and initiate other recovery and restoration efforts (fixed site collective protection, thorough decon, medical diagnosis and treatments, and logistics support)	Restore government services and protect military/civil infrastructure in support of lead agencies (support to federal/state/local emergency response, thorough decon, logistics support)	None—rely on DoD and other federal agencies responding as consequence management forces.	None—rely on DoD and federal agencies responding as civil support forces.

We can also examine the U.S. government's formation and execution of BioWatch, BioSurveillance, and BioShield programs, plus FEMA's active support of developing state and local emergency preparedness and response. Between these four national biodefense efforts, we can see the sense, shape, shield, and sustain concept emerge. Although there is no deliberate connection between the national biological defense strategy and the 4S concept, certainly the concept can serve as a general model for military applications across mission areas.

A PATH FORWARD

Brig. Gen. Stan Lillie, the Army's chief chemical officer, articulated a new vision for the Chemical Corps in October 2004. He envisioned an Army that is equipped, trained, and ready to fight and win, unhindered by threatened or real CBRN hazards. He wants the Chemical Corps to be tactically and technically unsurpassed, imbued with a warrior ethos. He intends to maintain CBRN defense capabilities as both vital and relevant for the combatant commander, the joint war-fight, and defense of the homeland. This is a noble vision, well worth working toward with all available assets and energy. It is the specific goals under which we might endeavor to reach this vision that now need to be stated and acted upon.

Unless we can outline an operational strategy that defense leadership can support and resource, the military will not get the necessary doctrine, training, and equipment to allow them to operate unhindered by CBRN hazards. Technical proficiency is important to understand and respond to these hazards, but it is not enough. We must understand how the enemy uses NBC weapons and how to employ CBRN defense assets and concepts under specific counterproliferation, antiterrorism, and homeland security concepts. Gen. Peter Shoomaker, Army chief of staff, and Lt. General Wallace have both stressed that the Army expects soldiers to be warriors first and technicians second. In 1972, Gen. Creighton Abrams decided to divest the Army of the Chemical Corps largely because he felt that it was the responsibility of the soldiers who had to live and die on the battlefield—not some technician's—to make sure the Army had a defensive capability against NBC weapons.[10] We need to avoid a repeat of that history. Hence the specific following long-term strategic goals:

Implement an aggressive education and outreach campaign to develop a senior leader constituency within the Army, OSD, and Congress. The Army must take the lead in championing CBRN defense, because the Army is the DoD Executive Agent for this mission and the overwhelming majority of full-time DoD CBRN defense specialists reside in the Army. The history, experience, and dedication for this mission is in the Army. Traditionally, the Army frowns on self-promotion, and it does not like the idea of lobbying Congress.[11] The Chemical Corps, as a part of the Army, mirrors that attitude and does not do a very good job of convincing senior Army, OSD, and Congressional leadership that investing in CBRN defense capabilities is worthwhile. The Chemical Corps believes that an honest appraisal of the threat should lead to funding increased personnel and equipment capability. Theirs is a fundamental misunderstanding of how U.S. defense policy is developed. Stationed at Fort Leonard Wood, in the middle of Missouri, and having only a few field grade officers within the Beltway, the Chemical Corps is unable to stay aware of and influence the current defense agenda. The Army leadership, failing to appreciate CBRN defense, has reduced the number of general officers in the Chemical Corps to one—the commandant of the Chemical School.[12] DoD WMD experts outside the Army are not looking out for the Army's CBRN defense interests. Meanwhile, funding for CBRN defense remains less than adequate to address the current military requirements of 1-4-2-1, resulting in an Army unprepared for NBC warfare.

Public policy experts could easily craft an effective engagement strategy, focusing on developing people, concepts, and things. This should begin by convincing Army senior leadership to actively support improvements in CBRN defense, to commit to working closely with OSD on developing critical policy and budget issues, and to work with Congress to address CBRN defense shortfalls that imperil protection of military service members. One immediate proof that this is needed is the Army's elimination of an NBC reconnaissance vehicle in the Future Combat System program. At the least, the Chemical Corps should encourage Army and DoD senior leadership to commit to the following:

- Add full-time Chemical Corps general officer positions to the JRO for developing capabilities, the Army G-3 for operational planning, and the

20th Support Command (CBRNE) for specialized operations.[13] All CINCs should have chemical officers at the rank of colonel rather than lieutenant colonel, and require dedicated, trained staffs to take on the expanded missions of antiterrorism and consequence management. Experience is desperately needed in those positions, and the lack of opportunities to advance to senior ranks is causing junior officers to leave the Chemical Corps and Army.[14]

- Document and discuss with senior OSD and congressional staffers how the projected levels of CBRN defense funding do not meet current military requirements for more than one major regional conflict. This may require analyzing and demonstrating the operational impact of CBRN hazards on personnel and equipment, but it works better than the vague statement, of "It's not a matter of if but when."

- Increase the visibility of joint CBRN defense training at the national combat training centers and education of senior military leaders and CINC staffs at Fort Leonard Wood.

- Become a strong advocate for the following suggestions below.[15]

Engage the four services and OSD agencies on the issues of the CBRN defense role within counterproliferation, antiterrorism, and homeland security missions. The CBRN defense community is very insular, in part because of the tendency to promote a "high wizardry" technological complex about this subject, and in part because many believe that CBRN defense is a stand-alone, unique capability. Those military and civilian experts in the areas of antiterrorism and homeland security don't understand technical issues, and because of that, often chose to either ignore or over hype the CBRN hazard. The belief that we need to focus on combating WMD implies the need to address a specific threat, one that usually requires development of specific technical equipment, and that flies in the face of Secretary Rumsfeld's instructions to switch from threat-based acquisition to capability-based acquisition. We need to stress that CBRN defense is a necessary component of the larger capabilities of counterproliferation, antiterrorism, and homeland security, and that these larger areas remain vulnerable as long as they remain segregated from the CBRN defense community.

At the Worldwide Chemical Conference in October 2004, Lisa Bronson (DUSD [TSP/CP]) stated that the Chemical Corps had four missions that had to be performed simultaneously: protecting the troops and sustaining operations in a CB warfare environment, assisting with civilian CB warfare casualties in theater, responding to a terrorist CB incident within the homeland, and dealing with WMD production facilities in theater. Reasonable people may disagree with the last item (depending on your views of how active the U.S. government will be in combating the proliferation of WMD programs), and antiterrorism specific to military installations needs to be on the list. At a 2005 conference in Washington, DC, staff officers of the combatant commands came together with the JRO and other subject matter experts to address CBRN defense issues. In articulating their mission needs, they identified the need for more specialization in CBRN defense as opposed to a more general technical specialist. This is the future for CBRN defense forces. The Chemical Corps needs to recognize and adapt to these new directions from OSD leadership. Developing the concepts for how CBRN defense should be executed under counterproliferation, antiterrorism, and homeland security is a necessary first step to get resources and to build an effective DoD program.

Design a joint enabling concept for CBRN defense that addresses the desired capabilities for counterproliferation, antiterrorism, and homeland security. We absolutely need to fix the current joint protection functional concept, in that it does not address CBRN defense capabilities outside of counterproliferation. More importantly, we need a document that can clarify to top defense leadership how CBRN defense supports these three mission areas and why combating WMD, at best, only applies to counterproliferation missions. Without a firm statement of how CBRN defense supports the national military strategy, this program will be mired in the lower tiers of defense spending and priorities. Without a clear definition of how CBRN defense works in the three major mission areas, the CBRN defense community will continue to be sidelined while representatives from OSD, Joint Staff, service staffs, and CINCs quarrel about what they need, who is in charge, and who should pay. Technicians won't be invited to these meetings. People who understand military strategy and priorities and who can talk operational military lingo will have seats at the table.

We need the right agencies to lead the development of these issues. STRAT-COM needs to address the evolution of counterproliferation (writ against nation states) as NORTHCOM takes on antiterrorism at military installations and JFCOM standardizes domestic and foreign consequence management practices. That leaves SOCOM to address combating terrorist CBRN threats, as is their specialty. Four complementary strategies would be far easier to understand and execute, as long as the Protection FCB keeps everyone from duplicating efforts and responsibilities while addressing all areas of concern. Meanwhile the JRO and Army address the CBRN defense issues across these four primary mission areas.

The current Joint Protection Functional Concept should be re-written immediately to acknowledge a concise group of the top protection niches, such as force protection, force health protection, combating WMD, homeland defense, and air and missile defense, without filtering specific mission capability elements into artificial tiers such as protection of personnel, protection of physical assets, and protection of information. This was originally done because of a poorly-executed attempt to start with a blank page, which was foolish considering the maturity of most defense protection capabilities. Once the links within this major concept are made clear, the JRO should articulate how the joint enabling concept of CBRN defense applies to these major niches. Table 10-2 demonstrates the need to apply specialized CBRN defense tools and expertise to specific missions. This table also illustrates the fallacy of developing a new BW concept—what value does a stand-alone BW concept provide if it is generally applicable and not focused on a specific operational need or mission area? Proponents of this concept do not recognize the necessity of clarifying whether they are discussing BW defense of a maneuver unit during combat or an installation during peacetime.

Base the 4S concept on operational capabilities, rather than on acquisition technologies. We need to change services' mindset from acquisition to a more operational focus. The technical focus of the Chemical Corps has resulted in categorizing all recon, detection, and identification equipment as contamination avoidance (*sense*), all modeling and simulation tools into another bin (*shape*), all medical and nonmedical protective equipment together (*shield*), and all decontamination equipment as restoration (*sustain*).

TABLE 10-2 *Specific CBRN Defense Roles in the Joint Operating Concepts*

Major Combat Operations	Stability Operations	Strategic Deterrence	Homeland Security
CBRN Defense Subcategories			
Passive defense	CBRN antiterrorism	Nonproliferation	Critical infrastructure protection
Foreign consequence management	Foreign consequence management	WMD interdiction	Military assistance to civil authority (domestic consequence management)
CBRN antiterrorism	WMD elimination	Counterproliferation	

This arrangement of technological rice bowls works well for acquisition agencies and budget analysts, but they do not make sense of operational analyses and capability assessments. The fact is some detectors aid more in protection than in identification and warning, that shaping is more than just decision tools and simulations, that shielding involves decontamination for mobile forces and personnel, and that sustaining involves fixed collective protection shelters. The current 4S concept does not reflect these complexities.

It may not be possible to assess the true impact of CBRN hazards on personnel and equipment, determine CBRN defense capability shortfalls, or develop joint strategies to correct capability shortfalls when people address manual detection techniques (such as M8 or M9 chemical detection paper) within the sophistication of automatic chemical standoff detectors. We cannot determine the impact of CBRN hazards on fixed sites' ability to sustain combat operations without addressing both decontamination capabilities and collective protection shelters. We cannot determine the impact of CBRN hazards on maneuver forces' shielding capability without considering the family of systems (including operational decon systems, collective protection systems, and NBC contamination survivability measures) that the crew of a tank or infantry fighting vehicle requires to maintain operations through contaminated environments. Because the analyses and assessments begin with the wrong assumptions, the resulting programming and budgeting recommendations remain biased toward contamination avoidance and protective equipment.

Conduct an operationally based assessment of DoD CBRN defense capabilities and prioritize funding to correct those deficiencies identified. In 2003, the JRO developed what they called a baseline capabilities assessment that used J-8 methodology to assess the health of the passive defense. The JROC reviewed and approved the baseline capabilities assessment and the 4S concept in the same meeting. The good news was that the brief held the JROC's interest, the JRO successfully used the J-8 methodology to assess passive defense, and the four services all participated in the assessment. The bad news was that the assessment used a technological categorization to assess current equipment and proposed future programs. It used an analytical construct, but the assessment was largely subjective. The assessment graded shape—information operations—as the weakest capability area that, with little investment, could be improved in the near term, with *sense*—detection— as the next-weakest capability area due to less-than-full performance in stand-off detection and next-generation agent detection. Shield—protection—was seen as critical but better off than the other two areas, and sustain—decontamination and medical treatments—was seen as the best of the four CBRN defense areas. The recommendation was to get the services to pay for JSLIST protective suits, use half of those freed-up funds on detection, and the other half on shape and sustain technology areas. This process was effective in establishing the JRO as a serious force in redefining the CB defense program priorities.

Yet during Operation Iraqi Freedom, critically-deficient decontamination and collective protection capabilities were all too apparent. One of the major faults of the assessment (other than subjectively assessing the technological capabilities) was that it was based on the values in service requirements documents, that is to say, on desired future objectives rather than on past and current capabilities. Had the JRO evaluated the CBRN defense capabilities against a baseline of what existed in 1991 during Operation Desert Storm, or as compared with other nations' CBRN defense capabilities, the assessment would have been far different. The U.S. military has perhaps the best CB detection systems in the world; additional improvements come in small increments. On the other hand, many other nations and even emergency responders have far better decontamination systems and collective protection shelters than the U.S. military does. The JRO's failure to recognize these shortfalls demonstrates an urgent need to revisit the assessment's methodology and to reassess passive defense capabilities.

The JRO assessment did note three specific must-do actions. First, the program has to fund the general cost of supporting joint CBRN defense acquisition, including fixing the aging and inefficient test and evaluation infrastructure at Dugway Proving Ground and developing a common data set for modeling and simulation efforts. These efforts would dramatically improve CBRN defense acquisition across the board. Second, the program has to reexamine the CB warfare agent challenge levels that were developed based on Soviet-style Cold War attacks. This included sensor mixes and employment, which might be different for a modern U.S. military force organization facing a modern adversary. The JRO still had to tackle the issue of the services' different practices regarding the issue and consumption of protective suits to establish future requirements. In the policy area, the JRO resolved to address the requirements for protecting a population other than U.S. forces in a particular theater of war. The "how clean is clean" issue remains unanswered, as does the JRO's role in supporting other defense acquisition agencies regarding NBC contamination survivability.

Third, the JRO needs to perform capability assessments for CBRN defense in the execution of consequence management, WMD elimination and interdiction, homeland security, and antiterrorism efforts, especially if the DoD plans to use different equipment, concepts, and risk management in those areas. These assessments, however, cannot be done correctly until the JRO adopts an operational mindset and revises the 4S concept accordingly.

Get Congress to lift restrictions on open-air tests of CB weapon systems and CBRN defense systems, or allow the U.S. military to conduct these tests in other countries. Saving the most radical idea for last, technical and tactical CBRN defense experts must be credible in regards to strategy, policy, and use of their unique equipment. A colleague of mine commented that CBRN defense may be one of the only areas where the twenty- to thirty-year veterans are all operating without any practical experience. While it is a good thing that U.S. military forces have not been attacked by another nation with CB weapons, it is impossible to predict what adversaries can do with their weapon systems and difficult to have confidence in our CBRN defense equipment, unless the U.S. government requires testing and evaluation trials in a realistic, open air environment. Although chemical and biological simulants have been extensively used in tests and evaluations, we will always doubt whether our equipment really works against CB weapons and warfare agents.[16]

Politically, this issue is probably dead on arrival, and that's unfortunate. Between the arms control agencies, Congress, and the media, it's doubtful that this idea would survive more than a few minutes' discussion. But think about it. Here we have CBRN defense specialists in the field advising their commanders about how the enemy could use CB weapons based on data that was developed in the 1960s. We have little to no practical idea how modern military CB warfare delivery systems work, other than in tests with simulants or exercises through computer models and simulations that we must assume are valid. Using simulants to test enemy weapon delivery systems may be adequate, but only if we use simulants that are validated to imitate the physical properties of the real CB agents in the environment. And the only way to know this is through open-air live agent testing. Do U.S. defense experts really understand what three SCUD rockets filled with VX agent are going to do to a seaport, or are they all guessing? Similarly, we know that our CBRN defense equipment works great in laboratories and in test chambers challenged with live agent, but what about with shifting weather patterns, particular terrain of the battlefield, and new chemicals used by the military that might interfere with CBRN defense equipment? Just as an infantry soldier's participation in computer simulations cannot replace live fire training, neither can chemical simulants replace live agent exposure. We believe that CBRN defense equipment will work as designed, but lacking verifiable and validated CB warfare agent exposure data coming from open-air tests and evaluation, it's all an estimate.

Could the U.S. government safely test offensive CB weapon systems and perform open-air trials of CB warfare agents? Absolutely. There has been a great deal of research on CB warfare agents and associated hazards, and certainly the U.S. government could find a vast, uninhabited territory in the West and conduct limited, small-scale, open-air tests without harming unprotected civilians outside of the installation.[17] The public trust may not be there, but certainly it is within our technical capability. As for the arms control concerns, let the inspection agencies come in and see what is going on for themselves. If the U.S. government were transparent about the process—that is, if they were developing and testing offensive delivery systems only to develop better defensive equipment and tactics—it would be within the letter of the law. If there are no agent stockpiles or numerous delivery systems at military installations, clearly there is no intent to develop an offensive CB weapons capability. The U.S. government could even share the data with its coalition allies to allow them to better protect their military personnel.

Limited open-air CB warfare testing would go far in developing the expertise and confidence required in today's CBRN defense specialists. In October 2004, Congress directed the secretary of defense to develop a plan to ensure the survivability of defense-critical systems to chemical or biological agent contamination.[18] For years, the major DoD weapon systems have gotten waivers from this requirement because it was too expensive to do, there wasn't enough material data available, and CB defense issues were too low a priority. If Congress is serious about this requirement, live-agent testing would improve the survivability of these major combat systems. Growing concerns about the adequacy of our response to terrorist CBRN incidents are pushing us to better understand the properties of CB warfare agents in urban and rural centers, how improvised CBRN devices work, and how to remediate a contaminated area back to preincident conditions.

In the early days of sea exploration, the people believed that sirens could lure sailors to their deaths, that ships could sail off the edge of the world, that horrible monsters would attack ships, and that no one would return from those long voyages. It was the experienced seafarers who could tell the difference between a sea siren and a walrus; knowledge gained by practical exploration and courage to face what was out there. We have to ask the Army, OSD, Congress, and the public the simple question—what are you afraid of? Chemical and biological weapons are only different weapons of war, and they can be successfully countered. The military can manage the response if their personnel are educated about the topic, can develop reasonable risk-based approaches to dealing with the hazard, and are equipped to sense, shape, shield, and sustain themselves against the modern CBRN threat. Otherwise, all we have to face is the fear of WMDs, and that's not a solution we can afford.

DEFENSE AGENCIES INVOLVED WITH CBRN DEFENSE

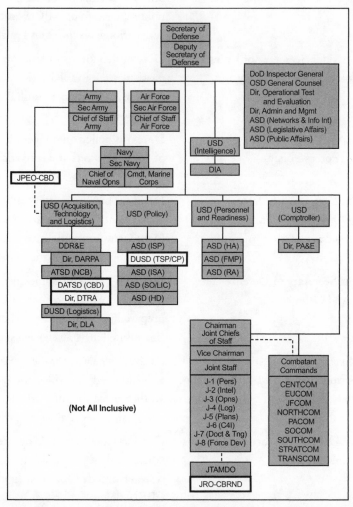

FIGURE A-1 *Organizational Structure of OSD Offices Involved with CBRN Defense*

TABLE A-1 *Organizations Involved with CBRN Defense and Their Responsibilities*

Organization	Responsibility
Under Secretary of Defense (Policy)	Formulates national security and defense policy. Develops, coordinates, and oversees department policy to counter WMDs.
Assistant to the Secretary of Defense (International Security Policy)	Develops, coordinates, and oversees policy for counterproliferation and nonproliferation of NBC weapons and conventional weapons and missiles.
Deputy Under Secretary of Defense (Technology Security Policy and Counterproliferation)	Develops counterproliferation policy, particularly for CBRN defense issues within military combat operations.
Deputy Assistant Secretary of Defense (Forces Policy)	Develops policy on nonproliferation of NBC weapons and conventional weapons and missiles.
Assistant Secretary of Defense (Special Ops/Low Intensity Conflict)	Develops policy on overseas consequence management, antiterrorism, and personnel survivability (including CBRN defense aspects).
Assistant Secretary of Defense (Homeland Defense)	Develops policy on domestic consequence management, installation preparedness, and homeland defense (including CBRN defense aspects).
Under Secretary of Defense (Acquisition, Technology and Logistics)	Establishes policies for the department's acquisition efforts. Milestone Decision Authority for all DoD CBRN defense efforts and chemical demilitarization.
Director, Defense Research and Engineering	Conducts analyses, develops policies, issues guidance on basic and applied research and development (including CBRN defense efforts). Oversees selection and execution of Advanced Concept Technology Demonstrations.

Organization	Responsibility
Assistant to the Secretary of Defense (Nuclear and Chemical and Biological Defense)	Develops policies, issues guidance, makes recommendations on CB defense programs. Primary staff officer and principal staff advisor to the SecDef on all CBRN defense matters, including NBC survivability. Oversees DTRA.
Deputy Assistant to the Secretary of Defense (CB Defense)	Provides DoD oversight and guidance for planning, programming, budgeting, and executing the DoD CBRN Defense Program.
Under Secretary of Defense (Personnel and Readiness)	Develops policies for personnel requirements, force preparedness, and training.
Assistant Secretary of Defense (Health Affairs)	Establishes policies, procedures, and standards for DoD medical programs including immunization of personnel against BW threats.
Assistant Secretary of Defense (Reserve Affairs)	Coordinates, develops, and oversees National Guard and Reserve consequence management and domestic preparedness programs involving military assistance to states, territories, and local authorities (including the WMD Civil Support Teams).
Director, Program Analysis and Evaluation	Analyzes and evaluates plans, programs and budgets in relation to defense objectives, projected threats, estimated costs, and resource constraints.
Chairman, Joint Chiefs of Staff	Principal military advisor to the president. The Joint Staff assists the chairman in providing unified strategic direction to the services, including their operations and integration under the combatant commands.

Organization	Responsibility
J-3–Operations	Develops consequence management and force protection policy, including CBRN defense aspects, and provides the lead for addressing operational readiness issues in CBRN defense matters.
J-4–Logistics	Develops policies and provides the lead for addressing medical CB defense issues and joint CB defense logistics issues.
J-5–Strategic Plans and Policy	Develops counterproliferation policy, including CBRN defense policy issues.
J-8–Force Structure, Resources and Assessments	Develops CBRN defense requirements for passive defense, force protection, consequence management, and homeland security. Coordinates with services and combatant commands on CBRN defense issues, capabilities, and priorities. Leads the review and development of joint and multi-service doctrine and training efforts.

ORDER OF BATTLE FOR OPERATIONS ENDURING AND IRAQI FREEDOM

OPERATION ENDURING FREEDOM (23 NOVEMBER 2003)

CFLCC HQ (Camp Doha)

310th Chemical Company (BIDS) (-) 1st Plt
2nd Plt, 51st Chemical Company (Fox)
1st Plt, 101st Chemical Company (Decon)
2nd Plt, 92nd Chemical Company (Decon)
1st UK BIDS Platoon

Uzbekistan

TEU Laboratory
1 TEU Joint Response Team

Afghanistan

2nd Plt, 310th Chemical Company (BIDS)
3rd Plt, 310th Chemical Company (BIDS)
2 TEU Joint Response Teams
26th Romanian NBC Detachment (Recon)
1st United Kingdom NBC Detachment
United Kingdom Decon platoon

Oman

Patient Decon Team

Operation Iraqi Freedom (circa April 10, 2003)

CFLCC Headquarters (Camp Doha)

CFLCC HQ Support Battalion
  1st Chemical Detachment (JA Team)
75th Exploitation Task Force (XTF)
  HHB, 75th Field Artillery BDE
  Combined/Joint Command and Control Exploitation (C2X) Cell
  Technical Escort Unit (TEU) Joint Response Team
  TEU Escort Team
  CBIST Teams
  SSE Teams 1-4
  Mobile Exploitation Team Alpha
  Mobile Exploitation Team Bravo
  Media Exploitation Team
  787th Ordnance Company (EOD)
  Direct Support Team (DTRA)
  JWICS Mobile Intelligence Communications System
513th Military Intelligence Brigade
  203rd Military Intelligence Battalion (Operations)
    Joint Captured Material Exploitation Center (DIA)

CFLCC Rear (Kuwait)

83rd Chemical Battalion
7th Chemical Company (BIDS) (-)
  4th Plt (Jordan)
51st Chemical Company (Recon) (-)
  2nd Plt
68th Chemical Company (Heavy) (-)
181st Chemical Company (attached from 2nd Chemical Battalion)
310th Chemical Company (BIDS) (-)
  4th Plt (Israel)
172nd Chemical Company (Mech Smoke)
59th Chemical Company (Smoke/Decon) (-)

MARCENT *(Djibouti)*

520th Medical Detachment (Theater Army Medical Laboratory)
1st Marine Expeditionary Force (Reinforced)
1st MEU Command Element
   3rd Plt, 7th Chemical Company (BIDS)
1st Marine Division
   431st Chemical Detachment (JB Team) (Main)
   Two squads, 1st Plt, 51st Chemical Company (Recon)
   101st Chemical Company (Smoke/Decon) (-)
      2nd & 4th Plts
1st Forward Service Support Group
   431st Chemical Detachment (JB Team) (Rear)
   One squad, 1st Plt, 51st Chemical Company (Recon)
   1st Plt, 101st Chemical Company (Smoke/Decon)
468th Chemical Battalion
   323rd Chemical Company (Smoke/Decon)
1st Armored Division (United Kingdom)
   UK NBC Regiment
      8 BIDS vehicles
      Decon Squadron
      Recon (Fuchs) Squadron
      Mobile Laboratory

V Corps

2nd Armored Cavalry Regiment
   87th Chemical Company (Recon/Decon)
3rd Armored Cavalry Regiment
   89th Chemical Company (Recon/Decon)
3rd Infantry Division
   92nd Chemical Company (Recon/Decon/Smoke)
   3rd Plt, 51st Chemical Company (Recon)
   2 plts, 59th Chemical Company (Smoke/Decon)
   6th Plt, 68th Chemical Company (Mech Smoke)
101st Airborne Division
   63rd Chemical Company (Smoke)

2nd Brigade, 82nd Airborne Division (-)
   2nd Plt, 21st Chemical Company (Smoke/Decon)
4th Infantry Division
   G/1-10th Cavalry (NBC Recon)
   44th Chemical Company (Recon/Decon) (-)
   46th Chemical Company (Mech Smoke)
2nd Chemical Battalion
   11th Chemical Company (Smoke/Decon)
   1 plt, 44th Chemical Company (decon)
   1 plt, 44th Chemical Company (recon)

Joint Special Operations Task Force (North)

3rd Plt, 310th Chemical Company (BIDS)
TEU Joint Response Team (-)
CBIST Team

Task Force-20

TEU Joint Response Team
1st Plt, 21st Chemical Company (Smoke/Decon)
Bio Research Program Lab (Naval Medical Research Center)
Mobile Chemical Laboratory (Edgewood CB Center)

Joint Task Force, Consequence Management (JTF-CM)

3rd Plt, 101st Chemical Company (Smoke/Decon) (Qatar)
750th German NBC Defense Battalion (recon/decon)
4th Czech NBC Defense Company (decon/medical support)
Ukrainian NBC Defense Battalion
Slovak engineer unit
Polish chemical defense unit (Jordan)
383rd Romanian NBC Defense Company and Italian decon platoon
   (Afghanistan)

Arriving after April 10

455th Chemical Brigade
450th Chemical Battalion
314th Chemical Company (Smoke/Decon)
371st Chemical Company (Smoke/Decon)

Acronyms

ABC	Atomic, Biological, and Chemical
ACADA	Automatic Chemical Agent Detector/Alarm
ACTD	Advanced Concept Technology Demonstration
AFRRI	Armed Forces Radiobiology Research Institute
AMC	Army Materiel Command
AMEDD	Army Medical Department Center and School
AOC	Army Operation Center
ASA (RDA)	Assistant Secretary of the Army for Research, Development and Acquisition
ASBREM	Armed Services Biomedical Research Evaluation and Management Committee
ASD (HA)	Assistant Secretary of Defense for Health Affairs
ASD (HD)	Assistant Secrety of Defense of Homeland Defense
ASD (ISP)	Assistant Secretary of Defense for International Security Policy
ASD (NS&CP)	Assistant Secretary of Defense for Nuclear Security and Counterproliferation
ASD (S&TR)	Assistant Secretary of Defense for Strategy and Threat Reduction
ASD (SO/LIC)	Assistant Secretary of Defense for Special Operations and Low Intensity Conflict
AT	Antiterrorism
ATNAA	Antidote Treatment Nerve Agent Autoinjector
ATSD (AE)	Assistant to the Secretary of Defense for Atomic Energy
ATSD (NCB)	Assistant to the Secretary of Defense for Nuclear and Chemical and Biological Defense
AVIP	Anthrax Vaccine Immunization Program
BAT	Biological Augmentation Team
BCJOC	Biological-Chemical Joint Operations Cell
BDO	Battle Dress Overgarment

BIDS	Biological Integrated Detection System
BMDO	Ballistic Missile Defense Organization
BW	Biological Warfare
CAM	Chemical Agent Monitor
CANA	Convulsant Antidote Nerve Agent
CB	Chemical and Biological
CBDCOM	Chemical and Biological Defense Command
CBIRF	Chemical and Biological Incident Response Force
CBIST	Chemical and Biological Intelligence Support Team
CBR	Chemical, Biological, and Radiological
CBRN	Chemical, Biological, Radiological, and Nuclear
CBRNE	Chemical, Biological, Radiological, Nuclear, and Explosives
CB-RRT	Chemical and Biological Rapid Response Team
CDC	Centers for Disease Control and Prevention
CENTCOM	Central Command
CFACC	Coalition Forces Air Component Command
CFLCC	Coalition Forces Land Component Command
CIA	Central Intelligence Agency
CINC	Commander-in-Chief (referring to the combatant commands)
CJCS	Chairman of the Joint Chiefs of Staff
CP DEPMEDS	Chemically Protected Deployable Medical System
CP MS SOG	Counterproliferation Mission Support Senior Oversight Group
CPRC	Counterproliferation Program Review Committee
CRDEC	Chemical Research, Development, and Engineering Center
CT	Counterterrorism
CW	Chemical Warfare
DARPA	Defense Advanced Research Projects Agency
DATSD (CBM)	Deputy Assistant to the Secretary of Defense for Chemical and Biological Matters
DATSD (CBD)	Deputy Assistant to the Secretary of Defense for Chemical and Biological Defense

DATSD (CP/CBD)	Deputy Assistant to the Secretary of Defense for Counterproliferation and Chemical and Biological Defense
DDR&E	Director, Defense Research and Engineering
DDS&P	Deputy Director for Strategy and Policy
DFU	Dry Filter Unit
DHHS	Department of Health and Human Services
DHS	Department of Homeland Security
DIA	Defense Intelligence Agency
DLA	Defense Logistics Agency
DoD	Department of Defense
DoE	Department of Energy
DoJ	Department of Justice
DOMS	Director of Military Support
DOT&E	Director for Operational Test and Evaluation
DPG	Defense Planning Guidance
DRI	Defense Reform Initiative
DTRA	Defense Threat and Reduction Agency
EOC	Emergency Operations Center
EOD	Explosive Ordnance Disposal
EUCOM	European Command
FBI	Federal Bureau of Investigation
FCB	Functional Capability Board
FDA	Food and Drug Administration
FEMA	Federal Emergency Management Agency
FORSCOM	U.S. Forces Command
FRP	Federal Response Plan
GAO	General Accounting Office (before 2004) Government Accountability Office (2004 and after)
GWOT	Global War On Terrorism
HAZMAT	Hazardous Materials
HMMWV	High-Mobility Multi Wheeled Vehicle
HPAC	Hazard Prediction and Assessment Capability
IAB	Interagency Board for Equipment Standardization and Interoperability

IAEA	International Atomic Energy Agency
IBAD	Interim Biological Agent Detector
IDA	Institute for Defense Analyses
IDLH	Immediately Dangerous to Life or Health
I MEF	First Marine Expeditionary Force
INC	Iraqi National Congress
IND	Investigational New Drug
INR	Bureau of Intelligence and Research (State Department)
ISG	Iraq Survey Group
ITF	International Task Force
JBPDS	Joint Biological Point Detection System
JBREWS	Joint Biological Remote Early Warning System
JCAD	Joint Chemical Agent Detector
JCS	Joint Chiefs of Staff
JDAM	Joint Direct Attack Munition
JFCOM	Joint Forces Command
JMPAB	Joint Material Priorities and Allocation Board
JNBCDB	Joint NBC Defense Board
JP-CBD	Joint Panel for Chemical and Biological Defense
JPEO	Joint Program Executive Office
JPO-BD	Joint Program Office for Biological Defense
JRO	Joint Requirements Office
JRO-CBRND	Joint Requirements Office for CBRN Defense
JROC	Joint Requirements Oversight Council
JSCC-CDE	Joint Service Coordinating Committee for Chemical Defense Equipment
JSIG	Joint Service Integration Group
JSIPP	Joint Service Installation Pilot Project
JSLIST	Joint Service Lightweight Integrated Suit Technology
JSLSCAD	Joint Service Lightweight Standoff Chemical Agent Detector
JSOTF	Joint Special Operations Task Force
JSMG	Joint Service Materiel Group
JSRG	Joint Service Review Group

JSTPCBD	Joint Science and Technology Panel for Chemical and Biological Defense
JTAMDO	Joint Theater Air and Missile Defense Office
JTF-CM	Joint Task Force for Consequence Management
JTF-CS	Joint Task Force for Civil Support
JVAP	Join Vaccine Acquisition Program
JWARN	Joint Warning and Reporting Network
JWCA	Joint Warfighting Capability Assessment
LAV	Light Armored Vehicle
LR-BSDS	Long Range Biological Standoff Detection System
MBPI	Michigan Biologics Product Institute
MDS	Modular Decontamination System
MEF	Marine Expeditionary Force
MET	Mobile Exploitation Team
NAAK	Nerve Agent Antidote Kit
NBC	Nuclear, Biological, and Chemical
NDA	New Drug Application
NDI	Non Developmental Item
NDPO	National Domestic Preparedness Office
NEST	Nuclear Emergency Support Team
NGIC	National Ground Intelligence Center
NIE	National Intelligence Estimate
NIOSH	National Institute for Occupational Safety and Health
NORAD	North American Aerospace Defense Command
NORTHCOM	U.S. Northern Command
NPR	Nuclear Posture Review
NSPD	National Security Presidential Directive
NSC	National Security Council
NSSE	National Special Security Event
O&M	Operations and Maintenance
ODCSLOG	Office of the Deputy Chief of Staff for Logistics
ODCSOPS	Office of the Deputy Chief of Staff for Operations and Plans
OEF	Operation Enduring Freedom

OIF	Operation Iraqi Freedom
ONE	Operation Noble Eagle
ONS	Operational Needs Statement
OSD	Office of the Secretary of Defense
OSP	Office of Special Plans
PA&E	Program Analysis and Evaluation
PACOM	Pacific Command
PAIO	Program Analysis and Integration Office
PB	Pyridostigmine bromide
PBD	Program Budget Decision
PCR	Polymerase Chain Reaction
PDD	Presidential Decision Directive
PEO	Program Executive Office
POM	Program Objective Memorandum
QDR	Quadrennial Defense Review
R&D	Research and Development
RAID	Rapid Assessment and Initial Detection
RDA	Research, Development and Acquisition
RDT&E	Research, Development, Test and Evaluation
RSCAAL	Remote Standoff Chemical Agent Alarm
SAF/AQP	Secretary of the Air Force for Acquisition, Global Power Programs Directorate
SASO	Stability and Support Operations
SBCCOM	Soldier and Biological Chemical Command
SERPACWA	Skin Exposure Reduction Paste Against CW Agents
SOCOM	Special Operations Command
SROC	Senior Readiness Oversight Council
SSE	Sensitive Site Exploitation
STRATCOM	U.S. Strategic Command
TEU	Technical Escort Unit
TIC	Toxic Industrial Chemical
TIM	Toxic Industrial Material
TP/CBD	Technical Panel on Chemical and Biological Defense
TRAC	Threat Reduction Advisory Committee
TRADOC	Training and Doctrine Command

TRANSCOM	U.S. Transportation Command
TSWG	Technical Support Working Group
UAV	Unmanned Aerial Vehicle
UN	United Nations
UNMOVIC	United Nations Monitoring, Verification, and Inspection Commission
UNSCOM	United Nations Special Commission
USACMLS	U.S. Army Chemical School and Center
USAMRICD	U.S. Army Medical Research Institute of Chemical Defense
USAMRIID	U.S. Army Medical Research Institute of Infectious Diseases
USANCA	U.S. Army Nuclear and Chemical Agency
USAREUR	U.S. Army Europe
USD (A&T)	Under Secretary of Defense for Acquisition and Technology
USD (AT&L)	Under Secretary of Defense for Acquisition, Technology, and Logistics
USD (I)	Under Secretary of Defense for Intelligence
USD (P)	Under Secretary of Defense for Policy
USD (P&R)	Under Secretary of Defense for Personnel and Readiness
VLSTRACK	Vapor-Liquid-Solid Tracking
WMD	Weapons of Mass Destruction
XTF	Exploitation Task Force

NOTES

CHAPTER 1   HERE BE DRAGONS!

1. See http://www.maphist.nl/index.html for a fuller discussion of this topic.

2. *Brewer's Dictionary of Phrase and Fable*, 1884, http://www.bootlegbooks.com/ Reference/PhraseAndFable/data/377.html.

3. See https://www.perscomonline.army.mil/tagd/tioh/Branches/Chemical%20Corps. htm. Note the Army Chemical Corps adopted the green dragon as its symbol, but certain chemical units, notably the 2nd Chemical Battalion, have used the red dragon in their patches. The 2nd Chemical Battalion's motto is *Flammis Vincimus*, or "Flame Conquers."

4. During World War II, the DoD CB warfare program grew into a massive military infrastructure for developing, producing, and testing CB weapon systems. The era for modern chemical weapons development was 1941–1990; for biological weapons development, it was 1941–1972.

5. Many people cite the number of more than 5,000 affected by the Tokyo subway incident. However, more than 4,000 were "worried well" cases who had not been exposed to sarin but who had been on or near the subway at the time and had panicked.

6. Scott Jones, "WMD Proliferation—More Than Nuclear," Defense News, October 18, 2004.

7. United Nations, "Resolutions Adopted on the Reports of the First Committee," January 26, 1946.

8. SIPRI, *The Problem of Chemical and Biological Warfare* (New York: Humanities Press, 1971) 4:193.

9. J. H. Rothschild. *Tomorrow's Weapons* (New York: McGraw-Hill, 1964), 111. The Soviets claimed that this statement was made in reference to U.S. military intentions to use these weapons in the future, which justified the Soviet Union's development of a retaliatory capability.

10. Albert J. Mauroni, *America's Struggle with Chemical-Biological Warfare* (Westport, CT: Praeger, 2000), 23. Camp Detrick, the birthplace of the U.S. BW program, was originally a temporary installation developed during World War II. At the end of the war, the Army shut down Dugway Proving Ground, where it had tested many of its chemical, biological, and incendiary munitions.

11. An excellent collection of documents covering the Nixon administration's deliberations on this issue can be found at the National Security Archives Web site, http://www.gwu.edu/~nsarchiv/index.html.

12. There were few dissentions over this decision outside of the Chemical Corps, perhaps because of the Congressional investigations into the use of Agent Orange and napalm in Viet Nam, the alleged poisoning of nearly 6,000 sheep near Dugway Proving Ground in 1968, the lack of any recent CB warfare against U.S. forces, and the presence of the U.S. military's strong nuclear retaliatory capability. Mauroni, *America's Struggle*, 56–60.

13. Report of the Secretary-General, *Chemical and Bacteriological (Biological) Weapons and the Effects of Their Possible Use* (New York: United Nations, 1969), table 4, 57. The UN report did not mention a specific chemical or biological warfare agent in its table, but it is my belief that they were referencing tularemia and VX nerve agent, as evidenced by the nature of the effects noted.

14. 18 U.S. Code section 2332a (2002), as amended by the Public Health and Bioterrorism Preparedness and Response act of 2002, section 231(d).

15. Joint Publication 1-02, *Department of Defense Dictionary of Military and Associated Terms* (Washington, D.C.: Joint Chiefs of Staff, 2004).

16. See Scott Jones, "WMD Proliferation—More Than Nuclear," *Defense News*, October 18, 2004, and Michael Heylin, "Weapons of Mass Destruction," *Chemical & Engineering News*, October 11, 2004 for two good discussions on this topic.

17. Notably, the Air Force Massive Ordnance Air Blast (MOAB) bomb with 18,000 pounds of tritonal explosives might be considered a WMD. See http://www.cnn.com/2003/US/03/11/sprj.irq.moab/ for the story and a photograph of the mushroom cloud created by this munition.

18. Al Mauroni, *Chemical and Biological Warfare: A Reference Handbook* (Santa Barbara, CA: ABC Clio, 2003), 99–100.

19. International Task Force (ITF) 25 defines *industrial chemical* as "a material capable of being produced in quantities exceeding 30 tonnes per year at one production facility. Otherwise, it is considered a specialty chemical." A *toxic industrial chemical* is defined as "an industrial chemical [that] has a LCt50 value less than 100,000 mg.-min/m^3 in any mammalian species and is produced in quantities exceeding 30 tonnes per year at one production facility."

20. Testimony before the Senate Veterans Affairs Committee, January 29, 1997, during a meeting on Gulf War illnesses.

21. The U.S. military budget is larger than those of the next twenty to twenty-five major powers combined. The United States owns the world's best tanks, armored infantry carriers, aircraft armed with state-of-the-art precision guided missiles, a dozen nuclear-powered aircraft carriers, and numerous submarines. See http://www.d-n-i.net/top_level/charts_and_data.htm.

22. The designation of 1,000 casualties (dead and injured) as "mass casualties" comes from DHHS, which states this number to define a mass casualty situation for planning purposes in establishing its Metropolitan Medical Response Teams. While 1,000 is clearly an arbitrary number, not based on any studies, it does at least set a standard for federal response. GAO/NSIAD-99-3, *Combating Terrorism: Opportunities to Improve Domestic Preparedness Program Focus and Efficiency* (Washington, DC: GAO, November 1998), 6.

23. See http://www.fooledbyrandomness.com/ for information on Dr. Taleb and his treatise on the black swan theory.

Chapter 2   An Evolving Management Structure

1. DoD Directive 5160.5, *Chemical Warfare/Chemical-Biological Defense Research, Development, Test and Evaluation*, signed March 30, 1976.

2. The Army focused on detecting and identifying radiological contamination from nuclear weapons used during tactical operations. The Air Force and Navy have similar requirements, but they justified keeping their radiological defense programs under their respective control by emphasizing the need to develop specific and unique devices to monitor the physiological health effects of radiation as a result of working around nuclear reactors and nuclear weapons. The Marine Corps basically procured anything the Army did, noting the similar ground force tactical combat requirements.

3. The U.S. national policy reserved the right for first use of nuclear weapons; to retaliate against the use of chemical weapons, not necessarily in kind. Under no circumstance would the U.S. military use biological weapons.

4. The overall NBC defense concept can be explained. Contamination avoidance incorporates and integrates standoff and early warning, reconnaissance, biological, radiological, and chemical point detection, and networked battlespace management system technologies. Individual protection includes ground and aircrew protective masks, and suits, and ancillary equipment. Collective protection seeks to provide a "clean" environment for personnel operating in aircraft, armored vehicles, ships, command-and-control centers, and other shelters. Decontamination provides protection and restoration capabilities after NBC weapons use for both personnel and equipment. Medical systems include the complete array of preexposure protection, NBC casualty management, and postexposure treatment and therapies.

5. At Edgewood, Maryland, the names change but the organizations do not. CRDEC (formerly known as the Chemical Systems Laboratory and then the Chemical Research and Development Center) became ERDEC (Edgewood RDEC) under the headquarters Chemical and Biological Defense Agency (CBDA) in 1992. CBDA then became CBDCOM in 1993 (incorporating the eight chemical stockpile sites), CBDCOM became SBCCOM in 1998 (incorporating Soldier Systems Command), and ERDEC became Edgewood Chemical-Biological Center (ECBC). SBCCOM became RDECOM (Research and Development Command) in 2004.

6. DoD Directive 5160.5, *Responsibilities for Research, Development, and Acquisition of Chemical Weapons and Chemical and Biological Defense*, May 1, 1985. This directive was updated primarily to address the Army's binary chemical weapons program responsibilities. It has not been updated since, despite DoD's intent to eliminate its chemical weapons and the public law that created the DoD CB Defense Program in 1994. See http://www.dtic.mil/whs/directives/corres/pdf/d51605_050185/d51605p.pdf.

7. The first official to fill this role was Dr. Tom Welch, a former scientist and program manager in the CB defense research community.

8. The ASBREM committee was chartered in 1981. This committee is cochaired by the Director, Defense Research and Engineering (DDR&E) and the Assistant Secretary of Defense (Health Affairs) (ASD [HA]). The medical R&D commands of the Army, Navy, and Air Force meet periodically in joint sessions to facilitate management, coordination, improve information exchange, and accomplish medical research, development, testing, and evaluation activities. (Source: DoD NBC Warfare/ Defense Annual Report to Congress, June 1994, page I-4).

9. AFRRI was created in 1981 as a subordinate organization to the Defense Nuclear Agency, now DTRA. DNA was to manage AFRRI, provide its operations and maintenance funding, and chair a board of governors, which included the service surgeon generals, service deputy chiefs of staff for operations, and the ASD (HA). See DoD Directive 5105.33, *Armed Forces Radiobiology Research Institute*, November 25, 1987.

10. GAO/NSIAD-91-197, *Chemical Warfare: Soldiers Inadequately Equipped and Trained to Conduct Chemical Operations*, Washington, D.C.: GAO, May 1991.

11. A more complete account of CB defense capabilities and lessons learned can be found in my book, *Chemical and Biological Defense: U.S. Policies and Decisions in the Gulf War* (Westport, CT: Praeger, 1998).

12. National Defense Authorization Act for FY 1994 (PL 103-160), passed on November 30, 1993.

13. Technically, the Marine Corps research and development effort is addressed in the Navy's budget.

14. These annual reports can be found at http://www.acq.osd.mil/cp/.

15. In 1995, ASD (NS&CP) would be eliminated and the ASD for International Security Policy (ASD [ISP]) would be responsible for overseeing counterproliferation policy issues.

16. This was directed under the National Defense Authorization Act of 1996, Title IX (DoD Organization and Management), Section 904 (Redesignation of the Position of Assistant to the Secretary of Defense for Atomic Energy), Public Law 104–106, January 3, 1996. "The ATSD (NCB) shall: 1) advise the Secretary of Defense on nuclear energy, nuclear weapons, and chemical and biological defense; 2) serve as the Staff Director of the Nuclear Weapons Council established by section 179 of this title; and 3) perform such additional duties as the Secretary may prescribe." See also DoD Directive 5134.8, March 1996. (http://www.dtic.mil/whs/directives/corres/ pdf/d51348wch1_060894/d51348p.pdf). Dr. Harold Smith, a political appointee, would fill the newly titled position. His deputy, the DATSD (CBM), was Dr. Ted Prociv.

17. Although titled the JSA for NBC Defense Management, the new management structure would focus on CB defense requirements and not radiological defense, other than procuring radiacs for the Army and Marine Corps.

18. The JSMG Executive Office would include a director, and process managers for research, development, and acquisition, logistics, NBC contamination survivability, and for intelligence. The Air Force, Navy, and Marine Corps did not agree that the JSMG should address NBC contamination avoidance or intelligence products, but General Friel insisted they were necessary and, because the JSMG Executive Office was formed on his dime, these positions were created.

19. Initial voting membership included BG Roy Beauchamp (USA), Deputy for Combat Service Support, ASA (RDA), RADM Lewis Felton (USN), Deputy Commander of the Engineering Directorate, Naval Sea Systems Command, Brig. Gen. John Hawley (USAF), Director, Fighter, C2 and Weapons Program, Assistant Secretary (Acquisition), and Maj. Gen. Carol Mutter (USMC), Commander, Marine Corps Systems Command.

20. SOCOM was the only combatant command that was a formal (although nonvoting) member. The rationale was that SOCOM had Title 10-like responsibilities, similar to the four services, and they had unique counterproliferation mission requirements that required a distinct voice. The Army OTSG sat at the table as the services' medical research and development agencies, although Air Force, Navy, and Marine Corps medical representatives often attended the meetings as well.

21. The eight milestone decision authorities included the Army's Soldier and Biological Chemical Command and Medical Material Development Activity, the JPO-BD, Air Force Material Command, Naval Aviation Systems Command, Naval Sea Systems Command, Naval Space and Warfare Systems Command (SPAWAR), and Marine Corps Systems Command. In 1999, the Defense Threat Reduction Agency joined this group to oversee counterproliferation ACTDs (making it nine milestone decision authorities for CB defense issues).

22. Initial voting membership included Col. Rick Jackson (USA), director of combat developments, USACMLS; Mr. Chuck Bogner (USN), director, ship safety and survivability, surface warfare division, and deputy chief naval operations; Maj. Gen. Jim McCarthy (USAF), Office of the Civil Engineers; and Maj. Gen. Anthony Zinni (USMC), deputy commanding general, Marine Corps combat development command.

23. The medical nuclear defense research program executed by the AFRRI did not receive any DoD CB Defense Program funding.

24. Initially, more than 40 percent was allocated for detection efforts until JSLIST procurement picked up.

25. GAO/NSIAD-96-103, *Chemical and Biological Defense: Emphasis Remains Insufficient To Resolve Continuing Problems*, Washington, D.C.: GAO, March 1996, p. 15.

26. See http://www.defenselink.mil/pubs/qdr/sec3.html.

27. The six "service-unique" detector projects included the Army's Individual Soldier Detector (ISD), the Air Force's Individual Vapor Detector (IVD) and Aircraft Interior Detector (AIDET), the Navy's Chemical Warfare Interior Compartment Sensor (CWICS) and Shipboard Chemical Agent Monitor-Portable (SCAMP), and SOCOM's Special Operations Forces Chemical Agent System (SOFCAS). This did not include the Marine Corps' Individual Chemical Agent Detector (ICAD),

which was bought directly from industry and not a formal research-and-development project. All of these requirements were, in the end, calling for a small, handheld chemical agent point detector that was sensitive enough to raise an alarm before a person could be overcome by CW agent vapors.

28. See John Deutch, Arlen Spector, et al., *Combating Proliferation of Weapons of Mass Destruction*, July 14, 1999, 24–25 and 55–56.

29. Section 228, Public Law 104-201, the National Defense Authorization Act for FY 1997, amended the U.S. Code addressing the DoD CB Defense Program (50 USC 1522) to exempt DARPA from its oversight.

30. Renamed in 1997 from DATSD (CBM) to DATSD (CP/CBD)—Counterproliferation and CB Defense programs.

31. From a CB defense perspective, the DRI was significant in what it did not do. That is, it did not mention chemical or biological weapons once in the entire document, focusing rather on nuclear proliferation issues. To maintain statutory compliance, the DDR&E (then Hans Mark) was dual-hatted as the ATSD (NCB). At that time, the DATSD (CBD) position was left vacant for nearly nine months and was subsequently filled by Dr. Anna Johnson-Winegar, who reported to DDR&E, until the ATSD (NCB) position was filled by Dr. Dale Klein in 2001.

32. In part this was because the Army CBDCOM had left the chair empty, and DTRA volunteered to take the duties over. DTRA stated that they could better coordinate CB defense science and technology with the nuclear defense science and technology executed by their organization, given the scope of the DoD counterproliferation initiative.

33. Renamed from DATSD (CP/CBD) to DATSD (CBD), focusing on CB Defense rather than on the broader area of counterproliferation, in 1998.

34. This figure shows a few changes made later to the OSD steering committee. The DDR&E was the acting chair for the ATSD (NCB) until OSD filled that position. The Joint Staff's J-5 directorate was added as a voting member in May 2000. The other two OSD positions shown were nonvoting advisors.

35. Although the current term is *combatant commands* or COCOMs, the traditional term is *CINCs*. Everyone understands that the president of the United States is the commander-in-chief of all military forces.

36. The Air Force and Navy had limited CBRN defense infrastructure, usually collocated with other defense laboratories. The Marine Corps had none. CBRN defense projects had been left to the Army, and, as such, the Army had developed the necessary infrastructure between 1941 and 1990 to research, develop, test, and evaluate these projects. There were no "pure DoD" labs other than DARPA that worked this area.

37. The four lead service action officers were nicknamed the "Four Horsemen" in deference to their influential decision-making authority during acquisition and budget discussions.

38. Zinni's farewell remarks at the U.S. Naval Institute in March 2000. See http://www.rcaca.org/News-Zinni.htm.

39. See Walter Boyne, *Operation Iraqi Freedom: What Went Right, What Went Wrong, and Why* (New York: Tom Doherty, 2003), 61–62. Forecasting what the military would need ten to twenty years out (the lifecycle of most defense programs) is a tricky business requiring dedicated professionals. A successful defense program required integrity, good judgment, connections, and sincere motivations of its backers. If the enemy came up with a new weapon or countermeasure that would force changes to the defense program, time and costs increased. External factors such as the fall of the Soviet Union or reductions in the size of the military would impact defense programs. Defense acquisition funds are inherently limited and have to be divided among the services and OSD programs. Competition is fierce, and is made more severe by increasing demands for operational and maintenance funds and other costs associated with deployments for the many missions American service members conduct every year. Congressional pressure does not always advance the best interests of the country, but rather often focuses on jobs within a certain constituency. The more sophisticated and advanced the defense program becomes, the more expensive it is. With increased visibility, the price of failure can be elimination. Technical expectations today are much greater than they were ten or twenty years ago, and again, results in more expensive devices that take longer to develop and produce. These issues affect all defense acquisition programs. Some affect the CB defense program more than others.

40. John M. Deutch et al., *Report of the Commission to Assess the Organization of the Federal Government to Combat the Proliferation of Weapons of Mass Destruction*, Washington, D.C., July 14, 1999. Hereafter called the Deutch Report.

41. The Air Force received funds to modify their aircraft to integrate the AERP masks with flight equipment, and received hundreds of thousands of consumable "second skin" covers for their MCU-2 masks. The Navy received funds to install the collective protection filters in their ships and used R&D funds to manufacture twenty IBADs. The Marine Corps took a one-year Congressional funding set-aside to seek alternatives to manufacturing JSLIST suits and kept it alive for years, although it produced no results. They also vigorously championed a CB dosimeter effort based on a failed advanced technology effort. The Army was content to allow these indiscretions as long as its heavy R&D infrastructure remained funded and its NBC reconnaissance program and BIDS program were not adversely affected.

42. Jon Anderson and Chuck Vinch, "Report: Many Gas Masks May Prove Useless in Combat," *Stars and Stripes*, June 22, 2000. Online at http://www.pstripes.com/jan01/ed010501f.html.

43. See DoD IG testimony to Congress on June 21, 2000, at http://www.dodig.osd.mil/audit/reports/fy00/00-154.pdf.

CHAPTER 3 REFORMING THE DoD CB DEFENSE PROGRAM

1. See http://www.fas.org/irp/offdocs/pdd18.htm for the text of the speech.

2. The National Defense Authorization Act of 1994 (PL 103-160, November 30, 1993) called for the establishment of an interagency review committee that included those agencies to report on nonproliferation and counterproliferation activities and programs.

3. Executive summaries of these annual reports can be found at http://www.acq. osd.mil/cp/.

4. See http://www.fas.org/spp/starwars/program/news98/b07151998_bt366-98.html. Notable members of the first TRAC: Ashton Carter, former ASD (ISD); Dr. Ted Gold, IDA; Dr. Harold Smith, outgoing ATSD (NCB); John Deutch, former Deputy Secretary of Defense and DCI, William Perry, former Secretary of Defense, and Paul Wolfowitz, John Hopkins University.

5. See also GAO/NSIAD-00-97, *Weapons of Mass Destruction: DoD's Actions to Combat Weapons Use Should Be More Integrated and Focused* (Washington, D.C.: GAO, May 2000).

6. In 1992, Powell told Congress, "The one [threat] that scares me to death—even more so than an attack of nuclear weapons and the one that we have even less capability against—is biological weapons." In 1993, a Defense Science Board report identified several shortfalls in biodefense, notably BW detection.

7. While the JPO leadership was in Virginia, much of the actual technical work on biological detection would continue at Aberdeen Proving Ground. Similarly, the overwhelming majority of vaccine research and development work would continue at Fort Detrick.

8. JROC Memorandum 93-00, *Department of Defense Chemical and Biological Defense Program (CBDP) FY02-07 Program Objective Memorandum (POM) Strategy*, May 17, 2000.

9. This exchange between reporters and a DoD official occurred during a DoD brief on the RAID teams in March 1998 (see http://www.dod.mil/transcripts/1998/t03191998_t317rcdp.html):

Q: What actual evidence do you have that the threat is increasing?

A: The FBI actually has the lead on the domestic threat. And of course, one of the things that we're preparing for is an item that Secretary Walker talked about. And that is we may, in fact, be attacked. And so if you look at terrorist activity worldwide, we are simply preparing for a mission that may come, may arrive. And so we do, obviously, listen to the FBI on a routine basis, a frequent basis, so that we get an update on the threat assessment as the activities occur. And so we clearly monitor the threat in terms of how much of the threat and the activity really—the FBI has release authority on that kind of information.

Q: Are you saying that the FBI has concrete evidence of an increasing threat of this type of an attack in the United States?

A: I really don't—I just simply can't describe the threat in terms of the lead agency because they have to react to that kind of question. We're saying the likelihood is changing, that we may have an attack in the continental United States, the likelihood. And so we're preparing for that question, might there be one. We're preparing for perhaps a mission that most hope never takes place.

10. See also http://www.defenselink.mil/pubs/domestic/toc.html for the full plan to execute this program.

11. Amy Smithson and Leslie-Anne Levey, *Ataxia: The Chemical and Biological Terrorism Threat and the U.S. Response* (Washington, D.C.: The Henry L. Stimson Center, October 2000), http://www.stimson.org/cbw/pubs.cfm?id=12.

12. Disclaimer—the author was a participant of the DoD Domestic Preparedness Program. See "A Rebuttal to Ataxia" at http://www.homelandsecurity.org/journal/Commentary/displayCommentary.asp?commentary=2.

13. In January 2005, the Marine Corps announced that it would be deactivating its CBIRF in response to the many WMD CSTs being stood up. My opinion is that this was not the sole decision point, but that practical manpower and resource constraints were also influential.

14. DoD Tiger Team, *Integrating National Guard and Reserve Component Support for Response to Attacks Using Weapons of Mass Destruction* (Washington, D.C.: DoD, December 1997).

15. The House Armed Services Committee Report 106-162 recommended that the Joint Staff and Army, as the DoD Executive Agent for the CB Defense Program, be added to the OSD CB defense steering committee. It also recommended that CBIRF's funding be integrated into the CB Defense Program. OSD only agreed with the Joint Staff joining the steering committee.

16. Within the Joint Staff, the J-3 (Operations) antiterrorism branch had an Army chemical officer to address planning for and response to terrorist WMD incidents. The J-4 (Logistics) had an action officer that watched CB defense logistics issues (but whose full-time job was managing munitions logistics issues) and a medical action officer who coordinated vaccine and other medical countermeasure issues for the Joint Staff Surgeon General. The J-8 (Programs and Resource Assessment) had an Army chemical officer who worked CB warfare issues in joint wargames and analyses.

17. The deputy CINC of SOCOM had communicated to the Joint NBC Defense Board twice, in writing, that the command was not getting the specialized, SOF-peculiar CB defense equipment their personnel required to conduct its counterproliferation missions. Specifically, the public law that created the DoD CB Defense Program was being cited as legal precedent to stop SOCOM from running its own CB defense research and development program to field specialized equipment, but the DoD program was not addressing special operations requirements.

18. DDR&E memorandum to Deputy Secretary of Defense, subject: Chemical and Biological Defense Program (CBDP)—Action Memorandum, April 21, 2000, with approval May 9, 2000.

19. See GAO/NSIAD-99-159, *Chemical and Biological Defense: Program Planning and Evaluation Should Follow Results Act Framework* (Washington, D.C.: GAO, 1999).

20. The Bush administration eliminated the ATSD (CS) position. Deputy Secretary of Defense Wolfowitz approved USD (P&R) as the program and policy oversight agent on November 21, 2001.

21. HAC markup to the DoD Appropriations for FY 2002, Title IX, *Counter-Terrorism and Defense Against Weapons of Mass Destruction*, November 2001, 253–54.

22. USD (AT&L) memorandum, subject: Chemical and Biological Defense Program Management, October 19, 2001.

23. This was an office under Lisa Bronson, the Deputy Under Secretary of Defense for Technology Security and Counterproliferation (DUSD [TSP/CP]), who reported to the ASD (ISP) under the USD (P).

24. Dr. Klein was sworn in as the ATSD (NCB) on November 15, 2001. Prior to his appointment by President Bush, Klein was a professor in the Department of Mechanical Engineering (Nuclear Program) at the University of Texas at Austin. He was the vice-chancellor for special engineering programs at the University of Texas System from 1995 until November 2001. His background was rich in areas of nuclear energy research.

25. USD (AT&L), "Organization Change Within the Office of the Under Secretary of Defense (Acquisition, Technology and Logistics)," memorandum, November 5, 2001.

26. Lisa Bronson, the DUSD (TSP/CP), reported to J. D. Crouch II, the ASD (ISP) (which had come back to replace the ASD (S&TR) in 2001), who in turn reported to Douglas J. Feith, USD (P). Ms. Bronson was the primary senior OSD Policy official who dealt with CBRN defense issues.

27. Defense Science Board, *Protecting the Homeland: Report of the Defense Science Board*, 2000 Summer Study. See executive summary at http://www.acq.osd.mil/dsb/protecting.pdf.

28. JROC Memorandum 061-02, April 29, 2002.

29. This is one reason why the JRO was not called the Joint NBC Defense Organization, which was the original proposed title—too many reminders of that other joint organization that "took away" the services' Title 10 responsibilities.

30. The director position would be filled by a general officer within the J-8, Joint Staff, as an additional duty.

31. By developing an Acquisition Corps, the Army eliminated the requirement to have a Chemical Corps general officer to head the Army laboratories at Aberdeen Proving Ground, Dugway Proving Ground, and the JPEO-CBD. As a result, the career progression for aspiring Chemical Corps officers is narrowing. Part of this was self-inflicted. When the Acquisition Corps was formed in the early 1990s, the Chemical Corps discouraged its officers from transferring to that organization, fearing that it would lose its talent. When the Army changed the leadership positions of those technical agencies to the Acquisition Corps, the Chemical Corps lost many of its traditional colonel and general officer slots.

Chapter 4   9/11 Changes Life as We Know It

1. See http://www.whitehouse.gov/news/releases/2001/09/20010914-5.html.

2. See http://www.defenselink.mil/transcripts/2001/t09252001_t0925sd.html.

3. The DFUs were (relatively) inexpensive portable air samplers that required operators to manually take samples at certain time intervals for testing. It weighed about thirty pounds and measured thirteen inches wide by thirteen inches long by fifteen inches high. The DFUs could be purchased on GSA schedule contracts. See http://www.osha.gov/dts/sltc/methods/onsite/osa7/osa7.html.

4. Each service had a different basis of issue for determining their suit requirements. The Army and Marine Corps stated that it needed two suits for deploying warfighters and two suits as backups in supply. The Air Force stated that it needed five protective suits per airman. The Navy stated the need for about two suits per sailor on ships and boats, and three suits for sailors at ports.

5. BBC News, "Anthrax 'may be linked to Bin Laden,'" October 13, 2001, http://news.bbc.co.uk/1/hi/world/americas/1596675.stm.

6. Paul Cabellon, "CBIRF Takes The (Capitol) Hill," *Marine Corps News*, December 3, 2001, http://www.usmc.mil/marinelink/mcn2000.nsf/main5/3CB6033EC5894 0BE85256B17007B27F5?opendocument.

7. Center for Counterproliferation Research, *Anthrax in America: A Chronology and Analysis of the Fall 2001 Attacks*, Washington, D.C.: NDU, November 2002, 10.

8. See http://www.fda.gov/bbs/topics/ANSWERS/ANS01030.html.

9. Anita Manning, "Anthrax Vaccine Found Safe for Troops," *USA Today*, March 7, 2002.

10. The full details on the FDA's animal efficacy regulation can be found at http://www.fda.gov/OHRMS/DOCKETS/98fr/053102a.htm.

11. Rick Weiss, "Army's Anthrax Material Surprises Some Experts," *Washington Post*, December 14, 2001.

12. The 7th Chemical Company deployed three platoons to Washington, D.C.. The other two had been deployed to Qatar and Uzbekistan. Due to personnel shortages and the need to provide continuous coverage, the three platoons of personnel operated two platoons worth of equipment.

13. PACOM and CENTCOM had instituted protective mask programs for their civilians prior to 9/11, using old M17 masks and Israeli civil defense masks, with their own discretionary funds. This was not an antiterrorism measure, but a combat measure intended to protect noncombatants in the area from an Iraqi or North Korean first strike using chemical weapons.

14. See http://www.quickmask.com/quick2000.htm for more details on this mask.

15. The mouthpiece, although providing the individual with filtered air, also prevents effective verbal communication.

16. Pamela Hess, "Pentagon staff getting gas masks," *United Press International*, February 20, 2002.

17. Associated Press, "20,000 Gas Masks Ordered for Capitol," June 26, 2002.

18. Here "Army staff" means the Army G-8 chemical officers and support from the USACMLS.

19. The services were eventually allowed to choose their own stateside installations, trying to comply with ASD (SO/LIC)'s guidance on choosing one small, one medium, and one large installation. The installations included Fort Gordon, Fort Lewis, and Fort Campbell; Robins Air Force Base, Pope Air Force Base, and Barksdale Air Force Base; Naval Surface Warfare Center (Dahlgren), Navy Region Southwest (San Diego), and Camp Lejeune.

20. See http://www.defenselink.mil/pubs/qdr2001.pdf and http://www.defenselink.mil/news/May2002/t05102002_t0510dpg.html.

21. Of the original 200 installations on the list, about 75 of them were overseas. It was explained off-line that cutting this number down to 15 was politically motivated and would be easier to implement, given the more fully developed relationships between installation and off-post emergency responders. The overseas CINCs were very upset about the slight, and continued to remind the Joint Staff about this incident for years.

22. The antiterrorism community uses force protection conditions (FPCONs) alpha through delta to manage resources in accordance to the perceived threat. They refused to develop similar guidance for terrorist CBRN threats (in my opinion because they didn't understand the concepts) but also refused to let the CBRN defense community develop a separate but parallel FPCON process to manage CBRN defense resources. As a result, the system was either fully on for CBRN threats or fully off. This lack of resolution should be unacceptable.

23. Congress has directed the DoD develop a QDR report every four years. Reference *National Defense Authorization Act of 2000 (PL 106-65), Title IX—DoD Organization and Management, Section 901—Permanent Requirement for Quadrennial Defense Review.*

24. DoD *Quadrennial Defense Review Report* (Washington, D.C.: GPO, 2001), 4–5. Hereafter referred to as the 2001 QDR report. See http://www.defenselink.mil/pubs/qdr2001.pdf.

25. Ibid., 30.

26. Ibid., 43.

27. See http://www.fas.org/irp/offdocs/nspd/nspd-17.html.

28. See: http://www.globalsecurity.org/wmd/library/policy/dod/npr.htm.

29. See http://www.lubbockonline.com/news/120897/LA0731.html.

30. The *National Security Strategy of the United States of America*, September 2002, available at http://www.whitehouse.gov/nsc/nss.pdf.

31. The conflict was more philosophical than different; the Air Force was introducing terms such as "proliferation prevention" and "contamination control" after the Joint Staff had successfully negotiated different joint terms and positions with all four services. Changing the vocabulary every few years was not acceptable.

32. The initiative has expanded to address ground interdiction scenarios as well.

33. See http://www.whitehouse.gov/news/releases/2002/12/WMDStrategy.pdf.

34. Guidance on military support to foreign consequence management was issued later as a Chairman of the JCS Instruction (CJCSI) to the services and combatant commands.

35. Franks with Macolm McConnell, *American Soldier* (New York: Regan Books, 2004), 269–72.

36. Associated Press, "CIA: al Qaeda Attacks Likely to be Small Scale," *USA Today*, June 3, 2003. http://www.usatoday.com/news/washington/2003-06-03-cia-alqaeda_x.htm.

37. See http://www.globalsecurity.org/military/ops/enduring-freedom_deploy.htm.

38. See http://www.globalsecurity.org/military/ops/enduring-freedom-ops.htm.

39. CNN, "U.S. Tests for Chemical Weapons in Afghanistan," November 27, 2001.

40. Associated Press, "Terrorists Said To Eye Biological Arms," *Washington Times*, May 24, 2003.

41. Barton Gellman, "U.S. Suspects Al Qaeda Got Nerve Agent From Iraqis," *Washington Post*, December 12, 2002. Also Mark Getler, "Here's Some News, But Be Careful," *Washington Post*, December 22, 2002.

42. Nic Robertson, "Tapes Shed New Light on Bin Laden's Network," *CNN*, August 19, 2002, http://www.cnn.com/2002/US/08/18/terror.tape.main/.

43. United Press International, "Chemical Atrocities Show Al-Qaeda's Lust for Weapons of Mass Destruction," *NewsMax.com Wires*, August 20, 2002, http://www.newsmax.com/archives/articles/2002/8/19/163452.shtml.

44. Franks, *American Soldier*, 331. In a CENTCOM press brief on March 22, 2003, Franks stated the military objectives of the campaign as "First, end the regime of Saddam Hussein. Second, to identify, isolate and eliminate Iraq's weapons of mass destruction. Third, to search for, to capture, and to drive out terrorists from that country. Fourth, to collect such intelligence as we can related to terrorist networks. Fifth, to collect such intelligence as we can related to the global network of illicit weapons of mass destruction."

45. Ibid., 350–55.

46. President Bush: "[Saddam] is a dangerous man who possesses the world's most dangerous weapons ... I hope that, of course, he allows inspectors to go into his country, like he promised he would do. Not for the sake of letting inspectors in, but to showing the world that he has no weapons of mass destruction." March 22, 2002, press conference by President Bush and President Fox.

CHAPTER 5   THE CASE FOR WAR

1. Prewar intelligence estimates of Iraq's nuclear, biological, and chemical warfare capabilities are discussed in the unclassified report of the Commission on the Intelligence

Capabilities of the United States Regarding Weapons of Mass Destruction (referred to after this point as the Commission on WMD Intel report), dated March 31, 2005. Their report can be found at http://www.wmd.gov/wmd.pdf. Also see the Senate Intelligence Committee's "Report on the U.S. Intelligence Community's Prewar Intelligence Assessments on Iraq," dated July 7, 2004, at http://www.gwu.edu/~nsarchiv/NSAEBB/NSAEBB129/senateiraqreport.pdf.

2. For one view of the Bush administration's deliberations on Iraq's WMD effort, I would refer the reader to Bob Woodward's *Plan of Attack* (Simon & Schuster, 2004).

3. For a more complete discussion of the Dugway sheep incident, see my book, *America's Struggle with Chemical-Biological Warfare* (Westport, CT: Praeger , 2000), 29–43.

4. This is especially true among many in the Chemical Corps and general CB defense community. This "unwritten code of silence" both perpetuates the ignorance within the Corps and the release of bad information by other, less reliable sources. Many of the best books on CB warfare printed prior to 1972 were by former Chemical Corps leaders, but that is no longer the case today.

5. A colleague of mine suggests that this issue could be resolved if we had technically trained and media-savvy professionals in the military, such as warrant officers in the Chemical Corps, rather than just tactically trained chemical specialists in the military units.

6. Mauroni, *Chemical and Biological Defense*, 122–25.

7. Kenneth Katzman, *Iraq: Weapons Programs, U.N. Requirements, and U.S. Policy* (Congressional Research Service: Washington, D.C.: September 2003), 1.

8. Ibid., 7–8.

9. See Scott Ritter, *Endgame: Solving the Iraq Problem Once and for All* (New York: Simon & Schuster, 1999) and http://www.un.org/Depts/unscom/Chronology/chronology.htm.

10. Tom Clancy, *Battle Ready*, with General Tony Zinni and Tony Koltz (New York: Putnam, 2004), 9–10.

11. See http://www.globalsecurity.org/wmd/library/news/iraq/1998/981219-end01.htm.

12. See http://www.gwu.edu/~nsarchiv/NSAEBB/NSAEBB80/wmd07.pdf.

13. Scott Ritter, "The Case for Iraq's Qualitative Disarmament," *Arms Control Today*, June 2000, available at http://www.armscontrol.org/act/2000_06/iraqjun.asp.

14. See an unclassified review of these countries' efforts at http://www.cns.miis.edu/research/cbw/possess.htm.

15. Clarification on terms: known—states have either declared their programs or there is clear evidence of NBC weapons possession, such as offensive use; probable—states have been publicly named as pursuing an offensive NBC weapons program, for example manufacturing capabilities and NBC weapons testing; possible—states have been identified as having an interest in developing NBC weapons and have the necessary technological and industrial capability to support such a program.

16. See Defense Secretary Rumsfeld testimony to HASC on September 18, 2002, http://www.defenselink.mil/speeches/2002/s20020918-secdef2.html.

17. See http://www.state.gov/secretary/rm/2001/933.htm.

18. John Pilger, "The Big Lie," *The Mirror*, September 22, 2003. For the text see http://www.mirror.co.uk/news/allnews/content_objectid=13434081_method=full_siteid=50143_headline=-THE-BIG-LIE-name_page.html.

19. James Bamford, *A Pretext for War* (New York: Doubleday, 2004), 287–90. Also see http://www.defenselink.mil/transcripts/2003/tr20031113-0874.html.

20. See http://www.theunelected.com/feith1.html.

21. Bamford, *A Pretext for War*, 317–18.

22. Douglas Jehl, "CIA Chief Says He's Corrected Cheney Privately," *New York Times*, March 10, 2004.

23. See Rep. Henry Waxman's report, "Iraq On The Record," March 16, 2004, at http://www.house.gov/reform/min/features/iraq_on_the_record/. A collection of many of these quotes can also be found at http://www.rotten.com/library/history/war/wmd/saddam/ and at http://www.ceip.org/files/projects/npp/pdf/Iraq/administrationoniraq.pdf.

24. Howard Kurtz, "The Post on WMDs: An Inside Story," *Washington Post*, August 12, 2004.

25. See http://www.namibian.com.na/2002/june/world/026AE664D1.html.

26. See *CNN Late Edition* transcript at http://www.cnn.com/TRANSCRIPTS/0209/08/le.00.html.

27. See http://www.whitehouse.gov/news/releases/2003/02/20030224-14.html/.

28. Remarks by Paul Wolfowitz to the Fletcher Conference in Washington, D.C., on October 16, 2002. See http://www.defenselink.mil/speeches/2002/s20021016-depsecdef.html.

29. See http://www.whitehouse.gov/news/releases/2002/09/20020912-1.html and http://www.number-10.gov.uk/output/Page1727.asp.

30. See "A Decade of Deception and Defiance," a State Department generated background paper for President Bush's speech to the United Nations, at http://www.gwu.edu/~nsarchiv/NSAEBB/NSAEBB80/wmd13.pdf.

31. Judith Miller, "Secret Sites: Iraqi tells of Renovations at Sites for Chemical and Nuclear Arms," *New York Times*, December 20, 2001.

32. See http://www.globalsecurity.org/wmd/library/news/iraq/1998/981219-uk-mod.htm.

33. David Rodgers, "Air Force Doubts Drone Threat," *Wall Street Journal*, September 10, 2003, http://www.house.gov/georgemiller/wsjarticle.pdf.

34. See the unclassified version of the DIA assessment at http://www.gwu.edu/~nsarchiv/NSAEBB/NSAEBB80/wmd12.pdf.

35. Tony Capaccio, "Pentagon 2002 Study Reported 'No Reliable' Data on Iraq Weapons," *Bloomberg.com*, June 6, 2003.

36. CIA, "Iraq's Weapons of Mass Destruction Programs," October 2002. See http://www.gwu.edu/~nsarchiv/NSAEBB/NSAEBB80/wmd15.pdf.

37. John Prados, "The Man Behind The Curtain," July 19, 2004, http://www.tompaine.com/the_man_behind_the_curtain.php/.

38. Michael Gordon and Judith Miller, "U.S. Says Hussein Intensifies Quest for A-Bomb Parts," *New York Times*, September 8, 2002.

39. *Commission on WMD Intel final report*, 55–56. In fact, the ISG later assessed the tubes to be designed for 81-mm rockets for Iraq's Nasser Multiple Rocket Launcher program. The DOE and INR still believed that Iraq was reconstituting its nuclear weapons program, but based their conclusions on factors other than the aluminum tubes.

40. *AP News*, "CIA Lacked Key Documents," July 17, 2003, http://www.cbsnews.com/stories/2003/07/17/iraq/main563752.shtml.

41. Johnathan Landay and Drew Brown, "Chalabi Group Gets Blamed for the Claims," Knight Ridder Newspapers, April 4, 2004, http://www.kansascity.com/mld/cctimes/2004/04/04/news/8352934.htm?template=contentModules/printstory.js p&1c.

42. Bob Drogin and John Goetz, "How U.S. Fell Under the Spell of 'Curveball,'" *Los Angeles Times*, November 20, 2005.

43. Johnathan Landay and Warren Strobel, "Report Links Ex-CIA Chief To A Defector," *Philadelphia Inquirer*, July 16, 2004.

44. Bamford, *A Pretext for War*, 314.

45. Michael Gordon and Judith Miller, "U.S. Says Hussein Intensifies Quest For A-Bomb Parts," *New York Times*, September 8, 2002.

46. David Rodgers, "Air Force Doubts Drone Threat," *Wall Street Journal*, dated September 10, 2003. http://www.house.gov/georgemiller/wsjarticle.pdf.

47. Bamford, *A Pretext for War*, 229-30.

48. White House, "President Delivers 'State of the Union,'" January 28, 2003, http://www.whitehouse.gov/news/releases/2003/01/20030128-19.html.

49. See http://www.cnn.com/2003/WORLD/meast/06/08/sprj.irq.main/.

50. Bruce B. Auster, et al., "New Questions about U.S. Intelligence Regarding Iraq's Weapons of Mass Terror," *U.S. News & World Report*, June 9, 2003.

51. James Risen, "CIA Aides Feel Pressure in Preparing Iraqi Reports," *New York Times*, March 23, 2003. Also see Bamford, *A Pretext for War*, 333–34.

52. Michael Isikoff, "Forget the 'Poisons and Deadly Gasses,'" *Newsweek*, July 5, 2004, 6.

53. Bamford, *A Pretext for War*, 344.

54. See http://www.scoop.co.nz/mason/stories/WO0306/S00131.htm.

55. See documents at http://www.downingstreetmemo.org.

56. Michael Gordon and Judith Miller, "U.S. Says Hussein Intensifies Quest for A-Bomb Parts," *New York Times*, September 8, 2002.

57. See http://www.americanprogress.org/site/pp.asp?c=biJRJ8OVF&b=24970.

58. See http://msnbc.msn.com/id/3080244/.

59. See http://www.whitehouse.gov/news/releases/2003/03/20030317-7.html.

CHAPTER 6   OPERATION IRAQI FREEDOM

1. For example, General Myers' testimony to the HASC on September 18, 2002. Question from Congressman Thornberry: "Are we ready to have forces in an environment where weapons of mass destruction may be used against them?" Answer: "Congressman Thornberry, let me first say that the short answer is yes. The longer answer is, over the past decade—and I will admit, early in the decade our capability to deal with weapons of mass destruction for our soldiers and sailors and airmen and Marines, Coast Guardsmen, was uneven, but in the last part of this decade, for the majority of it, we have made very good improvements in terms of sensors that detect attacks, in terms of being able to net those sensors together to provide, you know, area warnings for collective protection and in the kind of protective suits that our troops wear. So we've made improvements in all those areas. And without getting into much more detail, obviously our forces prepare for that, they train for that, and would be ready to deal with that type of environment." See http://www.defenselink.mil/speeches/2002/s20020918-secdef2.html.

2. That is to say, if an M8A1 chemical detector or a CAM was alarming or an M256A1 kit came up positive, there was a strong possibility of chemical agent contamination. There were two problems in using this standard; first, each detector used a different set of sensitivities, meaning there was no one exposure standard. Second, while military personnel could use this high-risk standard for military operations, it was not going to be acceptable for civilians. Occupational health standards were more applicable for post-conflict remediation and return to the United States, but military detectors do not detect low enough to what would be considered "safe" for civilian workers or the general population.

3. Gregory Fontenot, E.J. Degen, and David Tohn, *On Point: The United States Army in Operation Iraqi Freedom* (Annapolis, MD: Naval Institute Press, 2005), http://onpoint.leavenworth.army.mil/intro.htm.

4. STRATCOM, SPACECOM and JFCOM elected not to participate, since they did not have a heavy interest in maintaining a robust CBRN defense capability.

5. See Henry Sokolski, "Rethinking Bio-Chemical Dangers," Nonproliferation Policy Education Center, February 2000, http://www.npec-web.org/pages/2-00fpri-summary.htm.

6. The rationale here was based on the intelligence community's failure to accurately assess the Soviet Union's offensive CB weapons programs. So while OSD accepted the CIA and DIA assessments on Iraq's alleged WMD program, OSD policy was also saying that DoD needed to develop defensive capabilities for potential new, emerging threat agents that were not yet identified by the same intelligence agencies. They believed that if DoD could not accept the potential impact of these new agents, there had to be a ready defensive capability.

7. The commission on WMD intel's unclassified report references a National Intelligence Council report, "Iraq's Chemical Warfare Capabilities: Potential for Dusty and Fourth-Generation Agents: Memorandum to Holders of NIE 2002-16HC [the October 2002 NIE]" dated November 2002, at footnote 828 (p. 246). The footnote states that this report was to "cover certain aspects of the tactical CW

threat that the military wanted to have addressed" and that "NGIC took issue with some aspects of this NIE." I suggest that it was OSD policy that wanted this report, and not the military agencies (CENTCOM or Joint Staff).

8. *CBS News,* "U.S. Bio Weapon Defenses Vulnerable," January 8, 2002, http://www.cbsnews.com/stories/2003/01/08/attack/main535682.shtml. Identifying where U.S. forces are vulnerable with regard to CBW agents is not something he should have been trumpeting to the press.

9. The desired objective is pixie dust—100 percent effective against all CBW agents, harmless to the environment, equipment, and people, not reliant on water, and cheap to use in large quantities. The search for pixie dust is second only to the great search for a CBRN "tricorder"—an inexpensive, handheld detector that instantaneously detects and identifies all known hazards within seconds and without any false alarms.

10. Tony Capaccio, "U.S. Seeks Biological, Chemical Attack Cleanup Foam," September 24, 2002, www.bloomberg.com. Although Sandia Labs came up with the original concept, its foam was referred to as DF-100. The DF-200 used a different formula to develop its foam decontamination capability.

11. Joint Publication 4-06, *Joint Tactics, Techniques, and Procedures for Mortuary Affairs in Joint Operations* (Washington, D.C.: GPO, August 1996).

12. Interestingly enough, Britain was not one of those requesting anthrax vaccine. In fact, due to a voluntary vaccination program, more than half their forces had refused to be vaccinated against anthrax. Richard Norton-Taylor, "Troops shun anthrax jab," *The Guardian,* February 12, 2003.

13. *CNN,* "U.S. Officials: Iraq Ordered Nerve Gas Antidote," November 13, 2002.

14. Tony Capaccio, "U.S. Response: Army Replaces Defective Masks," *Bloomberg.com,* November 27, 2002.

15. *CBS,* "Bio, Chem Protective Gear Questioned," November 30, 2002, http://www.cbsnews.com/stories/2002/11/30/attack/main531271.shtml.

16. This included the DoD CB Defense Program quantity of 30,000 per month, plus DLA's purchases and increased production on the parts of existing JSLIST manufacturers. The JSLIST suit production would hit 88,650 in January 2003, due to an issue with the availability of fabric.

17. The soldier could wear the suit for 45 days while retaining full protection. An unworn suit from an open bag was good for 120 days. Within either period, the suit could be laundered six times and still be serviceable.

18. "There are three kinds of lies: lies, damn lies, and statistics." Attributed to Benjamin Disraeli. As to any claims that the BDOs were not effective, let the author note that he and many thousands of service members had worn the BDO suits in the presence of actual chemical warfare agents without ill effects.

19. The Air Force and Navy forces in Europe wanted fifty DFUs between the two of them. Army forces (led by Colonel Madere's urging) wanted the other three hundred DFUs predominantly for tactical uses even though this was NOT a tactical system. EUCOM had to assure the JRO that the DFUs would be used only for

installation CBRN defense purposes, i.e., antiterrorism support. It didn't make any sense to get this many DFUs (there had been no analysis to support the numbers), but the Army had committed itself to that number by then.

20. The SROC meetings included the under secretaries of defense, assistant secretaries of defense, the vice CJCS, and three-star general/flag officers from the four services, plus invited DoD executives from other agencies.

21. EUCOM had been a sponsor for a CB detection UAV between 1997 and 2004 under the Counterproliferation II ACTD. It was axed in 2004 for failing to meet operational expectations after spending a quarter of a billion dollars. DTRA is still marketing this capability to other defense agencies and combatant commands.

22. Initially, one site survey team was attached to 3rd Infantry Division. Eventually this would grow to three teams and both Mobile Exploitation Teams. MET Bravo would only support 3rd Infantry Division for two missions.

23. CWO3 Monty Gonzales, "The Search for WMD in Iraq," Center for Army Lessons Learned, 2003.

24. Anthony Cordesman, *The Iraq War* (Westport, CT: Praeger, 2003), 451–55.

25. The FDA's Naming Committee (yes evidently there is such a beast) didn't like the original name "Nerve Agent Antidote Delivery System" or NAADS.

26. See announcement at http://meridianmeds.com/press/100202.html.

27. By the end of January, two military members had shown "significant adverse effects" to the smallpox vaccine, although they were not life-threatening. About 3 percent of the immunized service members had lost one or more days at work or reported side effects. Sandra Jontz, "Two Show 'Significant Adverse Effects' to Smallpox Vaccine," *European Stars and Stripes*, January 30, 2003.

28. There were probably technical ways to do this, such as taking and documenting DNA samples to confirm the casualties, but the issue really was closure for the families without having a body to bury.

29. Reuters, "U.S. Rejects Gulf Battlefield Cremations," *Washington Post*, March 14, 2003. Interestingly, the British army was much more practical. Their practices included burying military casualties at overseas locations, and they had no issue with the idea of permanent internment of contaminated casualties.

30. See "Dr. Johnson-Winegar Interview with CBS 60 Minutes," February 18, 2003, at http://www.defenselink.mil/transcripts/2003/t02182003_t0216winegar60min.html.

31. During the interview, he referred to "defective training filters" used by troops in Kuwait, although the issue had been withdrawing defective gaskets stored in military warehouses located in the United States.

32. The media has often reported on the Army's alleged gassing of sheep at Dugway Proving Ground in 1968 when discussing current CB defense and chemical demilitarization issues today. It's sensationalistic to insinuate that the DoD culture in 1968 is somehow still pertinent in today's military, and therefore the same mistakes could happen. Of course, politicians also stretch the truth when convenient

—recall Defense Secretary Cohen's dramatic license with a five-pound bag of sugar, stating that it was enough anthrax to take out Washington D.C. It wasn't enough agent for total coverage and ignored dispersion physics necessary to achieve those casualties.

33. On May 8, I received word that Dr. Johnson-Winegar submitted her retirement papers to take effect at the end of June. Mr. Aldridge asked her to reconsider, but she was resolute. Perhaps this aggressive interview, and Representative Shay's lack of support in addressing this important issue, was part of the reason.

34. Vernon Loeb, "Troops Lack Protective Gear, Say Lawmakers; Safety Against Chemical, Biological Arms Doubted," *Washington Post*, November 30, 2002.

35. Specialist Jacob Boyer, "Threat of War Increases NBC Training in Kuwait," *Army News Service*, February 13, 2003.

36. Simon Robinson, "The Chicken Defense," *Time*, February 21, 2003, http://www.time.com/time/europe/me/daily/0,13716,423690,00.html. Also Ron Claiborne, "Chicken Warnings Aren't For the Birds," *ABC News*, February 25, 2002, http://abcnews.go.com/sections/GMA/Living/iraq030225_KuwaitFieldChickens. html.

37. BAE also gave four ChemSentries to the 4th Infantry Division to support an informal operational test. After receiving training on the systems and right before their deployment in March, the 4th Infantry Division told the Air Force project manager that they had the systems, and were told emphatically that they were not to conduct this test or even deploy with the detectors. BAE withdrew their offer and received the detectors back.

38. BAE's own test results reported to the Air Force indicated that the ChemSentry "had a high false alarm rate and the system failed high-temperature and humidity environmental tests," the audit said. The unit also had to be shielded from direct sunlight in order to operate, BAE test results cited in the audit said. Tests also showed that the detector "has an unacceptably high false alarm rate, particularly when exposed to insect repellant" and foam commonly found in Navy and Air Force fire extinguishers, Thomas Christie, the Pentagon's director of operational testing, said in his latest annual report on major systems." Tony Cappacio, "BAE Systems Chemical Detectors Recalled by Air Force," *Bloomberg News*, August 3, 2004.

39. The full transcript can be read at http://www.defenselink.mil/transcripts/2003/t03032003_t0303chembio.html.

40. One of the 68th Chemical Company's decon platoons was attached to the 3rd Infantry Division.

41. This was a contentious issue. The Chemical Corps insisted that two BIDS platoons (one from each of the two companies) should remain within the United States to support homeland defense missions. The political push to support Jordan's and Israel's requests for the BIDS assets and unwillingness to pull any CENTCOM-dedicated forces out overruled that concern, and the Army Operations Center agreed (and had the final word).

42. There were three active duty chemical battalions that could deploy for combat operations in 2004: the 2nd Chemical Battalion at Fort Hood, Texas, the 23rd Chemical Battalion in Camp Carroll, South Korea, and the 83rd Chemical Battalion at Fort Polk, Louisiana. In addition, there is the 82nd and 84th Chemical Battalions at Fort Leonard Wood (schoolhouse battalions), and the Army's Technical Escort Unit has now been turned into a battalion.

43. *Bloomberg.com*, "U.S. Says It Has Bomb To Safely Destroy Iraq's Chemical Agents," April 2, 2003.

44. Seymour Hersh, "Selective Intelligence," *New Yorker*, May 12, 2003, http://www.newyorker.com/fact/content/?030512fa_fact.

CHAPTER 7   WHO LOST THE WMDS?

1. Interview on CBS *Face the Nation*, March 23, 2003, http://www.defenselink.mil/transcripts/2003/t03232003_t0323cbs.html.

2. Christopher Cooper, "Chemical, Biological Weapons Still Haven't Been Seen In Iraq," *Wall Street Journal*, March 28, 2003.

3. Rick Atkinson, *In The Company Of Soldiers* (New York: Henry Holt, 2004), 95.

4. *Inside Defense*, "Commandant: Marines Prepared For Iraq's Chem-Bio Weapons," March 19, 2003.

5. Briefing by Lt. Gen. William Wallace at Fort Leonard Wood, MO, on October 15, 2004.

6. Stewart Stogel, "Iraq's WMD: How Big A Threat?" *Time*, March 27, 2003.

7. In actuality, the "forty-five-day wear" period referred to the actual time a service member could wear the suit, not the time once the bag was opened. The forty-five days included operational degradation caused by normal wear and tear associated with people running around and conducting combat missions in a 24-hour period, and was not related to the efficacy of the suit itself.

8. The Soviet-built Frog-7 missiles have a range of seventy kilometers, and as such, were legal for Iraq to retain under the UN resolution.

9. See Chapter 4 of "On Point" at http://onpoint.leavenworth.army.mil/ch-4.htm#3.

10. Boyne, *Operation Iraqi Freedom: What Went Right, What Went Wrong, and Why*, 86–87.

11. See http://www.cbsnews.com/stories/2003/03/23/earlyshow/main545538.shtml.

12. Jonathan Landay, "Evidence of Chemical Arms Found," *Philadelphia Inquirer*, April 2, 2003, and Jim Miklaszewski, "Avoiding attacking suspected terrorist mastermind," *MSNBC News*, March 2, 2004, http://www.msnbc.msn.com/id/4431601/.

13. Joby Warrik, "Banned Weapons Remain Unseen," *Washington Post*, March 27, 2003.

14. Associated Press, "Marines Find Weapons Cache, Chemical Suits, Gas Masks," March 31, 2003.

15. BBC News, "'Proof' of biological weapons found," March 27, 2003. Also see http://www.timesonline.co.uk/article/0,,1-629133,00.html. One might question this logic by noting that every Army unit has CB defense equipment, but the Army lacks an offensive CB weapons capability.

16. Tom Lasseter, "Troops, Journalists Undergo Cleanup for Nerve Gas Exposure," *Knight Rider Newspapers*, April 6, 2003.

17. To ensure that the national command authority (the president and the secretary of defense) could act confidently on the information of adversarial use of CBW agents, there was a very strict chain-of-custody process for transporting samples back to U.S. and U.K. laboratories (Aberdeen's ECBC, MRIID at Fort Detrick, and Porton Down in the United Kingdom). The laboratories were supposed to deliver ironclad analysis that could withstand the scrutiny of international courts within seventy-two hours. Often, if there was no confirmation of CBW agent presence, there was no official announcement of the results other than "it wasn't agent."

18. See, for example, Mauroni, *Chemical-Biological Defense: U.S. Military Policies and Decisions in the Gulf War*, Westport, CT: Praeger, 1998.

19. DoD News Transcript, Secretary Rumsfeld Remarks on ABC "This Week with George Stephanopoulos," March 30, 2003, http://www.defenselink.mil/transcripts/2003/t03302003_t0330sdabcsteph.html.

20. Bernard Weinraub, "Army Reports Iraq Is Moving Toxic Arms to Its Troops," *New York Times*, March 28, 2003.

21. Reese Dunklin and Richard Whittle, "Chemical Attacks Still A Top Fear," *Dallas Morning News*, April 4, 2003.

22. Bob Drogin, "Iraqi Chatter Threatens Use Of Chemicals," *Los Angeles Times*, April 4, 2003.

23. About April 15, V Corps would take 11th Chemical Company from 4th Infantry Division and assign it to the 2nd Chemical Battalion. The 4th Infantry Division kept the 44th and 46th Chemical Companies.

24. Guy Taylor, "False Alarm Puts GIs in Heavy Gear," *Washington Times*, April 4, 2003.

25. Atkinson, *In The Company Of Soldiers*, 242.

26. *Associated Press*, "U.S. Troops Find Signs of Chemical Readiness," *The Record*, April 5, 2003, http://www.globalsecurity.org/org/news/2003/030405-chem-readiness01.htm.

27. Bill Gertz, "U.S. Probes for Iraqi Chemicals," *Washington Times*, April 9, 2003.

28. Judith Miller, "U.S. Inspectors Find No Forbidden Weapons at Iraqi Arms Plant," *New York Times*, April 16, 2003.

29. See http://www.defenselink.mil/transcripts/2003/tr20030507-0158.html.

30. See http://www.whitehouse.gov/g8/interview5.html.

31. See the CIA special report on Iraq's mobile BW production plants at http://www.cia. gov/cia/reports/iraqi_mobile_plants/index.html.

32. DoD Briefing on WMD Exploitation in Iraq. See http://www.defenselink.mil/ transcripts/2003/tr20030507-0158.html.

33. "David A. Kay: America's Weapons Sleuth Talks about His Experiences Searching for Iraq's Weapons of Mass Destruction," *Chemical & Engineering New* 82, 31 (August 2, 2004): 28–33. See http://pubs.acs.org/cen/coverstory/8231/8231kay.html.

34. Donna Miles, "Roadside Bomb Releases Sarin Gas in Baghdad," *American Forces Press Service*, May 17, 2003, http://www.defenselink.mil/news/May2004/ n05172004_200405174.html.

35. See DoD briefing at http://www.defenselink.mil/transcripts/2003/tr20030530-0231.html.

36. See http://www.pm.gov.uk/output/Page3803.asp.

37. See White House transcript at http://www.whitehouse.gov/news/releases/ 2003/06/20030605-1.html.

38. Massimo Calabresi and Timothy Burger, "Who Lost the WMD?" *Time*, July 7, 2003.

39. *Associated Press*, "Iraq's Weapons Will Be Found, Insist Top White House Aides," June 9, 2003.

40. Dana Priest, "House Probers Conclude Iraq War Data Was Weak," *Washington Post*, September 28, 2003.

41. See http://www.cnn.com/2003/WORLD/meast/06/08/sprj.irq.main/.

42. Statement by David Kay on October 2, 2003, before the House and Senate. See http://www.cia.gov/cia/public_affairs/speeches/2003/david_kay_10022003.html.

43. Michael Dobbs, "Wolfowitz Shifts Rationales on Iraq War," *Washington Post*, September 12, 2003.

44. Remarks by the vice president at a Bush-Cheney '04 reception, Oklahoma City, October 9, 2003, http://www.whitehouse.gov/news/releases/2003/10/ 20031009-49.html. Mike Allen, "Chemical, Nuclear Arms Still 'Major Threat,' Cheney Says," *Washington Post*, December 17, 2003.

45. Simon Jeffery, "We Were All Wrong, Says Ex-weapons Inspector," *Guardian Unlimited*, January 29, 2004, http://www.guardian.co.uk/Iraq/Story/0,2763,1134290,00. html.

46. Some military colleagues insist that CB weapons were found in Iraq, but the facts remain classified. If this is true, it is hard to understand why the Bush administration would not publicize this finding, unless there are political factors involved.

47. Charles Hanley, "Anthrax Dumped Near Saddam Palace," *Washington Times*, March 29, 2005, http://washingtontimes.com/world/20050329-125828-2605r.htm.

48. Kenneth Pollack, "Spies, Lies, and Weapons: What Went Wrong," *Atlantic Monthly*, January/February 2004.

49. Center for Counterproliferation Research, 2003 Annual Symposium report, page 65. See http://www.ndu.edu/centercounter/docUploaded//2003%20Report.pdf.

50. Remarks of Secretary Rumsfeld to SASC on February 4, 2004, http://www.defenselink.mil/speeches/2004/sp20040204-secdef0843.html.

CHAPTER 8 LESSONS LEARNED

1. Just to clarify, having a renowned international laboratory and vast testing infrastructure does not necessarily mean DoD has led the way in innovative efforts. Many CBRN defense items have either foreign sources (the CAM, ACADA, the Fox vehicle, the M17 decon system, the Karcher) or origins from industry rather than the military labs (M291 decon kit resin, biodetection tickets). DoD has the capability and resources to do great things, but the acquisition process and lack of vision or ability to think out of the box has hurt the program. Often the DoD labs take industry's good ideas and tweaks them into finished products for the U.S. military.

2. An example of this is the past tests conducted by the JPEO for CBD off the Florida Keys to see whether Doppler radar could identify simulants representing a biological hazard cloud, released from a point off the coastline and allowed to drift toward the U.S. coastline.

3. The Army's AN/VDR-2 radiac meter is designed primarily for beta and gamma radiation detection. The AN/PDR-77 radiac is basically a jazzed-up VDR-2 with different probes. It detects alpha and x-ray radiation in addition to beta and gamma radiation.

4. Joint Publication 1-02, *DoD Dictionary of Military and Associated Terms*, June 9, 2004.

5. The Army is currently re-establishing tariff sizes for the JSLIST suits.

6. OSHA is concerned with occupational hazards, specifically chronic exposure over a period of years. For nerve agents, for instance, the OSHA standard for government workers (required for the chemical disposal facilities) is at least three orders of magnitude lower than the effective (not to be confused with lethal) dose. Since military personnel are not expected to routinely run into low levels of CW agents over their lifetime, it is inappropriate to use these standards (which would only imperil their ability to survive and sustain combat operations). All they are expected to do is survive the short, high-level CW attacks and complete their missions.

CHAPTER 9 CBRN DEFENSE POLICY

1. See the study done by Susan Moeller, "Media Coverage of Weapons of Mass Destruction," Center for International and Security Studies at Maryland, 2004, http://www.cissm.umd.edu/documents/WMDstudy_full.pdf.

2. For a better discussion on public policy aspects related to CBRN defense, see Mauroni, *Chemical Demilitarization: Public Policy Aspects* (Westport, CT: Praeger, 2003).

3. For a discussion on this topic, see http://www.acronym.org.uk/textonly/bwc/spec01.htm.

4. See http://www.defenselink.mil/speeches/2004/sp20040504-0321.html.

5. See the Commission's report at http://www.wmd.gov.

6. See http://www.downingstreetmemo.com for details.

7. Atkinson, *In The Company Of Soldiers*, 39.

8. DoD news briefing on April 21, 2003, http://www.defenselink.mil/transcripts/2003/tr20030421-secdef0121.html.

9. Lt. Col. Harry Conley, "Not With Impunity: Assessing US Policy for Retaliating to a Chemical or Biological Attack," *Air and Space Power Journal*, Spring 2003. Conley, to whom I give full credit for this section, has written a great paper on this topic. I strongly recommend it for professional reading.

10. Center for Counterproliferation Research, *At the Crossroads: Counterproliferation and National Security Strategy* (Washington, D.C.: NDU, 2004), 65.

11. The only active-duty chemical brigade as of 2005 is the 3rd Chemical Brigade at Fort Leonard-Wood, which primarily supports the Chemical School. An active-duty chemical brigade is programmed to stand up in 2007.

12. Secretary of Defense, "Designation of Responsibilities for Combating Weapons of Mass Destruction (WMD) to Commander, US Strategic Command (CDRUSSTRATCOM)," memorandum, January 6, 2005.

13. Scott R. Gourley, "Guardian Brigade," *Military Medical Technology*, 8, no. 4 (August 2004), http://www.military-medical-technology.com/articles.cfm?DocID=565.

14. See http://www.washingtonpost.com/wp-dyn/articles/A6245-2005Feb7.html?nav=rss_politics for mention of the funding for this facility.

15. Even if military chemical specialists are addressing a terrorist incident using industrial chemicals in a domestic setting, training and equipping them to work as Haz-Mat personnel, using occupational health standards, is wrong. The OSHA standards are overly conservative and intended to ensure a lifetime of health. Military personnel are focused on short-term exposure to complete the mission, and therefore need the flexibility of a higher risk standard in exchange for ability to perform quickly.

16. I built off the efforts of Lt. Col. Pat Sharon's 1999 Joint Staff memo.

CHAPTER 10   IMPROVING CBRN DEFENSE CAPABILITIES

1. For a good discussion on this topic, see Matthew Yglesias, "Why the Weapons Matter," June 19, 2003, http://www.techcentralstation.com/061903D.html.

2. Robert Scales, *Yellow Smoke: The Future of Land Warfare for America's Military* (Landam, MD: Rowman & Littlefield, 2003).

3. See transcript of the speech at http://www.thewashingtonnote.com/archives/000260.html.

4. Elaine Grossman, "Defense Board's 'Summer Studies' to Focus on WMD, Transformation," *Inside the Pentagon*, November 11, 2004.

5. Details and background reading can be accessed at http://www.dtic.mil/jointvision/index.html, but be warned, these documents are not easy reading. It may take

you a few attempts before the concepts become clear, and probably more than a few readings if you are unfamiliar with defense strategies and acquisition lingo.

6. See the document at http://www.dtic.mil/jointvision/jointfc.htm.

7. As another demonstration of failing to communicate, the Joint Staff's "Joint Operating Concept for Strategic Deterrence" uses the term "WMD/E" rather than "CBRNE" to describe force protection efforts. Clearly there remains a need to clarify how to address CBRN defense issues even within the Joint Staff.

8. This table does not reflect the JRO's 2004 modernization plan, although it incorporates aspects of that office's concepts. The JRO chose to retain the orientation along technological capabilities, rather than adopting an orientation toward operational capabilities more in the spirit of Rumsfeld's transformation planning guidance.

9. See http://www.whitehouse.gov/homeland/20040430.html.

10. Mauroni, *America's Struggle with Chemical-Biological Warfare*, 58.

11. The other services see no problems with informing Congress on important defense issues, while ensuring that they do not step over the line that forbids government agencies from trying to influence legislation or requesting additional funds.

12. The only other possibilities are that the general officer boards lack confidence in the Chemical Corps senior (colonel) leaders, or that the Acquisition Corps has siphoned off the talent. I don't believe either to be the case.

13. Currently, the director of the JRO is a dual-hatted position within the Joint Staff's J-8. There is no chemical general officer within the Army staff, and the 20th Support Command (CBRNE), which incorporates the Army's TEU battalion and several EOD units, is not led by a dedicated chemical general officer.

14. There is a general lack of lieutenant colonel command positions for operational battalion commands (as opposed to organizational commands that lack troops and do not deploy). This makes chemical officers less competitive in promotion boards when compared to their peers in other branches.

15. And if the Chemical School is not the main advocate for these actions, perhaps OSD Policy, the Joint Staff (J-8), STRATCOM, or DTRA should be. In any event, an advocacy group that actively campaigns on military CBRN defense capabilities and issues is sorely needed.

16. Although the U.S. Army's Chemical Defense Training Facility (CDTF) does give chemical specialists a good confidence level in their equipment, the CDTF is still a controlled environment without the impact of weather and external interferrents such as diesel fumes and industrial pollution for chemical detectors and high pollen counts and other natural biological organisms for biological detectors.

17. We also need to conduct data collection for urban environments. Building a "city" in the desert certainly could be done (and was done for nuclear testing during the Cold War). Gathering data for wooded terrain might be more tricky but not impossible. Outdoor testing of the adsorptive characteristics and decontamination of different contaminated surfaces would be invaluable in developing a better capability for understanding "how clean is safe."

18. National Defense Authorization Act for FY 2005, PL 108–375, Section 1053, signed October 28, 2004.

Selected Bibliography

Books

Atkinson, Rick. *In the Company of Soldiers*. New York: Holt, 2004.

Bamford, James. *A Pretext for War*. New York: Doubleday, 2004.

Clancy, Tom. *Battle Ready*. With General Tony Zinni and Tony Koltz. New York: Putnam, 2004.

Cordesman, Anthony. *The Iraq War*. Westport, CT: Praeger, 2003.

Fontenot, Col. Gregory, Lt. Col. E. J. Degen, and Lt. Col. David Tohn. *On Point: The United States Army in Operation Iraqi Freedom*. Annapolis, MD: Naval Institute Press, 2005.

Mauroni, Albert J. *America's Struggle with Chemical-Biological Warfare*. Westport, CT: Praeger, 2000.

_____. *Chemical-Biological Defense: U.S. Policies and Decisions in the Gulf War*. Westport, CT: Praeger, 1998.

Ritter, Scott. *Endgame: Solving the Iraq Problem Once and for All*. New York: Simon & Schuster, 1999.

Stockholm International Peace Research Institute. *The Problem of Chemical and Biological Warfare*. New York: Humanities Press, 1971.

Woodward, Bob. *Plan of Attack*. New York: Simon & Schuster, 2004.

Government Reports

Center for Counterproliferation Research. *At the Crossroads: Counterproliferation and National Security Strategy*. Washington, DC: National Defense University, 2004.

Department of Defense. *Quadrennial Defense Review Report*. Washington, DC: GPO, 2001.

Deutch, John M., et al. *Report of the Commission to Assess the Organization of the Federal Government to Combat the Proliferation of Weapons of Mass Destruction*. Washington, DC: GPO, July 14, 1999.

General Accounting Office. *Emphasis Remains Insufficient To Resolve Continuing Problems*. Washington, DC: GAO, March 1996.

_____. *Chemical and Biological Defense Chemical Warfare: Soldiers Inadequately Equipped and Trained to Conduct Chemical Operations*. Washington, DC: GAO, May 1991.

_____. *Chemical and Biological Defense: Program Planning and Evaluation Should Follow Results Act Framework*. Washington, DC: GAO, 1999.

_____. *Weapons of Mass Destruction: DoD's Actions to Combat Weapons Use Should Be More Integrated and Focused*. Washington, DC: GAO, May 2000.

Waxman, Rep. Henry. *Iraq on the Record*, Washington, DC: GPO, March 16, 2004.

JOURNAL AND MAGAZINE ARTICLES

Calabresi, Massimo, and Timothy Burger. "Who Lost the WMD?" *Time*, July 7, 2003, pp. 32-4.

Conley, Lt. Col. Harry. "Not with Impunity: Assessing US Policy for Retaliating to a Chemical or Biological Attack." *Air and Space Power Journal*. (Spring 2003), pp. 69-79.

"David A. Kay: America's Weapons Sleuth Talks about his Experiences Searching for Iraq's Weapons of Mass Destruction." *Chemical & Engineering News*, Vol 82, Iss. 31 (August 2, 2004), pp. 28-33.

Gonzales, CWO3 Monty. "The Search for WMD in Iraq." Center for Army Lessons Learned (CALL) database (2003).

Lofy, Maj. Pete. "Managing Sensitive Site Exploitation: Notes from Operation Iraqi Freedom." *Army Chemical Review* (September 2003), p. 22-5.

Lynch, Maj. Brian. "Task Force Environmental Cleanup." *Army Chemical Review* (September 2003), p. 26-7.

Pollack, Kenneth. "Spies, Lies, and Weapons: What Went Wrong." *Atlantic Monthly*, Jan/Feb 2004 (http://www.theatlantic.com/doc/200401/pollack).

Ritter, Scott. "The Case for Iraq's Qualitative Disarmament." *Arms Control Today* (June 2000) (http://www.armscontrol.org/act/2000_06/iraqjun.asp).

Stogel, Stewart. "Iraq's WMD: How Big a Threat?" *Time*, March 27, 2003 (http://www.time.com/time/world/article/0,8599,437398,00.html).

NEWSPAPER AND ONLINE ARTICLES

Associated Press, "Terrorists Said to Eye Biological Arms." *Washington Times*, May 24, 2003.

Auster, Bruce B., et al. "New Questions about U.S. Intelligence Regarding Iraq's Weapons of Mass Terror." *U.S. News & World Report*, June 9, 2003.

Capaccio, Tony. "Pentagon 2002 Study Reported 'No Reliable' Data on Iraq Weapons." Bloomberg.com, DoD Early Bird database, June 6, 2003.

_____. "U.S. Response: Army Replaces Defective Masks." Bloomberg.com, DoD Early Bird database, November 27, 2002.

_____. "U.S. Seeks Biological, Chemical Attack Cleanup Foam." DoD Early Bird database, September 24, 2002.

Gellman, Barton. "U.S. Suspects Al Qaeda Got Nerve Agent from Iraqis." *Washington Post*, December 12, 2002.

Gordon, Michael and Judith Miller. "U.S. Says Hussein Intensifies Quest for A-Bomb Parts." *New York Times*, September 8, 2002.

Hess, Pamela. "Pentagon Staff Getting Gas Masks." United Press International, February 20, 2002.

Jontz, Sandra. "Two Show 'Significant Adverse Effects' to Smallpox Vaccine." *European Stars and Stripes*, January 30, 2003.

Kurtz, Howard. "The Post on WMDs: An Inside Story." *Washington Post*, August 12, 2004.

Lasseter, Tom. "Troops, Journalists Undergo Cleanup for Nerve Gas Exposure." *Knight Ridder Newspapers*, April 6, 2003.

Loeb, Vernon. "Troops Lack Protective Gear, Say Lawmakers; Safety Against Chemical, Biological Arms Doubted." *Washington Post*, November 30, 2002.

Manning, Anita. "Anthrax Vaccine Found Safe for Troops." *USA Today*, March 7, 2002.

Miller, Judith. "Secret Sites: Iraqi tells of Renovations at Sites for Chemical and Nuclear Arms." *New York Times*, December 20, 2001.

Priest, Dana. "House Probers Conclude Iraq War Data Was Weak." *Washington Post*, September 28, 2003.

Rodgers, David. "Air Force Doubts Drone Threat." *Wall Street Journal*, September 10, 2003.

Warrik, Joby. "Banned Weapons Remain Unseen." *Washington Post*, March 27, 2003.

INDEX

About the Author

Al Mauroni, a senior policy analyst with Northrop Grumman, has more than twenty years of experience in military chemical, biological, nuclear, and radiological (CBRN) defense programmatic and policy issues. He has developed and coordinated joint concepts, strategies, plans, assessments, information papers, and briefings on DoD CBRN defense capabilities within passive defense, consequence management, force protection and homeland security mission areas. He graduated from Carnegie-Mellon University with a degree in chemistry in 1985 prior to joining the U.S. Army as a chemical officer. He has a master's in the science of administration from Central Michigan University. After seven years of active duty, he joined the ranks of the consulting industry, working for the U.S. Army Soldier and Biological-Chemical Defense Command, the Joint Chiefs of Staff J-5 Directorate (Strategic Plans and Policy) and J-8 (Force Structure, Resources and Assessment), and the Deputy Assistant Secretary of the Army for the Elimination of Chemical Weapons. Currently he is supporting the Defense Threat Reduction Agency's CB Directorate in the development and transition of CBRN science and technology efforts.

Mr. Mauroni is a member of the Army Historical Foundation, the Association of the United States Army (Life Member), the Chemical Corps Regimental Association (Life Member), and the National Defense Industrial Association (Life Member). He is the author of four other books and numerous articles on the topic of CBRN defense and chemical demilitarization. He lives with his wife, Roseann, and their dogs in Alexandria, Virginia.